Microcomputers for Educ
Second Edition

MW00709856

Microcomputers for Educators
SECOND EDITION

JAMES LOCKARD
PETER D. ABRAMS
WESLEY A. MANY

Northern Illinois University

HarperCollins*Publishers*

Library of Congress Cataloging-in-Publication Data

Lockard, James.
    Microcomputers for educators. / James Lockard, Peter D. Abrams.
    Wesley A. Many. — 2nd ed.
        p.   cm.

    Includes bibliographical references.
    ISBN 0-673-52030-7
    1. Computer-assisted instruction—United States.
    2. Microcomputers—United States.   I. Abrams, Peter D.   II. Many, Wesley A.   III. Title.
    LB1028.5.L575   1990   89-64339
    371.3'34'0973—dc20   CIP

Printed in the United States of America.

Library of Congress Catalog Card Number 89-064339

ISBN 0-673-52030-7

        3   4   5   6   MVN   95   94   93   92   91   90

1, photograph courtesy of IBM.

Trademark Acknowledgments

Every effort has been made to supply trademark information about company names, products, and services mentioned in this book. Trademarks indicated below were derived from various sources. The authors cannot attest to the accuracy of this information.

Writer's Helper Stage II is published by Conduit, the University of Iowa.
Bank Street Writer and The Print Shop are copyrighted by Broderbund.
COMAL-2.0 is copyrighted by Commodore Business Machines.
CompuServe is a registered trademark of CompuServe Incorporated, an H and R Block, Inc., company.
Crossword Magic is a registered trademark of L & S Computerware and Mindscape.
DB Master is a registered trademark of DB Master Associates.
dBASE II, dBASE III, and Framework are registered Trademarks of Ashton-Tate.
ESL Picture Grammar is copyrighted by Gessler Educational Software.
Facemaker is copyrighted by and a trademark of Spinnaker Software Corporation.
The Factory, The Incredible Laboratory, and Magic Slate are copyrighted by Sunburst Communications.
Fact Track is a registered trademark of Science Research Associates.
Friendly Filer is a registered trademark of Grolier Electronic Publishing, Inc.
Grammatik is distributed by Reference Software and is a trademark of Wang Publishing.
Homeword is a registered trademark of and copyrighted by Sierra On-Line, Incorporated.
Symphony, and Lotus 1-2-3 are registered trademarks of Lotus Development Corporation.
Courseware Series is copyrighted by Scott, Foresman and Co. and distributed by Mindscape, Inc.
Microsoft is a registered trademark of Microsoft Corporation.
Notebook is a registered trademark of Window, Inc.
One World—Countries Data Base is a registered trademark and copyrighted by Active Learning Systems.
The Other Side is a registered trademark of Tom Snyder Productions, Inc.
PFS: File, PFS: Report, PFS: Write and PFS: First Publisher are registered trademarks of Software Publishing Corporation.
Pilot is copyrighted by Earl Keyser, Jr., and available at Hartley Courseware, Dimond Dale, Michigan.
Appleworks is a registered trademark of Apple Computer, Inc.

(*Trademark information continues on page 442.*)

For Kathy, Barb, and Peg

□ *Preface to the Second Edition* □

The first decade of microcomputers in education was the 1980s. Those who experienced this period witnessed and participated in rapid technological development with enormous significance for educators. In ten years, American schools adopted microcomputers to the extent that it is now rare for a school to have none, and teachers who use computers are impressed with their benefits ("The Computer Report Card," 1989). As of 1989, 23 states and the District of Columbia required at least some teachers to have training in microcomputer use to become certified (Bruder, 1989). Considering that the 1980s began with virtually no computers in the classroom, we have clearly come a long way. The question is no longer *whether* to use computers in the schools, but how *best* to use them.

The potential of technology to advance education is much greater than its current application. We have made progress, but the ultimate goal is still far ahead. Although nearly every school in the United States has microcomputers, many have so few as to be able to achieve very little. More than half the states have not yet reached the inevitable conclusion that teacher training must include instruction and experience in the uses of technology in order to aid learners. In fact, teacher training was a major source of concern throughout the eighties; it promises to remain so during the nineties.

The pace of development in computer technology continues to be rapid. It would be easy for educators to feel like hunters shooting at a moving target. Yet is should be obvious that to do nothing is to opt to fall continually further behind. No matter what position one currently takes on the place of technology in the classroom, the course of action must be forward.

Noted educational futurist Christopher Dede (1990) cautioned against four misconceptions concerning emerging technologies of instruction. The "misconception of consolidation" is that the wave of innovation is over; in fact, it is only beginning. The "misconception of literacy" is that technologies are a medium like language, designed to manipulate and communicate symbols; in fact, they are "potential intellectual partners." The "misconception of power" is that students need computers with only limited power; in fact, to benefit from the next generation of software, they need systems *more* powerful than many adult users now have. Finally, the "misconception of timing" is that educators should wait until systems are well (or fully) developed before beginning preparations to use them; in fact, long advance planning is necessary to build new curricula and retrain teachers.

This book addresses many aspects of the challenges of educational technology. If has been prepared to help educators and educators-to-be become knowledgeable of and comfortable with microcomputer technology. The second edition has been thoroughly revised to reflect the developments of the past three years. The original philosophy has not changed from the first edition; hence, the book's organization and general structure remain unchanged as well. This is not to say that the first edition escaped the revisionist's hand. Changes have been extensive: ranging from updated citations, software references, research reports, and activities in all chapters to the total rewrite of several chapters. Many topics have been added or expanded significantly, including: telecommunications, hypermedia, optical discs, interactive video, multi-media, integrated learning systems, intelligent CAI, artificial intelligence, expert systems, publishing software, graphics tools, logic programming, and curriculum integration. More specific classroom applications have also been included. Part 5, "Microcomputers in Education," has been changed thoroughly to emphasize further the need for integration of computers throughout the curriculum and to reflect new views on implementation issues. In sum, the second edition is much more than a cosmetic refurbishing of the first.

We want to thank the many worldwide users of the first edition of this book and trust that this edition will suit their needs still better. We have made every effort to be accurate and current, but this is a fast-changing field. Adopters of this book are encouraged to obtain the accompanying *Instructor's Manual* from Scott, Foresman and Company, which contains some last-minute updates, as well as teaching tips, test items, and transparency masters.

Special thanks go to the following individuals who critically reviewed the first edition, suggested revisions, then critiqued the revised manuscript: Stephen M. Alessi, University of Iowa; Barbara Grabowski, Syracuse University; Michael Simonsen, Iowa State University; and Barrie Jo Price, University of Miami. Their suggestions were most valuable and we have implemented all that we possibly could. New photographs in this edition are the fine work of Barry Stark, Northern Illinois University, Art/Photo Department. At Scott, Foresman and Company we have enjoyed our association with: Chris Jennison, Education Editor; Anita Portugal, Developmental Editor; and Diane Beausoleil, Project Editor. We gratefully acknowledge their encouragement and guidance, as well as that of Gerri McGowan of Editorial Services of New England who helped oversee the editing and production of this edition.

Throughout this endeavor, our families were constantly with us behind the scenes, helping, encouraging, believing in our efforts. We cannot adequately thank them for their understanding.

J.L.
P.D.A.
W.A.M.

References

Bruder, I. "Ninth Annual Survey of the States." *Electronic Learning*, October 1989, p. 22–28.
"The Computer Report Card: How Teachers Grade Computers in the Classroom." *TechTrends*, October 1989, pp. 30–35.
Dede, C. J. "Educators, Take Hold of the Future." *Electronic Learning*, January 1990, pp. 8–9.

☐ *Preface to the First Edition* ☐

In the few short years since the first microcomputer reached the retail market, a technological revolution has swept across the United States. Computing has become a common term in the American vocabulary and a daily activity for millions of people. This is indicative of what has been called society's movement into a new Information Age. Within this framework, computers also have found their way into classrooms from coast to coast and at all levels in numbers large and growing rapidly.

While the blossoming of computer use in the schools may be viewed as a most proper response to the challenges of the 21st century, there is much reason to pause and consider its true significance. First, it is unique among educational advances in that the driving force is often external to the schools. Parents are demanding that their children learn to use microcomputers as an integral part of their education. Second, compared to any of the previous technologies introduced into the schools, computers require vastly more teacher training to be used effectively. One simply cannot place a microcomputer in the classroom, pat the teacher on the head, and leave expecting miracles to occur. Computer literacy has become a catch word of the 80s, despite its lack of a commonly accepted definition. Clearly teachers need to gain computer knowledge and skills *before* they can help their students toward the same goal. Software availability and quality are problems, to be sure, but improvements in this area will have limited impact unless teachers are educated to use the products. It is the human interface that will make or break this "revolution."

With so many books on the market today aimed at computers in education, is another really needed? Our search for a book to support our approach to educational computing has consistently come up empty-handed. Every volume we have examined fails in one way or another to address our concerns. Some are fervent proponents of the outmoded "literacy is programming" viewpoint; others fail to cover adequately the important tool uses of the computer; some ignore the elements of computer-assisted learning; and few give much attention to the vast research and practical experience literature on computers in education. Each term we have been obliged to rely on our own devices to meet the needs of our students. In this volume, we offer those devices to others with similar needs.

This book is the outgrowth of our experience in preparing teachers to use microcomputers in the classroom. It reflects much serious thought and experimentation as to what the initial step should be in learning to cope with these electronic marvels. In our model of how computers can be used most effectively, the computer as a tool is the cornerstone—those applications which make our everyday lives easier. The next most important application is the computer as an electronic tutor, an integral component of the learning process. Programming, the computer as learner, occupies third place. We disagree vigorously with the notion that computer literacy is synonymous with programming skills. Instead, we believe that programming is one of the viable elements of a school program, but not the primary one. We have long believed that the ultimate success of the microcomputer in education depends on its becoming an everyday classroom tool, much as chalk and pencils are, rather than being an object of special attention.

Our approach to computers in education is reflected strongly in the book's organization. In Part 1 we lay a foundation by looking at the emergence of computers and by describing microcomputer systems. Parts 2, 3, and 4 focus respectively on the computer as tool (e.g., word processing, databases, and spreadsheets), the computer as tutor (computer-assisted instruction, courseware evaluation, and computer-managed instruction), and the computer as learner (a conceptual approach to programming). In Part 5, we discuss computer literacy, implementing computer education, and issues and implications. We conclude the book with a look at trends which will affect computer education. We have attempted to prepare each section with relative independence from others, so that users can readily adapt the sequence to their own preferences and even omit sections which they choose not to include in their courses. To enhance the usefulness of the material, most chapters include activities and a bibliography.

This book is intended as background material for reading and discussion prior to hands-on laboratory experience, which is the heart of our approach to a beginning course in microcomputers for educators. We do not believe that teachers can be prepared to use computers through a lecture course. Instead, they must become thoroughly familiar with hardware and software which will be the basis of their own teaching. We have purposely not provided detailed recommendations for the hands-on component, since they would necessarily be machine and software dependent. Rather, the chapters and activities suggest the approaches we have found successful. They can be adapted to whatever hardware and software may be available.

Although the contents of this book reflect our own approach to the task of training teachers to make use of computers, our work on the manuscript was influenced by the careful reading and numerous suggestions of reviewers. We wish to express our gratitude to M. Vere DeVault, The University of Wisconsin-Madison; Jeffry Gordon, University of Cincinnati; Theodore M. Kellogg, University of Rhode Island; and David F. Salisbury, The Florida State University. All photographs are the work of Barry Stark and George Tarbay, Northern Illinois University, whose talents are evident despite the short deadlines given to them. In addition, we are indebted to Mylan Jaixen, Senior Editor, College Division, and Barbara Breese at Little, Brown and Co., as well as Julie Hotchkiss who helped oversee the production of the book. Without their encouragement and expert guidance, this project could not have been completed.

Finally, we gratefully acknowledge the continuous support and understanding of our families, from whom countless hours were taken to complete this work.

J.L.
P.D.A.
W.A.M.

□ Brief Contents □

PART 1   GETTING STARTED   1

1. Historical Perspectives   3

2. Microcomputer Systems   17

PART 2   THE COMPUTER AS TOOL   33

3. Word Processing   35

4. Data Bases and Filing Systems   61

5. Spreadsheets   89

6. Graphics, Classroom Publishing, Telecommunications, and Support Tools   113

7. Integrated Software   143

PART 3   THE COMPUTER AS TUTOR   161

8. Computer-Assisted Instruction   163

9. Courseware Evaluation   201

10. Computer-Managed Instruction   231

PART 4   THE COMPUTER AS LEARNER   243

11. The Concepts of Programming   245

12. Logo   265

13. BASIC   289

14. Beyond Logo and BASIC   315

PART 5   MICROCOMPUTERS IN EDUCATION   345

15. Computer Literacy and Beyond:
    Curriculum Integration   347

16. Implementation: How Do We Do It?   359

17. Issues and Implications   381

PART 6   LOOKING AHEAD   401

18. Today and Tomorrow   403

Appendices   417

Glossary   431

Index   443

□ Contents □

PART 1 GETTING STARTED 1

1 □ Historical Perspectives   3

Early Data Processing Devices 4
THE ABACUS 4 THE FIRST MACHINES 4 AUTOMATED
MANUFACTURING AND JACQUARD 4 THE ANALYTICAL ENGINE,
BABBAGE, AND LADY ADA 5
Two Lines of Development 6
UNIT RECORD DATA PROCESSING 6 THE START OF THE
COMPUTER 9
The Modern Computer Era 11
FIRST GENERATION—TUBES 11 SECOND GENERATION—
TRANSISTORS 12 THIRD GENERATION—INTEGRATED
CIRCUITS 12 FOURTH GENERATION—MICROELECTRONICS 12
The Microcomputer 14
REAL COMPUTER POWER 14 NEW APPLICATIONS 14 NEW
USERS 14
Summary 15
Bibliography 15

2 □ Microcomputer Systems   17

Hardware—The Physical System 18
CENTRAL PROCESSING UNIT 18 MEMORY 19 INPUT DEVICES 20
OUTPUT DEVICES 22 SECONDARY STORAGE DEVICES 24
MODEMS 26
Software—Making the System Work 26
PROGRAMS 27 OPERATING SYSTEMS 27

Summary 29
Chapter 2 Activities 30
Bibliography 31

PART 2   THE COMPUTER AS TOOL   33

3 □ Word Processing   35

An Overview of Word Processing   36
DEFINITIONS 36   BASIC CONCEPTS OF WORD PROCESSING 37
THE SPREAD OF WORD PROCESSING 37   WORD PROCESSOR
FUNCTIONS 39   WRITING AIDS 40

Benefits of Word Processing   45
EFFECTS ON QUANTITY AND QUALITY 45   IMPROVING
ATTITUDES 46   FINDING AN AUDIENCE 47   COPING WITH
WRITER'S BLOCK 47   OVERCOMING PAST EXPERIENCE 47
BUILDING READING SKILLS 47   SUMMARIES OF BENEFITS 48

Issues in Word Processing   49
THE APPROPRIATE AGE TO BEGIN 49   KEYBOARDING 49   THE
PROCESS APPROACH TO WRITING 51   CRITIQUES OF THE
TRADITIONAL APPROACH 51

Classroom Applications   52
LEARNING TO USE A WORD PROCESSOR 53   TEACHING
SEQUENCING 53   TOPIC IDENTIFICATION 54   LETTER
WRITING 54   PROMPTED WRITING 54   WRITING FOR
BEGINNERS 54   POETRY 55   GROUP PROJECTS 55   WRITING
ACROSS THE CURRICULUM 56

Summary   57
Chapter 3 Activities   57
References   58

4 □ Data Bases and Filing Systems   61

Challenges of the Information Age   62
THE TROUBLE WITH INFORMATION 62   THE NEED FOR DATA
MANAGEMENT 62   THE BENEFITS OF ELECTRONIC DATA
MANAGEMENT 63   DATA MANAGEMENT IN EDUCATION 64

The Technical Side of Data Management   65
CONCEPTS AND DEFINITIONS 65   DATA BASES 66   FILING
SYSTEMS 69   HYPERMEDIA 72   COMPACT AND LASER DISCS 74

Classroom Applications   75
TEACHERS AND DATA FILES 75   STUDENTS AND DATA FILES 76

Research on Learning with Data Bases   83
Summary 84
Chapter 4 Activities 84
References 85

5 □ Spreadsheets   *89*

   Development of Application Software   90
     COMPUTERS FOR PROGRAMMERS 90   COMPUTERS FOR NON-
     PROGRAMMERS 90   VISIBLE CALCULATORS 90   MORE POWERFUL
     SPREADSHEETS 91
   The Technical Side of Spreadsheets   92
     FUNDAMENTAL CONCEPTS 92   USING A SPREADSHEET 94
   An Example Spreadsheet—Class Recordkeeping   97
     CREATING THE SPREADSHEET 98   MANIPULATING THE
     SPREADSHEET 100   TEMPLATES 102   SUMMARY 103
   Categories of Spreadsheet Applications   103
     RECORDKEEPING 103   CALCULATION WORKSHEETS 104
     "WHAT IF" APPLICATIONS 104
   Classroom Applications   105
     FUNDRAISERS IN GRADE 2 AND HIGH SCHOOL 105   BUDGETS IN
     GRADE 5 106   HIGH SCHOOL MATHEMATICS 106   HYPOTHESIS
     TESTING OR WHAT IF? 106   WORD PROBLEMS 106   SPORTS
     STATISTICS 107   URBAN LIVABILITY 107   FAST FOOD
     COMPARISONS 107   PEER GRADING 107   HEALTH 108
     PERSONAL FINANCES 108   GROWTH MODELS 108   ENERGY
     USAGE 108   TEACHING SPREADSHEETS 108   MISCELLANEOUS
     APPLICATIONS 109
   Summary   109
   Chapter 5 Activities   110
   References   111

6 □ Graphics, Classroom Publishing, Telecommunications,   *113*
and Support Tools

   Graphics   114
     PRINT GRAPHICS 114   PRESENTATION GRAPHICS 117
   Classroom Publishing   118
   Telecommunications   120
     CONFERENCING 121   ELECTRONIC MESSAGING 121
     TELECOMMUNICATIONS APPLICATIONS 123
     IMPLEMENTATION 124
   Support Tools   124
     GRAPHING PROGRAMS 125   PUZZLE GENERATORS 131   TEST-
     GENERATING PROGRAMS 134   WORKSHEET GENERATORS 136
     READABILITY ANALYSIS 137   CLOZE 137   STATISTICAL
     PACKAGES 138   GRADE BOOKS 138   SPECIAL PURPOSE DATA
     MANAGERS 138   A CAVEAT 140
   Summary   140
   Chapter 6 Activities   140
   References   141

7 □ Integrated Software   **143**

The Rise of Integrated Software   144
FUNDAMENTAL DATA PROCESSING APPLICATIONS 144
APPROACHES TO MULTIPLE PROCESSING NEEDS 144

Concepts of Integrated Software   147
SIMPLE INTEGRATION 147   WINDOWS 148   COMPLEX
INTEGRATION 149

Assessing Integrated Programs   151
ADVANTAGES 151   DISADVANTAGES 152

Desktop Publishing   153
WHAT IS DESKTOP PUBLISHING? 153   ADVANTAGES AND
DISADVANTAGES 155

Classroom Applications of Integrated Programs   155
SINGLE-MODE APPLICATIONS 155   INTEGRATED APPLICATIONS
AND RESOURCES 156

Summary   159
Chapter 7 Activities   159
References   160

PART 3   THE COMPUTER AS TUTOR   161

8 □ Computer-Assisted Instruction   **163**

The Nature of Computer-Assisted Instruction   164
INTERACTIVITY 164   FLEXIBILITY 164   MEETING STUDENT
NEEDS 165

Evolution of Computer-Assisted Instruction   165
THE MAINFRAME BASE 165   OTHER EARLY INITIATIVES 166
TECHNOLOGICAL GAINS 166   MAJOR RESEARCH AND
DEVELOPMENT PROJECTS 166   MAJOR PROGRAM
EVALUATION 167

Common Types of CAI   167
DRILL AND PRACTICE 167   TUTORIALS 171   SIMULATIONS 174
INSTRUCTIONAL GAMES 178   PROBLEM SOLVING 181

New CAI Directions   185
MULTIMEDIA CAI 185   INTERACTIVE VIDEO 186   INTELLIGENT
CAI 188

What the Research Shows   190
ACHIEVEMENT 190   EFFECTIVENESS BY LEVEL OF
INSTRUCTION 191   LEARNING RETENTION AND TIME 191
ATTITUDES 192   PROBLEM SOLVING 192   PROBLEMS WITH THE
RESEARCH 193

Summary   193
Chapter 8 Activities   194
References   195

9 □ Courseware Evaluation   *201*

    The Issue of Quality   202
        SOFTWARE—THE CRITICAL ELEMENT 202   QUALITY TRAILS
        QUANTITY 202   WHY QUALITY IS PROBLEMATIC 203   THE NEED
        FOR EVALUATION 205   WHO SHOULD EVALUATE
        COURSEWARE? 206
    Approaches to Courseware Evaluation   206
        ADVICE OR RECOMMENDATIONS 206   PROFESSIONAL
        REVIEWS 207   HANDS-ON EVALUATION 209
    Evaluation Considerations   212
        INTENDED USE 212   LEARNING THEORY 212   SPECIFIC
        CRITERIA 217   EVALUATION OF SPECIFIC CAI TYPES 222
    Pulling It All Together   222
        EVALUATION FORMS 222
    Summary   226
    Chapter 9 Activities   227
    References   228

10 □ Computer-Managed Instruction   *231*

    An Overview of Computer-Managed Instruction   232
        BACKGROUND CONCEPTS 232   AN EARLY CMI SYSTEM—PROJECT
        PLAN 233
    Microcomputers and Computer-Managed Instruction 234
        CMI AS PERFORMANCE MONITORING AND ANALYSIS 234   CMI AS
        TEST-SCORING AND TESTING DEVICE 236   STUDENT USERS OF
        CMI 237   INTEGRATED LEARNING SYSTEMS 237   CONCERNS
        REGARDING CMI 238   EVALUATING A CMI SYSTEM 240
    Summary   240
    Chapter 10 Activities   241
    References   241

PART 4   THE COMPUTER AS LEARNER   243

11 □ The Concepts of Programming   *245*

    A Rationale for Programming   246
        PROGRAMMING AND TEACHERS 246   PROGRAMMING AND
        STUDENTS 247
    Fundamental Programming Concepts   248
        CONTROL 248   PLANNING 251   STRUCTURED
        PROGRAMMING 255   CODING 257   TESTING AND REVISION 259
    Programming and Languages   259
        LOW-LEVEL LANGUAGES 260   HIGH-LEVEL LANGUAGES 261
    Summary   262
    References   263

What is Logo?   266
   PHILOSOPHICAL AND PSYCHOLOGICAL FOUNDATIONS 266
   IMPLEMENTATION 267

Characteristics of Logo   268
   LOGO OFFERS MANY PRIMITIVES 268   LOGO IS PROCEDURAL 269
   LOGO IS RECURSIVE 272   LOGO IS INTERACTIVE 273   LOGO USES
   EASILY UNDERSTOOD WORDS 274   LOGO IS EASY TO USE 274
   OTHER CAPABILITIES OF LOGO 275

Logo Derivatives   275
   LOGOWRITER 275   LEGO® TC *logo* 276   LOGO PLUS 276

Why Teach Logo?   277
   LOGO IS UNIQUE 277   PROBLEM-SOLVING POTENTIAL 277
   RELATIONSHIP TO BLOOM'S HIERARCHY 278

Establishing the Logo Environment   279
   ROLE OF THE TEACHER 279   DIFFICULTY WITH TEACHER'S
   ROLE 279

Teaching Strategies   280
   USING ONE'S BODY AS "TURTLE" 280   TRANSPARENCY
   MAZES 280   DISPLAYING STUDENT WORK 281   EMPHASIZE PEER
   QUESTIONING 281

What the Research Shows   281
   METACOGNITIVE AND COGNITIVE DEVELOPMENT 281   PROBLEM
   SOLVING 282   REASONING ABILITY 283   SOCIAL-EMOTIONAL
   DEVELOPMENT 283   RESEARCH SUMMARY 284

Summary   284

Chapter 12 Activities   285

References   286

Development of BASIC   290
   COMPUTERS AND STUDENTS 290   THE SPREAD OF BASIC 290

Key Features of BASIC   291
   LINE NUMBERS 291   MODEST VOCABULARY 291
   INTERACTIVE 291

Structured BASIC   292
   THE SEQUENCE CONSTRUCT 292   THE SELECTION
   CONSTRUCT 298   THE ITERATION CONSTRUCT (LOOPING) 305

The Great BASIC Debate   309
   ADVANTAGES OF BASIC 309   DISADVANTAGES OF BASIC 311
   OUR RESPONSE TO THE DEBATE 312

Summary   313

Chapter 13 Activities   313

References   314

14 □ Beyond Logo and BASIC   315

Programming Languages   316
PASCAL 316   THE C LANGUAGE 318   FORTRAN 320   COBOL 321
AI, PROLOG, AND LOGIC PROGRAMMING 324
Authoring Software   326
WHY TEACHERS CREATE SOFTWARE 326   AUTHORING
LANGUAGES 328   AUTHORING SYSTEMS 331   HYPERCARD 334
EXPERT SYSTEMS SHELLS 336
Summary   338
Chapter 14 Activities   339
References   340

PART 5   MICROCOMPUTERS IN EDUCATION   345

15 □ Computer Literacy and Beyond: Curriculum Integration   347

Computer Literacy   348
THE PROGRAMMING MODEL 348 THE LITERACY CURRICULUM
MODEL 349 THE PROBLEM SOLVING MODEL 351   THE TOOLS/
APPLICATIONS MODEL 351   CONCLUSION 352
Curriculum Integration   352
WHAT IS THE SCOPE? 353   ADVANTAGES 354
The National View   355
Beyond Integration   355
Summary   356
Chapter 15 Activities   357
References   357

16 □ Implementation: How Do We Do It?   359

One View of Implementation History   360
THE EARLY 80s—GETTING STARTED 360   THE LATE 80s—
ASSESSMENT AND REFLECTION 361
Implementation for the 90s   362
THE GOAL 362   TEACHER INVOLVEMENT 363   HARDWARE AND
FACILITIES 365   BUDGETARY POTPOURRI 371   ARTICULATION—
WHAT'S THAT? 374   WHERE CAN I GET HELP? 374
Summary   375
Chapter 16 Activities   375
References   376
Selected Shareware or Public Domain Sources   379
Special Education Resources   380

17 □ Issues and Implications   381

Social Issues   382
IMPACT ON WORK 382   PERSONAL PRIVACY 383

Ethics 384
COPYRIGHT 385 HACKING 386 VIRUSES 387 WHITE COLLAR
CRIME 388
Equity 388
GENDER 388 ECONOMICS 389
Excessive Reliance on Computers 390
MATHEMATICS 390 WRITTEN COMMUNICATION 391 COMPUTER
INFALLIBILITY 392
Changing Roles 393
TEACHERS 393 STUDENTS 394 PARENTS 394
Summary 395
Chapter 17 Activities 396
References 397

PART 6   LOOKING AHEAD   401

18 □ Today and Tomorrow   403

Looking Back 404
GETTING STARTED 404 THE COMPUTER AS TOOL 404 THE
COMPUTER AS TUTOR 404 THE COMPUTER AS LEARNER 405
MICROCOMPUTERS IN EDUCATION 405
Looking Ahead 405
Trends in Microcomputer Hardware 406
MICROPROCESSORS 406 MEMORY 406 MASS STORAGE 406
INPUT/OUTPUT (I/O) 407 PHYSICAL SIZE 408
TELECOMMUNICATIONS AND NETWORKING 408 COSTS 408
The Future of Software 408
SELECTION 409 COMPLEXITY 409 COST 410 AS SOFTWARE FOR
LEARNING 410 MULTI-MEDIA 410
Computers in Education 411
GLIMPSES OF THE FUTURE 411 ASSESSMENT OF THOSE
FUTURES 411 TOWARD THE 21ST CENTURY 412
Reflections 413
Conclusion 413
Chapter 18 Activities 414
References 414

Appendices   417

Appendix A   Software Mentioned in the Text with
             Sources 417
Appendix B   Selected Software and Integrated Learning
             Systems Producers/Sources 420
Appendix C   CD-Rom Sources 424

Appendix D   Sources of Videodiscs and/or Related
             Products   424
Appendix E   Telecommunications Resources   425
Appendix F   Professional Associations and
             Organizations of Interest to Computer
             Educators   426
Appendix G   Publications of Interest to Computer
             Educators   428

Glossary   *431*

Index   *443*

□ PART 1 □
Getting Started

CHAPTER 1

☐ *Historical Perspectives* ☐

OBJECTIVES

After completing this chapter, you will be able to:

- ☐ *Define basic terms and concepts such as data, stored program control, mainframe, microcomputer.* ☐
- ☐ *Discuss the contributions to the development of computing by such major figures as Blaise Pascal, Charles Babbage, Hermann Hollerith, John Von Neumann.* ☐
- ☐ *Differentiate among the first four generations of computers in terms of their fundamental technology.* ☐

The microcomputers of today are the culmination of a long search for better and more efficient ways of getting things done. This chapter presents a brief history of this search and puts the present into perspective.

Humans have always sought more efficient ways of doing things. Just as we have created machines to ease our physical labors, we have also searched for ways to make mental work easier. The resulting devices are called *data processing machines.*

Data are meaningful pieces of information. Examples of data are names, addresses, ages, and similar descriptive information about individuals. *Processing* is doing something with data. Examples of simple *data processing* are alphabetizing names, ordering addresses, or calculating the average age of a group of people. While all these processing tasks can be performed manually, as either the amount of data or the complexity of the processing increases, a more efficient way of performing such tasks is not only desirable but often a necessity. Thus, the need for data processing machines.

EARLY DATA PROCESSING DEVICES

THE ABACUS

The abacus was invented and used by the Chinese centuries ago to speed up simple mathematical calculations. By moving little beads on wires, the process of addition and subtraction is facilitated. The abacus is probably the oldest data processing device.

THE FIRST MACHINES

Around 1650, Blaise Pascal constructed the tooth and gear adding machine, which consisted of a series of interlocking wheels with ten teeth around their outside rims. When one wheel made a complete revolution, its gearing caused the next wheel to turn a single notch. The teeth on each wheel represented the digits 0 through 9. As each wheel was turned forward to represent the numbers to be summed, this device served as a mechanical adding machine. If one turned the wheels in the reverse direction, it served as a mechanical subtracting machine.

Twenty years later, Gottfried Leibnitz enhanced Pascal's device, giving it the ability to multiply and divide. Thus, by the end of the seventeenth century a machine existed that could mechanically perform the basic operations of mathematics. The concept behind Pascal's machine remained the basis for the adding machines and calculators of the early twentieth century.

AUTOMATED MANUFACTURING AND JACQUARD

The next developmental step for data processing machines stems from the work of Joseph Marie Jacquard in 1790. Realizing the repetitive and time-consuming nature of hand weaving cloth, Jacquard designed and constructed an automated loom. This loom was controlled by a series of cards with holes punched into them. A single card directed the automated loom in constructing one row of the fabric. A set of such cards then directed construction of a series of rows of the fabric, eventually resulting in the desired pattern.

The advantages of such a process were many. First, the procedure was automatic. Once the cards had been prepared, they controlled the loom in making the desired fabric. Second, when a given fabric had been completed, the cards could be reinserted into the loom and used again to make an identical fabric. Third, by changing some of the cards, the operator of the loom could make material with variations in the original pattern. Fourth, an entirely new deck of punched cards could be inserted and used to create a totally different patterned cloth on the same machine.

Jacquard's concept, the use of a series of cards punched with holes that could be processed by machine, established one of the two paths that data processing machines would follow in the next 150 years. The other path developed from the ideas of Charles Babbage.

THE ANALYTICAL ENGINE, BABBAGE, AND LADY ADA

About the middle of the nineteenth century, an Englishman named Charles Babbage approached the processing of data from a different perspective. Living in the midst of the Industrial Revolution and aware of advances being made in motors and related devices, Babbage proposed a new concept for a processing machine. His machine would be capable of accepting a large amount of information. Once this information was stored internally, the machine would perform all the desired processing and output the results. Jacquard's processing was accomplished in small steps, each controlled by a punched card. Babbage's processing was to be accomplished all at once after all information was presented to the system.

Babbage called his machine the Analytical Engine, and while he drew plans for it, the engine never became fully operational. The concept was sound, but the technology of his time was inadequate for its implementation. About 100 years later, with much greater mechanical sophistication and the use of electricity, Babbage's concept served as the starting point in the development of modern data processing devices. It is for this reason that Babbage is often referred to as the "father of modern data processing."

Babbage was assisted in his work by Ada Lovelace, daughter of the poet Lord Byron and a gifted mathematician. In fact, much of what is known about the Analytical Engine's programming potential comes from an article written by Lady Ada in which she presented a fascinating analysis of the machine and Babbage's ideas. Her contributions to the development of computing were acknowledged when a computer language—Ada—was named in her honor.

TWO LINES OF DEVELOPMENT

UNIT RECORD DATA PROCESSING

The next advance occurred in the United States in the late 1800s and returned to the concepts of Jacquard. With the beginning of the great immigration period in the United States, the taking of the census every ten years became an increasingly difficult task. Officials noted that the 1880 census had taken nearly seven years to complete and projected that the 1890 census would require over ten years to complete if performed in the same manner. Clearly something had to be done!

The Census Bureau hired Hermann Hollerith to develop procedures for speeding up the processing of census data. To perform many of the data processing tasks, Hollerith designed a series of machines. They used a card punched with holes to represent the census information of one person. Other cards were punched representing the census information of other people, one card per person. These cards became known as *unit records,* since they contained the record of one person or unit. A group of these unit records was referred to as a file.

Hollerith's machines processed these cards automatically and completed the necessary census tasks faster and more efficiently than by hand. The machine that prepared the punched cards eventually became known as the keypunch. Examples of other machines Hollerith produced are the reproducer (which made copies of cards), the sorter (which rearranged cards in a file), and the tabulator (which counted the data on cards in files).

Commercial Applications

Utilizing his unit record processing machines, Hollerith was able to complete the 1890 census in approximately three years rather than the previously estimated ten years. This procedure for processing data clearly worked. In fact, it worked so well that in 1896 Hollerith left the Census Bureau and founded the Hollerith Tabulating Machine Company. Hollerith reasoned that if such machines could process census data efficiently, they would also find applicability in the general business community.

During the early part of this century, the Census Bureau discontinued using the Hollerith machines and hired another engineer, James Powers, to develop other ways to process census data. By 1910, Powers developed and put into use a series of machines that, while functioning on concepts similar to Hollerith's, were different enough to qualify for patents. The 1910 census was run using these machines and was completed efficiently and speedily. Powers also saw the benefit of these machines for the business community and in 1911 founded the Powers Accounting Machine Company.

The history of data processing for a good part of this century is the history of these two companies. In 1911, the Hollerith Tabulating Machine Company merged with the International Time Recording Company and the Dayton Scale

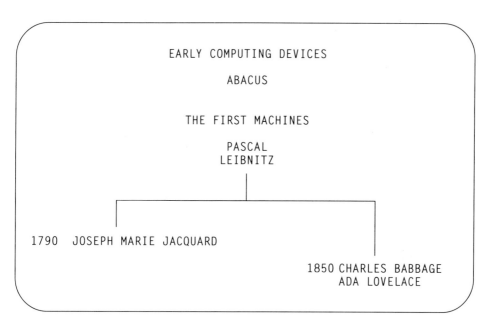

FIGURE 1.1. Computer history outline: From the beginning through the mid-nineteenth century

Company to become the Computing-Tabulating-Recording Company. In 1924, its name was changed to International Business Machines (IBM) to reflect the world-wide market served by the company.

The Powers Accounting Machine Company merged with several office supply companies to become the Remington Rand Company. Through mergers the Remington Rand Company became Sperry Rand and, most recently, Unisys.

The similar machines that these two companies produced served the data processing needs of the business community for many years. Their machines were continually upgraded to reflect technological advancements and finally became the full-fledged unit record data processing equipment that was available into the 1960s.

While unit record processing met the needs of the business community, it did not serve the somewhat different needs of the scientific community. In an oversimplified comparison, business often requires relatively straightforward and noncomplex processing of a large amount of individual data (such as payroll or billing), while scientific needs often focus on complex processing of a relatively small amount of data (as in statistics or engineering). There were many attempts to modify unit record machines to meet the demands of the scientific community. Examples include the upgraded unit record calculator and the card programmed calculator. Neither was completely successful. A scientific data processing machine had to be conceptualized differently from then-current business data processing machines.

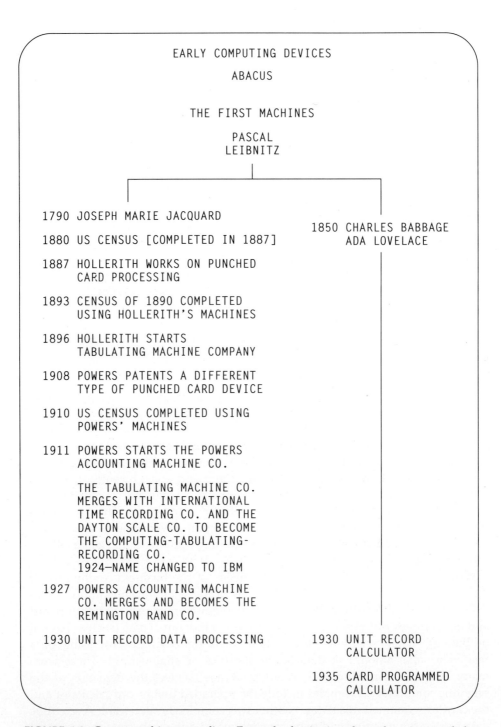

FIGURE 1.2. Computer history outline: From the beginning through unit record data processing

THE START OF THE COMPUTER

Machines suited to scientific applications began to appear in the mid-1930s. They were developed from the concepts of Babbage's Analytical Engine rather than from the concepts of Jacquard's automatic loom. The first electronic digital computer was designed and built by John Atanasoff and Clifford Berry at Iowa State College in 1942. In 1944, with funding from IBM, engineers and scientists at Harvard University designed and built the Mark I—The Automatic Sequence Controlled Calculator. These machines worked on the principle of data being input into a central processing unit where all processing was sequentially controlled until completed. The results were then output to the user. With the harnessing of electricity into vacuum tubes and electrical circuits, such a machine could not only be built, but worked as Babbage had predicted. For example, The Mark I could complete in approximately two minutes what had previously required over 20 hours of manual processing. Clearly, these were the types of machines that were needed by the scientific community.

About the same time the University of Pennsylvania was also developing and building a data processing machine following Babbage's ideas and geared to scientific processing. This machine was called the ENIAC—the Electronic Numerical Integrator and Calculator. It also worked successfully. Scientific data processing machines were becoming a reality.

The Control Problem

These early machines also had problems, the most serious of which was control. Setting them up to perform a specific processing job often required many hours of actual rewiring. Once rewired, the machines could perform quickly and accurately, but after completing a specific task, extensive rewiring was again necessary to perform a different processing task. Researchers had demonstrated that machines could be built that were capable of doing scientific processing. What was needed was a method of efficiently controlling them.

The Stored Program Computer

The control problem was eventually addressed by a mathematician and physicist named John Von Neumann. In 1945, Von Neumann published an article proposing a solution and outlining a machine that incorporated his new control concepts. This machine he called the EDVAC—the Electronic Discrete Variable Automatic Computer. The age of the unit record machine was ending; the age of the computer was about to begin.

Von Neumann's concept was termed *stored program control*. The idea was to build control capabilities into the machine and not view control as something external to the processing unit. The internal control unit would understand and use an instruction to direct the rest of the system to perform a desired operation. A series of instructions would make up a program which, when entered into the system, would be executed one instruction at a time to perform a complex processing task. Such computer systems were known as stored program computer systems to differentiate them from earlier machines.

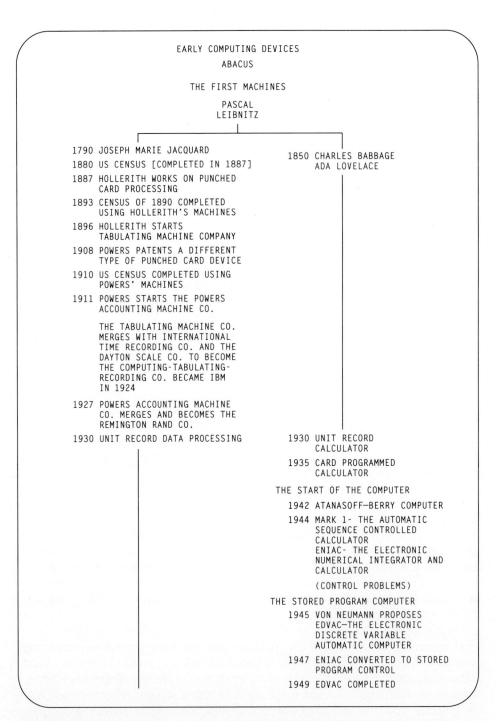

FIGURE 1.3. Computer history outline: From the beginning through the stored program computer

Work was begun on Von Neumann's EDVAC. While this machine was being built, the ENIAC at the University of Pennsylvania was converted to stored program control. In 1947, the redesigned ENIAC became one of the first functioning stored program computer systems. By 1950, the EDVAC was completed as were other stored program computers.

As the new computers were being developed, two fundamentally different approaches were proposed. Alan Turing and other British scientists argued that computers should be multipurpose. The multipurpose computer's instruction set would be based on *formal logic* and use *logical operators* such as AND, OR, and NOT to manipulate symbolic material, even ordinary language. Operators for arithmetic would be derived from the logical operators.

American scientists on the other hand, argued for computers that were based on mathematics. The fundamental instruction set for this type of computer would use numerical operators such as $+$, $-$, $<$. Such a computer would be less complex and, therefore, less expensive to build. It would better serve what was then thought to be the primary function of computers, that is, the processing of numerical data.

The American approach won out and serves as one of the conceptual bases of contemporary computers. There has always remained, however, a core of logic-based computer scientists. Recently, research in artificial intelligence has led to a resurgence of interest in logic-based computers.

THE MODERN COMPUTER ERA

Although the paths from Jacquard and Babbage existed in parallel for many years, they converged in the modern computer era, which is identified by four generations of technology.

FIRST GENERATION—TUBES

While a few stored program computers existed before 1950, they were still not widely available to the general scientific community. At that time, however, the Remington Rand Corporation hired some of the personnel who had worked on the ENIAC computer at the University of Pennsylvania. In 1951, Remington Rand introduced the first commercially available computer system, the UNIVAC I. The IBM 650 soon followed. Thus, by the middle 1950s both of the large unit record machine companies also built and distributed stored program computers.

The computers of this period are called the first generation of modern computer systems. They were constructed using vacuum tubes, were large and relatively expensive, and were prone to breakdown. But they did perform as indicated and started to gain acceptance in the scientific community and at least gained notice from the business world.

SECOND GENERATION—TRANSISTORS

The mid-1950s saw development of the transistor, which made vacuum tubes obsolete. Tubes were replaced with transistors that were cheaper, faster, more reliable, and easier to incorporate into complex electrical circuits. As a result, computers were re-engineered using transistors. Remington Rand introduced the UNIVAC 1102 while IBM introduced a series of machines (the IBM 1620 and 7090 for small- and large-scale scientific processing and the IBM 1401 and 7070 to meet small- and large-scale business data processing needs). All of these machines were faster and more complex than previous machines. At the same time, costs were held down by advances in technology. These computers, along with those of new companies in this period, are called the second generation of computer systems.

The introduction of business-oriented computers marked a significant change in direction. While first-generation computers were oriented toward scientific processing, computer manufacturers soon realized that their machines could also perform the functions of unit record equipment more quickly, more efficiently, and at lower cost. These new computers eventually took over all of the business data processing that had been performed for over 50 years by unit record machines.

THIRD GENERATION—INTEGRATED CIRCUITS

The early 1960s saw the development of solid logic technology and solid-state integrated circuits (ICs), which allowed many single-function electronic components of a computer to be combined into one device. Computers were redesigned to take advantage of these advances in technology and the third generation of computers was born.

Similar to the advances of the second generation, third-generation machines were more complex and faster, while their costs were not appreciably increased. Because of greater capabilities, the distinction between business and scientific computers slowly disappeared. There were simply small to large computers that could perform business or scientific processing with equal ease. Computers had become an integral part of both the business and scientific communities.

FOURTH GENERATION—MICROELECTRONICS

The early 1970s saw another technological leap, the introduction of the microprocessor, a tiny device that combined the functions of numerous integrated circuits on a single chip. The fourth generation of computers was upon us. Again machines were redesigned to make use of new technology and became even faster and more complex at stable cost.

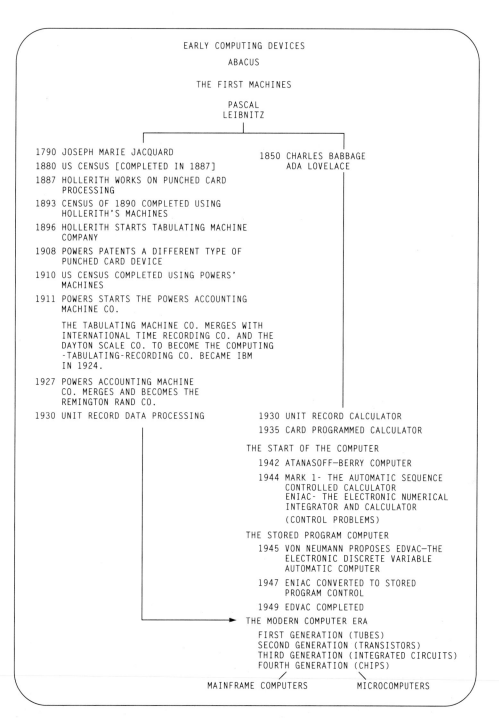

FIGURE 1.4. Computer history outline: From the beginning through fourth generation computers

THE MICROCOMPUTER

While computers were becoming increasingly complex, several individuals conceived of using microprocessors to build small, personal computers for individual use. The first of these machines appeared in the mid-1970s. They became known as *microcomputers* to differentiate them from the much larger computers which became known as *mainframe* computers.

The next few years brought innovation in the continual development and improvement of the microprocessors used in all types of computers. Both mainframe and microcomputers have continued to increase in power and capability. One can view mainframe computers as large systems serving multiple users and the complex needs of science and industry. Microcomputers can be considered personal systems serving the more modest needs of individual users.

REAL COMPUTER POWER

The microcomputers of today should not be thought of as toys or scaled-down mainframe computers with limited power and applicability. In the early years, typical first- and second-generation mainframe computers cost over $250,000, and in terms of their processing capabilities, they were worth it. Today, an individual could buy a more powerful microcomputer system for 1% of that price or less. Such has been the technological advancement and improvement in computer engineering.

NEW APPLICATIONS

Microcomputers are capable of doing more than just many of the same things that mainframe computers can. Many applications have been developed for microcomputers that are either inefficient or impractical on a mainframe, yet are extremely useful. Examples include word processing, spreadsheet management, and computer-based learning, applications that are more individual in nature and thus better suited to microcomputers than to mainframes.

NEW USERS

Low cost, remarkable processing power, and new applications have seen the movement of computers and computer power into areas with little or no prior access to computer capabilities. Such areas include education, small businesses, and the home. The microcomputer is already performing tasks that only a few years ago were not even thought of as potential applications for computers.

Microcomputers have extended computing power to a much wider audience than mainframe computers. Mainframe use had been limited to those who had access to such large computers. This excluded a great majority of individuals who, therefore, could not take advantage of the computer to satisfy their individual data processing needs. Microcomputers have changed this and have made computer power accessible to everyone.

This book will introduce you to this new type of widely available computer, the microcomputer. You will explore what it is, how it can be controlled, specific applications to education, and some of the implications as it finds its way more and more into our daily lives. It is only through an understanding of this new phenomenon that an individual can appreciate the capabilities available to all of us personally and professionally.

SUMMARY

The human search for easier ways to accomplish necessary tasks has produced many useful devices. Efforts to assist with mental tasks began with the abacus. Pascal and Leibnitz produced the first mechanical calculating devices in the seventeenth century. In the nineteenth century, the automation of weaving looms by Jacquard established one of two paths that led to the modern computer era. The other path stemmed from Babbage, who conceptualized the Analytical Engine.

Jacquard's concepts for automated looms guided the development of unit record data processing, which progressed rapidly from the work of Hollerith and Powers for the U.S. Census Bureau. From their government experience, both went on to form private firms that are known today as IBM and Unisys, respectively.

Unit record data processing satisfied the needs of business but was less viable for scientific needs. Scientific requirements led to the development of the stored program computer, an outgrowth of the work of Babbage. The paths from Jacquard and Babbage converged at the start of the modern computer era in the 1950s.

The modern era is divided into generations of computers based upon the underlying technology. The first generation relied on vacuum tubes. Transistors marked the second generation. In the third generation, solid-state technology and integrated circuits were the key features. Microelectronics, specifically the chip and microprocessors, created the fourth generation.

These four generations bring developments to our focal point, the microcomputer. Microcomputers have placed computing power into the hands of millions who before the late 1970s could never have dreamed of it. In addition, significant new applications have become available that hold special interest for educators. This book will acquaint you with the microcomputer and its applications in education.

BIBLIOGRAPHY

Bitter, G. G. *Computers in Today's World.* New York: John Wiley and Sons, 1984.

Capron, H. L. *Computers. Tools for an Information Age.* Menlo Park, CA: Benjamin/ Cummings, 1987.

Hicks, J. O. *Information Systems in Business: An Introduction.* St. Paul, MN: West Publishing, 1986.

Reiss, L. and Dolan, E. G. *Using Computers: Managing Change.* Cincinnati: South-Western Publishing, 1989.

Rohm, C. E. T., Jr. and Stewart, W. T., Jr. *Essentials of Information Systems.* Santa Cruz, CA: Mitchell Publishing, 1988.

Schnake, M. A. *The World of Computers and Data Processing.* St. Paul, MN; West Publishing Co., 1985.

Shelly, G. B. and Cashman, T. J. *Computer Fundamentals with Application Software.* Boston: Boyd and Fraser, 1986.

Shelly, G. B., and Cashman, T. J. *Computer Fundamentals for an Information Age.* Brea, CA: Anaheim Publishing, 1984.

CHAPTER 2

□ *Microcomputer Systems* □

OBJECTIVES

After completing this chapter, you will be able to:

□ *Differentiate hardware from software.* □
□ *List and briefly explain the basic components of a computer system.* □
□ *Name and describe at least four system input devices.* □
□ *Discuss the important characteristics of monitors and printers.* □
□ *List advantages and disadvantages of each type of secondary storage.* □
□ *Define the concept of a program and explain why programs are needed.* □
□ *Briefly explain the function of operating systems.* □

A microcomputer is a very sophisticated machine, one that can perform a wide variety of useful tasks. In order to comprehend how a computer performs its marvels, you must first understand what this machine is, how you communicate with it, and how it is controlled.

HARDWARE—THE PHYSICAL SYSTEM

Although the word "computer" implies a single machine, a computer is really a system of interconnected components, not just one piece of equipment. These components are collectively referred to as hardware. Figure 2.1 illustrates the basic hardware components of a microcomputer system. The primary component is the central processing unit (CPU), which includes the control unit and the arithmetic/logic unit circuits. In addition, the CPU contains circuits which connect to other internal and external units (memory, input devices, output devices, and secondary storage devices). We will consider these types of mechanical/electrical devices individually as they apply to a microcomputer system.

CENTRAL PROCESSING UNIT

The CPU is the key component, the "brain" of the system. This is where most of the work of the system actually takes place. The CPU of a microcomputer is a microprocessor that consists of two principal parts, the *control unit* and the *arithmetic/logic unit*.

Control Unit
Since a microcomputer system consists of many components, something has to assure that they work together properly. The control unit of the CPU is that manager of all the other pieces of the system. It can be likened to a police officer directing traffic. The basic need for control was described in the previous chapter.

Arithmetic/Logic Unit (ALU)
The power of a computer ultimately rests on its ability to perform arithmetic and logical operations. Microcomputer arithmetic is carried out in a series of steps by circuitry within the ALU. Arithmetic processing speeds can often be greatly increased by the addition of a special math chip that performs arithmetic operations directly rather than as a series of steps. Such chips are called *math coprocessors* because they supplement the basic arithmetic capabilities of the CPU.

The logic circuitry of the ALU handles the decision-making capabilities of the microcomputer. These capabilities are quite simple in nature. The seemingly complex functioning of a microcomputer system is actually the combination of many simple logic steps into a lengthy sequence.

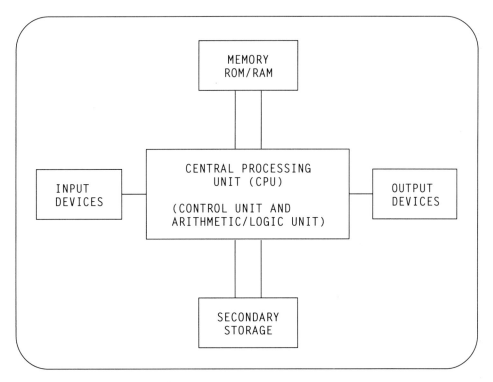

FIGURE 2.1. Components of a microcomputer system

MEMORY

In order for the CPU to do anything, its circuits must have data to process. Memory consists of those microchips that can accept data from external sources, retain them for a length of time, route them to and accept them back from the CPU, and finally relay the results through external devices to the user. There are two types of memory within a microcomputer.

Random Access Memory (RAM)

Random access memory (RAM) is a series of chips that can accept, retain, and have their data erased by the user when it is no longer needed. A simple analogy for RAM is safety deposit boxes into which one can place items for storage until retrieved. This type of memory is termed *volatile* since any data in RAM will be erased and lost when the computer system is turned off.

RAM has a capacity; that is, it can accept and retain only a certain amount of data. The basic unit of memory capacity is the *byte*, the space required to hold an individual number, letter, or special character. Because a useful computer must be able to hold and manipulate thousands of characters at once, RAM size is specified as a number followed by the letter K, the scientific symbol for 1000. Thus, a microcomputer with 128K bytes of RAM is capable of holding about 128,000 individual numbers, letters, and special characters simultaneously.

RAM is very important in any microcomputer system. The amount needed depends upon the job the computer is to do. Common memory sizes are 128K up through several megabytes (1 megabyte or 1 MB = 1 million or 1,000K). Memory can be increased in many computer systems by the addition of more RAM chips.

Read Only Memory (ROM)

The second type of memory in a microcomputer system is read only memory (ROM). ROM chips are programmed when the computer is manufactured and contain information that the system needs to function properly. ROM retains existing information but can neither accept new information nor have its contents altered. This type of memory is termed *nonvolatile,* since the data in it are retained even when the computer system is off.

INPUT DEVICES

The CPU of a microcomputer system is capable of performing a wide variety of tasks, but for most things to occur, it must be given data. Data are entered into the system through input devices. Most systems include one primary input device, a keyboard. Various secondary input devices are available.

Keyboard

The most common method of entering data into a computer system is through a keyboard. A computer keyboard resembles a typewriter, often with the addition of a calculator-like set of numeric keys, directional arrow keys for cursor movement, and other special purpose keys useful to the specific microcomputer.

Secondary Input Devices

A *light pen* resembles a ballpoint pen attached to the computer by a wire. It allows the user to select from choices displayed on the screen simply by touching the pen to the item.

A *mouse* is a hand-sized device with buttons that the user moves around a flat surface to move a corresponding marker (usually an arrow) on the video screen. The screen area pointed to can then be selected as input to the computer by simply pressing one of the mouse buttons. The mouse is increasing in popularity among manufacturers and users because it can simplify some input operations.

A *joystick* is a small box with a movable stick and usually one or two buttons. Moving the stick moves a marker on the screen, and pressing a button sends impulses to the system. It is most often used to play games on the computer.

A *graphics pad* is a board that the user touches and draws upon to communicate patterns to the computer system. These pads have gained wide popularity in art and computer-aided design (CAD).

In some systems, a *touch screen* allows the user to input information by simply

FIGURE 2.2. Graphics pads are used in art and design.

touching the video screen with a finger. This is much like using a light pen, only simpler.

To use a *mark sense scanner,* a user fills in special spaces on preprinted forms with regular pencils. The scanner then senses these markings and transmits the information to the microcomputer. The most common use of these devices is to "read" test answer sheets, a function of growing interest to schools implementing competency-based education programs. Some scanners process small cards, while others handle sheets of paper. Some can be loaded with a stack of forms; others require the user to feed each one separately.

An *optical scanner* is capable of "reading" typed or printed pages, including graphic images, and transmitting the scanned information into the system. This eliminates the need to type material. Such scanners may be hand held and physically moved across the material. More sophisticated page scanners "read" a whole page of inserted material at a time.

The future will probably bring additional innovative and creative methods of computer input. One major area of continuing research and development is voice recognition, which will have special benefits for the handicapped. The ability to control a computer by speaking to it will dramatically alter computer use.

OUTPUT DEVICES

When the computer has performed its tasks, the results of processing must be conveyed back to the user. Information from the CPU is converted into an understandable form through output devices. The primary output devices today are video monitors and printers.

Monitors

The most common way to receive information from a computer system is through a monitor. A monitor is a high-quality television set that displays text and graphics on its screen. Commonly referred to as screen, tube, or CRT (cathode ray tube), monitors vary considerably on several characteristics: color, resolution, and size. Color and resolution are controlled by the type of video circuitry in the system. The monitor itself must match the characteristics of that circuitry.

Color refers to whether the image is displayed in one color, much like black and white television, or in full color like color television. Monochrome monitors display images in one color. Depending upon the monitor selected, images may appear as white, green, or amber against a black background. Color monitors are capable of displaying a full spectrum of colors.

Resolution refers to the clarity of the text or graphic image on the screen. The higher the resolution, the sharper or clearer the image. Higher resolution increases readability and allows for more visually realistic graphic displays. There are many levels of resolution. The more common levels are:

Composite: lowest resolution text and graphics, comparable to TV, full color.
Color Graphics Adapter (CGA): Low resolution characters and graphics capability, full color possible.
Monochrome Display Adapter (MDA): High resolution characters, unable to display graphics, single color.
Hercules: High resolution characters and graphics, usually single color.
Enhanced Graphics Adapter (EGA): High resolution characters and graphics, full color possible.
Video Graphics Array (VGA): Very high resolution characters and graphics, full color possible.

Related to resolution is the number of characters that can be displayed across one line on the screen. While the standard display is 80 characters per line (a necessity for word processing and most advanced applications), most computers can be set to display fewer. This is especially useful with children, because each character is larger and therefore easier to read. Usually a screen displays 24 or 25 text lines.

Monitor sizes vary from five-inch screens in some portable microcomputers up through 25-inch screens for classroom use. For effective use by groups of more than four or five, the video output of a computer should be connected to a video projector to display the images on a large screen. The computer can also be connected to a liquid crystal display (LCD) viewer or panel that is placed on the bed of an overhead projector and focused on a large screen. LCD viewers are especially cost effective and easy to use.

Printers

A printer produces paper output, or *hardcopy*. Although the layout may differ, the contents of the hardcopy duplicate what could be viewed on the screen and may be saved for use after the system is turned off. Printers common to microcomputer systems differ from one another in print method, speed, range of capabilities, print quality, and interface method.

Several quite different methods of printing are widely used. Some printers form characters as a pattern of small dots and are referred to as *dot-matrix printers*. Others form characters by striking formed dies, just like a typewriter, and are referred to as *daisywheel* or *letter-quality printers*. Either type is capable of printing on multipart forms. Both are rather noisy.

Two other print methods are less common. *Ink jet* printers form characters by spraying droplets of ink onto the paper. *Thermal* printers "print" by heating patterns on special heat-sensitive paper. Neither of these can print on multipart forms but both are quieter than dot-matrix or letter-quality printers.

Becoming increasingly popular are *laser* printers, which operate on the principle of photocopy machines. While more expensive than most other printers, their flexibility, print quality, and speed make them desirable in many situations.

Printers differ greatly in speed. The speed of a printer is usually measured by the number of characters per second (CPS) that can be produced. Letter-quality printers are the slowest, printing at 10 to 60 CPS. Dot-matrix printers offer speeds of 100 to 300 CPS or more. The speed of ink jet printers varies widely, from 10 to over 200 CPS. (To estimate the time to print one page, figure that a double-spaced page contains about 1625 characters—25 lines of 65 characters.) Laser printers produce a full page at a time, so the CPS measurement is not used. These are the fastest printers available, commonly printing 8 to 12 pages per minute.

Print capabilities vary among printers in several ways. Some printers can print only characters while others can also create diagrams and illustrations. The latter type of printer is said to have *graphics capability*. Dot-matrix, thermal, and ink jet printers offer graphics printing. Letter-quality printers are not capable of sophisticated graphics. Depending upon the model, laser printers may produce text only, text and some graphics, or text and/or full graphics on a page.

Through the use of colored ribbons or special inking procedures, it is possible for some printers to print in colors other than the usual black or even in multiple colors. Full-color charts and graphics can significantly enhance printed materials.

Most printers allow changes in type size and form, such as pica, elite, italic, and so on. This can be accomplished (within limits) automatically on dot matrix printers and manually on letter-quality printers by changing the character element. On less expensive laser printers, additional type sizes and forms can be obtained from insertable cartridges. More expensive laser printers have the built-in capability for almost unlimited type sizes and forms.

The standard for comparison of print quality is usually the output of a good typewriter. Letter-quality printers produce results virtually identical to those of a typewriter. Thermal and ink jet printers do not print with formed dies; therefore, they produce characters that tend to look less perfect. This is also true of dot matrix printers, but most offer a *near letter-quality* (NLQ) mode. NLQ greatly improves the quality of the print, although at a greatly reduced speed. Some more expensive dot matrix printers utilize more pins within their print head. By single or multiple pass printing, they can produce output almost indistinguishable from letter quality. Laser printers offer the finest print quality available, virtually identical to professional typesetting.

The *interface method* between the computer and the printer is sometimes an important consideration. There are two basic ways that a computer can communicate with the printer: *serial* (one signal at a time) and *parallel* (multiple signals at a time). The computer, the connecting cable, and the printer must all use the same method. The parallel interface is easiest to install correctly and is most common.

With appropriate additional hardware, one printer may be shared by many microcomputers, providing maximum economy in labs or offices. Even the cost of a laser printer may be justified if it is *networked* to several computers, thus avoiding purchase of additional individual printers.

Secondary Output Devices

In addition to monitors and printers, the computer can provide processed information in graphic form or as speech.

Plotters produce output by controlling pens that draw on paper. There can be many different colors of pens on a single plotter, thus allowing very sophisticated graphs, charts, and maps. Only a laser printer can equal the graphic quality of a plotter.

Voice synthesizers convert output to ordinary speech that is intelligible to almost anyone. This is of special significance to the visually impaired.

SECONDARY STORAGE DEVICES

Secondary storage is another component of a microcomputer system. It is awkward to classify, since it functions as memory and also as input and output. There are cassette, floppy disk, hard disk, and optical drives in this category.

A secondary storage device is always accessible to the CPU. Data from the system can be sent to the device and stored. Stored data can be read by the device and sent to the CPU. In this way, these devices serve both input and output functions. Furthermore, the data stored externally remain until intentionally erased—an auxiliary memory function whose capacity may be far greater than the RAM size of the system. These capabilities make such components very important parts of the microcomputer system. Let's look at these components in more detail.

Cassette Drives

A cassette drive uses a cassette tape recorder to retrieve and store information on an audio cassette. The advantage of cassette drives is that they are relatively simple devices and quite inexpensive. Their disadvantages are that they are cumbersome to use when there is a lot of stored information and they operate slowly compared to the more common disk drives. Cassette drives are used in only the least expensive computer systems and are not suitable for most educational needs.

Another very different type of cassette drive is also available. These tape units (or tape "streamers") are high-speed precision units that can read and write large quantities of data at very high speeds. They are used on large microcomputer systems as back-up for the hard disk drives; that is, data from a hard disk drive is copied to a tape unit and stored in case any problems occur with the hard disk drive. If a problem arises, the data can be recovered from the back-up tape unit.

Floppy Disk Drives

Most disk drives use either a $5\frac{1}{4}$-inch flexible ("floppy") diskette to store information or a $3\frac{1}{2}$-inch diskette in a hard plastic case. The data storage capacity of a single floppy diskette depends upon whether data can be stored on both sides of the diskette (single vs. double sided) and the storage density of the data on each surface. Single-density disk drives store fewer data per area of surface than do double-density disk drives. Capacities range from around 100,000 bytes (100K) of data per diskette up to 1,500,000 (1.5MB). Multiple disk drives can be utilized on a system, further increasing storage capabilities.

When a diskette is full or no longer needed, it can be removed from the drive, saved, and replaced with another diskette. Diskettes can also be erased and reused.

Hard Disk Drives

Many microcomputer systems are equipped with hard disk drives. A hard disk drive's rigid recording surfaces are permanently sealed inside a container and therefore not removable. Hard disk systems can store a very large quantity of data (20 to 300 megabytes) that can be accessed at much higher speeds than with floppies. Such systems simplify and accelerate machine use by eliminating handling of diskettes, faster machine input/output operation, and much larger data files. Of course, hard disk systems are more expensive than their floppy disk counterparts. Microcomputer systems with one or more hard disk units and a single floppy disk drive (to interface with non-hard disk systems and for back-up) are becoming increasingly popular.

In an educational lab setting, one hard disk drive may serve many microcomputers in a cost-effective network. Individual microcomputer systems might not have to be equipped with floppy disk drives. With proper planning and foresight, an educational lab can be set up with the proper mix of hardware to maximize individual user capabilities at the minimum overall cost.

Laser/Optical Discs

Laser/optical disks provide an extremely high volume of storage, but are not yet widely available in forms that can record data as well as read prerecorded disks. One particular form, the compact disk-read only memory (CD-ROM), is being promoted as a means of inexpensively distributing large volumes of data, such as electronic encyclopedias. A capacity of 550 megabytes per disk is possible.

Other Devices

In addition to these common devices, there are other somewhat more exotic ones that can provide external storage for a microcomputer system. For similar input and output uses there are high-capacity storage devices (as exemplified by the *Bernoulli Box*, which uses a flexible diskette in a removable rigid case) and hard disk units with removable disks.

MODEMS

A modem (**mo**dulator **dem**odulator) is a device that allows one computer to communicate with another through phone lines. In this way, a modem provides for both input and output, much like secondary storage devices.

The single most important characteristic of modems is their speed; that is, how fast they transmit data through the phone lines. Common modem speeds are 300 baud (about 300 characters per second), 1200 baud (about 1200 characters), and 2400 baud. Faster modems continue to be developed and marketed. Although more costly to purchase, a higher speed modem pays for itself in reduced telephone costs by transmitting or receiving data more quickly. Modems have increased in importance as educators have developed telecommunications applications.

SOFTWARE—MAKING THE SYSTEM WORK

The physical elements of a computer system are actually isolated components. While connected, they do not work as an integrated unit unless directed to do so by the control section of the CPU. The obvious question then is how does one control the control section?

PROGRAMS

Getting a microcomputer system to perform a desired task is a matter of giving the CPU individual instructions concerning what should be done. The control section then directs and coordinates the rest of the system in executing the instructions. A *program* is a series of instructions designed to cause the system to perform a logical sequence of steps that will produce the desired result. The process of writing these instructions is called *programming*. Even if you do no programming personally, programming is still vital. Without programs, a microcomputer can do little more than decorate your desk.

The programs that cause a computer system to perform desired tasks are called *software* to distinguish them from the physical components of the computer system, or *hardware*. Programs come from two basic sources: They can be written by a user or they can be purchased. We will look at both ways of obtaining computer programs, but not just yet. You first need to understand how to get the computer system "up and running," before you can be concerned with programs of direct interest to educators.

OPERATING SYSTEMS

Before a computer system can perform the important tasks we desire of it, it must be prepared to accept and execute instructions. Initial preparation of the system is the task of a very special program called an *operating system*. An operating system is supplied with the computer or purchased for it. The control section of the CPU uses the operating system both to set itself up and to get information on how to perform various system-related tasks.

Some microcomputers have part of the operating system built into memory in ROM chips and only have to be supplied with the remainder when necessary. Other computers must load the entire operating system before anything can be done. Once the computer has the operating system (and has stored some of it in RAM), it is ready to perform the tasks contained in user programs.

The operating system is supplied to the user on one or more diskettes. On a floppy disk system, the programs needed to get the system started are read from a system diskette when the computer is turned on. This is called booting the system. On a hard disk system, the programs on the system disks are copied onto the hard disk and then read from it when the system is booted. Once the system is up and running, other parts of the operating system can be read from the system diskette or the hard disk as needed.

Operating systems differ greatly among makes and sometimes models of computers. There are several operating systems in common use. The Apple II series uses either DOS 3.3 or PRODOS. Most IBM-PC and related microcomputer systems use PC-DOS or MS-DOS while many newer models can also use OS/2. The Macintosh series uses a unique system of its own. UNIX, an operating system devloped for mainframe computers, is also available for some microcomputers.

FIGURE 2.3. Microcomputer software

Operating systems also differ in how they are used. Most are command-driven systems; the user must type the commands. Others are visual, with available commands displayed as text or icons on the screen. The user selects the desired command either by typing an abbreviated designator code or, if the computer system is equipped with a mouse, by clicking on the desired command.

This lack of standardization in operating systems is a major contributor to incompatibility among computers. The following information is therefore general in nature. You should gain a basic understanding from this generic information. Mastering the essential parts of the particular operating system for a specific microcomputer should not be too difficult.

There are two general categories of tasks that an operating system performs: system operation tasks and system utility tasks.

System Operation Tasks

System operation tasks are those that guide the most basic functioning of the computer. They occur through the operating system as needed, without direct requests from the user. Three examples will illustrate the concept.

□ *Screen Control.* The system must be able to place characters on the video screen.

□ *Keyboard input.* The system must be able to accept and interpret input from the keyboard.

□ *Interfacing.* The system must be able to control its various components and allow them to communicate with each other.

Other functions in this category are explained in the manual for the specific operating system.

System Utility Tasks

System utility tasks are functions that are often needed in the course of normal system use. These tasks are performed at the specific request of the user. The four most basic system utility tasks illustrate the concept.

□ *Directory.* The system lists on the screen or printer the contents of a disk.

□ *Format.* The system prepares a blank disk to accept information.

□ *Copy.* The system makes duplicate copies of programs or entire diskettes.

□ *Erase.* The system erases data from a disk.

There are other functions in this category, but they are too numerous or unique to cover here. These are explained in the operating system manuals. A user quickly becomes familiar with those most commonly needed.

Starting up the system and performing various necessary tasks are important functions of any operating system. Without them, a computer system could not function and run the various programs that direct it in the performance of an almost unlimited variety of tasks.

SUMMARY

A computer system consists of several physical components called hardware. The basic elements of a system are a central processing unit (CPU), memory, input and output devices, and secondary storage devices. The CPU handles such critical aspects of the system's operation as arithmetic, logic, and control. RAM and ROM are other critical components of the computer system. Input and output devices are essential to communication between the user and the computer. They exist in many different forms. In addition, to be useful most systems require secondary storage devices, which also provide essential input and output capabilities.

Making all the system components function as a unit is a control task. The heart of control is a series of instructions to the system called a program, or software. One highly specialized program that is essential in any computer system is the operating system. This must be available before the computer can do anything significant. There is a need for standardization of operating systems

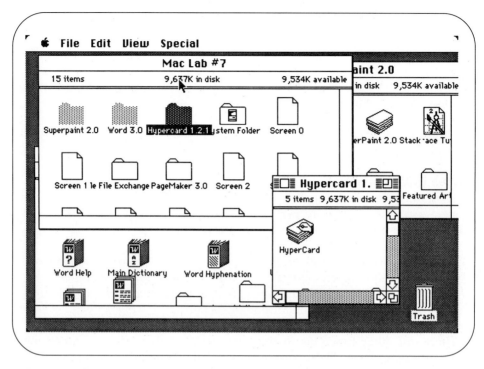

FIGURE 2.4. The Macintosh operating system uses a graphic interface.

among computer manufacturers to ease the problems of incompatibility across makes and models. Major functions of an operating system include system operation tasks that the user is largely unaware of and system utility tasks at the direct command of the user.

CHAPTER 2 ACTIVITIES

1. Using whatever computer system is available, identify the input and output devices.
2. Read any available article about microchips. If possible, physically examine a RAM or ROM chip and try to imagine its actual operation internally.
3. If alternate input devices are unavailable in your school, go to a computer store and request a demonstration of as many as possible. How do they differ? Which appeals most to you? Why?
4. Try to arrange demonstrations of ink jet and laser printing at a nearby dealer. You may also be able to observe a plotter at work. Would one be useful to you?
5. What types of monitors and printers are available in your school? If they are not ideal, what should you have access to? Why?

6. Make a side-by-side visual comparison of the displays from different color monitor types. How noticeable is the difference? (You may need to go to a dealer for this.)
7. Talk to someone who uses a modem. For what purposes is the modem used? What, if any, problems have been encountered in telecommunications?
8. If you have access to computers using different operating systems, try to familiarize yourself with their differences. You might want to make a wall chart for the computer area by listing system utility tasks and noting the corresponding command for each available system.

BIBLIOGRAPHY

Bozeman, W. C. *Computers and Computing in Education,* Chapter 3. Scottsdale, AZ: Gorsuch Scarisbrick, 1985.

Bramble, W. J., and Mason, E. J. *Computers in Schools,* Chapter 2. New York: McGraw-Hill, 1985.

Capron, H. L. *Computers. Tools for an Information Age.* Menlo Park, CA: Benjamin/Cummings, 1987.

Hicks, J. O. *Information Systems in Business: An Introduction.* St. Paul, MN: West Publishing, 1986.

Hofmeister, A. *Microcomputer Applications in the Classroom,* Chapter 8. New York: Holt, Rinehart and Winston, 1984.

Reiss, L. and Dolan, E. G. *Using Computers: Managing Change.* Cincinnati, OH: South-Western Publishing, 1989.

Richardson, R. L., and Gilchrist, J. *Introduction to Computers and Computing,* Chapters 2 and 7. Scottsdale, AZ: Gorsuch Scarisbrick, 1984.

Rohm, C. E. T., Jr. and Stewart, W. T., Jr. *Essentials of Information Systems.* Santa Cruz, CA: Mitchell Publishing, 1988.

Shelly, G. B. and Cashman, T. J. *Computer Fundamentals with Application Software.* Boston: Boyd and Fraser, 1986.

PART 2

The Computer as Tool

C H A P T E R 3

□ *Word Processing* □

O B J E C T I V E S

After completing this chapter, you will be able to:

□ *Explain the concept of word processing.* □

□ *Differentiate between a dedicated word processor and a microcomputer word processor.* □

□ *Define basic word processing functions.* □

□ *Explain the use of spelling, grammar, and style aids.* □

□ *Discuss the benefits of using word processors as contrasted to using other modes of written communication.* □

□ *Discuss the process approach to writing.* □

□ *Define the term* prewriting *and discuss possible uses of software to facilitate prewriting activities.* □

□ *Define the term* keyboarding *and explain the potential problems related to teaching keyboarding skills.* □

□ *Discuss possible classroom applications that make use of word processing.* □

□ *Analyze the role of word processing in the curriculum.* □

How many times have you finished writing a term paper or composition only to find that you have misspelled or omitted a word or phrase? Unfortunately, this omission forced you to retype the entire paper, or at least large segments of it, wasting considerable time and effort—to say nothing of the increased feeling of utter frustration! Just think how great it would be if a manuscript or document could be revised by redoing only those few parts that needed changing. Think of the time and effort that could be saved—not to mention the disposition of the writer! Such is the potential of the word processor. Writing has come a long way since the days of cave walls, cuneiform, hieroglyphics, and slate boards.

Among the potential uses of computers in the classroom, word processing has probably aroused the greatest interest. A bibliography of word processing-related articles in magazines and journals of just the past few years would fill pages. With each advance in technology have come both new potential and problems of application for the educator. Yet many teachers, for all the excitement, are still uncertain of what may be achieved or how to proceed. This chapter is written to provide information that will prove beneficial in reducing this uncertainty.

AN OVERVIEW OF WORD PROCESSING

DEFINITIONS

Early computers were valued for their "number crunching" capabilities, and even today many people think of computers primarily as numeric devices. However, the more wondrous and useful applications for the teacher and users in general relate to text manipulation—the control of words by the computer. The earliest efforts along this line were text editors, rather crude word manipulators with limited capabilities to ease the mechanical burdens of writing. They did, however, serve to whet the appetite of the early pioneers who used them for more powerful ways to control text.

The advanced application of computers for text manipulation is the word processor. As used in this chapter, a *word processor* is a computer program for writing, editing, revising, formatting, and printing text or a computer running such software. *Word processing* means using a word processor.

Dedicated vs. Microcomputer Word Processors
Beneath all word processors lies a computer. A *dedicated word processor* is a special-purpose computer whose functions have been preset and limited to word processing. Any microcomputer can become a word processor with the purchase of a word processing program. The major differences are cost (dedicated word processors are more expensive, even though they do less) and, for very skilled typists, ease and speed of use. Dedicated word processors offer many special-purpose keys to perform operations more quickly and easily.

BASIC CONCEPTS OF WORD PROCESSING

Improvements over Typing

A word processor uses a program to take away most of the mechanical problems associated with writing. Mistakes are corrected on the screen. Errors in the final printed copy should be a thing of the past. More complicated editing, such as moving words or blocks of text around, is a matter of a few keystrokes. The days of laboriously retyping an entire document because of a spelling error or changed organization are gone. Once typed, anything that is correct need never be retyped again. Any and all changes can be accomplished with relative speed and ease.

Some things never really feasible with a typewriter become commonplace. Boldface printing and aligned right margins (called right justification) are examples. Superscripts and subscripts generally require no more than a special command typed before the desired characters. Short lines of text can be centered on the page with a keystroke—no more counting characters to determine the number of spaces to indent. Block indentation of paragraphs requires a single command.

Control over Page Layout

Word processing differs from conventional typing in another important way. Much of typical typing instruction has focused on how to achieve the desired page format. Margins had to be controlled manually, and the typist had to be alert continually to the approaching end of a line to decide whether to hyphenate or move to the next line on the page. A later decision to use double spacing or change margins meant retyping the entire document. Footnotes, footers, headings, and page numbering were all tasks requiring much thought and planning.

These matters are now left for the word processor to determine. Even when entering text, the RETURN key on the computer's keyboard serves only to signal the end of a paragraph or a line that must stand alone. There is no need whatever to watch for the "end" of a line. The word processor manages all such concerns. The writer can focus on thoughts, organization, and style. Mechanics, once a primary concern, are strictly secondary and readily altered.

THE SPREAD OF WORD PROCESSING

Professional Users

Professional writers adopted word processing very quickly. It is likely that more personal computer systems have been sold strictly for use as word processors than for any other purpose, including game playing. Journalists have all but totally switched to word processors. The steno pools filled with typewriters in business offices are disappearing and being replaced with word processing centers. Word processing has significantly affected our communication efforts.

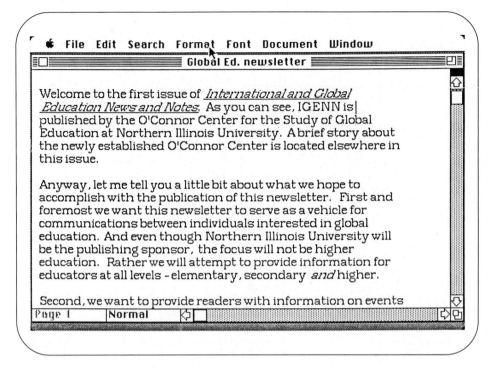

FIGURE 3.1. Word processing on a microcomputer

Casual Users

What about the rest of us, the "nonprofessional" writers? The steady decline in the price of microcomputers and the great improvements in word processing software have made this a tool for the masses. The level of sophistication available to the home user today rivals that of the most expensive systems used in industry. But sophistication has a price—complexity of operation. Many word processors in use today simply cannot be used on a once-a-month basis. The commands necessary to get them to perform their wonders are too numerous and difficult to remember without a lot of practice. Only through very regular use will the commands become automatic responses. For some people, then, there is a need for a less complex approach to word processing.

School Users

As the value of word processing became more apparent, educators began to consider its application to writing in the schools. The same complexity affecting the casual adult user made most word processing programs unsuitable for the classroom. Furthermore, there was a desire to extend the benefits of word processing to younger users. For them, however, a word processor with a densely printed multipage "Quick Reference" summary card showing the large number of commands available was an insurmountable obstacle.

Fortunately, programs such as *AppleWorks, Bank Street Writer, Homeword,* and *Magic Slate* were developed. Such programs were inexpensive compared with "professional" word processing software. They have proven to be versatile and, above all, very easy to use. These attributes have undoubtedly contributed to the increased use of word processing by significant numbers of adults as well as children and students. Furthermore, the early programs have been continually improved and enhanced so that they are now even more versatile and capable of achieving a greater number of tasks that make writing efforts—particularly those related to editing—even easier.

WORD PROCESSOR FUNCTIONS

Basic Functions of Most Word Processors

Much like automobiles, word processing programs come in different "sizes." Some are large and very powerful, while others are smaller with somewhat limited "horsepower." Regardless of size, nearly all word processors offer the same basic functions.

Word wrap or *wrap around* allows continuous typing of text without attention to the end of each line. When the end of a line is reached and the final word does not fit within the margin, it automatically moves to the next line, enabling the writer to continue with text entry. The RETURN key is pressed only when the writer wishes to begin a new paragraph or to move down to a new line prior to reaching the right margin.

With the *insert* function, space is created automatically. New material may be added anywhere in the document without retyping what follows.

The *erase* function removes unwanted words, phrases, paragraphs, and even more. Usually, the cursor is used to mark the beginning and end of the unwanted text. When this function is activated by specific key strokes, the unwanted text is immediately deleted and the remaining text appropriately rearranged so that the layout remains correct.

The *search and replace* function searches the document for a specified character, word, or phrase and allows this specific text to be replaced with another. Perhaps the writer has misused or misspelled a word. Assume an individual used the word "principle" when, in fact, the word should have been "principal." By using this function, each occurrence of the incorrect word "principle" can be located and replaced by the correct word "principal."

With the *move* function, a portion of the text is transferred from one location to another. Typically, all one needs to do is mark the beginning and end of the text block to be moved, then position the cursor at the desired new location for the text. On command, the block is moved. All text material is rearranged so that proper spacing and page format are maintained.

Additional Word Processor Functions

In addition to basic functions, most word processors provide such capabilities as centering text, automatic underlining, automatic page numbering, double

ERASE	PERMITS DELETION OF UNWANTED TEXT AND "CLOSES" THE GAPS.
INSERT	PERMITS ADDITION OF TYPED MATERIAL WHEREVER NEEDED BY "OPENING" SPACE IN THE DOCUMENT FOR IT.
MARGINS	NEW MARGINS MAY BE SET AND THE DOCUMENT REFORMATTED TO FIT THEM WITHOUT RETYPING.
MOVE	RELOCATES TEXT WITHIN THE DOCUMENT.
REPLACE	AFTER LOCATING DESIRED TEXT, CHANGES IT TO WHATEVER IS SPECIFIED.
SEARCH	LOCATES A SPECIFIED WORD, PHRASE, OR GROUP OF CHARACTERS WITHIN A DOCUMENT.
WORD WRAP	AUTOMATICALLY MOVES A WORD TOO LONG FOR THE CURRENT LINE TO THE NEXT LINE OF THE SCREEN OR PAGE. ELIMINATES USER ATTENTION TO THE RIGHT MARGIN.

FIGURE 3.2. Basic features of word processors

striking of text, and printing boldface characters. Other features produce variations in the document similar to typeset material. These include right justification of margins, proportional spacing of characters, and changing the pitch or type style during the printing process so that sections of the printed copy have fewer or more characters per inch or appear in, perhaps, italics. In addition, some packages such as *MacWrite, Multiscribe, TimeOut Superfonts* (a program that works within *AppleWorks*), and *Word Perfect* allow the writer to select from different type styles (fonts) to provide print style variety in the document. This ability to work with different fonts moved word processors in the direction of desktop publishing. Discussion of fonts and publishing software appears in Chapters 6 and 7.

It should be noted that some of these added features are dependent on the printer's capability as well as the word processor's. Not all printers can actually support all such functions, even if the word processing software offers them. Printer selection may depend on your needs for these features.

WRITING AIDS

In addition to the actual word processing functions so helpful in easing the writing process, several types of applications software packages have been

BOLDFACE	EMPHASIZES SPECIFIED TEXT IN THE PRINTOUT BY DARKENING AND SLIGHTLY ENLARGING EACH CHARACTER.
CENTERING	AUTOMATICALLY POSITIONS TEXT AT CENTER OF A LINE, E.G., TITLES OR HEADINGS
CHAIN PRINTING	PRINTS TWO OR MORE SEPARATE DOCUMENT FILES AS ONE TO OVERCOME SIZE LIMITATIONS ON INDIVIDUAL FILES.
COPY	ALLOWS TEXT TO BE DUPLICATED IN A NEW LOCATION IN A DOCUMENT WITHOUT RETYPING.
JUSTIFICATION	PRODUCES AN EVEN RIGHT MARGIN BY ADDING SPACES BETWEEN LETTERS OR WORDS TO RESEMBLE TYPESETTING.
MERGE PRINTING	CREATES PERSONALIZED DOCUMENTS BY INSERTING NAME, ADDRESS, OR OTHER MATERIAL INTO A BASIC "TEMPLATE," E. G., FORM LETTERS AND LEGAL DOCUMENTS.
PAGE NUMBERING	AUTOMATICALLY NUMBERS PAGES, OFTEN WITH CONTROL OVER WHERE ON THE PAGE, E.G., LOWER RIGHT OR TOP CENTER.

FIGURE 3.3. Additional features of many word processors

developed that assist with certain aspects of written communication. Beyond our treatment here, Wresch (1988) provides further information.

Prewriting

Considerable recent interest has focused upon the *process* of writing. The first step is prewriting, which has as its focus exploration, invention, and preparation. Prewriting programs are intended to help diminish that most difficult phase in writing—getting started.

One program aimed at helping students get started in the writing process is *Writer's Helper Stage II.* This program provides fast document analysis, pull-down menus and user modifiable prewriting and revision activities. According to Pogue (1989, p. 58), "The power of *Writer's Helper Stage II* is in its multitude of prewriting activities and collection of revising tools." The prewriting phase—helping the student to formulate a topic and organize facts and ideas—includes several helpful activities. "Idea Wheels" assists the writer by suggesting subjects and verbs. "Audience" asks the students questions that help to identify the readers for whom the writing is intended. Finally, "Organize" includes an

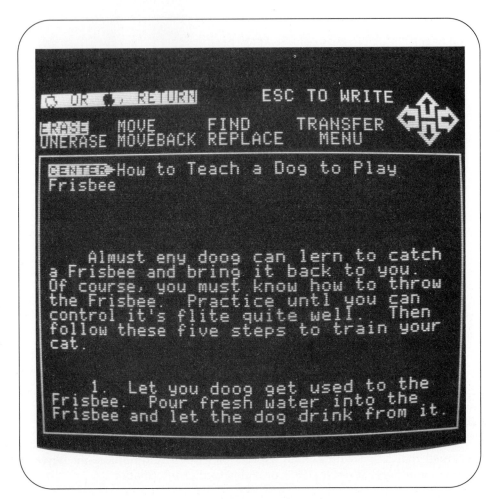

Basic word processing functions are selected from a menu.

outliner that helps students structure their writing ideas. These activities should prove invaluable in moving the student past staring at a blank sheet of paper with pencil poised but with "ideational blockage" preventing any meaningful writing activity.

Story Maker is a promising piece of software for prewriting in the elementary school. It allows children to build stories from previously defined story parts and to write, illustrate, and print their stories. Students focus on "theme, plot development, story structure, and coherence" (Solomon, 1985, p. 40). Children are freed from concern over handwriting and spelling skills and can concentrate on creating a complete story. They learn early in their writing experiences that they control the flow of the story by the choices they make. Shostak (1984, p. 8) stated, "Because this program provides an early experience with manipulating

```
┌─────────────────────────────────────────────────────────────────┐
│  ──────────── S P E L L I N G   C H E C K   M E N U ──────────   │
│   I ignore, check next word      E enter correction      ^U quit │
│   A add to personal dictionary   T turn auto-align off           │
│   B bypass this time only        G global replacement is off     │
│                                                                   │
│        Word:   "twa"                                              │
│  Suggestions:  1 two  2 tea  3 WA                                 │
└───────────────────────────────────────────────────────────────────┘
 L----!----!----!----!----!----!----!----!----!----!----!--------R

 left Mr. Bates, I went down to my father; where by the assistance

 of him and my uncle JOhn, and some other relations, I got forty

 pounds, and a promise of thirty pounds a year to maintain me at

 Leyden: there I studied "physic |twa| years and seven months,

 knowing it would be useful in long voyages.
```

FIGURE 3.4. This spelling checker suggests corrections.

language at a high cognitive level, it seems to have a great deal of promise for developing the kinds of skills one needs to become an effective writer."

Spelling Assistance

The *spelling checker* has become an indispensable word processing aid. Simply defined, a spelling checker is a program that searches for misspelled words in your document by comparing that text against a dictionary stored in the computer. Words that do not match those in the dictionary are then displayed as "misspelled." The time taken to check the spelling of words in the text is a fraction of the time required by the typical proofreading method.

Note that all words that do not match words in the electronic dictionary are reported as misspellings. When a spelling checker presents a misspelled word, you may correct or ignore it, depending on whether it is actually misspelled or is simply a word not found in the electronic dictionary. Most spelling checkers permit the user to add new words, if desired. Some programs even suggest alternatives for the "misspelled" word. When the correct spelling is found, a simple keystroke removes the error and inserts the correct word. In short, a spelling checker is not a complete substitute for spelling knowledge but rather a valuable helper in the spelling process.

Some spelling checkers display a total word count, a unique word count, and the frequency with which each unique word was used. This can help with the composition of the text by pointing out possible overuse of certain terms. Spelling aids *cannot*, however, tell you what you meant to say in your text. If you meant to use "there" and instead used "their," the spelling checker will not flag the error as long as the word is listed in its dictionary.

```
left Mr. Bates, I went down to my father; where by the assistance
of  him and my uncle JOhn, and some other relations, I got  forty
                    ^<<* 36. UNUSUAL CAPITALIZATION? *>>


pounds,  and a promise of thirty pounds a year to maintain me  at
Leyden:  there  I  studied "physic two  years  and  seven  months,
                    ^<<* 34. QUOTE NOT CLOSED *>>


knowing it would be useful in long voyages.
                <<* 31. COMPLEX SENTENCE *>>^
            <<* 17. LONG SENTENCE: 59 WORDS *>>^



                    <<** SUMMARY **>>

        OVERALL CRITIQUE FOR: gulliver

        READABILITY INDEX: 12.91
    Readers need a 13th grade level of education.
    The writing is complex and may be difficult to read.

            Total Number of Words in Document: 194
            Total Number of Sentences:    3
            Total Number of Syllables: 272

        STRENGTH INDEX: 0.56
    The strength of delivery is good, but can be improved.

        DESCRIPTIVE INDEX: 0.75
    The use of adjectives and adverbs is in the normal range.

        JARGON INDEX: 0.00

      SENTENCE STRUCTURE RECOMMENDATIONS:
            1. Most sentences contain multiple clauses.
               Try to use more simple sentences.
```

FIGURE 3.5. Output of a grammar and style assistance program.

Grammar and Style Assistance

There are also microcomputer programs to assist writers with punctuation, style, and clichés. They question word usage and analyze documents using a grammatical survey. While these programs have certain limitations in that they essentially emphasize mechanical and stylistic errors, the newer versions do represent a considerable improvement. Grammar programs no longer restrict the writer to only one primary writing style, but now offer several from which to select, depending on the intended purpose of the document.

One example is *Readability*, a program designed to accommodate the different writing styles required for different audiences and purposes. The program can analyze writing such as newspaper article style, advertising copy, novels, magazine feature stories, children's stories, children's books, and technical reports. *Readability* checks the writer's choice of words to ensure that at least 60 percent of them are commonly used English words. It evaluates the way long and short sentences have been mixed, identifies complicated sentences, compares the writer's style to that of other writers, computes a readability index, and displays a diagram of the entire document, with sentences numbered and plotted on a chart. The display also shows the "ideal" plot for that kind of writing for purposes of comparison.

Grammatik III has the ability to seek out 40 different types of bad phrasing, find typographical errors, locate and identify suspicious writing problems, display them in actual context, and offer advice for possible improvement. Armed with information of this kind, it is possible for the writer to edit the text to better fit the desired outcome.

MECC's *Ghost Writer* can display graphs of the lengths of sentences and mark those which, based on national norms, are longer than expected for the writing level. It can also generate a printout which keeps the first and last sentences of each paragraph. Words in between are replaced with dashes, but punctuation and transition words are retained. This can aid in assessing your writing patterns, or those of literary figures.

Other programs such as *RightWriter, Mac Proof,* and *Sensible Grammar* also analyze documents for errors in grammar, style, usage, and punctuation, thus providing the writer with a means for improving written text.

Vocabulary Assistance

Frequently a writer runs into the problem of overuse of a particular word or encounters the need for a word with precisely the right meaning. This need for vocabulary variety and precision is addressed by a thesaurus. Word processors such as *WordPerfect* and *Bank Street Writer III* include a thesaurus as an integral part of the program. *TimeOut Thesaurus,* designed to work within the popular *AppleWorks* program, offers approximately 50,000 synonyms for 5000 root words. The program removes and adds suffixes and allows the writer to request synonyms even for a synonym.

BENEFITS OF WORD PROCESSING

What is it that has caused countless computerphobic teachers at all levels to suppress their high tech anxieties and plunge into classroom word processing? Clearly the answer must be a belief that writing skills will develop more quickly or to a higher level among their students. Let's look at what educational users of word processing and researchers have found.

EFFECTS ON QUANTITY AND QUALITY

Both anecdotal and research findings concerning the effect of word processing on the quantity and quality of student writing are inconclusive, even contradictory. Teachers often perceive increases on both measures among their students (O'Brien, 1984; Feldman, 1984). Levin, Boruta, and Vasconcellos (1983) found significant differences favoring word processing, as did Morton (1988) and Zurn (1987).

On the other hand, Daiute (1985) found that students wrote less with a word processor, even after six months of weekly usage. Levin, Riel, Rowe, and Boruta (1984) reported similar findings. Roblyer (1988) summarized research and concluded that the use of word processing does not appear to improve the quality of writing.

Schramm (1989) conducted a meta-analysis of 14 studies pertaining to the use of word processing in writing instruction. Twelve of the studies reported findings related to the quality of student papers. Eight of the studies yielded a significant positive effect while three resulted in no difference. One study reported that the use of word processing equipment had a negative effect on quality of writing. Schramm also investigated whether students practicing word processing compose longer documents than students using traditional writing methods. Six studies involved in the meta-analysis reported effects on the length of student writings. All six authors reported that students wrote longer papers with word processing equipment than with traditional writing methods.

IMPROVING ATTITUDES

The impact of word processing on the attitudes of writers is much clearer (Pollitt, 1984; Palmer, Dowd, and James, 1984; Adams, 1985). Schramm (1989), in his meta-analysis, reported six studies that pertained to changes in student attitude towards writing after using word processing compared with that of students using traditional writing methods. Five of the six studies reported positive effects, while one study stated that the changes were negative. The overall finding resulted in a large, significant positive effect, suggesting that a larger number of the word-processing students had a more positive attitude toward writing than students using traditional writing methods. If one subscribes to the belief that students will perform better if they enjoy the task, then it seems reasonable to assume a relationship between student attitude and writing quality. Such a positive relationship was found by Schramm in those studies that also assessed the effects of using word processing on quality of writing in addition to attitude changes.

Although Roblyer (1988, p. 89) could not document improvements in the quality of student writing, she did find that word processing makes students want to write more and that they feel better about their writing. Roblyer concluded, "Since word processors make it generally easier for students to get their thoughts down on paper, this capability, in combination with improved attitudes toward writing, makes these tools among the potentially powerful uses of microcomputers for instruction."

FINDING AN AUDIENCE

Many writers experience difficulty in identifying an intended audience for their work. Writing is such an abstract process that they cannot relate their work to a specific audience and have trouble with their approach to this ill-defined recipient. Composing on the computer appears to provide the student with a sense that the computer is an audience. The interactive nature of the microcomputer is a major strength. The student and the computer can carry on a "conversation" face to face.

In addition, students view the computer as extremely unintelligent, requiring a much more thorough explanation of their ideas than the teacher (Loheyde, 1984).

COPING WITH WRITER'S BLOCK

Of special significance to Feldman (1984) was the virtual elimination of writer's block, even among students previously bothered by their inability to get started. She attributed this, in part, to the fact that the student never faced a blank sheet of paper. The screen always contained at least some text—the directives or menu of the word processor. Apparently, whatever minimal efforts the student had to make to load and activate the word processor helped to break the inertia present at the start. Collis (1988) also noted this benefit.

OVERCOMING PAST EXPERIENCE

Persons who work with students already experienced in writing at lower levels may be concerned that past failure and bad attitudes will carry over. Feldman (1984) found no evidence of this. The approach with word processing is so different that failures of the past are seemingly forgotten; a fresh start can be made.

BUILDING READING SKILLS

One of the most thoroughly tested of all computer-based writing approaches is *Writing to Read* which has been studied extensively by Educational Testing Service (ETS). The ETS study was conducted over a two-year period and involved more than 10,000 students in kindergarten and first grade. Although the focus of the program is more on reading than writing, several findings are significant for our purposes. First, although the program involves a complex technology system, this caused no problems in implementation even with such young children. Second, students in the program progressed faster in reading than national norm samples. Third, using specially developed techniques, ETS concluded that students in *Writing to Read* also wrote better than comparison groups. This finding held across all subgroups, including sex, race, socioeconomic status, and ability level (*The ETS Evaluation*, 1984).

SUMMARIES OF BENEFITS

Kleiman and Humphrey (1982, p. 98) reported the following outcomes when word processing was introduced in the East York School in Canada:

> The most important result is that students want to write more often and produce longer compositions. Teachers of young children have reported that the length of the average essay doubles. The next change occurs when the children become familiar with the editing capabilities of the word processor. First they start being more careful to correct typing, spelling, and punctuation errors. Then they begin to change words and sentences. Finally they learn to reorganize the material, moving, adding, and deleting large sections of text. They no longer just edit for details, but also pay more attention to the meaning of ideas and the order of presentation.

Jarchow (1984) summarized the positive arguments for using word processing. The most important are:

1. Students are motivated to spend more time writing.
2. Style of writing can be improved.
3. Students learn more about combining sentences and arranging content.
4. Students become less defensive at suggestions for change.
5. Clean drafts promote more objective revision by students and eliminate potential teacher bias against poor handwriting.
6. Self-confidence is boosted by printed drafts.

Womble (1984, p. 37) offered the following observations about students who wrote and revised using word processors:

1. Students tended to continue working longer on a piece of writing than they did with pencil and paper.
2. *Seeing* what they were writing on the screen appeared to be helpful in determining what changes and/or corrections were needed.
3. Actually making those required changes was so much easier using the word processor than pencil and paper that students often devoted more time to *revision* than previously.
4. Students who worked on the word processor appeared to find it easier to develop a sense of audience.

Clearly, word processing is a powerful tool with numerous benefits for writers of all ages. The differences in findings reported may have a rather simple explanation—differences in the approach of the teacher. Nothing suggests that the mere availability of word processors is a panacea for writing difficulties. To hope for improvements in quality and quantity, which are the long-term goal, students must still learn writing fundamentals *and* proper use of their new tool. "If [word processing] is presented only as an easy way of making editorial corrections (punctuation, capitalization, etc.), the advantages for encouraging creative thinking skills will be considerably diminished'' (Schiffman, 1986).

ISSUES IN WORD PROCESSING

THE APPROPRIATE AGE TO BEGIN

Teachers often ask, ''At what grade level should word processing be introduced?'' It appears that the development of the process is too new for a definitive answer to have yet emerged. Proponents of word processing for students tend to argue that it be used early in their schooling. Donald Graves, a prominent figure in composition theory, has stated, ''[O]ne can imagine starting kids off writing on the keyboard and saving handwriting until motor skills are more highly refined'' (cited in Green, 1984, p. 22).

A more acceptable view for many may be to wait until writing instruction has passed the point of sheer mechanics and at least a short paragraph is required of students from time to time. This approach differentiates the physical act of writing from writing as a visual representation of thoughts or writing as ''art.''

Another school of thought is that we should start a little sooner than just suggested, because word processing opens the doors to more significant writing activities at an early age by removing the physical barriers between thoughts and a visible product.

In the end, teachers must decide what they are most comfortable with. Word processing should never become artificial. It should support and enhance the curriculum as we know it. Yet we must not close our eyes to possible changes in the curriculum made possible by technology. Perhaps we can expect and elicit more from students at younger ages in this manner, but the answer is not clear at this point.

KEYBOARDING

The differences between typing and word processing have given rise to the term *keyboarding*. This means learning to use one's fingers correctly on the keyboard for rapid text entry, free from the formatting concerns of the past. At the very least, word processing is much easier for those with keyboarding skills.

Many writers and advocates of word processing in the schools now presume the need for keyboarding. Balajthy (1988) agrees, but thoughtfully presents the issues. If keyboarding is not taught early, other uses of computers may be less effective. Effective instruction can be very time consuming, both in sheer hours and in the level of monitoring required. Teachers must provide extrinsic motivation for many students, as the payoff may not be obvious. Keyboarding instruction should not be undertaken lightly.

For the youngest students, one must seriously consider keyboarding from the standpoints of both need and physical ability. Just as paper and pencil carry with them motor coordination concerns, so too will keyboarding. The physical ability to use the keyboard correctly may be the determining factor in selecting an appropriate age to introduce word processing.

The Computer as Keyboarding Tutor

One approach to the development of keyboarding skills is to let the computer teach the student. Balajthy (1988) has discussed six keyboarding programs suitable for school use. A particularly interesting keyboarding package is *Mavis Bacon Teaches Typing*. Incorporating aspects of artificial intelligence, the program keeps track of the student's strengths and weaknesses and alters the lessons accordingly, thus providing customized lessons. The program makes use of a monitor screen divided into two sections. Across the top section is the text to be typed. At the bottom are a pair of "hands" poised over a keyboard. The proper finger position for each letter to be typed is demonstrated by these "hands." To further motivate the student, "Mavis" makes use of state-of-the-art graphics and sound to involve the participant in a "race" to improve keyboarding speed and accuracy. This particular program appears to offer an excellent tutorial that should prove highly successful in helping students acquire essential keyboarding skills.

Collis (1988) reported on research on keyboarding instruction with fourth grade children. Over an eight-week-period, speed and accuracy improved significantly while using a commercial software program. However, when tested forty days after the instruction, the students had reverted to their preinstruction levels. This appears to demonstrate that keyboarding skills can be successfully taught to elementary age students, but underscores the importance of practice for skill maintenance at this level.

Perhaps the real question is not whether it is possible to teach keyboarding skills to elementary school children, but rather *when* is it most advantageous to do so. This question still receives considerable debate and no definitive answer has yet been obtained.

THE PROCESS APPROACH TO WRITING

For word processing to have maximum value in composition, a particular view of composition instruction is recommended. That view is often referred to as the *process approach* to writing. It has been developed and expounded by Donald Graves at the University of New Hampshire, among others. Writing is viewed as a continuous process of generating ideas, creating drafts, and revising them until finished. The focus is on the process all along, with revision central and all but endless (Graves, 1982).

Owens (1984, p. 128) also discussed writing as process rather than product. The teacher's tasks are to focus on the writers' strategies as they work and to deemphasize the finished document. He wrote:

Writing as process concerns itself with the flow and unfolding of the writing event, and for this reason, the teacher intervenes more frequently and attempts to probe, ask questions, and suggest strategies that stimulate a student's invention and lend it direction. . . .

The role of the teacher is not so much to tell a student how or what to write, but to suggest directions and to offer maps, pointers, cues. In this sense, the writing teacher is like a coach—a helper restricted to the sidelines.

When discussing the process approach to writing, Pon (1988) suggests that teachers focus on the steps of the process. Pon breaks the process into four discrete steps: prewriting, writing, editing/revising, and publishing. Further, not all of the steps are performed in every writing assignment; the teacher must decide which of the steps is appropriate for a given assignment.

CRITIQUES OF THE TRADITIONAL APPROACH

Overemphasis on Mechanics

One problem identified in more traditional approaches is an overemphasis on editing skills. After all, the stock in trade of the language arts and English teacher has been spelling, grammar, usage, and punctuation. These are important, even vital, to effective communication, but we may have stressed them to the detriment of what it really takes to compose well (Schiffman, 1986).

And yet we have tacitly acknowledged the truth all along. Consider this common scenario. Students are assigned a topic on which to write. They do so reluctantly and submit their work. The teacher evaluates the work and corrects it, sometimes writing more than the student did originally. The paper is returned to the student, who glances at the grade, mentally glowers at all the red ink, and stuffs the paper away, never to refer to it again.

What was the purpose of all the time spent writing comments on the page? Presumably, to stimulate better work the next time. But the next time will involve a different topic under different circumstances. The same problems may not reappear; the student may make no connection between the current writing task and previous critiques, if they were read at all. Comments have value only as they affect the *process* of writing, not the product itself. They are meant to prompt revised thinking, yet they should be aimed at a physical revision of the product. It is *revision*—frequent, bold, consistent—that is needed to improve writing skills.

Effects of Physical Appearance

The importance of appearance cannot be overemphasized. Graves (cited in Green, 1984) found that youngsters are bothered far more than ever imagined by the aesthetics of editing. Prior to word processing, markups on a page had a devastating effect on ego. However, Graves admitted fearing that the finished appearance of computer drafts might increase student reluctance to revise. He now believes the opposite is true, because the usual penalties for revision (erasure, cross-outs, recopying) are no longer present. Daiute (1985) and Harris (1985) also noted the appeal of clean drafts made possible by word processing.

Lack of Actual Revision

We have long known of the need for revision, but seldom required it. The reasons are simple—revision is entirely too physically difficult and frustrating to demand it of most students. How long did it take Alice to print her paragraph? How many hours went into typing that research paper, some of which are evident from the abundance of erasures and correction fluid visible on the page? Most teachers do not require revision, however beneficial it may be in the long run.

Word processing enables teachers to expect revision. Whether minor changes in wording or major structural alterations, the task need not be formidable because only new words need be typed. Thoughts can be expanded without penalty and without retyping what is already good. Changes to the document need not look like mayhem since they simply disappear from the screen.

However easily the word processor can enable revision, significant revision is not necessarily automatic. Although Levin, Riel, Rowe, and Boruta (1984) found that students corrected more errors in their computer drafts and that new versions seldom included new errors, Wolf (1985) reported that the nature of revision improved substantially with age. Wolf found that younger writers had little sense of the totality of their work and could only edit superficially. Levin, Boruta, and Vasconcellos (1983), Collier (1983), and Harris (1985) also found revision to be superficial. Haas (1988) confirmed this finding to be true with college freshmen and even faculty members, terming it "surface" revision. Finally, Kurth (1987) found *no* greater revision by students using word processing than by those writing by hand. However, the hand writers in that study had access to a photocopier to ease their revision tasks!

While the lack of revision in traditional writing is a valid criticism, it seems that writers using word processors will not automatically rise to the potential of their tool, regardless of age. The teacher has a critical role to play, if revision is to become meaningful. "The computer will not make better writers—only good instruction will improve a student's writing performance" (Loheyde, 1984). Just as the change from slates to paper had no profound effect, neither will the switch to word processing.

CLASSROOM APPLICATIONS

The following applications, including many experiences and ideas of other teachers, represent but a few possible uses of the word processor with school age students. The creative mind of the teacher and the desire to apply word processing techniques in the classroom will increase and immeasurably enhance this necessarily limited list of possible activities.

LEARNING TO USE A WORD PROCESSOR

Cursor Movement

In the early stages of learning to use word processors, cursor movements must be mastered. Teachers can prepare a document that is just a maze of characters on the screen through which students must steer the cursor. You might even allow them to "cheat" by providing certain characters in the walls of the maze that students are allowed to erase to make shortcuts through the maze.

Editing

To develop proficiency in editing with a word processor, prepare sample documents and give them to students on disk. Provide final printouts to read for content and organization and drafts. Use wide margins to enable easiest editing. This technique can be used effectively to stress the finalizing aspects of writing, rather than initial creating, as well as the mechanics of editing. It's a good way to approach word selection and overuse of subject-verb word order, especially when the same pronoun begins each sentence, as is often the case when young children write.

Locating Words in a Document

A word processor can be used as a crude data storage system. This offers a perfect excuse for mastering the SEARCH function when one wishes to locate a particular piece of information in the file. Students might enter their own personal list of bothersome spelling words, adding and deleting as their spelling improves and new lessons are begun. Name and address files, lists of belongings, and catalogs of collections all offer potential subjects for this use of a word processor.

TEACHING SEQUENCING

Scotchmoor (1984) was concerned about problems her seventh and eighth graders had with sequencing ideas. She prepared a 15–20 sentence story using a word processor, then rearranged the sentences randomly. Each student received a copy of the scrambled story on a disk, then used the word processor to place the events into a logical sequence. Students printed out their final versions. Ms. Scotchmoor then read them her original story. Students were given time to read their versions, since many had come up with variations. This led to discussion of often-subtle differences caused by sequence. Students could also write and scramble stories, then challenge their friends to find appropriate solutions.

TOPIC IDENTIFICATION

A major problem for writers is topic selection. Graves (1982) and many others have stressed the need for allowing students to select their own topics. Teacher-assigned topics often lack relevance and interest; it is better to work to help the student identify topics of personal significance.

At the very beginning of the term, have students prepare a list of possible theme topics. This will require prompting in most cases. Try to provide broad guidelines, which afford lots of flexibility. Here are some ideas that you can expand upon and adapt to various grade levels:

PEOPLE
    The person(s) I most admire
    My most unusual relatives
FOODS
    Foods I love to eat
    Foods I can't stand
    Foods I'd like to try

THE FUTURE
    Careers I am considering
    Places I want to visit
ACTIVITIES
    Jobs I have to do around the house
    My favorite TV show
    The best book I've ever read

LETTER WRITING

Letter writing could regain its old popularity thanks to the word processor. Have students develop this form of writing with letters to family or friends, thank-you notes following birthdays or Bar Mitzvahs or holidays, letters of praise or complaint to companies whose products they use or to government officials. You might even muster up a writing campaign to influence legislators on educational issues.

PROMPTED WRITING

Prompted writing entails providing instructions or questions to guide the writer, to stimulate thinking at various points. *FrEdWriter* (Free Educational Writer, for Apple II) includes provisions for creating files of prompts which the student cannot erase. The student loads a file created by the teacher and composes by responding to the prompts. Rodrigues (1986) provides suggestions for similar activities using any word processor.

WRITING FOR BEGINNERS

KidWriter exemplifies an approach to writing in the early grades. The program allows children to create first a picture about which to write. There are many colorful background scenes from which to choose and over 100 "clip art" graphics to complete the scene. Text may be placed on the picture or in the area reserved for it at the bottom of the screen. New pages can be added as needed, with or without further illustrations. Text editing is rudimentary; this is not a full-featured word processor. Final products can be printed easily, including the picture. Kids find this approach to writing very appealing.

POETRY

Consider poetry writing on the computer. Stress experimentation
   with word
      arrangements
               on the page
     as well as
  within the
poem itself.

Madian (1986) suggested writing poetry focusing on the use of homonyms. He contended that homonyms play a key role in developing writing and reading skills and that homonym poems provide an excellent means for building vocabulary, spelling skills, and composing ability. As an example Madian (p. 17) offered:

"A·gnu never knew
How to spell no
But I know how
to spell knew
What confuses me
Is how to spell gnu"

GROUP PROJECTS

Word processing can be used to enhance group activities. Older students can help teachers of younger students by entering teacher-selected text passages, then deleting words at a specified interval to yield cloze tests for reading. Teacher-created essay outlines can be used as group projects, as well as by individuals. A class can generate class stories from an outline. One student enters the first line or two, then another adds to it, and so on until a conclusion is reached. This activity can be extended over many days by saving and retrieving the partially completed story as needed. For the more adventurous, parts of a story might be assigned for independent development. They would then be combined by retrieving them together into one large file. Collis (1988) sees the social benefits of group writing significantly increased by the computer.

To stress the need for proofreading, have students routinely proof one another's work. The writer will benefit, and the reader will sharpen an important skill.

A class newspaper can be an appealing project, which may have been just too much work to bother with in the past. Whether it be contemporary news of class activities, a holiday issue on vacation plans, or a mock newspaper based on historical research in a social studies class, interest will run high. Effort devoted to it will likely exceed that given to more typical class assignments.

Could your class produce a mini-book of its own? Suppose you teach a unit

First page of an illustrated story from *KidWriter*.

on birds. Let each student research a particular bird and prepare the write-up on a word processor. Combine all reports in the appropriate order to create a bird encyclopedia. Publishing software (treated in Chapters 6 and 7) may be even better for these projects.

WRITING ACROSS THE CURRICULUM

Writing skills are critical to success in life for most individuals. They develop slowly and must be constantly nurtured. To teach writing skills in only one curriculum area is to deny their importance. Once students begin to write with a word processor, they should ideally use it for *all* writing assignments. This will contribute to maintenance of keyboarding skills, as well as extend the potential benefits of "electronic composing" to all writing endeavors.

For specific assistance in implementing word processing in your school, refer to Howie (1989), Collis (1988), and Turner and Land (1988). The Spring 1987 issue of *Computers in the Schools* is a special issue describing computers in reading and language arts. In addition, the chapter reference list contains many helpful entries. Finally, *The Writing Notebook* (Box 79, Mendocino, CA 95460; 707–937–2848) is a journal devoted to the teaching of writing with computers which goes beyond the language arts classroom. A collection of outstanding articles from the journal is also available (*Making the Literature, Writing, Word Processing Connection: The Best of The Writing Notebook, 1983–1987,* edited by S. Franklin).

SUMMARY

Word processing has significantly changed the writing process. If not yet obsolete, the typewriter will soon become a curiosity. Word processing has greatly diminished the tedium of mechanical editing and has provided total flexibility in reorganizing thoughts by moving and changing text. Revision need no longer be as difficult as previously.

Virtually all word processing software provides the same basic functions. Differences occur in such areas as control of fonts, handling of footers and headers, and integrated features like dictionaries. To further enhance writing, electronic assistance is available for prewriting, spelling and style proofing, even word selection with a thesaurus.

There are many benefits to writing with a word processor. The quantity and quality of writing may increase, attitudes may improve, writer's block may disappear, even reading skills may improve. However, little of this will occur effortlessly. Skillful instruction in composition remains essential. Unresolved are such issues as *when* word processing and keyboarding should be introduced. There is also much evidence that stimulating revision, so necessary to improved writing, is a difficult task. Those who use a word processor know from experience what a marvel it is. How *best* to bring its potential to our students is not yet clear.

CHAPTER 3 ACTIVITIES

1. Learn to use any available word processor. Some have their own on-line tutorials for self-instruction.
2. Using the word processing program you have learned, write a letter to the publisher of the software indicating what features you do not like about the program, what features you like and, if appropriate, suggesting changes that might make the program even better.
3. Explore the availability of spelling checkers and other word processing helpers in your setting. Read their manuals and determine their appropriateness for your use.
4. Using your word processing program, enter the following familiar rhyme:
   All the king's horses
   Humpty Dumpty had a great fall.
   Couldn't put Humpty together again.
   And all the king's men
   Humpty Dumpty sat on a wall.

Once entered, use the MOVE function to arrange the rhyme as it should correctly appear.

5. Bill and Mary watched intently as the bright light in the sky grew closer and closer. Suddenly. . . .
   Add a few sentences using your word processor to complete the story by providing your own ending.

6. Below is presented a definition of the term "word processor." Notice that it is indeed brief—too brief. Using your word processor, add to the definition to make it more meaningful: **word processor**—a program for writing and editing. . . .

7. How would word processing benefit you as a teacher? List several applications where you might use word processing in your work.

REFERENCES

Adams, C. "Composing with Computers." *Computers in Education*, November 1985, p. 18.

Balajthy, E. "Keyboarding, Language Arts, and the Elementary School Child." *The Computing Teacher*, February 1988, pp. 40–43.

Balajthy, E. *Microcomputers in Reading and Language Arts.* Englewood Cliffs, NJ: Prentice-Hall, 1986.

Boone, R. *Teaching Process Writing with Computers.* Eugene, OR: International Council for Computers in Education, 1988.

Calkins, L. M. *The Art of Teaching Writing.* Portsmouth, NH: Heinemann, 1986.

Collier, R. M. "The Word Processor and Revision Strategies." *College Composition and Communication,* 1983, 34(2), pp. 149–155.

Collis, B. *Computers, Curriculum, and Whole-Class Instruction.* Belmont, CA: Wadsworth, 1988.

Daiute, C. *Writing and Computers.* Reading, MA: Addison-Wesley, 1985.

The ETS Evaluation of Writing to Read. Executive Summary. Princeton, NJ: Educational Testing Service, 1984.

Feldman, P. R. "Personal Computers in a Writing Course." *Perspectives in Computing,* Spring 1984, pp. 4–9.

Graves, D. H. *Writing: Teacher and Children at Work.* Exeter, NH: Heinemann Educational Books, Inc., 1982.

Green, J. "Computers, Kids, and Writing: An Interview with Donald Graves." *Classroom Computer Learning,* March 1984, pp. 20–28.

Haas, C. "How Word Processing Affects Planning in Writing: The Impact of Technology." Reported in Collis, B. "Research Windows." *The Computing Teacher,* October 1988, p. 7.

Harris, J. "Student Writers and Word Processing: A Preliminary Evaluation." *College Composition and Communication,* 1985, 36(3), pp. 323–330.

Hawisher, G. E. and Selfe, C. L., eds. *Critical Perspectives on Computers and Composition Instruction.* New York: Teachers College Press, 1989.

Hoot, J. L. and Silvern, S. B., eds. *Writing with Computers in the Early Grades.* New York: Teachers College Press, 1988.

Howie, S. H. *Reading, Writing, and Computers: Planning for Integration.* Needham Heights, MA: Allyn & Bacon, Longwood Division, 1989.

Jackson, T. H. and Berg, D. "Elementary Keyboarding—Is It Important?" *The Computing Teacher,* March 1986, pp. 8–11.

Jarchow, E. "Computers and Computing: The Pros and Cons." *Electronic Education,* June 1984, p. 38.

Joslin, E. "Welcome to Word Processing." *The Computing Teacher,* March 1986, pp. 16–19.

Katz, C. and Hoffman, F. B. "Teaching Writing Through Word Processing." *Computers in the Schools,* Summer 1987, 4(2), pp. 99–115.

Kleiman, G. and Humphrey, M. "Word Processing in the Classroom." *Compute,* March 1982, pp. 96–99.

Kurth, R. J. "Using Word Processing to Enhance Revision Strategies During Student Writing Activities." *Educational Technology,* January 1987, pp. 13–19.

Levin, J. A., Boruta, M. J., and Vasconcellos, M. T. "Microcomputer-Based Environments for Writing: A Writer's Assistant." In Wilkinson, A. C., ed. *Classroom Computers and Cognitive Science.* New York, Academic Press: 1983, pp. 219–232.

Levin, J. A., Riel, M., Rowe, R. D., and Boruta, M. J. "Muktuk Meets Jacuzzi: Computer Networks and Elementary School Writers." In Freeman, S. W., ed. *The Acquisition of Written Language: Revision and Response.* Hillsdale, NJ: Ablex, 1984.

Loheyde, K. M. J. "Computer Use in the Teaching of Composition: Considerations for Teachers of Writing." *Computers in the Schools,* Summer 1984, pp. 81–86.

Madian, J. "Word Processing and Curriculum Renewal." *The Computing Teacher,* August/ September 1986, pp. 17–19.

Milone, M. N. *Every Teacher's Guide to Word Processing.* Englewood Cliffs, NJ: Prentice-Hall, 1985.

Morton, L. L. "Word Processing and the Editing–Revising Process." *Computers in the Schools,* 1988, 5(1/2), pp. 165–178.

Neuman, S. B. and Cobb-Morocco, C. "Writing with Word Processors for Remedial Students." *The Computing Teacher,* December/January 1987–88, pp. 45–47, 61.

O'Brien, P. "Using Microcomputers in the Writing Class." *The Computing Teacher,* May 1984, pp. 20–21.

Owens, P. "Creative Writing with Computers." *Popular Computing,* January 1984, pp. 128–132.

Palmer, A., Dowd, T., and James, K. "Changing Teacher and Student Attitudes through Word Processing." *The Computing Teacher,* May 1984, pp. 45–47.

Pogue, L. "More Power for Less Money on your IBM." *Electronic Learning,* January/ February 1989, pp. 58–59.

Pollitt, A. H. "Warming to the Wonders of the Word Processor: An English Teacher's Introduction to the Computer." *The Computing Teacher,* May 1984, pp. 48–49.

Pon, K. "Process Writing in the One-Computer Classroom." *The Computing Teacher,* March 1988, pp. 33–37.

Roblyer, M. D., "The Effectiveness of Microcomputers in Education: A Review of the Research from 1980–1987." *T.H.E. Journal,* September 1988, pp. 85–89.

Rodrigues, R. J. "Creating Writing Lessons with a Word Processor." *The Computing Teacher,* February 1986, pp. 41–43.

Rodrigues, D. and Rodrigues, R. J. *Teaching Writing with a Word Processor, Grades 7–13.* Urbana, IL: National Council of Teachers of English.

Schiffman, S. S. "Productivity Tools for the Classroom." *The Computing Teacher,* May 1986, pp. 27–31.

Schramm, R. M. "The Effects of Using Word Processing Equipment in Writing Instruction: A Meta-Analysis." Unpublished doctoral dissertation, Northern Illinois University, 1989.

Schwartz, H. J. *Interactive Writing: Composing with a Word Processor*. New York: Holt, Rinehart and Winston, 1985.

Scotchmoor, J. "Order out of Chaos." *Classroom Computer Learning*, March 1984, p. 69.

Shostak, R., ed. *Computers in Composition Instruction*. Eugene, OR: International Council for Computers in Education, 1984.

Solomon, G. "Writing with Computers." *Electronic Learning*, November/December 1985, pp. 39–43.

Watt, D. "Tools for Writing." *Popular Computing*, January 1984, pp. 75–78.

Wolf, D. P. "Flexible Texts: Computer Editing in the Study of Writing." In Klein, E. L. *New Directions for Child Development, No. 28*. San Francisco: Jossey-Bass, 1985, pp. 37–53.

Womble, G. "Process and Processor: Is There Room for a Machine in the English Classroom?" *English Journal*, January 1984, pp. 34–37.

Wresch, W. *A Practical Guide to Computer Uses in the English/Language Arts Classroom*. Englewood Cliffs, NJ: Prentice-Hall.

Wresch, W. "Six Directions for Computer Analysis of Student Writing." *The Computing Teacher*, April 1988, pp. 13–16, 42.

Zurn, M. R. *A Comparison of Kindergartners' Handwritten and Word Processor-Generated Writing*. Unpublished doctoral dissertation, Georgia State University, Atlanta, 1987.

CHAPTER 4

□ Data Bases and Filing Systems □

OBJECTIVES

After completing this chapter, you will be able to:

□ *Explain why information management has become a serious problem.* □
□ *Give several examples of data management tasks relevant to teachers.* □
□ *Discuss benefits of electronic data management over manual systems.* □
□ *Define the terms field, record, file, and data base.* □
□ *Explain the differences between a data base management system and a filing system, including SQL and relational capability.* □
□ *Discuss the significance of student use and creation of data files.* □
□ *Discuss the potential and problems of using information services to access data.* □
□ *Explain the concept of hypermedia and discuss its unique character.* □
□ *Suggest several optical disc applications.* □
□ *Define student data base use in terms of three stages and discuss the potential and difficulties of each.* □
□ *Outline factors in selecting data management software.* □
□ *Outline basic steps in setting up a data base or file.* □
□ *Discuss research on learning with data bases.* □
□ *Develop classroom data base applications.* □

This chapter presents the computer as a highly sophisticated tool for data storage and retrieval. You will consider society's growing problems in information management and ways in which computers are assisting with the task. After examining concepts of electronic data storage, including hypermedia and optical discs, you will learn how computerized data management can assist you in your teaching. Finally, you will also consider how students may benefit from using data bases or data filing systems in the classroom based on current research.

CHALLENGES OF THE INFORMATION AGE

THE TROUBLE WITH INFORMATION

Among all of the human faculties, none is more impressive, or at times exasperating, than our memories. Everyone has many thousands of individual bits and pieces of information stored away in memory. We manage remarkable tasks of retrieving this information, associating it correctly with other items, and even combining pieces into new relationships. Regardless of whether one understands the neurological aspects of the mind, it is truly an amazing thing.

For all of its marvels, the human mind is also quite fallible. Just as we achieve great feats of remembering, so we also commit great blunders of forgetting. The written word is clearly important as a means of transferring knowledge and information across time and space, but for us individually and daily, it is also an essential aid to our fragile memories.

As more and more written information has come into existence, problems in storing and retrieving the ever-increasing pool of knowledge have led to all manner of new devices—drawers in which to place papers, file folders and cabinets, and Rolodex cards and containers, to name a few. Today we are swimming in a sea of paper, and new industries have sprung up to try to handle it.

However, our advances have been less than perfect. How irritating it is to be able to store that valuable document safely in the file cabinet, only to discover later that the labeling on the folder has slipped your mind! "I know it's here, Ruth, but I can't seem to put my hands on it just now. I'll call you back when it turns up." There goes another valuable hour spent searching file cabinet drawers.

THE NEED FOR DATA MANAGEMENT

By now you should realize that information and data are somewhat synonymous terms. The search for better ways to "process data" has gone on for many years already and is certain to continue. John Naisbitt summarized the need in *Megatrends* (1982, p. 24): "We are drowning in information but starved for knowledge." Mountains of raw data do not necessarily convey meaning.

Let's consider briefly a data management problem related to the life of a teacher. Libraries are among our most hallowed repositories of knowledge. In medieval times, keeping track of the collection was no great intellectual challenge. Today, the library of one million or more volumes is relatively common, to say nothing of nonbook materials. The task of finding what one needs is hardly trivial. For the librarian, tracking what is in the collection, on loan, on order, lost, strayed, or stolen is formidable.

Considering only the user's need for books, we have long depended on the card catalog as our road map to the collection. For many, even most, purposes it is quite adequate. But consider its limitations. Books are categorized in three ways: author, title, and subject. This necessitates three different cards for each book, differing primarily in the order in which the information is recorded on each. Typically, the three cards are housed in at least two distinct sections of the card catalog, if not three. Thus, adding a new book to the collection means preparing three cards, *and* placing each one in the *correct* place alphabetically in the *correct drawer* of the card catalog. Hardly an impossible task for a human, but somewhat inefficient and clearly open to error.

THE BENEFITS OF ELECTRONIC DATA MANAGEMENT

Although we describe the benefits of electronic data management in terms of our card catalog example, the principles behind each one are applicable in other situations as well.

A Single Data Set
From the paper conservation viewpoint, or simply as a labor-saving aid, the use of a computer to replace the library card catalog is a natural idea. What may be overlooked are other benefits of computerization. Not only are cards unnecessary, there is also no need for three versions of the same information. The computer stores only one copy of the basic information and can easily retrieve that data based on a user-specified criterion. You need only go to the nearest terminal and enter a request.

More Information
Unlike the card catalog, the computer may also tell you whether the book is currently on loan, saving a futile search of the shelves. Some systems can also search for materials in many libraries across the region or nation, a feature not available with physical card catalogs. Interlibrary loans are encouraged and facilitated by such a system. Finally, in many cases the results of the search can be printed by the computer, eliminating the need to copy down call numbers by hand before going to the stacks, an operation again open to possible error.

Greater Manipulation Potential
Reports on the status of the collection or items on loan can be easily produced. Need an alphabetical list of all titles in the collection? A modest request for the

computer, a nearly impossible task otherwise. A list of all authors represented? Readily available! That one set of data on the collection can be reordered at will with no disruption of service to the patron. In addition, book orders can be tracked and new acquisitions made available to users much more quickly by transferring on-order data electronically to the "available" pool. Small wonder that libraries ranging from the Library of Congress to modest school libraries are going computer.

Easier Access to Data

There is another even less obvious benefit to a computerized card catalog, to stay with our example. When searching for materials manually, certain types of requests require sifting through the available data to find just what you are seeking. For instance, suppose you wanted to find all books by Mickey Spillane with a copyright date no older than 1975. You would go to the author section of the catalog, find the Spillane entries, then read each one to determine which are of interest. Not impossible, but a needless chore. Computerized data can be readily retrieved based on a *combination* of criteria, such as Spillane *and* 1975 or newer.

To return briefly to the file cabinet concept, each item placed in a folder can be stored under only one heading. Locating the material later depends on one's recall of the chosen heading or folder label. The ability to do so quickly and accurately is a hallmark of an outstanding secretary in most offices; the boss could never manage alone! Yet deciding on that heading initially is often difficult, since few materials worth filing are clearly linked to only one possibility. The computer solves this problem by providing the equivalent of multiple headings per item.

Enhancing Human Capacity

Computerized data storage and retrieval are big business and growing in importance. Starting with the capabilities of the human mind, the computer may be seen as a logical, valuable extension of our native abilities. It is not a replacement for mental ability, but rather an aid, much as other tools aid us in everyday living. Computers are not a crutch, as some contend, but merely the latest in an evolutionary chain of tools stretching back to the first stone ax. Early man's major task was mastery of the environment. Many writers have concluded that our largest tasks in the near future, in the Information Age, relate to information management. The computer is a key to this future.

DATA MANAGEMENT IN EDUCATION

The Administrative Level

If data manipulation as described is the heart of present-day computer usage, what is its relationship to education? Schools have used the data processing power of computers in such administrative applications as scheduling, budgeting, grade reporting, and attendance for many years.

The Classroom Level

Stop to consider your own data management needs and problems as a teacher or future teacher. A few items are fairly obvious. Most teachers maintain various types of student records. Gradebooks are a prime example. Other forms of student records may be kept: anecdotal information for reports to parents, mandated records on exceptional children, team data in athletics. The list goes on and on. Think of what is or could be in your file cabinet or desk drawers and consider whether a computer might help you manage better.

The Issue of Appropriateness

Just because a computer *can* do something does not mean it is the best or even the better way of doing it. Many home computer owners were attracted to the idea of storing recipes on their new gadget, only to realize that it really didn't work well unless they intended to place the computer in the kitchen alongside the range! Personal mailing lists can be computerized, but there is little gain over an address book, unless the list is long and a printer and blank mailing labels are always at hand. A computer file of phone numbers may sound good, but chances are you can look up what you need in the telephone directory more quickly than you can turn on the computer, locate and insert the proper disks, get the system running, enter your request, and digest the response. This is an example of where the computer's capabilities require human judgment in determining *appropriate* usage.

THE TECHNICAL SIDE OF DATA MANAGEMENT

CONCEPTS AND DEFINITIONS

Before considering other, perhaps more significant, educational data processing applications, let's look at some of the technical aspects of data storage and retrieval. When data are stored in a computer, the computer assumes much of the responsibility for organization of the data. The user is unconcerned with exactly how or where the data are stored on a diskette. The only concern is that they be stored correctly and be retrievable when needed.

The smallest meaningful unit of information to be stored is a *field*. A field contains an individual piece of information, such as first name or phone number. Data are entered into a data management system by fields.

A *record* is a group of related fields such as all the data for an individual student (Figure 4.1). All student records form one *file*. Figure 4.2 shows the three level structure of a data file. (Figures 4.1 and 4.2 appear on the following page.)

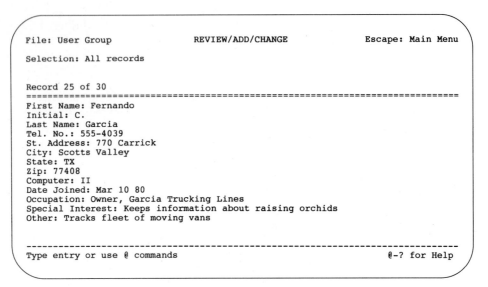

FIGURE 4.1. Screen of an *AppleWorks* data base record

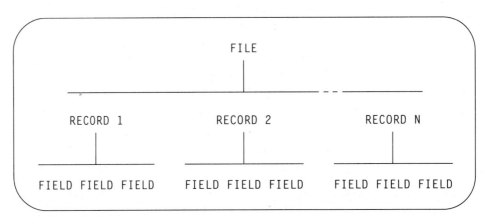

FIGURE 4.2. Generalized file structure

Figure 4.3 presents a more concrete example, a student personal data file. All data on one student constitute a record within one file. Within one record, each category of information about a student is a field which contains the correct data for that student. Try to keep these concepts clearly distinguished in your mind. Figure 4.4 illustrates sample content of such a personal data file.

DATA BASES

Problems with Data Files
Data files have existed for a long time. In most businesses, daily operations dictated a need for many different files—employee data, payroll, inventory,

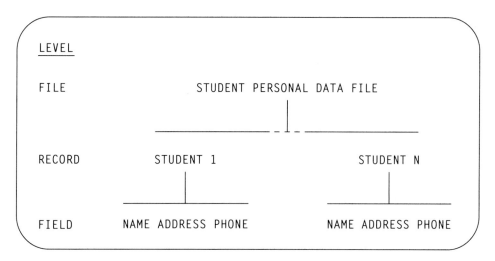

FIGURE 4.3. Student personal data file structure

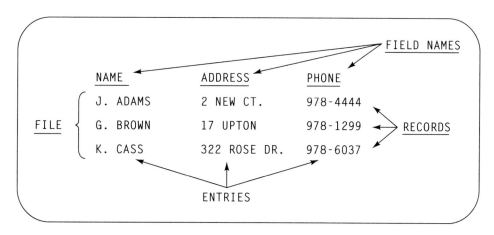

FIGURE 4.4. Student personal data file—sample contents

and so on. Many of the files necessarily contained considerable identical information—employee name or Social Security number, parts names or numbers, and so forth. This is called *data redundancy*.

In the early days of data processing, this was no great concern, but as data volume increased, redundancy became very expensive. Disk storage space is costly. Updating files became expensive and complex; each file had to be updated separately and consistency from one to the next became problematic. Hardware changes and upgrades often necessitated redesigning the files and rewriting the application programs that used them because the programs were written specifically for the structure of the files. It all cost too much.

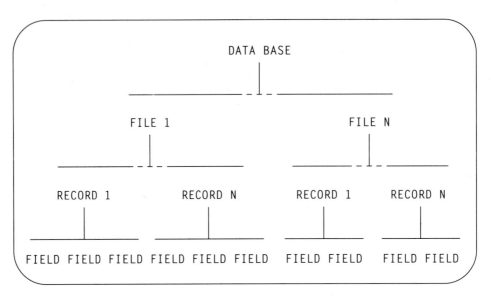

FIGURE 4.5. Generalized data base structure

Data Base Concepts

The solution to redundancy in individual data files was the concept of a data base. *Data base* can be synonymous with file, but the term often refers to a collection of related files, as illustrated in Figure 4.5. Data bases are quite complex. Access to them is controlled by a *data base management system* (DBMS).

A *relational* DBMS links separate files or even data bases though a common "key" field; for example, a social security number field in both personnel and payroll files. Reports draw needed information from both files, yet only the key field is duplicated. This removes as much redundancy as possible. Although most familiar to MS-DOS users in products like *dBase* and *Paradox*, *DB Master Version 5 Professional* offers relational capabilities for the Apple II world.

A DBMS shelters the user and application programs from the actual structure of its files. The user need know only how to make a request of the DBMS to store or retrieve a record. A DBMS may also include *Structured Query Language* (SQL), a simplified user interface. SQL permits a user to get information from the data base quickly, and simplifies data entry applications (Apfelstadt, 1989). Unlike most software, SQL does not depend on the computer itself or its operating system. Data bases on different types of microcomputers, such as MS-DOS and Macintosh, as well as minicomputers and even mainframe computers, can all use SQL to access data stored on any or all of the systems. This interconnectivity makes SQL important to many users.

Finally, the most sophisticated data base systems are *programmable*. Complex applications can be developed to meet virtually any need. Software like *dBase*, *Oracle*, *Paradox*, and *Double Helix* include their own programming languages for this purpose (Crabb, 1989).

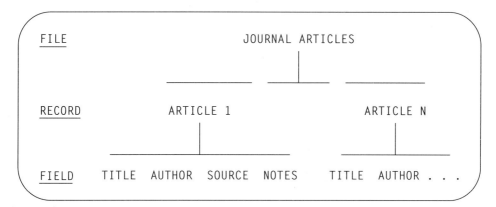

FIGURE 4.6. Filing system structure

FILING SYSTEMS

Data Bases and Microcomputers

Teaching is a world of microcomputers. Where does the data base concept fit? Although the term *data base* is often applied to microcomputer applications, it is seldom, if ever, technically correct. Major data base systems require faster CPUs, more RAM, and larger disk drives than are common to school micro-computer systems. Microcomputers are not quite ready to handle the data management needs of Standard Oil.

A Compromise—the Filing System

Where microcomputers are commonly used, a scaled-down version more properly called a *filing system* is the norm. Such a system is an intermediate step between personally programmed data files and the complexity of a DBMS.

Generally, a filing system does not seek to interrelate multiple files, but it provides many of the same kinds of sheltering of the user from the nitty gritty details of physical structure, storage, and retrieval. A mainframe data base is usually accessed through applications programs that are written in COBOL, assembler, PL/1, or another language. A microcomputer filing system is self-contained and the user interacts directly with it through its own command structure. Thus, a filing system allows the user to create and manipulate a data file without programming. Figure 4.6 shows the structure of data in a filing system. It is identical to our original explanations of data storage concepts.

Filing System Software

Highly specialized filing systems such as a mailing list manager, an electronic grade book, and a test item bank are treated in Chapter 6. General purpose filing systems include *AppleWorks, Bank Street Filer, FrEdBase, Notebook,* and *File-Express.* One unusual product is *Reference File* which is a memory-resident, pop-up data base for MS-DOS. It works with any other application and allows you to cut and paste information across applications. All these systems provide

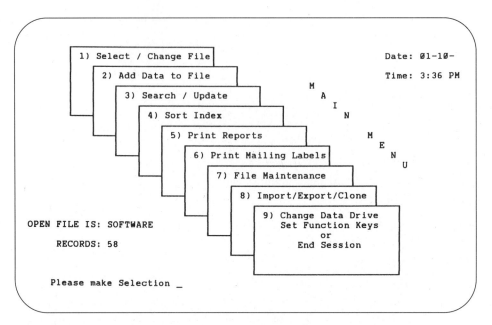

```
  ┌─────────────────────────┐                    Date: 01-10-
  │ 1) Select / Change File │                    Time: 3:36 PM
  │ ┌─────────────────────────┐
  │ │ 2) Add Data to File     │
  │ │ ┌─────────────────────────┐        M
  │ │ │ 3) Search / Update      │      A
  │ │ │ ┌─────────────────────────┐      I
  │ │ │ │ 4) Sort Index           │        N
  │ │ │ │ ┌─────────────────────────┐
  │ │ │ │ │ 5) Print Reports        │          M
  │ │ │ │ │ ┌──────────────────────────┐    E
  │ │ │ │ │ │ 6) Print Mailing Labels  │      N
  │ │ │ │ │ │ ┌─────────────────────────┐      U
  │ │ │ │ │ │ │ 7) File Maintenance     │
  │ │ │ │ │ │ │ ┌──────────────────────────┐
  │ │ │ │ │ │ │ │ 8) Import/Export/Clone   │
  │ │ │ │ │ │ │ │ ┌─────────────────────────┐
  OPEN FILE IS: SOFTWARE    │ 9) Change Data Drive    │
                            │    Set Function Keys    │
      RECORDS: 58           │         or              │
                            │    End Session          │

  Please make Selection _
```

FIGURE 4.7. Main menu of a general purpose filing system

general data handling capabilities on varying levels of sophistication. In turn, they require much more work on the part of the user to tailor them to a specific application. The trade-off is doing more work in return for the ability to handle widely varying needs with a single piece of software.

Selecting Filing Software. It is beyond the scope of this book to go into great detail on selecting filing software, but you should be alert to some of the key dimensions.

A major concern when selecting a filing system is the capacity of the software. Most systems have specific limits on the total data volume that can be accommodated. This may be a result of conscious decisions by the developer to limit the system or it may be a reflection of hardware limitations. Some filing systems are RAM-based, meaning the program and all data must fit within the computer's RAM capacity. This allows for very rapid manipulation of the data but will usually provide the least storage capacity. Other systems are disk-based, typically limiting file size to the storage capacity of the disk drive in use. Storage and retrieval are slower, because of frequent input/output operations involving the disk drive.

Beyond total storage capacity of the system, some software allows only one file per diskette, regardless of the amount of data actually entered. Many systems place limits on the size of individual records or even fields within records. This is often expressed as maximum bytes per record or field. Thus, you must have a clear idea of the exact requirements of a given application before selecting filing software.

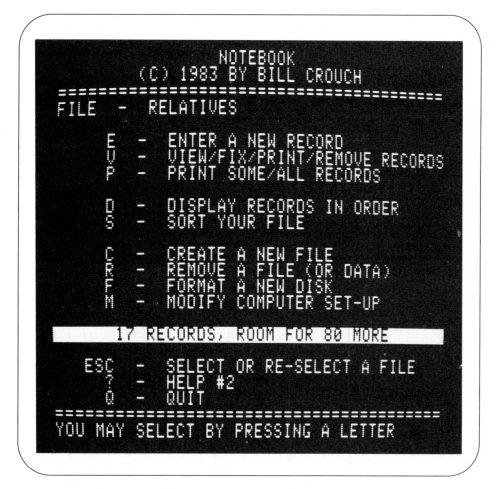

```
                    NOTEBOOK
          (C) 1983 BY BILL CROUCH
=========================================
FILE  -  RELATIVES

     E  -  ENTER A NEW RECORD
     V  -  VIEW/FIX/PRINT/REMOVE RECORDS
     P  -  PRINT SOME/ALL RECORDS

     D  -  DISPLAY RECORDS IN ORDER
     S  -  SORT YOUR FILE

     C  -  CREATE A NEW FILE
     R  -  REMOVE A FILE (OR DATA)
     F  -  FORMAT A NEW DISK
     M  -  MODIFY COMPUTER SET-UP

      17 RECORDS, ROOM FOR 80 MORE

   ESC  -  SELECT OR RE-SELECT A FILE
     ?  -  HELP #2
     Q  -  QUIT
=========================================
YOU MAY SELECT BY PRESSING A LETTER
```

The record capacity of this filing system is clearly shown.

Filing systems vary widely in their ability to customize output to your needs, ranging from little more than displaying your data in the precise form in which you entered it to rearranging and manipulating it in almost any fashion. Many have no arithmetic capabilities, making them unsuitable for recording any numeric data from which even a simple sum might be required. Others even allow fields whose content is derived from one or more other fields, perhaps the mean of some set of numeric fields.

Such factors will determine the suitability of a filing system for your needs. It should come as no surprise that the more flexible, versatile, and powerful a filing system, the more difficult it will be to master and use. When we turn to specific application suggestions, keep in mind the ramifications of these selection factors for ideas that appeal to you.

Setting Up a File. To create a new file, you must first analyze the requirements of the application and determine what fields are to be included in each record. This task requires a thorough understanding of the system's capabilities and your desired output. For instance, if you need to be able to sort an address file by zip code, then zip code will probably have to be a field of its own. If this does not matter, you could store in just one field both state and zip code or even more of the address. Similarly, if you anticipate the need for an alphabetical list of the names in the file, then you will probably require separate fields for first and last names.

The order in which fields are arranged within the file may also be important. If the system can display the contents of records only in their physical order, then entering Doe before John would make it impossible to ever display John Doe, say for a mailing label.

It may be necessary to specify the number of characters (bytes) allowed per field, either numerically or, in the case of *PFS: File,* as visible space on the screen. Some systems reserve all of the space specified for a field, regardless of what is actually entered. Thus, the name Doe consumes as much memory as Schwartzendruber. In such cases, you would try to select the smallest practical size for a field. Other systems use little more storage than the actual entries require, so that one can afford to be generous in setting field sizes.

When setting field sizes, one initially makes the best guess possible, but later use may turn up fields too small to hold some data elements. Systems vary in the ease with which a field may be enlarged; in some cases, it is not even possible. Further, suppose you discover long after a file was created and all the data have been entered that you forgot an important field. Perhaps something has changed in your use of the system and you need to add a new field. Systems differ widely in how easily new fields may be added later, if at all.

It should be apparent that there are many pitfalls in learning to work with data filing systems. Experience is clearly the best teacher, but the flexibility of the system you use makes a big difference as well. It is wise to create a file using your best judgment and intuition, then enter only a few records before thoroughly testing your application. If you have made a major error that the system will not allow you to correct easily, at least you will not have invested a lot of data entry time before going back to replan and reimplement the file.

HYPERMEDIA

Data bases are simply means of organizing text; that is, alphanumeric information. Storage and retrieval methods are essentially linear in nature; one piece of data follows another. But is that how the human mind works? Hardly! The human mind stores far more than just text. People often say something like "I can picture that in my mind." You can "hear" a familiar song whenever you think of it. Further, human retrieval processes are not linear, that is, one need not recall A before one can recall B. The human mind is a web of associations which are interrelated far more complexly than data bases.

In 1945 Vannevar Bush, an electrical engineer, described an integrated workstation he called a memex, "an extended physical supplement for man's mind, [which] seeks to emulate his mind in its associative linking of items of information, and their retrieval as a result" (Forrest, 1988). Bush was far ahead of his time, but today's *hypermedia* is much like his dream. Imagine reading a biography of Mozart, viewing his portrait, following a score as you hear the music, then taking a quiz on the material, all at your own PC! Gery (1989) provided this description of hypermedia.

> Hypermedia is an umbrella term . . . for a way to organize various data formats—text, sound, video, etc.—into elements that represent a particular concept, content area or point of view. Each data element is then 'linked' or associated with related elements (irrespective of form) into a lattice of relationships. When a user accesses a particular piece of information, all associated and related data elements become available through simple access methods (for instance, clicking with a mouse on a screen icon). This relational data base permits associative exploration of vast amounts of related and linked information in a seamless flow by the user (p. 51).

Gery suggested that one could conceivably get from John F. Kennedy's inaugural address to Joe DiMaggio's baseball batting average through their mutual link to Marilyn Monroe.

If such an associative lattice or web is limited to just text, the term applied is *hypertext*. Carr (1988) explained the significance of hypertext as data base in this way: "Formal databases use formal access systems; these usually require knowledge of both the material in the database and knowledge of how to use the database itself. Hypertext, however, requires a minimum of the former and virtually none of the latter."

Hypermedia includes non-text data. Its significance lies in the closer parallel to how our minds work, the ability to pursue answers as questions arise, to extend or contract the search virtually at will. Possible analogs for hypermedia are Tinker Toys and erector sets. Clearly, hypermedia offers entirely new possibilities to educators and learners alike.

The first major software for hypermedia was Apple's *HyperCard* for the Macintosh, introduced in August 1987. *HyperCard* has already become somewhat synonymous with hypertext or hypermedia, but just as all tissues are not Kleenex, not all hypermedia use *HyperCard*.

In the data base context, the *HyperCard* terms "stacks" and "cards" are significant. *Cards* are roughly comparable to records, while *stacks* are related or linked cards, somewhat like a file. Potentially, anything on a card can be linked to anything on any other card, even in other stacks. This flexibility is the lattice or web in action. See Figure 4.8 on the following page.

Although pioneered on the Macintosh, hypermedia software exists for the Apple II and MS–DOS computers as well. Chapter 14 contains a brief description of these products in the presentation of hypermedia as a programming environment.

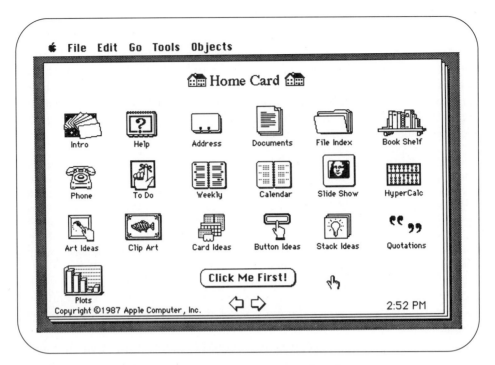

FIGURE 4.8. The *HyperCard* Home Card is a directory of stacks.

COMPACT AND LASER DISCS

One of the problems mentioned previously concerning microcomputers and data bases was *limited disk storage*. The data storage capacity of floppy disks is clearly very modest. Using multiple diskettes is hardly satisfactory, as it greatly increases retrieval time. Hard disks are a big step up, but even 40 megabytes or more quickly becomes too little for storage needs. Optical discs provide a viable means of dealing with large amounts of data, *as long as you do not need to change or update it*. Within limits of affordability, these are read-only media, but look for erasable or re-recordable systems in the near future.

The read-only nature of the medium is clear from the name of one major optical technology, CD–ROM. A disc the size of an audio compact disc (CD) has a capacity of 550 megabytes (MB). That is equivalent to 270,000 pages of text, nearly 5000 Apple 5¼-inch diskettes, or seventeen 40MB hard disks! To use this technology, the user must add a relatively inexpensive CD drive to the computer system. CD-ROM discs normally include the retrieval software (the data base management system) appropriate for the application. With care in designing the software as well as the layout of the data on the disc, that vast amount of data can be searched for any random piece of information easily and quickly. As Bitter (1988) maintains, this technology is of enormous importance to education, as it can truly put primary source data into the hands of students in ways never before possible.

Technically, there is no real limit to what can be stored on compact discs (CDs). Audio CDs are the most familiar. CD–ROM applications are usually all text. Other formats include CD–V (V = video) and CD–I (I = interactive) which are much like miniature laser discs with full photo quality analog images. DVI (Digital Video Interactive) is a competing format in which video images are digitized and can be fully manipulated. Refer to Bitter (1988) and *PC Magazine* (Staff, 1989) for basic information on these variants.

One major benefit of the CD size is that a drive can fit in the floppy disk drive space of most microcomputers. The small discs are also convenient to carry and store. Yet, despite the enormous text capacity explained previously, computer graphics require so much memory that a CD can hold only about 1000 images (Staff, 1989). For still images, this is still impressive, but not for motion.

The 12-inch laser disc remains the choice for randomly accessible motion segments. Its capacity of 54,000 individual frames offers enormous *visual data base* potential. One disc can easily contain photos of the entire collection of the National Gallery of Art or enough images to support an entire science curriculum without microscope and other slides. That same capacity provides about 30 minutes of motion playback. Combinations of still and motion are easily possible.

While applications are still somewhat limited for educators, optical storage systems are almost certain to have a major impact on education as the 21st century nears. The sheer storage capacities involved magnify Naisbitt's concern about data. The retrieval software is critical to our hope of turning so much data into something meaningful, that is, into knowledge.

With hypermedia interfaces, teachers can create ideal learning systems. As Gery (1989) explained, CD–ROM "permits random-access structure and inquiry-based learning" which computer-based learning promised, but failed to deliver, with its linear frame approach. Optical discs become a relational data base of text, data, graphics, still images, audio, and video. Computer-based learning ". . . automated the past. CD–ROM and related technologies redefine the future." The data base becomes a unique, highly flexible learning tool.

For more information in this exciting area, refer to Lambert and Ropiequet (1986), Ropiequet (1987), and especially Ambron and Hooper (1988). Truett (1988) provides a very short educator's introduction.

CLASSROOM APPLICATIONS

TEACHERS AND DATA FILES

Data bases can help teachers "work smarter." Possibilities include computerizing any of the data you now keep in file folders, on index cards, on a Rolodex, or in an address book. It requires some experience with filing systems to be able to judge the worthiness of computerizing any specific set of data. Honeyman (1985) describes a project to utilize *PFS:File* to cope with the reporting and recordkeeping requirements of federal law related to special education students. Computerization was a sound choice in the face of the massive requirements of such programs.

Perhaps you have difficulty recalling where you saw an article or other resources for class use. A personal annotated index to journals and other materials might be invaluable. If you work with student organizations, you may deal with mailing lists or membership rosters which are difficult to maintain manually. Slides, negatives, and prints for the newspaper or yearbook can be tracked with a data base. The possibilities are endless; the specific applications of benefit to you may be unique.

The EPIE *Integrated Instructional Information Resource* is a group of data bases designed to help educators identify and use all manner of educational materials. It is described further in Chapter 16.

Testing offers many possible applications, such as a data bank of test items to draw upon as needed. The *Test Center Database* provides access through an ERIC-based key word search to all tests and surveys available through the Northwest Regional Educational Laboratory Test Center (NWREL). TESTNET, also from NWREL, links users to individuals who have actually used the test instruments identified via the Test Center Database. For details, contact NWREL Test Center, 101 S.W. Main St., Suite 600, Portland, OR 97204.

STUDENTS AND DATA FILES

A Rationale

To limit discussion to those things that make a teacher's life a little easier is to miss the area of greatest potential—student involvement with data files. Hunter (1985, p. 21) suggested several purposes for using data bases in the classroom:

Discovering commonalities and differences among groups of things
Analyzing relationships
Looking for trends
Testing and refining hypotheses
Organizing and sharing information
Arranging information in more useful ways

Each of Hunter's purposes is an exercise in problem solving. Who would disagree that students need to learn problem-solving skills? The question is how to help students gain them. Collis (1988, pp. 17–60) presents the computer as an outstanding tool for developing the skills to organize, display, summarize, extend, and evaluate information. The goal is to apply critical thinking to information using data bases.

A Three-Stage Approach

If students are to learn with data bases, Hunter (1985) suggests a three-stage process. First, the student learns to use data files created by someone else. Once students are skilled in retrieving and manipulating data, they proceed to stage two—building their own file from a design prepared and tested by the teacher or someone else. This stage focuses on planning a research project, gathering data, and entering it into the filing system. Only then is it ready to use as before. In the third stage, students plan, design, create, and use a totally original data base.

Parker (1986) noted that the way in which the students must use a data base also determines the level of intellectual skill involved. Searching is a low level skill, regardless of the source of the data base. Interpretation, seeking trends, and testing hypotheses are all higher level skills, even if one uses an existing data base.

Applications and resources have three stages according to Hunter (1985). However, many listed as stage one could become stage two or three. The stage alone does not define the skill level.

Stage One Resources

Partly in response to the growing interest in data management among educators, software houses have created specialized resources that meet the needs of Hunter's stage one—using data files.

Disk File Resources. Scholastic supports an inquiry approach to science and social studies with data base files, activity packages, and lesson plans. Products are available for *PFS: FILE/REPORT* in physical and life science, U.S. history and government, and world geography, cultures, and economics. *AppleWorks* products include the topics of weather, climate, the Congress, and the Constitution. Sunburst offers many data bases for *Bank Street Filer.* Examples include endangered species, space and astronomy, and colonial times.

The MECC *Dataquest* series does not require a separate filing system. Among the offerings are *The Presidents, Fifty States,* and *The World Community.* For Apple IIgs only, *World GeoGraph* is a visual data base providing 40 colored maps and 55 categories of information on 177 nations. Active Learning Systems' *One World* is self-contained and offers 33 categories of data on over 170 nations.

The National Collegiate Software Clearinghouse (Box 8101, Raleigh, NC, 27695; 919/737–3067) has databases in *Lotus, dBase, SPSS,* and *ASCII* formats for cultural anthropology, crime and corrections, and various aspects of the United States. The World Bank provides primary data for social studies with its *World Development Indicators* files. Contact World Bank Publications, Department 0552, Washington, DC 20073–0552.

BOOKBRAIN and *BookWhiz* are interactive, annotated data bases of children's books designed to encourage readers in grades 4–9. Users can seek books likely to interest them and add their own annotations.

HyperCard Stack Resources. The Association for Educational Communications and Technology has established the *HyperCard* Instructional Stackware Exchange to serve as a clearinghouse and library for quality instructional stacks. For information, contact Scott Grabinger, University of Colorado at Denver, Campus Box 106, 1200 Larimer Street, Denver, CO 80204–5300. Teachers can submit stacks to the Exchange for possible distribution as well as obtain stacks from it.

Among stacks from the International Society for Technology in Education is *World Data*, which includes 47 fields on nearly 170 nations. *Presidents* augments basic data with maps on the westward movement during relevant terms.

SchoolArt is a collection of 200 images in stack format. *StateFacts* includes maps as well as basic state data. Both are from P-Productions. *Amanda Stories* from the Voyager Company may stretch the data base idea some, but is a fascinating demonstration of *HyperCard* to create interactive fiction. Voyager also supplies stacks with many of its videodisc products. Heizer Software is another stack source.

Watch for rapid expansion of hypermedia resources.

CD–ROM Resources. Because CD–ROM is a read-only technology, resources in this format are fixed and cannot be altered, but are ideal for stage one applications. This is a fast growing field; therefore, this section highlights only selected sources and products.

Many familiar products are now available in compact disc format. Among them are Grolier's *New Electronic Encyclopedia* and *Compton's Encyclopedia*. The full text of the hardcopy forms is provided, but not the illustrations. Grolier's includes a form of hypertext which allows users to locate related information easily. Search results often far exceed what one would typically find manually. Dishnow (1988) describes using this CD with students in grades 7–12.

Common reference works available on CD include ERIC, *A–V Online, Reader's Guide to Periodical Literature, Education Index*, and various versions of *Books in Print* and related works.

U.S. Census data is now on CD. *Compact Disclosure* is a CD data base detailing over 10,000 companies traded on major stock exchanges. *Geovision Maps* provides thousands of maps in various scales and configurations. *The Constitution Papers* is a unique and inexpensive CD resource for social studies. NATASHA, the National Archive on Sexuality, Health, & Adolescence, provides access to 109 sets of data from 82 major studies relevant to teenage pregnancy. It includes a user's guide on microfiche. *The First National Item Bank & Test Development System* contains many thousands of validated test items, including graphics, linked to curricular objectives from multiple item banks.

University Microfilms International offers CDs containing journal article abstracts covering a wide range of fields. These are usable on any CD hardware. Its *Business Periodicals Ondisc* demonstrates a future direction—full text of articles which the user can print as needed. Special hardware is required. Over 300 popular business periodicals were initially covered, representing an estimated half of the citations in the abstracts disc. The research potential is staggering. One day you will be able to search through abstracts for what you need, then retrieve and *print* the full text of each article, all without leaving your computer!

Keeping up with CD developments is difficult. *CD–ROM Review* (IDG

Communications, 80 Elm Street, Peterborough, NH 03458; 603–924–9471) is a helpful resource for non-music CDs.

Telecommunications and Information Services. Telecommunications offers computer users the ability to access digital information services around the world. From a microcomputer equipped with a modem, telecommunications software, and a printer, the user can connect to such well-known services as *CompuServe* and *Dow Jones.* Newer services include *Prodigy* and *Dialog/Classmate,* the latter geared especially to educational uses.

Through these services you can tap almost unlimited data resources. As one example, *Dialog/Classmate* offers access to U.S. Census data, the complete text of over 50 popular magazines, a magazine index akin to *Reader's Guide,* an index to major US newspapers, a daily index to over 2000 news stories, UPI news stories, historical research information on the U.S., and articles on the world since 1450. There are more than 1400 publicly accessible data bases. Even CD–ROM pales in comparison for sheer volume. Consult Parisi and Jones (1988) or Reinhold and Vernot (1987) for greater detail.

Along with the original hardware and software expenses required for telecommunications, there are specific costs to use information services. Usually there is an initial subscriber or membership fee. In metropolitan areas, you may be able to reach one or more services with a local phone call. If not, then add long distance charges. For some services, although the actual computer may be located anywhere, you can call a phone number in the nearest metropolitan area. There may be an additional charge for the special "packet-switching" network that connects you to the information service. Once connected, you pay for "connect time," the actual minutes your computer spends "talking" to theirs. Some services have a minimum monthly service charge, even if you do not call. Others charge monthly or annual subscription fees.

On-line information brings primary data into students' hands. One intriguing application is the program *Weather Machine* from National Geographic. Although it includes 30 days data from the National Weather Service, you can use its telecommunications component to obtain real-time weather data. (On an Apple IIgs, this program even produces color weather maps.)

Perceptions of cost have been a major inhibitor of educational use of these services, along with teacher ignorance and lack of skill in their use. Sheer logistics of setting up for telecommunications in the classroom or lab can dull enthusiasm. However, Collis (1988), Wigley (1988), and Scrogan (1987) offer sound advice on meeting these problems. Slatta (1985) and Friedlander (1985) have also researched this area.

Until CD–ROM, there were no rivals to the resources of information services. Today, educators must assess their applications carefully. If your only interest is data bases, you may be able to meet your goal more cost effectively and flexibly with CD–ROM. However, other online services presented in Chapter 6 may justify membership for some schools.

For more information refer to Wigley (1988) and Motamatsu and Newman (1987), and the *CompuServe* experiences reported by Riedl (1986). Included are many practical ideas on cost containment and time management. While it is still early in educational telecommunications, the potential is impressive.

Stage Two Resources and Applications

At stage two, students extend or build data bases designed by others. Few commercial products exist at this level. *Hometown: Local Area Studies* provides survey forms and lesson plan ideas easily adapted to any situation. Students collect information about their own town, then store it in and manipulate a local area database. Sunburst has a similar product in its *Bank Street Filer* data bases. *GeoWorld* from Tom Snyder Productions also requires students to extend the basic information provided.

Many teachers have developed applications which can be either stage two or three, depending on who develops the record structure. Barbour (1988) had students gather data from headstones in a local cemetery. Uses included looking for epidemics and how average age of death has varied by time periods.

Lynch's (1988) sixth graders surveyed the residents of their community about attitudes toward their state's mandatory seat belt law. Students learned about social science procedures and practiced interviewing skills. They gathered and entered data, then manipulated it and graphed the results. This idea of "doing" social studies could be applied to countless topics.

In language arts, teachers can maintain a student reading database. You can record such things as title, author, fiction/non-fiction, subject area of the book, name and gender of reader, assessment, etc. You can even help students determine the most popular books or authors, make a display, or include results in a newsletter to parents. Students can find interesting books based on searchs by reviewer gender, subject, and rating. Variations on the book report data base for different grade levels are given by Bilyeu (1984), Dunfey (1984) and Wasylenki (1985).

Two different approaches to the study of minerals in earth science are given by Woerner (1987–1988) and Hirschfelt (1987–1988). Woerner used an *AppleWorks* database to help students experience the process of science through discovery or inquiry learning. She also provided lesson plans for using the database, a source for the actual minerals needed, and an offer to share all of her materials. Hirschfelt had the same goal, but chose to develop a program in BASIC to meet it. Students must examine a specimen of an unknown mineral. The program then asks questions about their findings, and matches that against its stored mineral characteristics. The program could be modified to work with most categorical data.

Krueger (1987) created a computer unit for 4th–6th grades called *Datasaurs— An Experience with Dinosaurs*. An *AppleWorks* data base covers 40 different dinosaurs. Emphasis is on carefully designed activities aimed at higher-order thinking, not the data base itself.

For election years, Schiffman (1986) outlined a data base activity to explore voting trends, population shifts, etc., as well as project the election outcome based on prior voting records.

The Kids Network Project is a joint effort of Technical Education Research Centers (TERC) and the National Geographic Society. Instructional units contain one month's activities on science topics like water pollution. Students collect data and report it through the network. For information, contact TERC, 1696 Massachusetts Avenue, Cambridge, MA 02138.

Seventh graders in British Columbia created a *HyperCard* yearbook (*DBKids*, Winter 1989). The principal designed stacks, students digitized their own photos, "pasted" them onto cards, and added autobiographies. What other creative ideas can you envision based on hypermedia?

Stage Three Resources and Applications

The most personal experience with data manipulation occurs at Hunter's stage three, when students create and use their own personal data banks. Possibilities include cataloging coin or other collections; maintaining reading lists with annotations; lists of spelling words that need extra study; and records of individualized assignments started, in progress, and completed.

Thomas (1988) explained the significance of stage three activities. Students learn that "the shape of the question is as important as the answer. . . . They learn to examine both questions and answers in light of their own biases and habits. . . . (T)hey learn that they can organize large amounts of data in a systematic fashion and derive meaning from it." Schiffman (1986) concurred and noted that "conceptualizing a database requires breaking a body of information into critical attributes, pinpointing key concepts and eliminating peripheral or nonessential ones."

Virtually any idea previously presented could be a stage three application. You must decide whether your situation, including student computer access and available time, permits this level of activity. Stage three demands more resources than stages one or two.

Here are a few more applications at stage three. Worster and Morrison (1986) describe the derivation of a geography data base from, and ties back to, traditional materials. Thomas (1988) carefully covers and illustrates the steps in designing a data base using an example based on prime-time television. For language arts classes, Collis (1988, pp. 99–102) suggests a poem data base containing keywords, time period when written, author, title, style, or format. When students learn to do research papers, they might jointly develop a bibliography of books or articles. Collis provides a lesson plan for this idea.

An unusually extensive project is reported by Modla (1988). An interdisciplinary medieval life unit captivated social studies, language arts, and gifted classes. At the heart of the project was a *Bank Street Filer* data base on life in the 1200s. Fields included home, clothing, food, and social status. Students also created their own files of fictional persons and places. Besides the data base, the total plan encompassed 31 other software programs, including word processing and computer-assisted instruction.

Perhaps the ultimate local, or even district, application would be extending basic data base concepts into a complete educational information system. Such a system could provide the empirical decision support data routinely expected in business, but seldom available in education. Such data could be vital to meeting demands for increased accountability and is now feasible with PCs. For more information on this kind of application, consult Deck (1987).

Teaching Resources

Although many educators think of computers as individual tools, data base activities offer unlimited potential for group work as well. With group projects, students experience the importance of team work and the requirements for group decision making.

Consider the possibilities of dividing a class into teams, assigning a continent or some other area to each, and having each group design and create a data file on the countries in their area. The entire class could have access to all completed files and use them for further study of the topic. In the process, they may experience directly how the structure of data affects one's ability to use it.

If the goal were strictly the ultimate usefulness of the data, then you should provide at least minimal guidelines for structuring the data file to assure some level of compatibility across projects.

There are numerous resources to assist the teacher wishing to use data bases in the classroom. An outstanding one is Beverly Hunter's newsletter *DBKids*. This is a subscription resource of up-to-date classroom application ideas, sources of data bases, information on networks and products, even bibliographies. Write Targeted Learning Corporation, Rt. 1, Box 190, Amissville, VA 22002. Contributions help pay for the newsletter.

Resource assistance can be found in *Correlating Computer Database Programs with Social Studies Instruction* and *A Review of Database Software for Science* (available with or without detailed product descriptions). Both are publications of the Northwest Regional Educational Laboratory.

Warner (1988) has provided a coherent approach to in-school data base development, including practical advice and sample worksheets which help assure that students learn from the results. Sopp (1985) and Pon (1984) have related experiences working at the third and fourth grade levels.

Starting from basic data base operations, *Teaching Thinking Skills with Databases* (Watson, 1988) offers a carefully sequenced approach to developing higher order skills in grades 3–8. The book includes scripted lesson plans, worksheet and transparency masters, and data files on disk. It is available in *AppleWorks* and *FrEdBase* versions. Lesson plans sequenced across grade levels and designed for a single computer classroom are featured in Collis (1988).

Hannah (1987) gives classroom and team activities useful for grades 5–12. A complete data base on US presidents and vice-presidents is included, with copyable worksheets!

Hunter and Lodisch (1988) offer a wealth of practical and tested projects using online data bases. Ideas aim at transferable skills practiced in a variety of contexts: chemistry and health, American history and government, global studies, and contemporary issues. Another useful resource is Epler (1989).

RESEARCH ON LEARNING WITH DATA BASES

Too little research on learning with data bases has appeared to warrant generalizations. However, four studies offer some insights. Based on 665 subjects, White (1985) found that use of a data base in social studies resulted in significantly higher performance on a test involving such tasks as evaluating the relevance of data to a problem, its sufficiency for reaching a conclusion, and ways to organize data to more readily solve a problem.

Rawitsch (1988) sought empirical evidence to support anecdotal claims that data base use aids development of higher-order thinking skills. His study of 339 eighth graders examined their work styles, their attitudes, and had them perform exercises with both paper and computer data bases. Rawitsch found that students solved more problems correctly when using the computer, but they took longer to do so. They preferred using the computer. Students with an unstructured work style were less efficient using the computer than those with a structured style. He also found evidence of transfer of learning to more life-like contexts. Rawitsch stressed that "problem solving with computer data base use . . . cannot effectively be learned as a one-time activity. . . ." Rather, the skills should be taught and used repeatedly throughout the curriculum for maximum effect.

Rawitsch, Bart, and Earle (1988) examined how use of data bases affected hypothetical-deductive and proportional reasoning. The study used *The Oregon Trail* simulation with part of the seventh grade subjects, an *AppleWorks* data base file with the others. The data base group was further divided, with one subgroup receiving debriefing before the post-test, the other after. Although there were modest gains in the data base groups, with the largest found on hypothetical-deductive reasoning in the group with debriefing after the post-test, they were not statistically significant. Actual computer time involved was only three successive days. The researchers believe this was insufficient to truly develop the anticipated changes. They also believe teacher behaviors played a role and require further study.

In a study by Eastman (1986), a group of eighth graders had access to an online encyclopedia via *CompuServe* for three weeks. The intent was to provide a new way to glean information for writing a theme. Instead, students came to focus on their printouts—getting one was success, not getting one was failure. Many spent a lot of time pouring over their printouts, cutting and pasting, marking them up, probably at the expense of the library follow-up hoped for by the teacher. They were also willing to accept whatever the computer gave them as "enough" information, provided that their printouts were about the same length as others! Clearly educators have a lot to learn about effective use of online information sources.

Although research evidence is limited, observation and anecdotal reports strongly suggest that data bases have the potential to be an extremely powerful educational tool. Their optimal use must yet be determined. Gooler (1987) provides a glimpse of what may one day exist.

SUMMARY

Existing school microcomputers and inexpensive filing system software can ease many common data management burdens for the teacher. Whatever paper and pencil recordkeeping a teacher now does should be carefully examined as a candidate for computerization. However, the fact that data can be filed electronically does not guarantee a better result. The use must be compatible with software limitations and hardware accessibility. Common sense must prevail over sheer potential.

Teachers should also consider classroom uses of computer filing systems. Projects relevant to students can be devised readily, which may yield a clearer understanding of the significance of information in our society. Students can experience the ramifications of their decisions concerning what information is worth storing and how it should be handled. Group or class research projects may become more exciting as students are able to benefit individually from the data gathered and entered by all. Class files become exercises in problem solving. Applications of hypermedia and the massive storage capacity of CD–ROM are being developed and the potential is enormous. Beyond what compact discs can offer, telecommunications links to data bases through information services offer exciting possibilities for student access to primary data, something often reserved for advanced graduate students. All data base projects should aim at higher order thinking skills to the extent possible.

Research concerning learning with data bases is scarce. Still, of all the computer skills and knowledge that students may gain in school, working with data base or electronic filing systems may be one of the most beneficial in terms of application during their adult years.

CHAPTER 4 ACTIVITIES

1. Take any common blank form used in your environment for recordkeeping and analyze it in data base concepts. Write a brief explanation of it in terms of files, records, and fields.
2. Using the same form, jot down the fields that would be included in a computerized version and suggest the number of characters of space each would require in a computer file. Total the field requirements to determine the approximate size of one record.
3. List three or more data management tasks of your own that you could consider for computerization. Are they appropriate for the computer? Why?
4. Select your most appropriate personal data management task. What sort of information would you need to retrieve from your system for it to help you?

This is the information you would minimally put into your file or data base. Can you think of additions that would give you potential for answering questions you currently cannot?

5. Explain how your selected application would be improved by using a computerized system. What would you lose in the process?

6. Examine software reviews or advertising literature for a variety of data bases or filing systems. Compile a list of features allowing comparison of the systems. Which seems best to you, considering capabilities, ease of use, and cost?

7. Create a small data file using any available computer filing system and one of your own application ideas.

8. Explore any CD–ROM or hypermedia application to which you have access.

9. Obtain sign-up literature from information services of interest to you. Compare and contrast them for cost and services.

REFERENCES

Ambron, S. and Hooper, K., eds. *CD ROM. Vol 3. Interactive Media.* Redmond, WA: Microsoft Press, 1988.

Apfelstadt, M. "Higher Education Applications" *Call–A.P.P.L.E.*, February 1989, pp. 8–13.

Barbour, A. "A Cemetery Data Base Makes Math Come Alive." *Electronic Learning*, February 1988, pp. 12–13.

Bilyeu, L. M. "Computer Tracks Second Graders' Book Preferences and Accomplishments." *Reading Teacher*, 1984, 38(3), pp. 358 359.

Bitter, G. G. "CD–ROM Technology and the Classroom of the Future." *Computers in the Schools*, 1988, 5(1/2), pp. 23–34.

Bitter, G. G. and Camuse, R. A. *Using a Microcomputer in the Classroom*, Reston, VA: Reston Publishing Company, 1984.

Carr, C. "Hypertext: A New Training Tool?" *Educational Technology*, August 1988, pp. 7–11.

Coburn, P., Kelman, P., Roberts, N., Snyder, T. F. F., Watt, D. H., and Weiner, C. *Practical Guide to Computers in Education.* Reading, MA: Addison-Wesley, 1982.

Collis, B. *Computers, Curriculum, and Whole-Class Instruction.* Belmont, CA: Wadsworth, 1988.

Crabb, D. "SQL: Promise or Panacea?" *MacWeek*, 31 January 1989, pp. 30–32.

Deck, D. *Designing Information Systems in Educational Settings.* Portland, OR: Northwest Regional Educational Laboratory, July 1988.

Dishnow, R. "*Electronic Encyclopedia* Helps Prepare Students for Automated Card Catalog." *The Computing Teacher*, November 1988, pp. 37–39, 49.

Dunfey, J. "Using a Database in an English Classroom." *The Computing Teacher*, February 1984, pp. 26–27.

Eastman, S. T. "A Qualitative Study of Computers and Printouts in the Classroom." *Educational Communication and Technology Journal*, Winter 1986, 34(4), pp. 207–222.

Eaton, N. L., MacDonald, L. B., and Saule, M. R. *CD–ROM and Other Optical Information Systems.* Phoenix, AZ: Oryx Press, 1989.

Epler, D. M. *Online Searching Goes to School.* Phoenix, AZ: Oryx Press, 1989.

Forrest, C. "Technological Convergence." *TechTrends*, November/December 1988, pp. 8–12.

Friedlander, B. "Get Your Class In-Line and On-Line with a Modem." *Electronic Education*, November/December 1985, pp. 14–15, 23.

Gery, G. J. "CD–ROM. The Medium Has a Message." *Training*, January 1989, pp. 45–51.

Gooler, D. G. *The Education Utility: The Power to Revitalize Education and Society.* Englewood Cliffs, NJ: Educational Technology Publications, 1986.

Hannah, L. "Teaching Data Base Search Strategies." *The Computing Teacher*, June 1987, pp. 16–23.

Hannah, L. "The Database: Getting to Know You." *The Computing Teacher*, August/September 1987, pp. 17–20.

Hirschfelt, J. M. "A Mineral Database Program." *The Computing Teacher*, December/January 1987–88, pp. 22–24.

Honeyman, D. S. "Data Bases and Special Education IEP Reports." *Electronic Learning*, March 1985, pp. 24, 26.

Hunter, B. *My Students Use Computers.* Reston, VA: Reston Publishing Company, 1983.

Hunter, B. "Problem Solving with Data Bases." *The Computing Teacher*, May 1985, pp. 20–27.

Hunter, Beverly and Lodish, Erica K. *Online Searching in the Curriculum.* Santa Barbara, CA: ABC–CLIO, 1988.

Krueger, S., SNJM. "Brontosaurus Meets the Computer." *The Computing Teacher*, June 1987, pp. 13–15.

Lambert, S. and Ropiequet, S., eds. *CD ROM. Vol. 1. The New Papyrus.* Redmond, WA: Microsoft Press, 1986.

Lynch, C. "The Andover Seat Belt Project." *The Computing Teacher*, February 1988, pp. 31–32.

Motamatsu, N. R. and Newman, J. A. *Research Goes to School: Teaching Students to Go Online*, ERIC, ED 288 531, 1987.

McClelland, J. "A New Twist on an Old Skill: Retrieving Information with Computers to Enhance Decision-Making Processes." *Computers in the Schools*, Spring 1986, pp. 83–88.

Moberg, T. F. *Databases in the Humanities and Social Sciences.* Osprey, FL: Paradigm Press, 1987.

Modla, V. B. "Using Computers in 'Medieval Life'." *Media and Methods*, January/February 1988, p. 18.

Naisbitt, J. *MegaTrends.* New York: Warner, 1982.

Parisi, Lynn S. and Jones, Virginia L. *Directory of Online Databases and CD–ROM Resources for High Schools.* Santa Barbara, CA: ABC–CLIO, 1988.

Pon, K. "Databasing in the Elementary (and Secondary) Classroom." *The Computing Teacher*, November 1984, pp. 28–31.

Ragan, L. C. "HyperCard—A User's Description." *TechTrends*, September 1988, pp. 38–39.

Rawitsch, D. "The Computerized Database: Not a Simple Solution." *The Computing Teacher*, December/January 1987–88, pp. 34–37.

Rawitsch, D. "The Effect of Computer Use and Student Work Style on Database Analysis Activities in the Social Studies" In *Improving the Use of Technology in Schools: What Are We Learning. Research Bulletin #1* St. Paul, MN: MECC/University of Minnesota Center for the Study of Educational Technology, November 1988, pp. 1–3.

Rawitsch, D., Bart, W. M. and Earle, J. F. "Using Computer Database Programs to Facilitate Higher-Order Thinking Skills." In *Improving the Use of Technology in Schools: What Are We Learning. Research Bulletin #1* St. Paul, MN: MECC/University of Minnesota Center for the Study of Educational Technology, November 1988, pp. 7–9.

Reinhold, F. and Vernot, D. "Online Information Services: You've Come a Long Way. Baby!" *Electronic Learning,* November/December 1987, pp. 36–36.

Riedl, R. "CompuServe in the Classroom." *The Computing Teacher,* March 1986, pp. 62–64.

Ropiequet, S., ed. *CD ROM. Vol. 2. Optical Publishing.* Redmond, WA: Microsoft Press, 1987.

Schiffman, S. S. "A Strategy for Helping Students Draw Conclusions." *The Social Studies,* Vol. 77, No. 2, pp. 74–76.

Schiffman, S. S. "Productivity Tools for the Classroom." *The Computing Teacher,* May 1986, pp. 27–31.

Scrogan, L. "Telecomputing: How to Overcome the Roadblocks." *Classroom Computer Learning,* February 1987, pp. 40–45.

Slatta, R. "The Banquet's Set." *Electronic Education,* January 1985, pp. 12–13.

Sopp, N. P. "Do You Really Need a Children's Data Base?" *The Computing Teacher,* November 1985, pp. 43–45.

Staff. "Archives in Miniature." *PC Magazine,* 31 January 1989, pp. 185–200.

Thomas, R. "The Student-Designed Database." *The Computing Teacher,* February 1988, pp. 17–19.

Truett, C. "What Is This Thing Called CD–ROM?" *The Computing Teacher,* August/September 1988, pp. 30–31.

Warner, M. "Developing Database Files for Student Use." *The Computing Teacher,* April 1988, pp. 44–47.

Wasylenki, L. "The Electronic Book Report." *Computers in Education,* January 1985, p. 15.

Watson, J. "Database Activities in a One-Computer Classroom." *The Computing Teacher,* August/September 1988, pp. 21–23, 50

Watson, J. *Teaching Thinking Skills With Databases.* Eugene, OR: International Council for Computers in Education, 1988.

Watson, J. and Strudler, N. "Teaching Higher Order Thinking Skills with Databases." *The Computing Teacher,* December/January 1988–89, pp. 47–50, 55.

Woerner, J. J. "The Database as a Resource in the Earth Science Classroom." *The Computing Teacher,* December/January 1987–88, pp. 20–22.

Worster, B. and Morrison, D. M. "Using *AppleWorks* in the Geography Class: From Transparent Maps to Sortable Electronic Data." *Computers in the Schools,* Spring 1986, pp. 63–73.

White, C. "Developing Information-Processing Skills Through Structured Activities With a Computerized File-Management Program." *Journal of Educational Computing Research,* 1987, 3(3), pp. 355–375.

White, C. S. *The Impact of Structured Activities with a Computer-Based File-Management Program on Selected Information Processing Skills.* Unpublished doctoral dissertation, Indiana University, 1985.

Wigley, J. "Telecommunications Planning Guide for Educators." *The Computing Teacher,* November 1988, pp. 24–29.

CHAPTER 5

□ *Spreadsheets* □

O B J E C T I V E S

After completing this chapter, you will be able to:

- □ Briefly discuss the development of application software. □
- □ Explain the concept of a spreadsheet. □
- □ Describe the basic elements of a spreadsheet. □
- □ List and describe generic functional commands used to construct and manipulate a computer spreadsheet. □
- □ Explain the significance of spreadsheet templates. □
- □ Explain the significance of "what if" applications. □
- □ List and discuss several educational uses of computer spreadsheets. □
- □ Detail at least one application that you would like to try or explain why you see no personal application for spreadsheets. □

This chapter examines one of the earliest and most useful types of application program ever written for the microcomputer, the electronic spreadsheet. This fascinating application is first placed in the context of application software, followed by an overview of what a spreadsheet is and what a spreadsheet program can do. A sample computer spreadsheet is developed step by step. Applications of spreadsheets in the educational setting conclude this chapter.

DEVELOPMENT OF APPLICATION SOFTWARE

COMPUTERS FOR PROGRAMMERS

When microcomputers became generally available in the latter part of the 1970s, computer languages were the first software. These programs presented the user with a variety of programming approaches patterned after the languages then in use on mainframe computers. Users were obliged to plan and write their own application programs, a topic discussed in a later section of this book. At that time, microcomputer usage was viewed as a downward extension of mainframe computing, with expertise in programming and programming languages being required for machine usage. This made it appear that considerable technical knowledge and experience would also be necessary for the average person to make use of rapidly developing microcomputer technology.

COMPUTERS FOR NON-PROGRAMMERS

Word processing programs were the first major microcomputer software development to approach usage from a different perspective, that of the computer as a tool. *Tool* or *application* programs allowed the user to perform desired tasks without the necessity of doing the actual programming. Someone else had already created a general purpose tool for a common need. By learning how to use a specific application program, the user could benefit from a microcomputer without having to learn or even be familiar with a computer language. This simplified computer usage and made the microcomputer directly accessible to a wide variety of potential users. Rather than devoting weeks, months, or years to mastering programming skills, users could achieve useful results in a period of hours or, at most, days.

VISIBLE CALCULATORS

Business Origins
The introduction of the *VisiCalc* program in 1979 continued and accelerated the trend toward application software. The creators of *VisiCalc* recognized that many common tasks entail working with a calculator and a sheet of paper to record and organize information in a row and column format. This was especially true

in the world of business finance—accounting ledgers, forecasting documents, and so on. Their new product was a *visible calculator*, and much more.

The program presented the user with a simple and direct way to construct and manipulate a computer work area of rows and columns called a *spreadsheet*. A wide variety of useful tasks could be performed with no knowledge of a complicated computer language. *VisiCalc* was an immediate success and ultimately became a best seller in all major areas of potential computer usage: business, education, and the home. It helped to convince countless mainframe users that microcomputers were more than toys. It also created a whole new generation of first-time computer users.

An Educator's Application

Although most teachers are far removed from business finance, they typically use a spreadsheet every day without realizing it. Recall that a spreadsheet is an arrangement of rows and columns that stores data. What, then, is a teacher's grade book? It is a *manual* spreadsheet. Figure 5.1 shows how grade book data might appear in an *electronic* spreadsheet. Spreadsheets have found varied uses quite apart from their origins in finance.

MORE POWERFUL SPREADSHEETS

Today spreadsheets are a major generic form of computer software, along with word processing and data management programs. Since the creation of *VisiCalc*, improved versions of spreadsheet programs have been introduced by a variety of companies. Each new version and upgrade have built upon previous spreadsheet developments and introduced a wider range of more powerful capabilities. These capabilities represent improvement in two directions. The

	A	B	C	D	E	F
1	Student Name	Quiz 1	Quiz 2	Quiz 3	Student Total	
2						
3	Brown, Sally	29	19	28	76	
4	Roberts, Kevin	25	25	13	63	
5	Smith, Betty	20	18	22	60	
6	Taylor, James	23	21	25	69	
7						
8	Quiz Average	24.25	20.75	22	67	
9						
10						
11						
12						
13						
14						
15						
16						
17						
18						
19						
20						

FIGURE 5.1. Spreadsheet implementation of a grade book

first adds more features to the basic spreadsheet, turning it into a "power" spreadsheet of large size with a wide variety of commands and functions available. The second adds tools to the spreadsheet, turning it into some level of integrated program. The most common of such additions are the capability to produce graphs and charts directly from the data within a spreadsheet, and the capability to surround spreadsheet data with appropriate narrative to serve as introductions, headings, or explanations. There are even programs that integrate full-fledged generic applications such as word processing and data base management within the same program. Such programs that go beyond basic spreadsheet processing are discussed in Chapter 7. The basic "stand alone" spreadsheet (or the spreadsheet portion of a more complex program) is the focus of this chapter.

THE TECHNICAL SIDE OF SPREADSHEETS

FUNDAMENTAL CONCEPTS

While most spreadsheet programs are basically similar in their underlying concept and use, there are numerous terminology and technical differences among them. What is presented here is a generic spreadsheet description; that is, the basic concepts that underlie most spreadsheets. There is enough commonality among all spreadsheet programs to allow a user with a conceptual understanding to adapt quickly to the specific characteristics of any particular one.

Electronic Paper

A spreadsheet (also called a *worksheet*) can be thought of as a large piece of paper where data can be stored in rows and columns and manipulated by the computer. While spreadsheet processing can be accomplished by hand, using a computer spreadsheet is considerably easier and faster in all but the simplest cases. Many tasks become feasible that simply would be too time-consuming or complex for a manual worksheet.

Cells

Once a spreadsheet program has been booted on a computer, the user views a nearly blank screen. A typical empty spreadsheet is presented in Figure 5.2. The workspace is divided into columns and rows. Columns are usually designated by one or two letters (starting with A), and rows are generally designated by numbers (starting with 1). The intersection of a row or column is called a *cell*. A cell is typically referred to by its column and row designation, e.g., A1 or K25, which is its unique "address" within the total spreadsheet.

A cell may contain one of three types of entries:

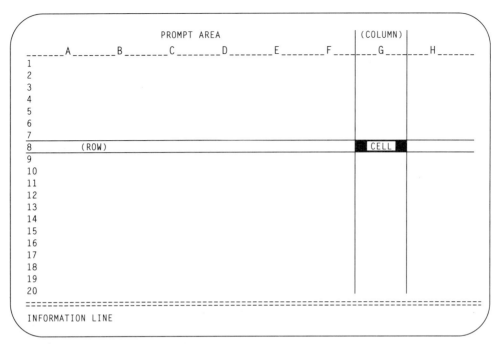

FIGURE 5.2. An empty spreadsheet

1. Numbers or *values* (numeric data)
2. *Labels* (alphabetic or alphanumeric data)
3. *Formulas* (expressions of calculations or relationships among cells). Predefined formulas are called *functions*.

Numbers and labels are displayed in the cell as entered. With a formula, the cell displays the result of the calculations.

To check your understanding of the cell concept, look at Figure 5.1 again and count the number of cells that actually contain data. Did you find 30? Five columns (A–E) and six rows (1, 3–6, 8) yield 30 cells. The types of entries are identified for you in Figure 5.3.

Prompt Area

Typically, there are additional lines above the worksheet referred to as the *prompt area*. In some programs, these lines are below the worksheet. The prompt area is used to show commands to alter or manipulate the spreadsheet and also to display the contents of the current cell. Formulas are displayed in the prompt area only; the cell displays the result of the calculation. (See Figure 5.3.) There may also be a line under the spreadsheet that is used to display current information about the spreadsheet.

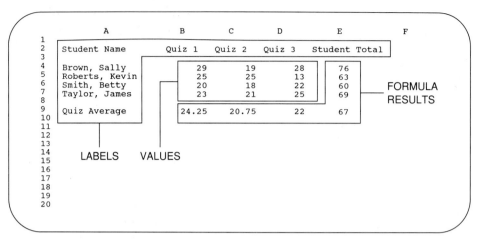

FIGURE 5.3. Types of cell entries in a sample spreadsheet

Cell Pointer

When working within a spreadsheet, the *cell pointer* or cursor keeps users visually informed as to their location within the spreadsheet. The cell pointer is a highlighted rectangle on the screen that identifies the user's current cell location. The cell pointer can be moved around the spreadsheet with either arrow keys or by special commands on the keyboard. New entries can be made in the cell currently shown by the cell pointer.

The Window

Actually, only a portion of the complete spreadsheet can be seen at any time on the screen. As the user moves the cell pointer around the spreadsheet, previously hidden parts become visible and previously visible parts are hidden. The screen can be thought of as a movable window or frame looking upon a much larger spreadsheet (see Figure 5.4). While only a portion can be seen at one time, the entire spreadsheet is nonetheless still there and can be examined and manipulated by moving the cell pointer to change the location of the window on the spreadsheet.

USING A SPREADSHEET

To understand how to use a spreadsheet, first recall the three types of entries that a cell may contain. They are numbers or values, labels, and formulas.

Entering Data

Two types of data can be entered into a spreadsheet. The most common is simple numeric information, placing a specific *number* or *value* in a cell. This is accomplished by moving the cell pointer to a desired cell and entering the required digits.

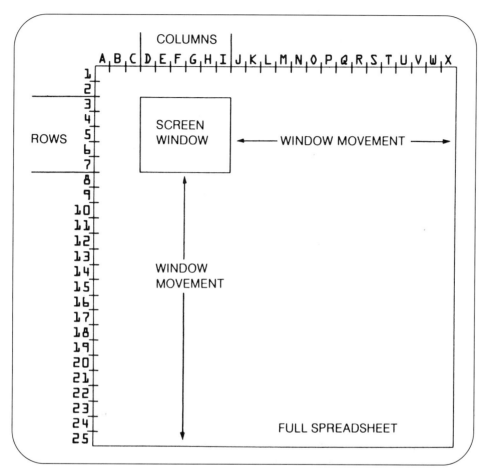

FIGURE 5.4. The spreadsheet window

Alphabetic information, called *labels,* can also be entered into a cell in a similar manner. Labels make a worksheet easy to read and understand.

If the first digit of a cell entry is a number, the program interprets the entry as a value; if the first digit of a cell entry is not a number, the program interprets the entry as a label. Formula and function entries are preceded by special coding.

Generating Data from Relationships

Information in a cell can also be generated by *formulas* that cause a cell to display the result of a calculation. The calculation may involve the contents of other cells in the worksheet, or specific values and cell contents. For example, the formula A1 + B7 produces the SUM of the values in the indicated cells. The formula 3.1416*Q6*Q6 would yield the area of a circle if cell Q6 contained the

```
  File: Winter Grades         REVIEW/ADD/CHANGE           Escape: Main Menu
 ========A========B========C========D========E========F========G========H====
  1|
  2|         Winter Grades
  3|
  4|                           Score    Score    Score    Score
  5|         Students          Test 1   Test 2   Test 3   Test 4   Average
  6|         Avenir, George      98       95       88       94       94%
  7|         Balder, Marsha      88       87       92       85       88%
  8|         Cleveland, Mark     77       83       80       67       77%
  9|         Edwards, Bret       83       80       85       84       83%
 10|         Hegley, Elaine      85       88       87       88       87%
 11|         Jenred, Jack        77       80       79       84       80%
 12|         Lofter, Laura       99       98       99       95       98%
 13|         Matthrews, Orem     91       90       89       92       91%
 14|         Normans, Cuz        66       70       74       80       72%
 15|         Prince, Perry       77       60       66       75       69%
 16|         Serenski, Bob       81       83       80       85       82%
 17|         Winthrop, Nigel     98       95       99       98       97%
 18|
 ---------------------------------------------------------------------------
  H6: (Value, Layout-P0) (+D6+E6+F6+G6/4)/100

  Type entry or use @ commands         ↑                    @-? for Help
```

FIGURE 5.5. The arrow points to the *formula* contained in cell H6. Note the prompt area location.

radius value. Remember, the cell contains a formula, which is displayed in the prompt area, but the worksheet shows the result of the specified calculation.

Analogous to formulas are built-in spreadsheet *functions*. Functions are special commands that allow a user to achieve often complex processing without personally creating the necessary formulas. Some spreadsheet programs provide an extensive list of functions for many diverse needs, including mathematical functions, trigonometric functions, statistical functions, and financial functions. Statistical functions useful to most educators include SUM (add part of a row or column of numbers) and AVERAGE (compute the average of part of a row or column of numbers).

Formulas and functions are powerful and important aspects of spreadsheets and will be used in the next section to create a practical example of spreadsheet use. They underlie the concept that the power of a spreadsheet stems from the user's ability to define *relationships* among the many values and cells.

Spreadsheet Commands

Simple data entry and manipulation alone are inadequate to make a spreadsheet powerful and relatively easy to use. There are numerous commands at the user's disposal that perform manipulation and ''housekeeping'' tasks, offering enormous flexibility over paper methods of work. These commands are displayed in the prompt area on the screen when requested. The user can then select the command needed. After supplying all necessary information, the computer will automatically execute the command on the spreadsheet. A generic name for

```
  ┌─────────────────────────────────────────────────────────────────────────┐
  │  File: Personal Worth          REVIEW/ADD/CHANGE          Escape: Main Menu│
  │  ========B========C========D========E========F========G========H========I====│
  │   1│                                                                        │
  │   2│Personal Financial Net Worth Statement                                  │
  │   3│                                                                        │
  │   4│                                                                        │
  │   5│ASSETS                                        LIABILITIES               │
  │   6│                                                                        │
  │   7│Fluid Assets:                                 Bills Due:                │
  │   8│        Cash on Hand            500               VISA                  │
  │   9│        Checking Accounts       435               Sears                 │
  │  10│        Savings Account        2050               Medical Bills         │
  │  11│                           ---------              Dental Bills          │
  │  12│                               2985               Homeowner's Ins.      │
  │  13│                                                  Auto Ins.             │
  │  14│Long Term Assets:                                 Life Ins.             │
  │  15│        Certif. Deposit        5000                                     │
  │  16│        U.S. Savings Bonds     1000                                     │
  │  17│        Life Insurance       175000                                     │
  │  18│                           ---------          Taxes We Owe:             │
  │  ---------------------------------------------------------------------------│
  │  E12: (Value) @SUM(E8...E10)                                                │
  │                                                                             │
  │  Type entry or use @ commands                           @-? for Help        │
  └─────────────────────────────────────────────────────────────────────────┘
```

FIGURE 5.6. The arrow points to the *function* contained in cell E12.

each commonly available spreadsheet command and a brief description of its use are presented in Figures 5.8 and 5.9.

Many other commands are available within specific spreadsheet programs, but these are the most basic types and are adequate to develop a concrete illustration in the next section.

Verification of Results

Depending on one's needs and skills in developing spreadsheet applications, the result can become very complex. Spreadsheets developed for projecting trends, for instance, may involve hundreds and hundreds of cells with complex interrelationships expressed in the formulas used. The possibility of errors in setting up the spreadsheet cannot be overlooked. It is vital to enter test data into any spreadsheet to verify against known results that the spreadsheet has been correctly designed. It is only too easy to believe that an answer produced by the computer is always correct.

AN EXAMPLE SPREADSHEET—CLASS RECORDKEEPING

For a practical introduction to electronic spreadsheets in education, let's stay with the familiar and use a simple class recordkeeping or grade book example. This example addresses the need to keep data on the three quiz results of a small group of students. Also desired are the sum of the three test scores for each of the students and the class average on each test.

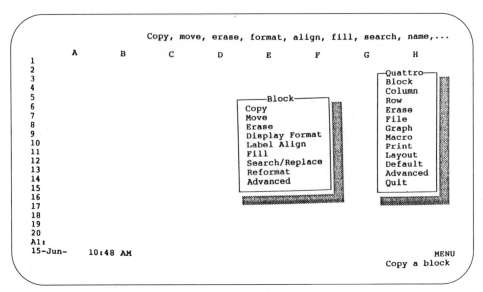

FIGURE 5.7. Available spreadsheet commands are clearly displayed and easily selected.

CREATING THE SPREADSHEET

While this simple example could clearly be done by hand, a computer spreadsheet offers a more flexible and efficient approach to this type of problem. A step-by-step guide to creating it follows, using our generic spreadsheet commands. The completed worksheet is shown in Figure 5.10.

1. Use the ERASE command to clear the entire worksheet area.
2. Widen column A and column E using the WIDTH command to provide enough room for appropriate headings and data.
3. Enter the following headings into the spreadsheet at the specified locations:

COLUMN	ROW	ENTRY
A	1	STUDENT NAME
B	1	QUIZ 1
C	1	QUIZ 2
D	1	QUIZ 3
E	1	STUDENT TOTAL

4. Skip row 2 (for visual clarity) and enter in each following row a student's name, score 1, score 2, and score 3. In Figure 5.10, four students have been entered on the worksheet.
5. Skip another row for visual clarity and enter the label QUIZ AVERAGE in column A row 8.
6. Use the SUM function in column E row 3 to cause this cell to display the sum of the data in row 3, columns B, C, and D, i.e., the sum of the three

```
COPY          DUPLICATES THE CONTENTS OF ONE OR MORE CELLS
              IN ANOTHER LOCATION ON THE SPREADSHEET.

DELETE        REMOVES EITHER A COLUMN OR A ROW FROM A
              WORKSHEET. THE REMAINING COLUMNS MOVE TO
              THE LEFT; ROWS MOVE UP TO CLOSE THE GAPS.

ERASE         DELETES THE CONTENTS OF A CELL, A GROUP OF
              CELLS, OR THE ENTIRE WORKSHEET.

FORMAT        SPECIFIES HOW INFORMATION WILL BE DISPLAYED
              WITHIN A CELL, E.G., INTEGER VALUE, FIXED DECIMAL
              PLACES, FLOATING DECIMAL POINT, FLUSH AT LEFT
              EDGE OF CELL, FLUSH RIGHT, AND SO ON.

INSERT        INSERTS EITHER A COLUMN OR A ROW INTO A
              WORKSHEET. ORIGINAL COLUMNS MOVE RIGHT AND
              ROWS MOVE DOWN AS NECESSARY TO ACCOMMODATE
              THE ADDITION.

MOVE          RELOCATES THE CONTENTS OF ONE OR MORE CELLS
              TO ANOTHER LOCATION ON THE SPREADSHEET.

WIDTH         INITIALLY, ALL COLUMNS ARE THE SAME NUMBER
              OF CHARACTERS WIDE. THE WIDTH COMMAND
              IS USED TO WIDEN OR NARROW A COLUMN ON THE
              SPREADSHEET TO MEET THE USER'S NEEDS.
```

FIGURE 5.8. Spreadsheet manipulation commands.

test scores for this student. You have just established the first relationship among cells! You could, of course, enter your own formula in cell E3, but functions are easier to use and more versatile.

7. For cells E4, E5, and E6, again use the SUM function or comparable formulas. The simplest approach is to use the COPY command to duplicate the function or formula in E3. When the COPY command is used, any cell references are automatically adjusted to indicate the cells containing the appropriate data. The designated cells in column E would then display the sum of the three test scores for each of the students.

8. Enter either a formula or a function in column B row 8 indicating that this cell is to contain the average of the data in column B rows 3 through 6. Cell B8 would then contain the average of the four student scores for test 1, a more complex relationship among cells.

9. Finally, use the COPY command to duplicate the function or formula in cell B8 into row 8 columns C, D, and E. As before, the COPY command automatically adjusts the cell references to reflect the appropriate data cells. The designated cells in row 8 would now contain the averages of the four

```
┌─────────────────────────────────────────────────────────────┐
  PRINT              DIRECTS THE SYSTEM TO PRODUCE A PRINTED
                     COPY OF THE WORKSHEET ON THE SCREEN.
                     WHEREAS THE SCREEN CAN DISPLAY ONLY AS
                     MUCH OF THE WORKSHEET AS ITS WINDOW HOLDS,
                     A PRINTOUT MAY CONTAIN THE ENTIRE
                     WORKSHEET OR ANY DESIRED PORTION.

  RETRIEVE           CAUSES THE SYSTEM TO LOAD THE CONTENTS OF A
                     WORKSHEET FROM A DISK AND DISPLAY THEM AS
                     THE CURRENT WORKSHEET DATA.

  SAVE               DIRECTS THE SYSTEM TO SAVE THE CURRENT
                     SPREADSHEET IN A DISK FILE FOR FUTURE USE.
└─────────────────────────────────────────────────────────────┘
```

FIGURE 5.9. Spreadsheet housekeeping commands

student scores for each of the tests as well as the average total score for all three tests.

10. The worksheet is now complete. Use the SAVE command to store a copy of this worksheet on the disk for future access and use.

11. If desired, use the PRINT command to obtain a hard copy of this spreadsheet.

MANIPULATING THE SPREADSHEET

The spreadsheet is basically complete at this point, much like a grade book at the end of a term. While useful as a recordkeeping tool, this is only the beginning of what can be done with this computer spreadsheet. The following is a partial list of additional operations that could be done within this illustration.

Changing Data
If you discovered that any of the data entries in this table were incorrect, you would simply reenter the correct data in the appropriate cell. With each new entry the spreadsheet program would automatically recalculate all affected cells to reflect this data change. *Automatic recalculation* is one of the most important features of a spreadsheet program. Specifically, changing the score in cell B3 would also automatically alter the result in cells B8, E3, and E8 since each of these is based in part on the contents of B3. Figure 5.11 illustrates this. In a manual system, you would have to recall which cells to change and, eraser in hand, make all adjustments yourself. Recalculation becomes increasingly valuable as worksheet size and complexity grow.

Adding a Student
If another student needed to be added, you would use the INSERT command to open up a blank row at the desired location on the spreadsheet and enter

```
        A              B        C        D        E           F
 1  Student Name    Quiz 1   Quiz 2   Quiz 3   Student Total
 2
 3  Brown, Sally        19       19       28          66
 4  Roberts, Kevin      25       25       13          63
 5  Smith, Betty        20       18       22          60
 6  Taylor, James       23       21       25          69
 7
 8  Quiz Average     21.75    20.75       22        64.5
 9
10
11
12
13
14
15
16
17
18
19
20
```

FIGURE 5.10. Example spreadsheet—class recordkeeping

the data for this student. Normally, this would be done so as to insert the student in the proper place alphabetically in the list. Functions would be adjusted automatically to include this new student. The whole spreadsheet would be recalculated to include the new data in the sum and average cells. Not only does this save you a lot of work, but your records are always in the correct order. Additions to a grade book must normally be made at the bottom of the list, which can be confusing.

Removing a Student
If a student already on the spreadsheet left the class, you would use the DELETE command to remove the row containing that student's data. Functions would again be adjusted automatically to omit this student, and the whole spreadsheet would be recalculated to exclude these data in the sum and average cells. This results in a set of records that is easier to read than a typical grade book with lines drawn through rows no longer needed.

Adding a Quiz
To add another quiz, use the INSERT command to open up a blank column at the desired location on the spreadsheet. Enter a heading in row 1, and enter the student data for this quiz. Functions would automatically be adjusted to include this new quiz. The sum and average cells would be updated appropriately.

New Features
Adding more features to this application would be quite easy. Column F could become the STUDENT AVERAGE. Row 10 might be test standard deviation or some other statistic. You need only determine and enter the formula or function

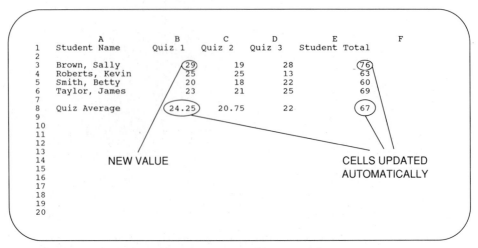

FIGURE 5.11. Results of changing data in example spreadsheet

once, then COPY it into all appropriate cells. This flexibility to establish new relationships among cells with very little extra work is a major attraction of spreadsheets.

TEMPLATES

It is not always necessary to develop an original spreadsheet to meet a need. There are books and journal articles that offer ready-to-use spreadsheet *templates.* A template is simply a spreadsheet file (or the directions for creating one) with no data provided. First, you load the template from a disk file, then enter your own data into the appropriate cells. As data are entered, automatic recalculation occurs, and the appropriate results are displayed in cells containing formulas. When all data have been entered, the spreadsheet is saved onto the disk *using a new name* for the file. In this way, the template is available for further use.

By using templates, the person who despairs of being able to create an original application can still benefit from the power and versatility of a spreadsheet. Sticking with our example, a template for a grade book could be developed by one teacher and shared by any others interested in this approach to student recordkeeping.

Add-in Programs

Since spreadsheet programs are so popular, an after-market has developed of programs that can be attached to spreadsheet programs to either extend their capabilities or allow them to perform some useful task. Examples include:

Sideways Printing Programs: These programs allow the printer to print a spreadsheet sideways on the output paper, thereby allowing very wide spreadsheets to be printed in a more readable form.

Screen Management Programs: These programs allow the screen to display more of a spreadsheet by decreasing the size of the characters on the screen.

File Compression Programs: These programs compress spreadsheet data during file saving, allowing large spreadsheets to be stored in a smaller form on a disk. File writing and reading may also be accelerated in the process.

Other more specific add-in programs are available (such as statistical routines) and new ones continue to be introduced. Such programs add to the power, flexibility, and applicability of the basic spreadsheet program.

SUMMARY

It should be apparent that once a spreadsheet has been set up, it can be modified quickly and easily, whether changing existing data, adding new data, or deleting data. Our example used only a small data set to illustrate some of the capabilities of a computer spreadsheet. Since some spreadsheets have thousands of rows and hundreds of columns available, it is possible to work with rather large data sets. The automatic adjustment of formulas to reflect modifications, as well as the automatic recalculation of all formula cells after changes, makes a computer spreadsheet a powerful tool.

CATEGORIES OF SPREADSHEET APPLICATIONS

For simplicity, possible uses for spreadsheets may be summarized under three headings: recordkeeping, calculation worksheets, and "what if" applications.

RECORDKEEPING

A computer spreadsheet might be used simply as a big scratchpad, a place to easily record information that is not manipulated at all. For example, a complete record of one's students, relatives, or business associates and any related data could be stored on a spreadsheet. Related data could be anything to which a user wished to have easy access. A spreadsheet can be used to handle a mailing list or telephone numbers or to store other routine personal data. Room or department inventories could also be kept on a spreadsheet. The spreadsheet becomes a rudimentary data base.

Advantages of using a spreadsheet in this manner include ease of changing data already on the sheet, ease of adding new data anywhere on the sheet, and ease of deleting unneeded data. Moving around to view data within this type of computer spreadsheet may be more efficient and easier than working with large amounts of paper. A very large amount of information can be stored on a single diskette, taking much less storage space than equivalent paper records. A hard copy of all or some of the spreadsheet can then be printed as needed. Even using a computer spreadsheet in this very simple manner can be advantageous for the user, although it would hardly justify purchasing spreadsheet software. Such applications do not make use of the inherent power of a spreadsheet.

A computer spreadsheet becomes much more powerful as a "complex" recordkeeping system. In addition to storing various amounts of information, simple and complex calculations can be performed on the data. The student grade book illustration included two types of calculations: sum of each student's scores and average of scores on each test. Many more calculations based upon the data in the spreadsheet could have been included.

In addition to performing the indicated calculations efficiently, the spreadsheet's ability to allow for data correction, addition, and/or deletion and the automatic recalculation of all formulas and functions after data changes have made this use of computer spreadsheets invaluable in a wide variety of diverse applications. Many educators find a spreadsheet grade book much easier, more flexible, and faster to use than special-purpose grade book programs that are described in Chapter 6. Inventory records were mentioned under simple recordkeeping, but they may be more valuable if counts and/or sums of item values are added.

CALCULATION WORKSHEETS

Computer spreadsheets are not restricted just to recordkeeping areas. They were developed to speed up and ease many business applications primarily involving complex calculations. There are many specialized functions included in most spreadsheet programs that are useful in particular application areas. Of course, you could construct your own formulas or use those published in the general literature regarding spreadsheets.

An example is loan amortization calculations. This involves specifying the amount of a loan, the interest rate, and the length of the loan. A spreadsheet function or series of functions then calculates the amount of each payment under the entered parameters and displays the amount of each payment, the principal and interest components of each payment, and the remaining balance. In addition, other functions could produce the sum of all principal and interest payments to provide a clear picture of the total cost of a loan as well as the monthly details. Such applications can be very useful when considering whether to borrow money, perhaps in a business math, economics, or family living class.

"WHAT IF" APPLICATIONS

This type of application can be thought of as an extension of the calculation worksheets just discussed. Being able to answer "What if . . . ?" questions is another reason why spreadsheets were created and is a major factor in their popularity. Instead of looking at only one possibility, the user can have the computer calculate the results for different entered parameters.

From our loan example, the user could direct the computer on the same spreadsheet to generate amortization data to answer many questions. What if the amount of the loan were increased or decreased? What if the interest rate were 2 percent higher or lower? What if the repayment period were extended or shortened? The results could all be examined and compared and decisions made appropriately based upon this comparison.

There are two different methods for handling "what ifs." If the worksheet is not too large and the number of different parameters of interest is small, you can create multiple worksheets in one by COPYing the first set into unused areas of the sheet. For example, if the initial area used was cells A1 through G25, it could be duplicated from H1 through N25 or from A26 through G50.

In a more complex situation, "what if" questions are often explored interactively. Create a worksheet, enter one set of parameters, and print the results. Next, enter a new set of parameters and print the result. This is done as many times as necessary, after which the printouts are compared to see the effects of the changes. For a quick look at alternatives, the printouts may not be needed.

Even a spreadsheet grade book has "what if" uses. Suppose you have set up your worksheet to compute total scores and average marks. Your students know that their grades will be based on their final averages. With one test remaining, your worksheet shows each student's average to that point. If students ask what score they must achieve on the last test to earn a certain grade, you could very quickly enter any number of different scores for the final exam and watch the resulting average change. Many teachers regularly face such questions but can give an answer only after finding time to do several sets of calculations. A spreadsheet offers almost instantaneous responses.

Can you think of other applications where this type of "what if" comparison would be important, even indispensable? Consider how often you must make decisions based on incomplete data. How could a spreadsheet help you weigh your options?

CLASSROOM APPLICATIONS

The preceding section on application categories may have stimulated your thinking about potential uses in your teaching. Other concrete examples should further help expand your thinking in an area admittedly foreign to many teachers.

FUNDRAISERS IN GRADE 2 AND HIGH SCHOOL

If you think spreadsheets are only for advanced high school students, an example from Alaska may change your mind. Sopp (1985) described how students and staff were involved in a fund-raising effort. A second grade teacher created a simple spreadsheet file and taught his students to enter the figures reported by students from all classes. These second graders managed the recordkeeping for the project for the entire school!

Kneen (1987) used a spreadsheet to plan a high school fund raising project, which was tracked with a data base. The students sold personalized Christmas gifts they had made using *Print Shop,* a graphics program described in Chapter 6.

BUDGETS IN GRADE 5

Wilson (1985) was interested in whether a spreadsheet could be used with elementary school students to explore mathematical relationships and use of formulas, as well as to facilitate problem solving and decision making. Fifth grade students worked with *VisiCalc* to develop a simple budget based on a template provided by the teacher. She reports a challenging and enjoyable experience and goes on to offer a variety of application suggestions in science, mathematics, and social studies.

HIGH SCHOOL MATHEMATICS

Bratton (1988) describes concrete ways to allow students to "do math" at a precalculus level using spreadsheets. Among the topics are the remainder theorem and synthetic division, graphing polynomial functions, and approximation of irrational roots.

Russell (1987) suggests ways of using spreadsheets to extend the normally limited treatment of probability, while Choate (1986) focuses on modeling and problem solving. For extensive applications in math, see Arganbright (1985).

HYPOTHESIS TESTING OR WHAT IF . . . ?

You already have read about the power of spreadsheets to allow for hypothesis testing as you vary one or more values within your worksheet. Collis (1988) and Schiffman (1986) both discuss this approach to exploring personal finance issues such as interest and loan amortization. Hoelscher (1986) describes how students may build new analytic skills by re-examining data from new perspectives. Karlin (1988) brought life to time and distance problems by using as a topic the running speed of dinosaurs. This example included "doing science" by starting with human movement, which was videotaped for analysis.

WORD PROBLEMS

Math students often encounter much difficulty in learning to deal with word or story problems. Arad (1986–87) suggests use of spreadsheets to allow students "to focus on the solution process and dynamics underlying the problem" rather than the typical abstractions of algebra. Students could apply a trial-and-error approach to solving word problems. Collis (1988) also supports this idea. However, one might legitimately ask what the student is actually learning from such experimentation. One might well consider Schiffman's (1986) observations on how a spreadsheet can shift the focus from product (an answer) to process. Taken together, interesting outcomes seem likely.

SPORTS STATISTICS

Miller (1988) found it difficult to interest students in typical spreadsheet applications like budgeting. However, interest soared when the application became following major sports teams based on weekly newspaper data. Miller describes both basic activities such as determining which team has the best record in various categories to more advanced concepts like predicting upcoming events from past performances.

URBAN LIVABILITY

A project concerning "quality of life" was developed with junior high students in California. Hannah (1985–1986) first asked his students to rank a variety of cities across the country as to their livability. This was a subjective judgment. A simple spreadsheet was used to tally and weight the votes. He then introduced students to published livability ratings, which led to lively discussion of the factors used in these judgments. A livability rating spreadsheet was developed based on commonly used factors. Much discussion also went into the weighting of each factor.

   After practice with this spreadsheet, Hannah introduced to the students a competition. Students were divided into teams and each drew the name of a city to represent. Using available data, each team was to devise a spreadsheet which would demonstrate that its city was the most desirable in which to locate a new research center.

FAST FOOD COMPARISONS

A brief tutorial on the use of *VisiCalc* is provided by Blank (1985). The application developed is very simple—comparison of the costs of similar meals at a variety of fast food restaurants. While the topic should interest most students, especially the necessary "research" into current prices, the result could be more easily determined with a hand calculator because of its simplicity.

   This idea could be expanded and made more challenging by also researching nutritional information about such food, which has been published in *Consumer Reports.* One could then devise a more complex spreadsheet to analyze fast food along several dimensions including cost, healthfulness, and so on. Daily dietary needs might also be included in the analysis.

PEER GRADING

Another intriguing application is provided by Dribin (1985). He finds a spreadsheet invaluable in his public speaking class. The spreadsheet has allowed him to implement a complex peer grading system, which requires students in the class to become "responsive and responsible listeners." Peer evaluation requires a solid set of evaluation criteria. Dribin teaches the students how to evaluate a speech using a critique sheet based on the criteria. Students' final grades for a unit depend not only on their own performance, but also on their critiques of other students. The entire process required tabulation and posting of results as quickly as possible. Only use of a spreadsheet made implementation possible. The system is complex but fully described in Dribin's article.

HEALTH

A model worksheet to analyze data gathered on the effects on heart rate and blood pressure of smoking or being in a smoky environment is offered by Flake, McClintock, and Turner (1985, pp. 215–217).

PERSONAL FINANCES

Another common application is developing a personal budget, with cells provided for entering both budgeted and actual expenses in each category. With appropriate formulas, you can quickly determine how real spending compares to your planned budget.

Advanced students could develop a spreadsheet model of the IRS 1040 tax form. What might they discover about the bases of the income tax as well as the interrelationships of various sections of the form?

GROWTH MODELS

Social studies or science students might develop a spreadsheet to investigate human or animal population growth according to some chosen model. Economic growth patterns might be explored as well. A specific example is given by Schwinge (1985) for studying growth rates of closed populations in biology.

ENERGY USAGE

A spreadsheet could be devised to study energy usage. Students could inventory their home appliances and record their energy use in kilowatts per hour. After estimating hours of use for each appliance over some time period, an energy consumption model could be developed.

Also in the area of energy, students might take measurements of their home, recording or calculating square footage of the residence and all windows and doors as well as thickness of attic insulation. Based on published R-values and formulas for heat loss or gain, home heating and cooling requirements could be determined. The effects of increasing insulation could also be estimated.

TEACHING SPREADSHEETS

Perhaps one day you will find yourself in a situation where you need to teach others to use spreadsheets. Just as you were probably mystified by the concepts at first, so will your students be. An excellent introduction to spreadsheets is carefully laid out, complete with lesson plans, activities, and copiable handouts, by Brown (1986–1987, 1987). Lesson plans are also provided in Collis (1988) and Luehrmann (1986). Other sources of suggestions include Carey and Carey (1986) and Dyrli (1986).

MISCELLANEOUS APPLICATIONS

Wright and Forcier (1985, pp. 255–277) offer very brief looks at using spreadsheets to:

☐ Weight alternative fundraising activities.
☐ Project equipment replacement costs based on longevity, original cost, and inflation.
☐ Calculate costs of setting up a new computer lab.
☐ Maintain an expenditure journal.

Caffarella (1985) devotes an entire book to the many administrative applications of spreadsheets. Virtually any school administrator not already using spreadsheets could benefit from this book.

The grade book concept is expanded by Riedesel and Clements (1985, pp. 249–252) to include minimum and maximum scores on each assignment. They also mention enrollment projections, checkbook balancing, mapping time on task, and study of relationships among numbers as possible applications. Metric-English conversions can also be studied, as can the effects on area, perimeter, and volume of changes in the dimensions of two- and three-dimensional shapes.

This roster of potential educational applications of spreadsheets is in no way complete. Individuals are using spreadsheets in many other areas to simplify and solve a wide variety of data processing needs. The flexibility of such programs combined with the ingenuity of the user is one of the things that make spreadsheet programs such popular and powerful processing tools. Today's uses far exceed the original financial applications of the creators of *VisiCalc*.

SUMMARY

Spreadsheets are a major form of application software, joining word processing and data bases as productivity tools. They were developed to cope with often difficult and time-consuming financial calculations but have found wide usage in other situations as well.

A spreadsheet is simply an arrangement of rows and columns in which data may be stored and manipulated. The intersection of a row and a column is termed a cell. Each cell may contain numeric or alphabetic data, or a formula or function that establishes a mathematical relationship among cells. The latter is one key to the power of spreadsheets. Templates offer this power to users without the need to create original applications.

Spreadsheets quickly become larger than can be displayed on a computer screen at once. The screen then becomes a window or frame, which can be moved about on the spreadsheet as needed. Changing the contents of any cell in the spreadsheet will automatically alter any other related cell. This is a major advantage of electronic spreadsheets over their manual counterparts. It opens the way to answering "What if . . . ?" questions to check the results of varying assumptions or projections.

Spreadsheets seem very alien to teachers, who tend not to see applications for a "financial" tool. Yet there are many viable classroom applications of spreadsheets. Examples illustrated uses across many subject fields and at various grade levels from elementary through high school. While it may require more effort for a teacher to become comfortable with a spreadsheet than with word processing or data bases, the benefits are worth the effort. The potential of spreadsheets in education is limited only by the creativity of the teacher.

CHAPTER 5 ACTIVITIES

Use any available spreadsheet for the following activities.

1. Compare the specific screen format of your spreadsheet to the general design in Figure 5.2. What are the differences? Determine the maximum size of a worksheet, i.e., what is the maximum row and maximum column?
2. Make a list of the actual commands used with your spreadsheet in place of the generic commands described in this chapter. You may want to create a wall chart for your computer room.
3. Create a functional grade book similar to the illustration given.
4. Expand your basic grade book by determining what additional functions your spreadsheet offers and adding those you consider potentially useful.
5. Develop a personal budget. You'll need both an income and an expenditure part. Divide the expenses into major categories such as housing, food, automotive, clothing, etc. Set up a "base" budget and leave space to record actual expenses for several months. Be sure to include cells that compare expenses to budget each month.
6. Develop any specific application that interests you personally or professionally.
7. Develop a lesson plan for using a spreadsheet with your students.

REFERENCES

Arad, O. S. "The Spreadsheet: Solving Word Problems." *The Computing Teacher*, December/January 1986–87, pp. 13–15, 45.

Arganbright, D. *Mathematical Applications of Electronic Spreadsheets*. New York: McGraw-Hill, 1985.

Blank, D. E. "Stepping through Fast-Food Land: A Spreadsheet Tutorial." *The Computing Teacher*, June 1985, pp. 26–28.

Bratton, G. "Spreadsheets and Synthetic Division." *The Computing Teacher*, March 1988, pp. 38–40, 61.

Brown, J. M. "Spreadsheets in the Classroom." *The Computing Teacher*, December/January 1986–87, pp. 8–12.

Brown, J. M. "Spreadsheets in the Classroom Part II." *The Computing Teacher*, February 1987, pp. 9–12.

Caffarella, E. P. *Spreadsheets Go To School*. Reston, VA: Reston Publishing, 1985.

Carey, D., and Carey, R. "Make Spreadsheets Make Sense: A Model for Introduction." *The Computing Teacher*, February 1986, pp. 62–64.

Choate, J. "Using *VisiCalc* and *DYNAmo* to Make Models and Solve Problems in High School Math Classes." *Computers in the Schools*, Spring 1986, 3(1), pp. 75–81.

Collis, B. *Computers, Curriculum, and Whole-Class Instruction*. Belmont, CA: Wadsworth, 1988.

Dribin, C. I. "Spreadsheets and Performance: A Guide for Student Presentations." *The Computing Teacher*, June 1985, pp. 22–25.

Dyrli, O. E. "Electronic Spreadsheets in the Curriculum." *Computers in the Schools*, Spring 1986, 3(1), pp. 47–54.

Flake, J. L., McClintock, C. E., and Turner, S. V. *Fundamentals of Computer Education*. Belmont, CA: Wadsworth, 1985.

Hannah, L. "Social Studies, Spreadsheets and the Quality of Life." *The Computing Teacher*, December/January 1985–1986, pp. 13–17.

Hoelscher, K. "Computing and Information: Steering Student Learning." *Computers in the Schools*, 1986, 3(1), pp. 23–34.

Karlin, M. "Beyond Distance = Rate * Time." *The Computing Teacher*, February 1988, pp. 20–23.

Kneen, T. J. "A Computerized Fund Raising Project." *The Computing Teacher*, May 1987, pp. 11–12, 56.

Luehrmann, A. "Spreadsheets: More Than Just Finance." *The Computing Teacher*, April 1986, pp. 24–28.

Miller, M. "Using NFL Statistics to Teach the Spreadsheet." *The Computing Teacher*, March 1988, pp. 45–47.

Riedesel, C. A., and Clements, D. H. *Coping with Computers in the Elementary and Middle Schools*. Englewood Cliffs, NJ: Prentice–Hall, 1985.

Russell, J. C. "Probability Modeling with a Spreadsheet." *The Computing Teacher*, November 1987, pp. 58–60.

Schiffman, S. S. "Productivity Tools for the Classroom." *The Computing Teacher*, May 1986, pp 27–31.

Schwinge, S. "Spreadsheets and Simulations." *The Science Teacher*, 1985, 52(9), pp. 27–28.

Sopp, N. P. "Do You Really Need a Children's Data Base?" *The Computing Teacher*, November 1985, pp. 43–45.

Wilson, J. W. "VisiCalc in the Elementary School." *The Computing Teacher*, June 1985, pp. 29–30.

Wright, E. B., and Forcier, R. C. *The Computer: A Tool for the Teacher.* Belmont, CA: Wadsworth, 1985.

CHAPTER 6

☐ Graphics, Classroom Publishing, Telecommunications, and Support Tools ☐

OBJECTIVES

After completing this chapter, you will be able to:

☐ *Differentiate between print and presentation graphics.* ☐
☐ *Identify varied applications of print graphics software.* ☐
☐ *Discuss the concepts and applications of classroom publishing.* ☐
☐ *Explain at least three distinct applications of telecommunications.* ☐
☐ *Explain what a support tool is.* ☐
☐ *Give at least two examples of support tools and explain how they would be of use to you.* ☐
☐ *Describe several ideas for student use of support software.* ☐

Preceding chapters have shown numerous ways for teachers and students to benefit from use of common general-purpose computer applications. In this chapter, we look at more specialized software of interest in the classroom. First we present single page *print* and *presentation graphics,* then whole document manipulators known as *classroom publishers.* The rapidly developing uses of telecommunications and *support tools* (which serve very limited purposes by design) are also discussed. These programs provide means to accomplish common, even daily, tasks in less time. In many cases, teachers can produce results of which they could once only dream. None of these tools replaces the more general ones discussed previously. Rather they are important additions to a teacher's software collection. No one teacher is apt to find all such programs useful, but all teachers will find something of value among the available resources.

GRAPHICS

Although early computers were limited to alphanumeric input and output, they have now entered the age of graphic communication. Macintosh initiated a move toward graphics interfaces between user and computer. This section deals with graphics not as art, but as basic communication; it introduces software that produces individual pages (or screens) of text and/or images.

PRINT GRAPHICS

Print graphics describes those ingenious, inexpensive products that allow you to create banners to festoon your room and bulletin boards; posters (single pages) to announce coming events and dates; signs to serve as certificates of recognition for some achievement; letterhead for your own personalized stationery; and greeting cards for all occasions. Since the original *Print Shop,* competitors have appeared, including *PrintMaster, Print Magic,* and *SuperPrint.* The latter can produce wall-size calendars and graphics nearly six feet high.

Common to all such software is a choice of text fonts in different styles and sizes, border designs, and a selection of ready-to-use "clip art." The latter is a great benefit to those of limited artistic skill. Enhancements to the original concept have been minor, but new collections of art work appear regularly.

Applications

Beyond the obvious uses of these programs, educational applications abound. How many classroom posters, handouts, even worksheets might be done more attractively, more "professionally" using a graphics program? You can also make great transparency masters!

"Kids on Computers" (*The Computing Teacher,* October 1986) illustrated creation of a *rebus,* a story in which graphics replace some words in sentences. A later issue (*The Computing Teacher,* November 1987) showed creation of titles for video

FIGURE 6.1. Poster or sign style

A SNOWFLAKE

I AM ICY COLD &
TOO SMALL FOR
YOU TO SEE MY
SHAPE EASILY.

NO TWO OF ME
ARE EVER ALIKE.

KIDS USE ME TO
TO MAKE THINGS.

WHAT AM I?

FIGURE 6.2. Card style: A single sheet of paper becomes a card when properly folded.

recordings. Still another (*The Computing Teacher,* March 1988) used the greeting card format to create animal riddle cards. The cover gives clues to the graphic answer inside. Children rarely choose not to put borders around their print graphics products. Lamb (1988) capitalized on this natural interest to enhance a unit on book illustration for children.

Print graphics software lends itself to fund raising projects, too. Turn your students' creations into iron-on T-shirt images using special heat transfer ribbons (Pixellite Computer Products, Inc., 5221 Central Ave. Suite 205, Richmond, CA 94804. 1-800-643-0800.) Stationery, notepads, calendars, and other personalized products can be made and sold (Kneen, 1987). Could you create and laminate menus for local restaurants? Signs for garage sales or a realtor's open house? There is no limit to extracurricular uses.

Whatever your idea, planning your project before going to the computer will reduce wasted paper and save time at the machine, something critical when computer access is limited. Hubert, Winebrenner, and Qualkenbush (1987) offer planning suggestions and helpful reproduceable worksheets.

PRESENTATION GRAPHICS

Presentation graphics software has many of the same preparation capabilities as print graphics—multiple fonts, clip art, even manipulation of image size or orientation. However, it produces individual "screens" which can be printed but often are not. Rather, they are put together into "computer slide shows" for electronic delivery. For small groups, shows are viewed on a regular monitor. For larger settings, a video projector or LCD panel is used.

Envision replacing all of your physical transparencies with graphics files. As necessary, you can quickly and easily update your images. Unlike plastic transparencies which are usually monochrome, colors are basic design tools of presentation graphics. The software also provides transitions from one screen to the next which rival special effects seen in films and on television—wipes, fades, dissolves, checkerboard, starburst, and so on. Graphics shows are impressive, and development is easier than you may imagine.

Products of this type vary considerably. Scholastic's *Slide Shop* for Apple II has the basic features and some sound segments to enliven its shows. *ThunderView* is inexpensive and can incorporate images from *ThunderScan,* a low cost scanner which replaces the print head in an ImageWriter printer. MS-DOS products like *StoryBoard Plus* include memory resident software which will "capture" any screen you can produce with any other software product. You can illustrate your presentations with real screens rather than trying to simulate them. *PowerPoint* for Macintosh takes a different approach, perhaps because projecting Mac screens was uncommon until recently. This product lets you create screens, enter notes concerning each, and print out the screens as full size transparency masters. It also produces audience handouts, aligning your notes with miniature versions of the screens!

Presentation graphics add a whole new dimension to teaching if you take the time to explore the possibilities and master a software product. You could bid farewell to chalk, transparencies, and other teaching tools. With battery powered portable computers and light-weight LCD panels, you can even take your show on the road!

CLASSROOM PUBLISHING

Classroom publishing may not be widely recognized as a category of software. We mean software products which resemble print graphics, but which are better suited to newsletters, small scale newspapers, and so on. The biggest distinction is page layout capabilities. There are three critical attributes. One is that your text wraps into columns like a newspaper, perhaps as many as 6 on ordinary paper. *NewsMaster,* for instance, defaults to a two-column format. Second, you place your graphics on the "page" as desired and the text will "flow" around it. Third, you work on a whole document at once, not just a single page at a time. Products of this type include *Publish-It!, Springboard Publisher, Newsroom, The School Publisher,* and *PFS: First Publisher.*

You may have heard of desktop publishing and question our distinction here. We categorize as classroom publishing software products within the easy financial grasp of schools, say $150 tops, and intended primarily for dot matrix output. We reserve the term desktop publishing for much more expensive products with greater capabilities and an expectation of laser printing. You will meet this category of application in the next chapter. (If just variable text fonts are required, a word processor with fonts, such as Scholastic's *MultiScribe,* Microsoft *Word,* or *Word Perfect,* may meet your need.)

Publishing software includes its own *text editor.* We purposely do not use the term *word processor* here because the features of a text editor are limited to inserting, deleting, and word wrapping. Some publishing software products can import text from a word processor. This is a desirable feature because you can then create your text like any document and enhance it with the publishing features—fonts, page composition, graphics—as you see fit. Be sure, however, that the products you wish to use are compatible.

Some publishers require a mouse; others simply are easier to use with one. If you have no mouse, evaluate how well and easily the software performs using keyboard commands.

Can you get by with print graphics or a publishing system alone? Probably not. Educators regularly use both! Column layouts and graphics in the midst of text require a publisher. Banners, cards, and calendars require print graphics. Either can produce signs and transparency masters.

Classroom publishing software can produce professional quality newsletters and newspapers, without tedious manual cut and paste work. For schools that teach the process approach to writing, a publisher is ideal for the dissemination aspect. Schools may also find that some items previously produced by commercial printers can now be done in-house—directories, certificates, and tickets are

THE
𝕾𝕸𝕴𝕿𝕳 𝕾𝕮𝕳𝕺𝕺𝕷
FAMILY NEWS

Well, the new school year is off to a roaring start for all of us here at Smith School. Every fall at this time, we like to inform the parents and friends of Smith Students about all the latest happenings.

Kindergarten

The big news for our youngest pupils is the addition of ballet to our already long list of gym activities. Many parents have requested this move over the years, and we were fortunate to be able to hire a new kinder-garten teacher, Sue Smith, who once danced with the Geoffrey. We know the boys will be especially excited by this development.

First Grade

The first graders will be busy little bees this year. We will be extending the range of activities for them in both math and science. Look for many requests from their teacher, Shirley Smith, for help with field trip transportation, butterfly net repairs, etc. You intrepid ichthiologists may want to join the group on their visit to the Smith Shark Sanctuary.

Grade 2

We know there has been some controversy about our decision to add driver training to the second grade curriculum this year. However, our curriculum expert, Sheila Smith, insists that it is important to get an early start. We are grateful for the cooperation of Six Sox Over Smithville in allowing us access to their excellent bumper car facility for this new class. Transportation will be provided.

Third Grade ?

Due to unusual circumstances, the third grade has been cancelled.

Grade IV

In a move certain to provoke discussion for days to come, Principal S. Sophokles Smith has instituted a sweeping change in the writing curriculum for fourth grade. Word processors are forbidden and all students will learn quill-manship.

FIGURE 6.3. Use *NewsMaster* for your class or school newsletter.

examples. McCarthy (1988) and Stanley (1986) are sources for further reading on this topic.

A word of caution: Classroom publishing software does not substitute for knowledge of, sensitivity to, and skill at graphic design, just as your word processor did not turn you into Shakespeare. Bad design is bad, whether done by hand or computer. Rose (1988) offers useful guidelines for those not trained in graphic design.

TELECOMMUNICATONS

Chapter 4 briefly introduced telecommunications as the means of accessing large public data bases. That is but one application. Telecommunications are a part of everyday life: Automatic teller machines, lottery ticket terminals, cable television, and news wire services are common examples (Wigley, 1988).

The mechanics of telecommunications are fairly simple. By connecting a modem to your computer and phone lines, then running communications software, your computer is ready to call countless other computers around the world. The interesting part is what happens once you connect to that other computer. According to Bruder (1988), this is one of the hottest technologies in education today. Let's look at applications.

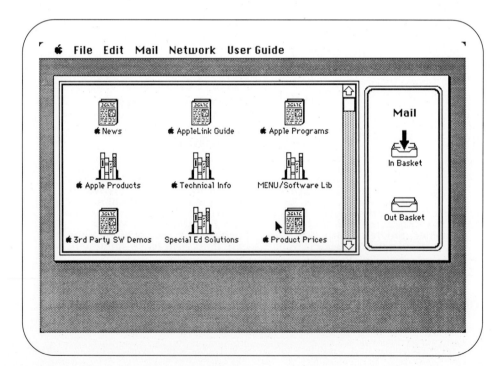

FIGURE 6.4. *Applelink* offers many services.

CONFERENCING

Conferencing is interacting with others in real time via computer. It is like talking on the telephone, except that you "speak" with your keyboard and "listen" with your monitor. This can be as simple as calling and conversing with a friend. If a school wires its computers into a Local Area Network (LAN), conferencing among multiple participants becomes possible.

On a larger scale, major information services host conferences. CompuServe calls theirs *forums*. Education Forum features weekly opportunities to visit with "expert" guests. You can be an active participant by submitting questions or an "eavesdropper" who merely reads the on-going interaction.

Because a 60-minute conference means 60 minutes of telephone time, conferencing can be expensive. There may be local or long distance charges, packet switching network charges, and CompuServe charges. To minimize costs, conferences are typically held evenings and weekends when rates are lowest.

Elementary pupils often go on field trips or have class guests. With conferencing, the potential expands. CompuServe's Student Forum handles conferences during school hours. Handler (1988) described her experience with second graders and an author whose book the children were reading. This is not likely to be a routine activity in most schools, but it is affordable on occasion as a unique variation on activities.

For information about CompuServe's education-related services, including their Educator's Forum, contact: Director of Information Services, LINC Resources Inc., 4820 Indianola Ave., Columbus, OH 43214. A smaller network for educators is BreadNet, a service of the Bread Loaf School of English, Middlebury College (Middlebury, VT 05753). Though not specifically geared to education, Apple users should investigate *Applelink* through their dealer.

Telecommunications and conferencing are the basis for *electronic distance learning*. In this form of instruction the teacher and pupil interact from different locations via computer. For an overview, see Batey and Cowell (1986). According to Bruder (1988), Alaska and Idaho are among states exploring electronic distance education to deal with problems of providing education in rural, remote areas. Distance education appears to be as effective as traditional instruction (De-Loughry, 1988).

ELECTRONIC MESSAGING

Electronic messaging includes *electronic mail* (E-mail) and the more general *bulletin board systems* (BBS).

Electronic Mail
Electronic mail is communicating with others via computer, but not in real time. Rather, you compose your message (memo, letter, report, first draft of the Great American Novel) with your word processor. Then, using a local area or information service network accessible to both you and the recipient, you

transmit the document as a file to the other party. The network computer stores it in the recipient's "mail box" until retrieved at that person's convenience. If E-mail were as universal as the phone itself, it could be the end of telephone tag! A speech professor at Penn State even conducted a class entirely by E-mail (Staff, 1988).

Bulletin Boards

E-mail is usually used for private communication directed to an individual or group of mail boxes. Public messages are simply "posted" on an electronic bulletin board system (BBS). The host computer stores them in categories, and allows anyone calling in to "read" them. Unless part of an information service, a BBS is normally free of charge except for the cost of the telephone call. Such systems are operated by individuals, computer clubs, and computer retailers, among others. Through a BBS you can contact kindred spirits. Many computerists have solved their hardware or software problems with advice obtained on a BBS.

BBS possibilities are as endless as all the physical bulletin boards you have ever seen. Similar to classified ads in the newspaper, or the garage sale notices at the local supermarket, bulletin boards serve buyers and sellers. They are sources of lists of other BBS's. You can often *download* (transfer to your computer) public domain software and shareware, which are discussed in Chapter 16. Regrettably, BBS's have also been used to publicize the telephone numbers and secret passwords of government and business computers around the world, an issue addressed in Chapter 17.

Examples

NASA Spacelink exemplifies the potential of a bulletin board system (BBS). Dedicated to educators, Spacelink offers instructions on how to use the system plus vast information resources categorized as current NASA news, aeronautics, space exploration before and after the shuttle, and space program spinoffs, to name a new. Lesson plans and suggested classroom activities are available. You can also post questions and receive answers another day. The only cost is your call to Huntsville, Alabama (205-895-0028). Spacelink operates at 300, 1200, or 2400 baud with 8 data bits, 1 stop bit, and no parity. To download files, your software must support the XMODEM protocol. (Clark [1988] explains the technical aspects of telecommunications well.)

A different sort of BBS is *CSUPER-NET*, California State University Profiles in Educational Resources Network. The system provides information on the nineteen CSU campuses, including degrees, programs, cost, financial aid, campus phone directories, and sources of further information. Questions receive next day replies.

SPIN, the Student Press Information Network, is for journalism students, editors, and advisors. It offers a national student newswire, bulletin boards, a reference library, and E-mail. There is no charge for SPIN itself. For information, contact School Management Arts, P.O. Box 1, Boston, MA 02195.

Kimmel, Kerr, and O'Shea (1987) describe the Electronic Information Exchange System, a network for educators based at the New Jersey Institute of Technology. Services include E-mail, conferences, "notebooks" for collaborative development of materials, text editing and document preparation. The project was conceived to enable teachers to more freely exchange ideas and materials.

TELECOMMUNICATIONS APPLICATIONS

Telecommunications activities may contribute to cross-cultural understanding. Electronically, students can "meet" their peers in other parts of the country or world. Solomon (1989) reported positive results from both domestic and international contacts. Sayers and Brown (1987) described linking California, New England, Puerto Rico, and Mexico in bilingual education. They also explained how costs were kept down to about $1 per transmission! Butler and Jobe (1987) brought together students in the U.S. and Australia. By communicating through The Source, there were no international telephone costs for either group—a real advantage to a world wide information service. Riel (1987) also described links around the world via The Source. Hagar and Thoren (1987) bypassed telecommunications and established a "diskpals" relationship between the U.S. and Egypt. Their experiences with exchanging diskettes by mail merit consideration where telecommunications is not feasible.

Many applications involve writing beyond just the essential typing. Solomon (1989) claimed students' writings benefit when shared with a broad, if unseen, audience. Stories may begin with one writer, then grow as others add their ideas from wherever they are. Tamashiro and Hoagland (1987) called this chain writing. They found that students benefitted from risk-free self-expression. They were able to focus on content, not the story teller. Lake (1988–89) also reported successful "round robin" writing projects. One produced a 21-page booklet of student work across grades 3–6. Another was a simulated bike trip which focused on the geography and history of the area traveled as students from two schools "biked" toward each other, meeting halfway.

Thread writing begins with a single "memo," which the next person reads and responds to. Each participant reads all that has been written before and adds another memo, referencing the previous ones as appropriate. Dodge and Dodge (1987, "Readiness") presented both chain and thread writing without computers as readiness activities to simulate E-mail and bulletin board communication.

Telecommunications can be integrated into many curriculum areas. Schrum, Carton, and Pinney (1988) describe how students in various locations held a plant growing contest, planting the same kinds of seeds at the same time, then reporting growth data on the network for all to share and compare. Goldberg (1988) discusses telecommunications instructional models and what has been implemented in the New York City schools.

IMPLEMENTATION

For anyone considering telecommunications in instruction, Schrum, Carton, and Pinney (1988) offer five suggestions based on their experiences. First, projects must tie to a specific curriculum need or opportunity. Second, telecommunications must be more effective than any other possibility. Third, conference participants must get acquainted before meaningful communication will occur. Fourth, the teacher must be committed to the lesson and its use of telecommunications to cope with inevitable difficulties. Finally, teachers must be willing to share their results with others afterward.

There will be administrative issues to resolve. What about costs? Will the phone line be abused? Scrogan (1987) claims there are dozens of roadblocks, but offers assistance in meeting them, as does Riedl (1986). For encouragement and advice on setting up a BBS, read Clark (1988). For guidance in selecting communications and BBS software, refer to Dodge and Dodge (1987, "Selecting").

If you cannot get telecommunications off the ground in your school, you can simulate the experiences with a variety of software. *Electronic Village* includes tutorials on telecommunications concepts and a bulletin board simulator. *Electronic Mailbag* is an E-mail simulator. *Windows on Telecommunications* is a tutorial on concepts plus a simulation of going on-line. It sells complete with site license for disk duplication.

Less expensive yet are public domain materials available from Softswap. *KidMail* is an E-mail simulation that encourages writing skill development. *SimuComm* offers both E-mail and bulletin boards, plus a modifiable database for learning search strategies. *Modemless CMS* simulates a BBS with two message boards, E-mail, a news and features display, and the ability to conduct user polls.

As a final resource, Lake (1986) describes use of *Newsroom* to share student writing among schools. This article clearly presents the project, it outcomes, and the pros and cons of telecommunications.

SUPPORT TOOLS

Support tools are those special purpose programs whose output:

☐ Is useful to a teacher.
☐ Can be produced more quickly than by traditional means.
☐ May be more varied than is reasonable to produce otherwise.
☐ Relieves a teacher of time-consuming, non-professional work.

These programs normally produce a specific paper product.

Although we stress the value of this software group to the teacher, one should also consider potential student uses. We will offer suggestions at various points.

GRAPHING PROGRAMS

We all know the value of seeing information presented graphically, yet how many teachers ever attempt to produce graphs for student use? One major deterrent is the time it takes to produce a good graph by hand, not a lack of appropriate uses for graphs. Software like *MagnaCharta, Imaginator 3-D,* or Microsoft *Chart* are easy, powerful graphing tools. Let's talk about applications.

Data Interpretation

How much are we influenced by numbers alone? Suppose a student was to be graded based on five separate assessments, each with a maximum value of 100. Further assume that the student's five scores were 85, 94, 92, 86, and 90. What impression do you obtain from just the values? Now look at Figure 6.5. Does it appear that this student is quite erratic in performance, given to significant swings? It does to many observers. Next examine Figure 6.6. The data are unchanged, but the vertical axis divisions have been altered. How does this affect your impression of this student? What could you (and your students!) learn about data representation from this exercise?

Could graphics be used to help students see the effects of extreme values in a set of data? Figures 6.7–6.9 present essentially the same data, beginning with a relatively normal distribution, then including extreme high and low values. Does this tell more than a verbal description of the results would? The time involved in producing the first graph is a few minutes; the time to modify and replot the data is trivial.

As a final example, consider the effects of graph type on interpretation of the data. Schiffman (1986) notes the impact of viewing data in differing formats, something rare before microcomputers. Figures 6.10–6.16 show the same figures presented in some common formats. What is the effect on initial interpretation? What exercises are students already doing that might gain new meaning from the ability to graph the results quickly and easily, changing scales and even formats until the desired result is achieved?

Student Applications

Student applications for graphing programs are virtually unlimited. Any time visualization of data would be helpful, consider graphing. Students might graph their own performance on class activities over some time period, similar to the examples in Figures 6.5 and 6.6. If there is a class fund-raising project, income or sales might be tracked on a daily or weekly basis similar to Figures 6.7–6.9.

In social science classes, what might students learn by graphing stock market activity over a specified period? How about trends in voting over a span of elections? Population trends? Inflation? The possibilities are endless. While some of these examples may be found in graphic form already in area newspapers, there is learning value in having students collect the raw data and develop their own representations.

Science classes also offer countless data gathering opportunities from which

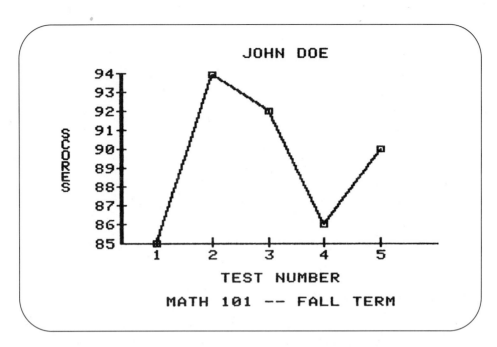

FIGURE 6.5. Student performance using small vertical axis divisions

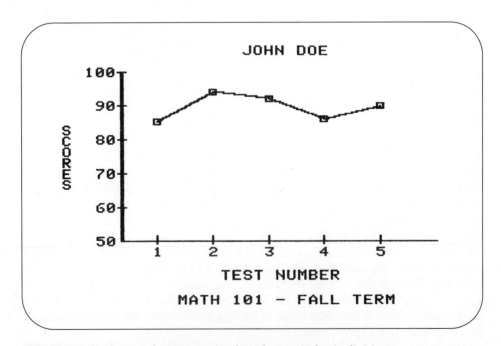

FIGURE 6.6. Student performance using broader vertical axis divisions

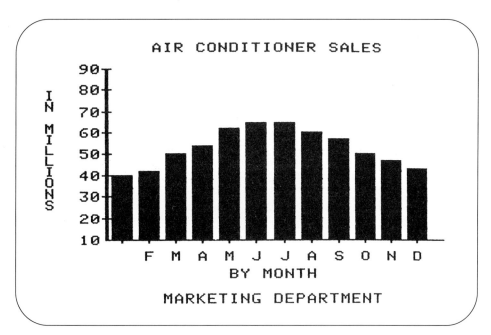

FIGURE 6.7. A relatively normal data distribution

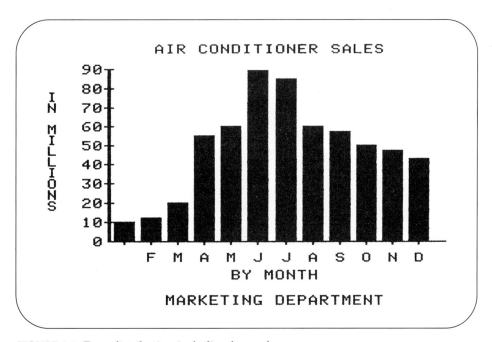

FIGURE 6.8. Data distribution including low values

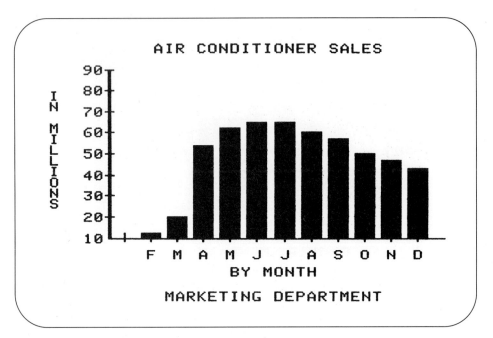

FIGURE 6.9. Data distribution including high values

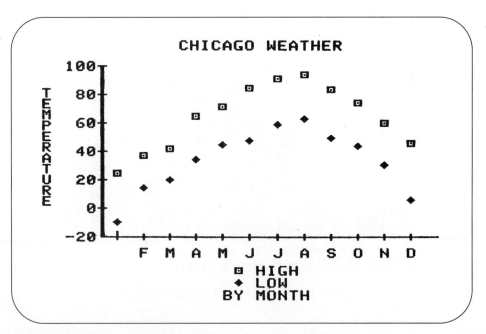

FIGURE 6.10. Data plotted as individual points

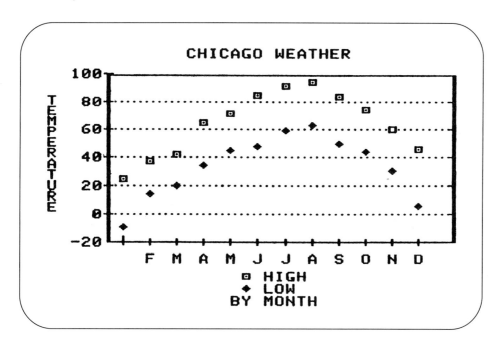

FIGURE 6.11. Data plotted as individual points with a reference grid

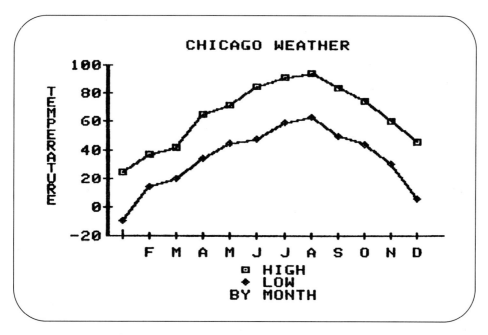

FIGURE 6.12. Line chart

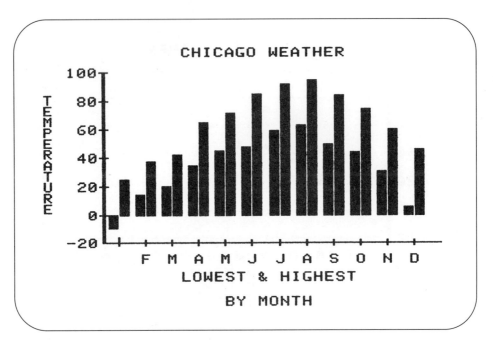

FIGURE 6.13. Bar graph

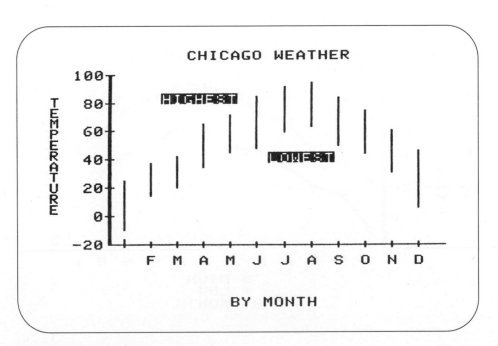

FIGURE 6.14. Hi-lo chart

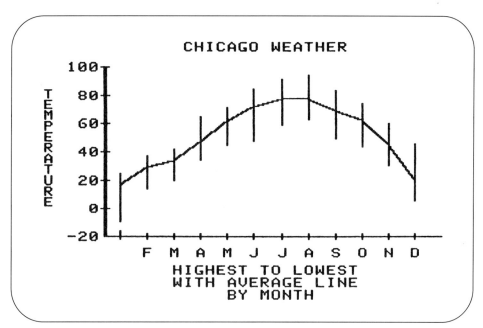

FIGURE 6.15. Hi-lo chart plus line chart

graphs might be developed to good advantage. "Kids on Computers" (*The Computing Teacher*, August/September 1986, p. 12) illustrated two specific applications. Fourth graders in Eugene, Oregon, tracked their diets (in bites of food eaten from each food group) and graphed findings to analyze nutrition. Middle school students graphed weather information obtained from the local paper, as well as a variety of information about classmates from their own student database.

A final note of caution. In one study (Machmias and Linn, 1987) researchers found that eighth graders accepted graphs generated from data collected by the computer, even when they should have spotted obvious problems such as scaling that failed to show all the data, or results that had to stem from errors in equipment usage. Computer-generated graphs simply were not questioned as they should have been. This study points out the need for explicit teaching of data interpretation. For extensive reviews of graphing software, see Johnson (1988) and Mathis (1988).

PUZZLE GENERATORS

The most common types of teacher-created puzzles are word searches and crossword puzzles. Both can be done by hand, of course, but these are labor-intensive activities! Teachers can "work smart" with special programs to meet this need, devoting more effort to content and virtually none to layout and printing.

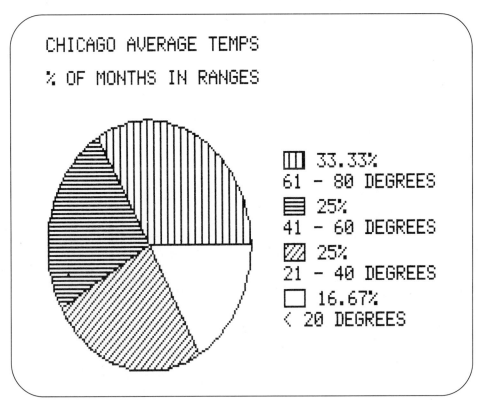

CHICAGO AVERAGE TEMPS
% OF MONTHS IN RANGES

▥ 33.33%
61 - 80 DEGREES

▤ 25%
41 - 60 DEGREES

▨ 25%
21 - 40 DEGREES

☐ 16.67%
< 20 DEGREES

FIGURE 6.16. Pie chart

Word Searches

A word search puzzle can be created very easily following prompts from the program. First, of course, you must compile the list of words to be hidden in a rectangular grid of letters. The program may ask that you specify the dimensions of the puzzle in advance, or it may calculate what is necessary as you go. Since words may be positioned vertically, horizontally, diagonally, and going either forward or backward, it is necessary to first enter the entire list. The computer then arranges the words into the puzzle and fills the blank spaces with random letters.

The computer may have to cycle through your list of words more than once to find a suitable place for each entry. Sometimes, it may be impossible to include all words within the specified puzzle size. At that point, you have the option of increasing the dimensions or doing without the words that did not fit. Despite such minor problems, the entire process is much faster than manual puzzle creation.

The final printout will contain the puzzle and the list of words to be located within it. An answer key is provided as Figure 6.17 shows. Word searches and

COMPUTER LANGUAGES

```
F Y F E S L F W Q H
E Y T R C O O A D A
G D U I R Z Y G S M
R I S T L L I L L M
F A R O A Y P O U A
B A B C R P P G Z S
N O S P M S I O J I
C A G V I U B L M Z
P T S L U X Y P O T
U T M R U P Z V F T
```

FIND THESE WORDS IN THE ABOVE PUZZLE:

ADA	ALGOL	BASIC	COBOL	FORTRAN
LISP	LOGO	PASCAL	PILOT	RPG

HERE IS THE ANSWER KEY:

```
.  .  .  .  .  L  F  .  .  .
.  .  .  .  C  O  O  A  D  A
.  .  .  I  R  .  .  G  .  .
.  .  S  T  L  L  .  .  L  .
.  A  R  O  A  .  .  O  .  A
B  A  B  C  R  P  P  G  .  .
N  O  S  P  .  S  I  O  .  .
C  A  G  .  I  .  .  L  .  .
P  .  .  L  .  .  .  .  O  .
.  .  .  .  .  .  .  .  .  T
```

FIND THESE WORDS IN THE ABOVE PUZZLE:

ADA	ALGOL	BASIC	COBOL	FORTRAN
LISP	LOGO	PASCAL	PILOT	RPG

FIGURE 6.17. A word search puzzle

activity sheets are the specialities of the program *Activitymakers,* which also produces cryptograms. Its files are compatible with *FrEdWriter.*

Crossword Puzzles
Word searches are generally used just for a change of pace. Crossword puzzles, on the other hand, can serve to reinforce learning by presenting content review

in an entertaining, alternative format. Any fan of such puzzles already appreciates the difficulty involved in creating them. It's not hard to come up with words and clues, but fitting it all together and coordinating clues to puzzle locations is a real challenge.

Enter the computer once again. A crossword puzzle generator requires little more effort than a word search program. Armed with your items and clues, let the machine prompt you for both. Again, sizing is often automatic but can usually be specified if there is a reason to do so. The final printout is achieved so easily as to be all but unbelievable to anyone who has ever made such a puzzle by hand. Of course, an answer key is also provided—not that you need one!

Crossword Magic not only does all of the above, but also shows you the puzzle on screen as it is being created. If you do not like its choice of location for a particular word, ask the computer to move it. Words that do not fit at the time of entry are retained and tried again as the puzzle grows. If no fit is ever found, leftover words can be saved for another puzzle, rejected entirely, or exchanged for new words.

Student Applications

If you have access to puzzle-generating software, do not keep it all to yourself. Have your students create puzzles to demonstrate their knowledge and challenge their classmates. Virtually any field of study and all but the lowest grade levels offer lots of material for such puzzles. With some creative guidance from the teacher, preparing a puzzle can be a meaningful learning experience. In fact, even the teacher may find a new challenge in student-created materials!

TEST-GENERATING PROGRAMS

In Chapter 10, the potential of the computer in testing is described in the context of computer-administered examinations. Other programs allow the teacher to create paper and pencil tests with variation in the formats but with a potentially significant savings of time.

Capabilities

Programs for creating paper tests generally accommodate such formats as multiple-choice, matching, true/false, and fill-in-the-blank. Some programs handle short answer and essay exams, although a word processor may do just as well. Questions are typically entered into an item bank. They may be grouped as a specific test, by objective, by unit, or by subject. *All of the Above* does both printed and on-screen tests in five formats and can create end of unit tests by selectively choosing items from earlier tests. *TestMaker* is a set of *AppleWorks* templates for multiple choice, matching, and true-false formats. Questions can be scrambled, formatting is handled, and an answer key provided.

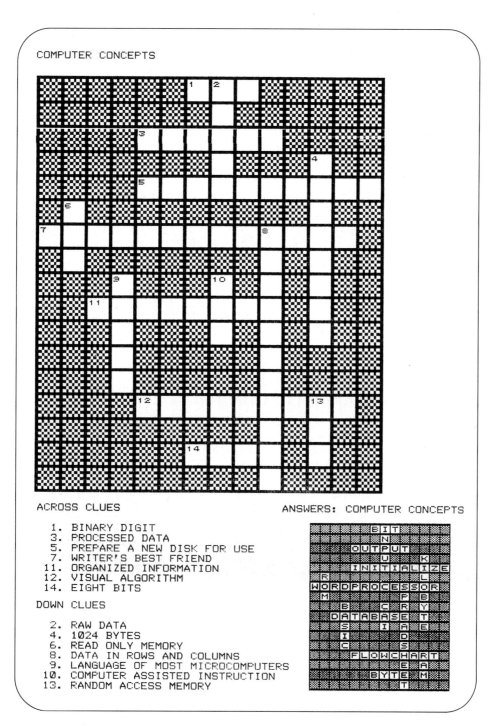

COMPUTER CONCEPTS

ACROSS CLUES

1. BINARY DIGIT
3. PROCESSED DATA
5. PREPARE A NEW DISK FOR USE
7. WRITER'S BEST FRIEND
11. ORGANIZED INFORMATION
12. VISUAL ALGORITHM
14. EIGHT BITS

DOWN CLUES

2. RAW DATA
4. 1024 BYTES
6. READ ONLY MEMORY
8. DATA IN ROWS AND COLUMNS
9. LANGUAGE OF MOST MICROCOMPUTERS
10. COMPUTER ASSISTED INSTRUCTION
13. RANDOM ACCESS MEMORY

ANSWERS: COMPUTER CONCEPTS

FIGURE 6.18. A *Crossword Magic* puzzle

Advantages

One great advantage of a test-generating program is the ability to produce alternate forms of a test with little effort. Once an item bank of sufficient size exists, the computer could easily prepare a unique test for each student in the class, if desired. However, even if the idea appeals to you, it is apt to be impractical without access to a very fast printer. It is far more sensible and feasible to think in terms of a basic exam with alternate forms for each class section and for make-up or retesting purposes.

Programs of this type often allow you to select specific items from the pool, with the program performing only the clerical service of arranging everything on the page in an appropriate layout. Items in the bank can be deleted, modified, and added easily, with the current pool always available for the next exam on the subject.

Since the test item bank is normally prepared with both questions and answers, most such programs also provide a complete answer key printout along with the test. This may be little more than a memory crutch, which some of us need more than others. However, consider the potential time savings of complete answer keys when alternate forms of a test have been generated.

Even if you do not need multiple versions of a test, you may still find a test generator useful. The final printout will be free of typographical errors, if you proofed your items carefully when you created the item pool. The computer assists with matters of page layout, so that the test is well-formatted. If you must duplicate using a spirit (ditto) master, you can insert the master into your printer and avoid purple fingernails from correcting typos on a master.

WORKSHEET GENERATORS

There are many similarities between test generators and worksheet generators. In fact, for many purposes, there might be no need for separate software at all. There may be no major difference between the content of a unit exam and the practice items one would give to students during the teaching of the unit. One area for which specialized programs are available is arithmetic practice worksheets. These amount to little more than software that can generate an infinite variety of arithmetic problems within a specified range of parameters (times tables, single digit factors, answers less than 100). Teachers have long typed out such practice sheets by hand. While no great intellectual challenge, the time can be better spent on other duties.

More than just a worksheet generator, Prentice-Hall's *Reading Strategy Series* enables teachers to create reading exercises that can be completed at the computer or printed for desk or home work. Text is created with a word processor. Cloze and fill-in formats are possible with the *Super Context* system, while *Super Skills* handles speed reading, scrambled letters, scrambled words, and completion types. Although reading selection files are included, the teacher may input any content.

READABILITY ANALYSIS

Teachers may be interested in the readability level of text for many reasons. Perhaps a student or group of students is having difficulty with assigned material. The cause could be a reading level that is too high. When selecting material for a class, the reading level should be determined as part of the assessment. Even materials we develop for students ourselves should be analyzed to be sure they are appropriate.

Readability analysis is very straightforward and well-suited to a computer. A typical program is *Readability Machine* which requires the user to type in three passages of 100 words each. The program analyzes word frequency, syllabication, long words, number of sentences, and so on. Eight different readability formulas are calculated. This is beneficial because each follows differing assumptions. Results can vary significantly. When finished, you can save and print both your text passages and the analysis scores!

Writing aids such as *Grammatik, RightWriter,* and *Readability* also analyze reading level among their numerous assessments.

Some teachers approach creative writing assignments for older students by having them write stories for others, usually younger children. This is an excellent opportunity for use of readability analysis to assure that the materials are suitable for their intended audience. Beneficial insight into language use could easily be developed in such exercises.

CLOZE

For the language arts, the *cloze* technique presents the student with a written selection from which words have been deleted at a regular interval. The student must determine each missing word from the context of the passage.

Similar to readability software, cloze programs require the user to input passages and specify the interval for deleting words. The program generates blank spaces in the output, as well as an answer key. Interactive programs using cloze are also available, so that the student benefits both from the technique and from immediate feedback as responses are made. *Cloze Plus* includes a management system permitting teachers to assign specific lessons to students and to collect performance data.

STATISTICAL PACKAGES

The use of statistical analysis by the classroom teacher is a highly individual matter. Teachers who have been exposed to such analysis are often enthusiastic about the potential benefit of calculating minimally the mean and standard deviation on their tests. Enthusiasm generally wanes in the face of hand calculation. You, of course, have long since realized that there must be programs to calculate all the common statistics that a classroom teacher could ever desire. You are correct again!

What less than ten years ago could be achieved only on a mainframe computer is now available in microcomputer statistics packages. With the right package, the teacher can proceed from the simplest mean all the way to complex analysis of variance, multilinear regression, multiple and partial correlation, even factor and time series analysis.

For MS-DOS computers with ample hard disk space, microcomputer versions of the legendary *SPSS* and *SAS* mainframe programs are available. Both are extremely powerful and priced to match. Apple II users will find all the power they are likely to need in products like *APPSTATS* or *STATISTIX* (Apfelstadt, 1989). It is not the purpose of this book to suggest what statistical applications you should find beneficial, but to convey that anything you might desire is likely to be available in one package or another for your school microcomputer.

GRADE BOOKS

Among the earliest of teacher support programs to appear on the market was the grade book. Although similar to an actual grade book on the surface, any grade book software worth considering will have far greater flexibility and capability.

Naturally, you will have to enter student names and specify the number of values (assignments) to be entered per student. Good grade book software then allows weighting of the individual assignments (e.g., tests are worth four times as much as quizzes) and provides alternate methods of dealing with missing values or late work. The weighting factors can generally be changed at any point, allowing great flexibility in overall grading with no modifications to the data.

Some programs also perform common statistical procedures. *GradeBook Deluxe* and *Gradebook Plus* are representative products.

Many such packages permit up-to-the-minute standings to be requested. Thus, a student may pose the perennial question "Where do I stand in this class?" and the teacher can actually respond as of that time. Beyond this potential, grade book programs often include report-generating capacity— possibly in narrative form for student and parents, as graphic displays with appropriate statistics, or as a report card.

If you perceive a need for some of these extensions to normal recordkeeping in a grade book, then by all means seek out the best package you can find. On the other hand, if all you really want is an automatic calculator of final grades, which can also allow experimentation with weights, use a spreadsheet as your grade book, as described in Chapter 5.

SPECIAL PURPOSE DATA MANAGERS

Although the general data management tools you met in Chapter 4 can meet virtually any need, some applications are more easily handled with limited, specialized products.

Mailing List Managers

In most schools, major mailing lists are a problem for the central office, not individual teachers. However, some teachers wish to keep a handy record of their students' addresses for their own purposes. A mailing list manager could be just right.

Such a program would typically begin with a menu. For example:

1. Create a mailing list.
2. Add to an existing list.
3. Delete from an existing list.
4. Delete an entire list.
5. Print out a list.

Depending on your choice, the program would then prompt you for the information needed to perform the specified task. A good list manager should allow for varied processing of the information, such as producing the list on paper for proofing or on labels for easy mailing. You should also be able to specify whether output will be in alphabetic order, sorted by ZIP code, or as entered. Such a program is limited in potential but will be simpler to use than a general filing system.

A mailing list manager might be used with elementary students to reinforce learning regarding components of addresses and how envelopes are properly addressed. For young pupils just learning to remember their own address or writing for the first time, having them enter their personal information into such a program might offer useful practice. Older students involved in school organizations might benefit from access to such a program, using it for membership lists, mailings to past supporters of group activities, or comparable purposes.

Research Bibliographic Aids

Many data bases do not support fields and records of sufficient size for academic researchers. *Notebook II* was designed to store and manipulate article abstracts, research and lab notes, then aid in compiling bibliographies and reading lists. A companion product, *Bibliography*, uses *Notebook II* database information to construct a bibliography from citations in manuscripts. Another companion imports data from on-line data bases.

A CAVEAT

A word of caution is in order as we conclude this chapter. Because graphics and support programs are so easy to work with, there may be a tendency to rely on them more than is pedagogically warranted. Teachers should not fall into the trap of allowing easy creation of varied yet simplistic materials to substitute for other potentially more demanding ways to treat subject matter.

Use these programs thoughtfully, but do not abuse them. Keep curriculum foremost, not software capability.

SUMMARY

In this chapter you were introduced to applications that are fun, powerful, practical, and useful across the curriculum. Print and presentation graphics offer new ways to communicate and new levels of sophistication in the outcome. Classroom publishing software offers enormous benefits to those who need its special layout facility. The concept of the global village becomes real and personal through telecommunications, especially when connections extend beyond your own country. The potential of telecommunications warrants the effort which will be required to obtain the necessary budget in most schools.

Beyond these major applications, you also were introduced to other specialized software that can make your life as a teacher a bit easier. Whenever the computer can assist with a routine task, you reclaim time for other duties. Whether you want to help students interpret data better, apply statistics to your data, determine the approximate reading level of some new materials, or create puzzles and other desk work, helpful tools are readily available.

Best of all, most of these applications require only inexpensive, easy-to-use software.

CHAPTER 6 ACTIVITIES

1. Create a newsletter with at least two columns to bring your family up to date on your activities. Illustrate it with appropriate clip art.
2. Produce at least one example from each of the formats available with your print graphics program, e.g. card, poster, calendar. Suggest several potential fund raisers using this package.
3. Experiment with any presentation graphics package. Create a slide show of at least five frames, using varied transition effects.
4. Your school budget will only permit purchase of one graphics package. Will you choose print graphics, presentation graphics, or classroom publishing software? What factors must you consider? Explain and justify your choice.
5. Write a persuasive argument for the school board to justify the hardware, software, and operating expenses to use telecommunications in your school. Modify your appeal to suit the parent-teacher organization.
6. Log on to a bulletin board (BBS) or information service. Spend as much time as possible experimenting with the available services or options. If there is no local BBS, would you consider starting one? Why?
7. List several uses you can project for programs described in this chapter. Which seems to have the most applicability to your needs? Why?

8. Plan a unit of instruction in your field where a graphing program would provide an interesting and valuable change of pace.

9. Develop a short "policy" statement regarding your approach to student use of graphics, telecommunications, or support programs. Where would you draw the line between legitimate student use of school hardware and software and uses that the school should not permit or support?

10. Depending on software available to you, learn to use at least one support tool.

REFERENCES

Apfelstadt, M. "Higher Education Applications." *Call-A.P.P.L.E.*, February 1989, pp. 8–13.

Batey, A. and Cowell, R. N. *Distance Education: An Overview.* Portland, OR: Northwest Regional Educational Laboratory, 1986.

Bruder, I. "Electronic Learning's 8th Annual Survey of the States, 1988." *Electronic Learning*, October 1988, pp 38–45.

Butler, G. and Jobe, H. "The Australian-American Connection." *The Computing Teacher*, April 1987, pp. 25–26.

Clark, C. "Confessions of an Educator/SysOp." *The Computing Teacher*, June 1988, pp. 11–12.

Clark, C. "Telecommunications is Here and Now." *The Computing Teacher*, May 1988, pp. 24–25.

DeLoughry, T. J. "Remote Instruction Using Computers Found as Effective as Classroom Sessions." *Chronicle of Higher Education*, 20 April 1988, pp. A20–A21.

Dodge, J., and Dodge, B. "Readiness Activities for Telecommunications." *The Computing Teacher*, April 1987, pp. 7–9, 22.

Dodge, J., and Dodge, B. "Selecting Telecommunications Software for Educational Settings." *The Computing Teacher*, April 1987, pp. 10–12, 32.

Ellenwood, W. C. "Commodore Users: On Line." *The Computing Teacher*, April 1987, pp. 13–14, 60.

Gittinger, J. D., Jr. "A Telecommunications Simulation." *The Computing Teacher*, April 1987, pp. 15–16.

Goldberg, F. S. "Telecommunications and the Classroom: Where We've Been and Where We Should Be Going." *The Computing Teacher*, May 1988, pp. 26–28.

Hagar, M. J. and Thoren, C. "Egypt and the Floppy Disk." *The Computing Teacher*, April 1987, pp. 17–18.

Handler, M. "Meeting an Author Online." *The Computing Teacher*, October 1988, pp. 17–19.

Hubert, E., Winebrenner, J., and Qualkenbush, D. "Planning Your Print Shop Projects." *The Computing Teacher*, February 1987, pp. 18–20, 26.

Johnson, J. "Graphing Packages for Mathematics Teachers: An Overview." *The Computing Teacher*, November 1988, pp. 50–53.

Kimmel, H., Kerr, E. B., and O'Shea, M. "Computerized Collaboration. Taking Teachers Out of Isolation." *The Computing Teacher*, November 1987, pp. 36–38.

Knapp, L. R. "The Computer Chronicles. A Newswire Network for Kids." *Classroom Computer Learning*, March 1986, pp. 38–41.

Knapp, L. R. "Teleconferencing: A New Way of Communicating for Teachers and Kids." *Classroom Computer Learning*, March 1987, pp. 37–42.

Kneen, T. J. "A Computerized Fund Raising Project." *The Computing Teacher*, May 1987, pp. 11–12, 56.

Lake, D. T. "Telecommunications From the Classroom." *The Computing Teacher*, April 1986, pp. 43–46.

Lake, D. "Two Projects That Worked: Using Telecommunications as a Resource in the Classroom." *The Computing Teacher*, December/January 1988–89, pp. 17–19.

Lamb, A. "Borders: Expanding Children's Interest in Illustration." *The Computing Teacher*, November 1988, pp. 30–33.

Machmias, R., and Linn, M. C. "Evaluations of Science Laboratory Data: The Role of Computer-Presented Information." *Journal of Research in Science Teaching*, 1987, 24(5), pp. 491–506.

Mathias, J. "Turning Data into Pictures: Part I." *The Computing Teacher*, October 1988, pp. 40–48.

Mathis, J. "Turning Data into Pictures: Part II." *The Computing Teacher*, November 1988, pp. 7–10, 56.

McCarthy, R. "Stop the Presses." *Electronic Learning*, March 1988, pp. 24–30.

Mendrinos, R. "Computers as Curriculum Tools: Exceeding Expectations." *Media & Methods*, January/February 1988, pp. 14–18.

Ohler, J. "Getting Your Computers to Talk to Each Other." *The Computing Teacher*, May 1987, pp. 16–18, 54.

Resta, P. "Europe On Line." *The Computing Teacher*, August/September 1988, pp. 54–56.

Riedesel, C. A., and Clements, D. H. *Coping with Computers in the Elementary and Middle Schools*. Englewood Cliffs, NJ: Prentice-Hall, 1985.

Riedl, R. "CompuServe in the Classroom." *The Computing Teacher*, March 1986, pp. 62–64.

Riel, M. "The InterCultural Learning Network." *The Computing Teacher*, April 1987, pp. 27–28.

Rose, S. Y. "A Desktop Publishing Primer." *The Computing Teacher*, June 1988, pp. 13–15.

Sayers, D. and Brown, K. "Bilingual Education and Telecommunications: A Perfect Fit." *The Computing Teacher*, April 1987, pp. 23–24.

Schiffman, S. S. "Productivity Tools for the Classroom." *The Computing Teacher*, May 1986, pp. 27–31.

Schrum, L., Carton, K., and Pinney, S. "Today's Tools." *The Computing Teacher*, May 1988, pp. 31–35.

Scrogan, L. "Telecomputing: How to Overcome the Roadblocks." *Classroom Computer Learning*, February 1987, pp. 40–45.

Solomon, G. "A Writing Class Taps Into a World of Knowledge." *Electronic Learning*, March 1989, pp. 16–17.

Staff. "For Professor at Penn State, Class Lectures Do Not Compute." *Chicago Tribune*, 20 March 1988, Section 1, p. 28.

Stanley, M. "Desktop Publishing." *The Computing Teacher*, November 1986, pp. 46–48.

Tamashiro, R. and Hoagland, C. "Telecomputing a Chain Story." *The Computing Teacher*, April 1987, pp. 37–39.

Wigley, G. "Telecommunications Planning Guide for Educators." *The Computing Teacher*, November 1988, pp. 24–29.

CHAPTER 7

□ *Integrated Software* □

OBJECTIVES

After completing this chapter, you will be able to:

□ Briefly explain the history and development of integrated software. □
□ Describe the common characteristics of programs that integrate two or more microcomputer applications. □
□ Discuss the advantages and disadvantages of integrated programs and the integrated approach to multiple software applications. □
□ Explain the concept of desktop publishing and its advantages and disadvantages. □
□ Present and discuss educational uses of integrated software. □

In this chapter, you will meet software that integrates multiple major applications into a single product. After considering the need to exchange data among applications, you will learn why this can be difficult. Approaches to solving problems of data exchange will be presented, focusing on integrated programs. Next, we'll look at the advantages and disadvantages of such programs as compared to individual specific application programs. After a brief look at desktop publishing, we conclude with selected educational uses of integrated software.

THE RISE OF INTEGRATED SOFTWARE

FUNDAMENTAL DATA PROCESSING APPLICATIONS

The previous four chapters have discussed most of the common general application areas for which microcomputer software is presently available. These were word processing (using the microcomputer as a sophisticated typewriter), data management (using the microcomputer as a sophisticated file cabinet), spreadsheets (using the microcomputer as an electronic worksheet), and specialized programs for such tasks as graphics and telecommunications.

While there is software available to perform a wide variety of additional tasks, those applications represent the tools that are of general concern to a wide spectrum of users. In each of these areas, there are numerous software products available that differ considerably in their scope and power although designed to perform a similar basic function. The user must pick and choose from among them in order to meet specific needs.

APPROACHES TO MULTIPLE PROCESSING NEEDS

Consider now the situation when a user wishes or needs to use the same data in two or more different applications. For example, a user might have a spreadsheet file and need to perform data management procedures on this file. There are five possible alternatives in such a situation.

Make Do
The user could attempt to make do with any data management procedures already contained within the spreadsheet program itself. Some contain simple routines, such as basic sorting, within their command options. However, not all spreadsheet programs contain such commands, and even if a specific program does, the commands tend to be limited and do not perform more than a minimal function. Most spreadsheet programs are not very capable data managers.

Reenter Data
The spreadsheet data could be reentered as input into a data management program; that is, the data could be typed again as required by the data

management program. Then the data management program could manipulate such data and perform any type of file-oriented processing desired. There are at least two major problems with this approach.

First, the user has to input the data completely a second time. This is obviously a time-consuming and tedious task that does not take advantage of the fact that the data already exist in computer form, i.e., as a spreadsheet file. The potential for typing errors during data entry is clear as well.

Second, even if the data were entered a second time, after data management processing was completed, it would not be possible to directly access the altered file from within the spreadsheet program, a possibility that has many benefits. Rather, the user would have to again reenter all the data manually into the spreadsheet program. Even for very small files, this would be a nuisance at best, and on medium to large files it would be totally impractical.

Share the Data File

There is, though, a third possibility that can be used to solve this data transfer problem—file sharing. Once a data set has been created, the same file serves as input to varied applications and can be processed appropriately within each. The terminology that is often used to describe this file transfer process is *exporting* or *importing* files between programs. This procedure overcomes the limitations of the first two alternatives and is a viable approach to multiple processing requirements.

However, there are potential problems with this approach. File sharing requires that one program be able to access the files of another program. Unfortunately, there is little standardization of file structures on microcomputers. Many software packages utilize unique procedures in setting up their files. While this is understandable as an attempt to make files as efficient as possible within the context of a specific program, such files usually cannot be directly read and used by another program that employs a different file structure.

Many programs can both read and write files in ASCII and DIF formats, two generalized file structures created just for data exchange. ASCII and DIF files are "flat" files of just alphanumeric characters. They do not include specialized codes that are stored when a file is saved in program-specific format, such as those which control output formatting or fonts. Thus, some information is "lost" when using ASCII or DIF files.

Transform the File

In order to overcome the problems of file sharing, special programs have been developed that can input a file of one type, modify it to conform to the parameters of another file structure, and then output this transformed file. The newly created file can then be used as input by the program that requires the different structure. The process can also be reversed. Files may be transformed even further for use in additional programs.

The difficulty is availability of such transformation programs. Some are provided as part of comprehensive application packages. Other transformation

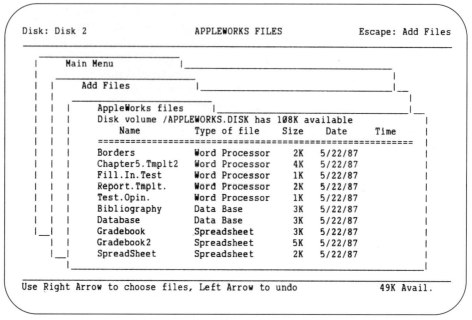

```
Disk: Disk 2                    APPLEWORKS FILES            Escape: Add Files
_____
 |      Main Menu            |_____
 |    _____ |                                        |
 |   |   Add Files           |_____ |__
 |   |  _____  |                                        |  |
 |   |  |   AppleWorks files   |_____|__
 |   |  |   Disk volume /APPLEWORKS.DISK has 108K available            |
 |   |  |     Name          Type of file   Size   Date     Time       |
 |   |  |   ======================================================    |
 |   |  |   Borders          Word Processor   2K   5/22/87            |
 |   |  |   Chapter5.Tmplt2   Word Processor   4K   5/22/87            |
 |   |  |   Fill.In.Test      Word Processor   1K   5/22/87            |
 |   |  |   Report.Tmplt.     Word Processor   2K   5/22/87            |
 |   |  |   Test.Opin.        Word Processor   1K   5/22/87            |
 |   |  |   Bibliography      Data Base        3K   5/22/87            |
 |   |  |   Database          Data Base        3K   5/22/87            |
 |__|  |   Gradebook         Spreadsheet      3K   5/22/87            |
    |  |   Gradebook2        Spreadsheet      5K   5/22/87            |
    |__|   SpreadSheet        Spreadsheet      2K   5/22/87            |
       |_____|
_____
Use Right Arrow to choose files, Left Arrow to undo            49K Avail.
```

FIGURE 7.1. *AppleWorks* integrates the three basic tool applications.

programs are available individually as stand-alone programs. While file transformations are available for popular programs, there are many situations involving more specialized programs where none exists, or if available, only limited types of file transformation are possible. Even if file transfer programs are available to meet a specific need, some can be relatively difficult to use.

Integrated Applications

While file transformation enables data sharing among programs, there is another approach to meeting this same need. It involves not two different programs using the same file but one program performing many different applications on a single file.

This approach was pioneered in the early eighties by the Lotus Development Corporation with the program *Lotus 1-2-3*. While basically a spreadsheet program, *Lotus 1-2-3* also has data base management and graphics capabilities. That is, this program functions as three programs (spreadsheet, data management, and graphics), all within the context of a single package. This avoids completely the problems of file transfer. None is necessary since only one program performs these different applications on the same data and files.

This first "combination" program was soon followed by others that integrated two or more separate applications within the same package. Examples include *SuperCalc, Excel,* and *Quattro* (spreadsheet, graphics, and data base) and *AppleWorks* (word processor, data base, spreadsheet). Other combination programs include even more applications within their integrated structure. Programs such as *Symphony, Framework,* Microsoft *Works* for both MS-DOS and Macintosh, and *PC–Quintet* offer five different applications within the same program structure—word processing, data base, spreadsheet, graphics, and data communications.

CONCEPTS OF INTEGRATED SOFTWARE

Integrated software is any program that performs the functions of more than one of the specific applications that have been discussed previously. Such a program can function on various levels.

SIMPLE INTEGRATION

A common approach is to treat the computer memory as a single workspace that is viewed differently depending upon which program function the user has specified. Let's look at some examples of simple integration.

Spreadsheet and Data Management
In the spreadsheet mode, the user can set up a typical spreadsheet. By switching to the data management mode, the user manipulates this spreadsheet as if it were a data base file. Data management tasks such as record sorting and specific record selection can be carried out more easily than within the spreadsheet mode.

Word Processing and Spreadsheet
In the word processing mode, the user can type in the headings for a table. Then, within the spreadsheet mode, the actual table is constructed. Finally, by going back to the word processing mode, the user easily can enter any notes and commentary at the bottom of the table.

Spreadsheet and Graphics
The user can enter and manipulate data in the spreadsheet mode. A switch to the graphics mode permits construction of a graph from all or part of the spreadsheet data. The graph may be displayed on the screen or printed.

Data Management and Communications
The user can create a data base and, by switching to the communications mode, transfer the data to another microcomputer or to a mainframe computer. In a similar manner, from within the communications mode users can transfer data from another microcomputer or mainframe computer to their microcomputer for use within the integrated program.

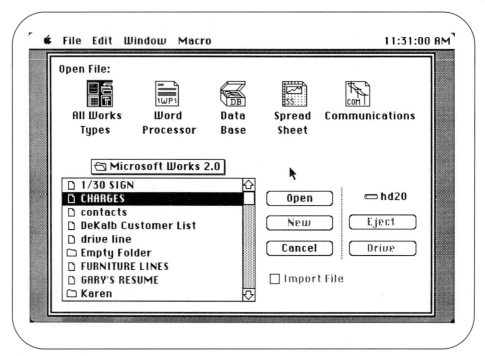

FIGURE 7.2. *Works* integrates multiple applications.

WINDOWS

A feature of some integrated programs called *windowing* allows the user to simultaneously display different parts of the same workspace on the screen but in different modes. The user can then work within each of these mode windows. For example, the screen could be split in half horizontally. In the lower window, a spreadsheet could be displayed, while in the upper window the user could be working within the word processing mode, typing a report based upon the spreadsheet data.

An even more interesting example of window use would be displaying a spreadsheet in one while the second displays a graph of the spreadsheet data. By changing some figures on the spreadsheet, the user could then immediately observe the effect of this change on the graph. The integrated program would reconstruct the graph to reflect the spreadsheet change.

Some integrated programs allow more than two windows, affording the user even greater flexibility in achieving desired results.

It should be obvious that the integration of different applications within the context of a single program allows the user to perform many different operations on the same data in a direct and efficient manner. While our examples have illustrated use of two modes, the next section illustrates more complex integration.

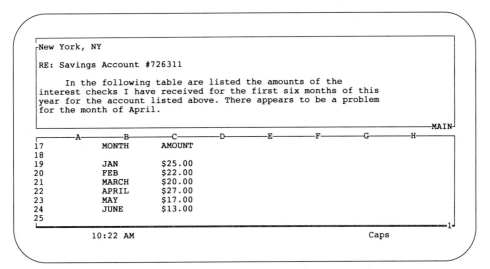

```
┌──────────────────────────────────────────────────────────────────┐
│ ┌New York, NY                                                      │
│ │                                                                  │
│ │RE: Savings Account #726311                                       │
│ │                                                                  │
│ │     In the following table are listed the amounts of the         │
│ │interest checks I have received for the first six months of this  │
│ │year for the account listed above. There appears to be a problem  │
│ │for the month of April.                                           │
│ │                                                          ┌MAIN┐  │
│ │  ──A────────B────────C─────────D──────E──────F──────G──────H──   │
│ │17              MONTH      AMOUNT                                 │
│ │18                                                                │
│ │19              JAN        $25.00                                 │
│ │20              FEB        $22.00                                 │
│ │21              MARCH      $20.00                                 │
│ │22              APRIL      $27.00                                 │
│ │23              MAY        $17.00                                 │
│ │24              JUNE       $13.00                                 │
│ │25                                                                │
│ └                                                             1┘   │
│          10:22 AM                                     Caps         │
└──────────────────────────────────────────────────────────────────┘
```

FIGURE 7.3. Differing applications can operate in each window
of some integrated software.

COMPLEX INTEGRATION

Some programs allow more than two functions to be carried out within one
program. Spreadsheet, data base, word processing, telecommunications, and
graphics functions are commonly included. Such programs are truly multifunc-
tional and extremely versatile.

Assume that you want to write a report that includes within the text a
spreadsheet table and a graph derived from it. The following is a brief generic
description of how this might be done with an integrated program.

1. Enter word processing mode and type the text up to the beginning of the
spreadsheet table. When you are in word processing mode, the program
allows you to perform the typical word processing functions discussed in
Chapter 3.
2. Switch to spreadsheet mode and enter the table data. In spreadsheet mode,
you can perform common spreadsheet functions described in Chapter 5.
3. To continue with the text after the table, switch back to word processing
mode and continue entering text up to the location where the graph is to
appear in the report.
4. Switch to graphics mode and direct the system to construct a graph with
the data from the spreadsheet table. In graphics mode, the program performs
many of the typical graphing functions illustrated in Chapter 6.
5. To continue with text after the graph, switch back to word processing mode
and enter text to the end of the report.
6. The report can now be printed, as illustrated in Figure 7.4.

```
                                        123 Maple
                                        Brooklyn, NY


      XYZ Bank
      Savings Account Department
      97 West 59th Street
      New York, NY

      RE: Savings Account #726311

          In the following table are listed the amounts of the
      interest checks I have received for the first six months of this
      year for the account listed above. There appears to be a problem
      for the month of April.

          MONTH           AMOUNT

          JAN             $25.00
          FEB             $22.00
          MARCH           $20.00
          APRIL           $27.00
          MAY             $17.00
          JUNE            $13.00

          Since I have withdrawn some principal each month, a slight
      decline in interest each month is expected. However, April shows
      an increase. The graph below illustrates even more clearly the
      possible problem.
```

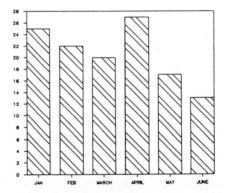

```
          It appears that something may be wrong with the April
      figure. Will you please check this and let me know as soon
      as possible.

                                        Yours truly,


                                        John Doe
```

FIGURE 7.4. Output of an integrated package

This is not the end of what can be done with this report using an integrated program. The data management mode could manipulate the table to arrange the data in alternative ways. If the person who is to receive the report also has a microcomputer, instead of sending a printed copy of the report to this individual, the communication mode could be used to send the report over phone lines directly to the person's microcomputer for immediate access. The recipient would then decide whether to print it or just read it on the screen.

It should be obvious from these examples that an integrated program allows the user to perform quickly and easily various processing possibilities far beyond the scope of individual application programs. And these were only simple examples! With integrated programs, one can perform a vast array of complex processing tasks on the same data without being limited to programs that can share files or having to rely on file transformation programs to act as a link between various application programs.

There are numerous add-in programs that can be used in conjunction with integrated software. Common examples are *Sideways* for *Lotus 1-2-3* and the *Timeout* series for *AppleWorks*. The latter is an ever-growing collection of programs which add sideways printing and graphics to the spreadsheet, a spelling checker and thesaurus to the word processor, multiple font capability, and so on. Add-ins further increase the power, flexibility, and applicability of the base program.

ASSESSING INTEGRATED PROGRAMS

ADVANTAGES

Following this brief overview of integrated software, let's consider several major advantages of such programs.

1. *No file transfer problems from one application to another.* All processing modes (spreadsheet, word processing, data management, graphics, communications) function on the same data and data file.
2. *One command structure that is reasonably similar among all applications.* Since integrated software is one program with different modes, the operating command structure tends to be similar across all modes. For instance, cursor movement and file saving or retrieving would use the same commands regardless of mode. Separate application programs usually have considerably different command structures, which force the user to master many varied procedures. This is confusing and inefficient at best, counterproductive at worst. Using integrated software should be much easier.
3. *The integrative nature of a single multipurpose program.* With a true integrated package, the same data can be handled in many different ways within the workspace. As previously described, a set of data may be presented in a spreadsheet table and also be shown as a graph on the same screen. Adjustments to achieve the desired result are simple. This flexibility is seldom available with separate programs.

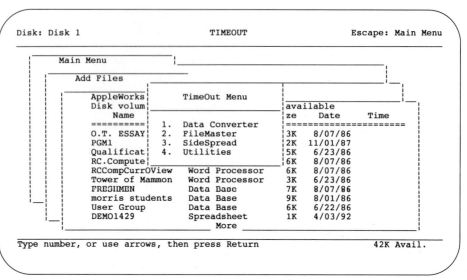

FIGURE 7.5 *TimeOut* programs work within *AppleWorks*.

4. *An integrated program may be more cost effective.* Although an integrated package costs more than a single-purpose application program, one must buy several separate programs to obtain similar capabilities. When the total cost of a number of such single-purpose programs is considered, the integrated program may be considerably less expensive.

DISADVANTAGES

On the other hand, integrated software also has disadvantages that the potential user must be aware of.

1. *Less powerful or flexible than single purpose application programs.* In the design of integrated packages, some compromises are inevitable. While some modes of an integrated program may be as powerful as their single application counterparts, this is usually not true of every mode. A single-purpose program may have more features or particular features that are lacking in the corresponding mode of the integrated program. A potential user must carefully assess the suitability of a package, checking especially the critical features of the primary applications envisioned.

2. *Difficulty of learning.* Integrated programs tend to be relatively difficult to learn because of their complexity. With so much capability comes a lot to master in order to take full advantage of these capabilities. This can be overwhelming, especially to beginners. Overall, there may actually be less to learn than with comparable separate packages, but it looks overwhelming all gathered together.

3. *Greater memory requirements.* It should be apparent that combining so many functions into one package will necessitate a computer with more memory than otherwise. This poses no great problem for MS–DOS and Macintosh computers, but users may need to expand RAM on machines like the Apple IIe, IIc, and IIgs. It may limit use of complex integrated programs in schools.

4. *Difficulty in selection.* It may be confusing and difficult to find an integrated program that satisfies one's needs. There may be modes within an integrated program that are unlikely to be used, perhaps communications. Of course, one could argue that having this mode included in the package means the user can later expand into this area without new software. A more serious problem is an integrated program that lacks a particular mode that the user needs.

If an integrated program approach is to be taken, the selection of the appropriate package involves many dimensions. All software programs have advantages and disadvantages. In selecting software, whether single-purpose application programs or a multipurpose integrated programs, these strengths and weaknesses as well as alternatives must be taken into consideration.

DESKTOP PUBLISHING

Before turning to educational applications, let's look briefly at a rather different type of program that also integrates functions. In Chapter 3 you learned that some word processors support multiple fonts, producing text variety that, until recently, could only have been typeset. Used with a laser printer, they give very professional-looking results, but are generally limited to just text or simple line drawings. In Chapter 6 you were introduced to classroom publishing programs. These low-cost products offer font control and add graphics libraries and drawing capabilities. They output to dot matrix or laser printers, yielding a neat but less than typeset quality. For more professional results, there is desktop publishing.

WHAT IS DESKTOP PUBLISHING?

The ultimate programs of this type are called desktop publishing (DTP) or page layout programs. Major examples are *PageMaker* and *Ventura Publisher.* Although such programs typically offer integrated text entry and art creation capabilities, their real strength is importing and combining output from other programs to create pages which truly rival professional printing.

Text may be created with your favorite word processor and graphics with a program like *Publisher's Paintbrush.* Scanned images are also widely used, offering unlimited graphics capabilities. The DTP program offers total control to vary text styles, sizes, and fonts, to arrange page content, and to incorporate graphics in the size and location desired. A laser printer then produces output that is

Ventura Scoop

Xerox Shows Off Ventura Publisher at Conference

BEVERLY HILLS (VP) — Xerox Corporation has introduced version 1.1 of its first electronic publishing software product that runs on industry standard personal computers. Xerox chose the Seybold Conference to announce the price and availability of the new revision to the industry standard software package. Conference attendees were impressed by the eighty-one new features, all of which were added without compromising the speed of the product and its depth of functionality.

Product now widely available.

The Xerox Desktop Publishing Software Series: Ventura Publisher Edition is available through Xerox authorized dealers (including ComputerLand, Microage, and Pactel), and the Xerox Business Software Center via (800)-822-8221, and the Xerox general line sales force. Commented one observer, "This breadth of distribution represents Xerox's commitment to the mainstream of the PC-based market."

Ventura Publisher Edition allows personal computer users to merge text and graphics to create publishing-quality documents, such as newsletters, technical manuals, books, bids and proposals, that might otherwise be sent to a print shop or typesetter. The package runs on the Xerox 6065, IBM PC/XT, IBM PC/AT, and other PC compatibles. It supports popular laser printers, including the Xerox 4045, the Apple Laser-Writer and the HP Laser Jet.

Pioneers in the field

"As one of the pioneers in the field of electronic publishing, Xerox fully understands users' requirements for a

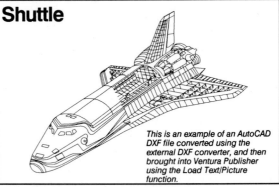

Shuttle

This is an example of an AutoCAD DXF file converted using the external DXF converter, and then brought into Ventura Publisher using the Load Text/Picture function.

Version 1.1 Redefines Desktop Publishing — Again

MORGAN HILL (VP) — Xerox Ventura Publisher Edition version 1.1 has added new meaning to the term "Desktop Publishing." Before the introduction of Ventura Publisher Edition, desktop publishing referred primarily to advanced drawing packages that were extended to handle different text fonts.

These types of packages were characterized by a hand-intensive approach that attempted to mimic what graphic artists and typesetters were used to doing using the personal computer screen as an electronic paste-up board. While this approach was easy for artists to pick up, it did not result in much time-saving because the user was still faced with the drudgery of hand-adjusting each piece of text on the page.

Fortunately, the software developers at Ventura Software Inc. recognized this and adopted a **style sheet** approach. In

Illustration of nozzle produced in AutoCAD. Line-Art can also be brought in from Mentor Graphics EE CAD, DXF compatible CAD packages, Lotus 123, GEM Draw or GEM Graph. Images can be brought in from PC Paintbrush, GEM Paint, MicroTek, Dest, and other scanners.

the same way that a spreadsheet defines the rules for a complex set of repetitive calculations, a Style Sheet defines the rules for complex layout. Once these rules are defined, non-typesetters can quickly achieve typesetter-quality results simply by applying or tagging each paragraph as a Headline, Sub-

This complex page, formatted with Xerox Ventura Publisher, uses many fonts used in combination with graphics. Some printers cannot print everything on this page, e.g. the headline, which is 72 point, will only print on PostScript printers.

FIGURE 7.6 Desktop publishing compares well to professional typesetting and printing.

hard to distinguish from typeset copy. Color laser printers permit full color production right in your office!

With DTP you virtually can become your own publisher. Tasks involving page sizes other than 8-1/2 × 11 may still be better left to professionals who can cut their output to size. There are also issues of binding and speed for large quantities. However, reports, pamphlets, and guide books can easily be produced with DTP. This application has become so popular that it has spawned all manner of support ranging from auxiliary programs to specialized magazines like *Personal Publishing*.

ADVANTAGES AND DISADVANTAGES

The positive side of DTP is that you are in complete control of the process from start to finish. Often products can be completed on very short deadlines compared to those a printing company would require. There is also an increase in flexibility, limited only by the capacity of your software and printer, and your own knowledge of both. Schools with print shops as part of their vocational education program should be teaching desktop publishing today.

The negative side of DTP is also that you are in complete control. To get the most out of such a system, you must learn both the software and hardware thoroughly, not a trivial task. These programs are quite complex. Furthermore, use of DTP software does nothing for one's initial artistic skill or design sense. Part of the professional printer's service is in those areas. Just as giving a typewriter to a monkey is unlikely to produce a new Hemingway, DTP in no way guarantees a quality product, only one that looks professional in its print quality. In addition, true DTP systems are expensive—software runs hundreds of dollars, laser printers with full graphics capabilities are costly, and many systems work best with special page-size monitors. Before buying into DTP, you must weigh cost and benefits carefully.

CLASSROOM APPLICATIONS OF INTEGRATED PROGRAMS

SINGLE-MODE APPLICATIONS

Since an integrated program is essentially a single package made up of various modes, each concerned with the tasks of a single-purpose application program, some educational uses of integrated software parallel the uses of each mode. These have been treated in earlier chapters. Rather than reiterating ideas here, refer to the appropriate chapter for application ideas. While not taking advantage of the unique potential of integrated software, the potential cost effectiveness may suggest use of an integrated package for non-integrated purposes.

☐ Word processing—refer to Chapter 3.
☐ File management—refer to Chapter 4.

□ Spreadsheets—refer to Chapter 5.
□ Graphics—refer to Chapter 6.
□ Telecommunications—refer to Chapters 4 and 6.

INTEGRATED APPLICATIONS AND RESOURCES

The following are some areas where the unique strengths of an integrated program might be useful in an educational setting.

Administration

An integrated program might be useful for particular administrative applications. The concept of setting up one big file (for instance, a class or school student list with appropriate data) and then processing this file in many different ways would allow an administrator to manage effectively many aspects of record reporting as well as possibly to approach the task of achievement management in a more systematic fashion. Presentations to the school board or state agencies might well be more effective with greater use of graphic representations of data. Direct communication of data and reports to state offices is already possible in some states.

Business Education

With a realistic desire to expose business education or office practice students to the most contemporary work methods possible, it may be highly desirable to bring integrated software into these curricula. The business world has adopted integrated software widely.

Science

Weather and Climate Lab from Scholastic is a series of data base and spreadsheet files for *AppleWorks*. Included are units that teach the basic mechanics of *AppleWorks* so prior instruction is not required. The files contain real data collected every three hours for each of two different months by the National Oceanic and Atmospheric Administration. Guided use of the data base files, for example, progresses from the simple "When was it coldest?" to higher-order inquiries such as "What would you have been wearing on this date?" Observations become the basis for generating hypotheses, which can be tested by further querying the files and plotting or graphing data. The set of nine weather experiments involves science concepts of growing difficulty, demanding increasingly sophisticated manipulations of the files. The seven climate experiments are conceptually more difficult. A side benefit of this software is the skill in using *AppleWorks* which will result, including a clear picture of when a data base or a spreadsheet is the appropriate tool.

Strickland (1987) described an excellent elementary science unit using all the capacities of *AppleWorks*. Children did actual field observation near their school, recorded and analyzed the data on flora and fauna with the data base and spreadsheet, and completed integrated writing assignments with the word processor. Similar activities could be planned for many curriculum areas.

Social Studies

The Power of Nation States makes *AppleWorks* a classroom learning tool. Two spreadsheets, three data bases, lesson plans, handouts, and more cover 167 nations of the modern world. Print materials are provided as both hard copy and disk files to encourage users to modify the materials to suit their exact needs. This set is also available for the Macintosh version of Microsoft *Works*. It is the work of three teachers in Eugene, Oregon. Anyone interested in possibly developing such materials will want to read their description of the process (Jagger, Layton, and Veeck, 1988).

Immigrant is a set of middle school social studies materials produced at the Harvard Educational Technology Center (ETC, 337 Gutman Library, Harvard Graduate School of Education, Cambridge, MA 02138) to exploit the potential of integrated software. It utilizes all three modes of *AppleWorks*. The setting is the wave of immigration in the 1840s. Immigrant families are selected from a data base file containing the ship's passenger lists. Other files deal with employment and housing issues. The spreadsheet is used to explore income and expenses over a period of 10 years. Instructions for working through the experiences are provided in word processor files. Aside from the use of *AppleWorks* as a learning tool beyond its own merits, this is an excellent example of materials designed to promote group work among users. *Computers in the Schools* published extensive articles on experiences with *Immigrant* (1988, 5(1/2), pp. 179–211).

Special Education

K-12 MicroMedia Publishing offers *IEPWorks*, a part of the *SchoolWorks* series of *AppleWorks* template files for teachers. An individualized IEP can be developed quickly from these stock formats.

Elementary Education

The winter 1989 issue of *DBKids* describes how a zoo can be a source of inspiration for many types of projects. Children work with the teacher to design a data base, then use reference materials to obtain initial data. Data are expanded, even modified, based on field observations at the zoo. Extended projects include comparing animal sizes with the spreadsheet and writing stories about animals or from the point of view of a zoo animal. Although designed for *AppleWorks*, other integrated packages would work equally well.

Resources

The popularity of *AppleWorks* in schools has led to many resources for teachers. Most of the ideas presented can be adapted to other integrated software, and portions may also be useful ideas for stand alone applications software. Here are some selected examples.

The International Society for Technology in Education is the source for two *AppleWorks* publications. *AppleWorks for Educators—A Beginning and Intermediate Workbook* aims at those needing to learn the software. It includes many integration activities and reprints of articles on tool software from *The Computing Teacher*. *ClassWorks* provides resources for teaching *AppleWorks* to students, including lesson plans, transparency masters, handouts, test materials, and data disks. All may be duplicated for class use and files may be modified as desired.

For grades 7–12, there is *AppleWorks in Your Classroom: A Student Introduction* by David Chesebrough, from J. Weston Walch, Publisher, 321 Valley St., P.O. Box 658, Portland, ME 04104-0658. Claris has released through Scholastic *The AppleWorks Resource Guide for Teachers and Parents,* which includes a directory of sources of ready-to-use templates, actual lesson plans, directions for creating templates, and other useful information.

WorksBox is a complete kit for teachers who wish to introduce Microsoft *Works* into the 7–12 curriculum. MS-DOS and Mac versions each contain a teacher's edition of the respective *Works* student workbook, transparency and handout masters to copy, and a disk of demonstration files. *Worksbox* is available directly from MicroSoft Corporation, Inside Sales, Box 97017, Redmond, WA 98073-9717. For information, call the Microsoft Information Center at 800-426-9400.

Heizer Software offers templates and data files for *Excel* and Microsoft *Works* as well as a series of tutorials on getting the most out of *Works*. Microsoft has encouraged use of *Works* in schools. Beginning in 1988 *Works* was bundled with the IBM PS/2 Model 25, the system aimed at the school market.

Disks of user-developed *AppleWorks* files and templates are available from many sources. Quality may vary, but prices are low, and the inevitable treasures make it worth searching through some marginal items. Naturally, these do not offer the level of documentation support that accompanies commercial *AppleWorks* resources, but that's part of the price difference. Sources include:

CUE Softswap, Box 2087, Menlo Park, CA 94026.
Teachers Idea and Information Exchange, P.O. Box 6229, Lincoln, NE 68506.
Apple Library Users Group, 10381 Bandley Dr., Cupertino, CA 95014.
Resources for AppleWorks, Box 24146, Denver, CO 80224.
The AppleWorks Users Group, c/o Computer C.A.C.H.E., P.O. Box 37313, Denver, CO 80237-7313.
National AppleWorks Users Group, P.O. Box 87453, Canton, MI 48187.

The Works is a monthly newsletter produced during the school year that focuses on educational applications of *AppleWorks*. For information, contact *The Works*, Box 72, Leetsdale, PA 15056.

Strudler (1988) makes a strong case for the value of macros to automate processes in *AppleWorks* and describes using them to make templates, such as for business letters. The article is a good resource if you are ready to get more out of *AppleWorks*.

SUMMARY

Integrated programs are a relatively recent innovation in microcomputer software. They were developed to address two aspects of total software utilization. The first was the problem of using a single file as input/output for more than one program. The second was a desire for the convenience of a single program to perform the functions of many individual application programs.

There is no doubt that the first concern has been efficiently solved by integrated programs. However, software to transform files for compatibility among different programs has also been improved to the point that such an approach is less of a problem than in the past.

As for the second aim of integrated software, a single integrated program can indeed perform the functions of multiple individual applications programs. However, there is considerable debate as to whether programs within an integrated software system are as comprehensive as the most common and popular of their single application counterparts.

Since there are both advantages and disadvantages to the use of single application software as well as integrated software, it remains for the user to decide which approach to take when setting up a total application software environment.

CHAPTER 7 ACTIVITIES

1. If you have access to an integrated program, use this program to develop a report using at least two different functions of your program.
2. Develop a lesson plan for your content area that uses at least two functions of an integrated program. You may need to review application ideas presented in earlier chapters.
3. Integrated packages vary in the number of functions provided, and prices differ considerably. Prepare a comparison report on at least three packages. Printed reviews, publisher's literature from a dealer, software manuals, and/ or "How to Use XYZ" type books are possible resources.
4. If availability were equal, would you choose separate application programs or an integrated package for your personal use? For use with your students? Why?
5. Redo any product of a classroom publisher (Chapter 6) with a desktop publisher. Compare the effort and the result.

REFERENCES

Jagger, A., Layton, T., and Veeck, B. "Making Sense of World Power." *The Computing Teacher*, June 1988, pp. 16–18.

Strickland, A. W. "*AppleWorks* Afield." *The Computing Teacher*, November 1987, pp. 9–11.

Strudler, N. "Adding Macro-Power to *AppleWorks*." *The Computing Teacher*, February 1988, pp. 33–34.

PART 3

The Computer as Tutor

CHAPTER 8

☐ Computer-Assisted Instruction ☐

OBJECTIVES

After completing this chapter, you will be able to:

- ☐ Define computer-assisted instruction. ☐
- ☐ Discuss the historical development of computer-assisted instruction. ☐
- ☐ Identify the principal types of computer-assisted instruction and cite appropriate applications of each. ☐
- ☐ Explain the issues surrounding each type of computer-assisted instruction. ☐
- ☐ Discuss current research findings relating to computer-assisted instruction. ☐
- ☐ Explain the nature of multimedia CAI. ☐
- ☐ Discuss interactive video instruction and its potential. ☐
- ☐ Contrast CAI and ICAI. ☐

The microcomputer is a highly versatile tool. Thus far, we have discussed its potential as a *personal productivity tool*—word processor, spreadsheet, and file management system along with more specialized programs. This chapter presents still another important use—that of an *instructional tutor,* or learning tool. In this chapter, you will examine the nature and evolution of computer-assisted instruction (CAI), the major types of such instructional packages, their primary characteristics, their potential strengths and weaknesses, new directions in CAI, and research findings related to CAI.

THE NATURE OF COMPUTER-ASSISTED INSTRUCTION

Computer-assisted instruction (CAI) is the most common term for what is also known as computer-aided instruction, computer-assisted learning, computer-based instruction, and other combinations of these words. Regardless of label, the concept is that of the computer in a direct instructional role. According to Wright and Forcier (1985, p. 96), "Computer-assisted instruction is a term applied to a learning environment characterized by instructional interaction between computer and student. . . . The teacher . . . sets up the learning environment, ensures that each student has the necessary skills to engage in a particular activity, and adjusts the learning activities according to students' needs."

Alessi and Trollip (1985, p. 60) note that effective instruction requires presenting information, guiding the learner, practice, and assessment of student learning. The use of a computer to provide any combination of these factors may be termed computer-assisted instruction. It should be noted that there is no requirement that the computer provide *all* of these elements. Rather, any combination of them can be appropriate computer intervention in the learning process.

INTERACTIVITY

Interactivity refers to the user engaging in direct and continual two-way communication with the computer, responding to questions and receiving feedback to answers provided. The computer user is an *active participant* in the learning process. The potential for a student merely to observe the learning activity is largely removed in CAI. The interactive capability of the microcomputer offers considerable potential to both the learner and teacher.

FLEXIBILITY

Another appealing aspect of CAI is the flexibility to teach higher thought processes such as problem solving, as well as relatively simple learning usually associated with stimulus-response learning theory. CAI software can be used for instruction directly related to the ongoing curriculum, for enrichment and supplementary instruction, or for remediation.

MEETING STUDENT NEEDS

CAI offers the teaching tool so essential to more effective efforts to meet the learning needs of individual students. We have long known that students do not learn at the same rate. Unfortunately, typical classroom instruction does little to take this into account.

Our schools are not well-equipped to deal with individual differences. Children typically start school at about the same chronological age, advance one grade per year, use similar textbooks, do the same assignments, follow the same curriculum, and are expected to attain essentially the same standards. Furthermore, one teacher with 20 or 30 students per class is seldom able to devote significant attention to just one student at a time. These facts all *minimize* rather than capitalize on individual differences.

The greatest instructional strength of the computer is adaptivity, according to Siegel and Davis (1986, pp. 24–27). With most other formats, there is only one route through the instruction, which never varies in any significant way. A teacher working one-to-one with a student can adapt the instruction continuously based upon learner responses. However, the teacher generally must address the needs of the individual within the context of group instruction. The computer has the potential to provide instruction adapted to the needs of the one current user of the program, which may vary greatly from the needs of the next.

Computer-assisted instruction should, then, contribute significantly to meeting student needs. As Barger (1983) aptly pointed out:

> With the computer, students can pace themselves. They can linger over material that they need more time to absorb or they can speed through material that they quickly understand. In fact with the computer it is possible to branch a student to remedial material or to jump the student ahead to more advanced material on the basis of the student's response. Also, with the computer, students can be allowed choices concerning the format of content within a lesson (p. 109).

For an extensive treatment of computers and student needs, we suggest *Computers and Individualized Learning* by Robbat (undated).

EVOLUTION OF COMPUTER-ASSISTED INSTRUCTION

THE MAINFRAME BASE

The first major instructional application of the computer appears to have occurred in 1950 when MIT scientists designed a flight simulator for training combat pilots. Large and expensive, the simulator conceptually paved the way for future CAI efforts by industry, primarily for staff development and training. Such mainframe efforts were expensive and accessible only to limited numbers of users.

OTHER EARLY INITIATIVES

In 1959, IBM adapted its staff development CAI technology for use with school children in New York State. At approximately the same time, CAI courses in physics and statistics were developed and offered for credit at Florida State University. It was also at this time that the BASIC language was created at Dartmouth College. This was an important development because it provided a rather simple programming language that could be used to develop CAI programs.

In 1960, the PLATO (Programmed Logic for Automatic Teaching Operation) project at the University of Illinois was initiated. Its goal was to demonstrate the technical feasibility, manageability, and economic viability of an extensive computer-based education network. High cost, however, contributed to a somewhat limited acceptance by educational institutions.

At Stanford University, Patrick Suppes and his team developed a small tutorial system in mathematics and language arts primarily for disadvantaged elementary school students. Parallel to this, the Stanford Drill and Practice System was introduced. The fundamental assumption of the drill and practice program was that the teacher would first present basic concepts. The computer system was then used to provide intensive drill and practice at a level of difficulty suitable for each student.

Despite limited accessibility, these pioneering efforts did generate considerable interest in and awareness of the potential of the computer as an instructional tool.

TECHNOLOGICAL GAINS

The potential for CAI grew with significant technological advancements. In 1964, IBM developed a cathode-ray tube appropriate for computer-assisted instruction use and in 1966 marketed the IBM 1500—the first computer system designed expressly for CAI. Late in 1971, INTEL Corporation introduced its "computer on a chip." This laid the groundwork for low-cost, readily accessible microcomputers appropriate for instructional use.

MAJOR RESEARCH AND DEVELOPMENT PROJECTS

At about this same time, the enthusiasm for CAI declined. Cost continued to be a serious deterrent to greater use. Accessibility to a mainframe using terminals was limited. Educational software was scarce and of questionable quality.

In 1971, the National Science Foundation decided to invest some $10 million in two CAI programs: the previously mentioned PLATO project and Time-shared Interactive Computer Controlled Information Television (TICCIT). The aim of TICCIT was to demonstrate in community colleges that computer-assisted instruction could provide better instruction in mathematics and English at less cost than traditional instruction. Intended for adults, TICCIT was based on an educational philosophy called Learner-Controlled Instruction (LCI). LCI stressed the need for students to be able to adapt the sequence of instruction to their own pace and learning style. Furthermore, students were encouraged to control the content by making sequencing decisions at their terminal keyboards (Alessi and Trollip, 1985, p. 48).

MAJOR PROJECT EVALUATION

Both PLATO and TICCIT were evaluated by the Educational Testing Service (ETS). In community colleges using PLATO, positive achievement effects were obtained in mathematics, chemistry, and biology. Attitudes of teachers and students were favorable toward PLATO. In elementary schools, significant math achievement was found at all grade levels involved (4, 5, and 6). Attitudes toward subject matter tended to be more positive in the PLATO group than in a group that received traditional instruction.

The TICCIT system also yielded positive achievement results with community college students, a 10 percent improvement over conventional mathematics classes and, a 5 percent improvement in English. Attitudes toward the subject matter were also positively affected.

The key ingredients were beginning to accumulate—experience with CAI in different settings using different instructional models and new hardware technology, and in 1977, the introduction of successful microcomputers by Radio Shack, Commodore Business Machines, and Apple Computer. Microcomputers made CAI *economically* viable in education.

COMMON TYPES OF CAI

Today, several CAI formats are available. We will consider drill and practice, tutorials, simulations, instructional games, and problem solving. These categories are not necessarily clear-cut. It can be quite difficult to label some pieces of software.

DRILL AND PRACTICE

Drill and practice is the most common and best known form of instructional program. The name appropriately suggests its purpose—to help learners remember and use information they have *previously* been taught. Teachers assign students to use these programs for extensive repetitive work with selected skills or knowledge.

It would be erroneous to assume from this that drills apply only to lower level tasks. While this is often true, drill and practice can also develop skills that are vital to more complex tasks. For instance, work on subword and word recognition is important in the development of reading comprehension. Even what appears to be routine practice on arithmetic facts can be essential preparation for coping with more difficult skills at a later time.

Appropriate Learning Tasks

Essentially, drill and practice activities present a stimulus to the student, elicit a response, and provide immediate reinforcement. One appropriate use of drill and practice programs is when the learning objectives relate to multiple discrimination learning. This type of learning involves, first, perceptually differentiating among events and, second, attaching the proper labels to each of them. Discrimination learning emphasizes the ability to distinguish among members of a set of stimuli and to make an appropriate response to each.

Paired associate tasks are also appropriate for drill and practice. In these tasks, the computer helps to create meaningful links between related items or ideas. Overlearning is the goal, to enable the student to perform a task automatically with very little mental activity. Examples of this type of desired overlearning are addition and multiplication facts, sight vocabulary words, and correct spelling of commonly used words.

Types of Drill and Practice

Let's take arithmetic as a content field to which drill and practice is often applied. Three types of programs may be identified, paralleling the adaptivity concepts of Siegel and Davis (1986).

At the lowest level, a computer program resembles traditional flashcards or programmed instruction. A fixed number of problems is presented to every user of the program. The student who has already mastered the material must perform the same tasks as one who truly needs the experience. Only after completing this can the student move on to the next task.

Slightly better is the program that uses an arbitrary mastery criterion, perhaps ten correct responses in a row. The best students should complete the program in just ten items, while a student needing more practice might require several times that number to achieve the criterion. Upon completion, the student is able to select the next level of drill.

The most highly adaptive program might assume "mastery" after relatively few responses and automatically increase the difficulty level, or even move on to the next topic, say from addition to multiplication. If performance falters, the difficulty is decreased or the student returns to the previous topic. Such continual adjustment seeks to assure mastery throughout, while neither boring the student with needless repetition nor causing frustration by demanding more than the student is capable of.

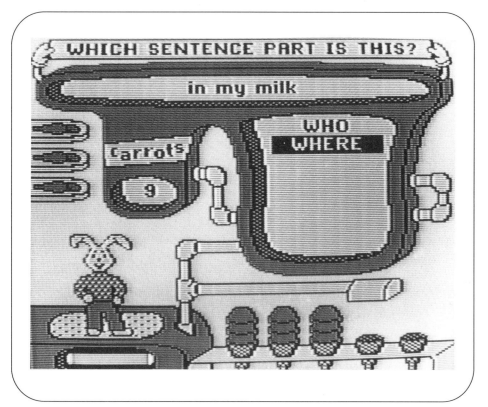

FIGURE 8.1. Drill and practice in language arts

Examples of Drill and Practice

For students of English as a second language, *ESL Picture Grammar* (from Gessler Software) provides practice with potentially troublesome English verb tenses. The program helps the student develop simple sentences by pairing pictures and verbs. The student writes a sentence using the words depicted in the pictures and the suggested verb. As students progress through the 24 levels of the program, sentences become increasingly complex. In addition, the program tests students on content and stores their performance scores, allowing the teacher to check learning progress.

A third grade teacher noticed that several of her students were still having trouble with basic mathematics skills. An arcade game format built motivation for math operations and facts drill in *Math Man*. The student must decide which number and operation sign to pick to match a target number. Correct responses move a construction worker through a network of beams connected by ladders. There are variable difficulty levels, and students race against the clock.

In *All Star Drill* the context is a baseball game. You enter multiple-choice or open-ended questions for the content of your choice. Questions can be printed for study, and the teacher guide includes lesson plans.

The Drill and Practice Debate

Drill and practice programs have attracted considerable criticism. Critics claim that they are often boring, very narrow in their pedagogical approach, drill all students the same way regardless of their ability or level of functioning, interfere with desired remembering, and often provide undesirable negative feedback.

Proponents argue that drill and practice already exists as flash cards and worksheets in most classrooms. Software motivates students better and can effectively reduce the tedium of learning many skills which require extensive practice for retention or speed. Further, traditional approaches usually permit a student to repeat errors, even to the point of learning incorrect material, since feedback is delayed. Alessi and Trollip (1985, p. 158) note the computer's potential to target practice where it is needed most without dwelling on items mastered—something difficult at best with other methods.

In sum, drill and practice is desirable, even essential, but many such programs are the work of individuals who know little about sound learning principles. The problems cited by critics are attributable to specific software, not the idea of computer drill and practice. Admittedly, numerous drill and practice programs are of minimal educational value. Design flaws in such programs can lessen, even negate, the impact of a product which is sound in its basic concept. Collis (1988, p. 70) reports such problems in the widely known *Writing to Read* program. Still, good drill and practice programs are available, with the quality and quantity continuing to improve. Teachers must personally *evaluate* software prior to purchasing it for classroom use. The next chapter will deal with evaluative procedures and criteria.

Characteristics of Good Drill and Practice

Viable drill and practice programs possess certain characteristics. Summarizing a variety of sources, these characteristics typically include:

☐ Appropriate use of graphics, sound, and color.
☐ Use of appealing gaming elements to provide motivation.
☐ Inclusion of tutorial "help" options.
☐ Effective feedback for correct and incorrect responses.
☐ Control over the rate of presentation.
☐ Provision for reviewing directions or previous information.
☐ Random generation of items.
☐ Application of appropriate learning theory and pedagogy.
☐ Presentation of accurate content with correct language.
☐ Ability to stop at will and resume at the same point later.

For in-depth treatment of drill and practice, read Chapter 8 of Alessi and Trollip (1985).

Applicability in the Curriculum

Given the previous descriptions of drill and practice computer-assisted instruction (CAI), it may be apparent that this format is not equally common in all areas of the curriculum. While one can undoubtedly find drill materials for virtually any content, much currently available software is for arithmetic and language arts at the elementary level. Basic arithmetic facts, spelling, and punctuation, for example, are required learning for all students and fit the appropriate learning tasks previously described.

The teacher's task in using drill and practice is to determine that a program is compatible with the curriculum, then to assure that students have adequate preparation to benefit from the program. Drill and practice should not introduce material, but rather provide needed work with already familiar items.

Drill and practice can serve important learning goals. These goals need not focus on greater achievement than those for traditional instruction. Rather, if software is simply "as good," it can free the teacher for other activities and contribute to the total learning situation. How you implement drill software is also important. Govier (1988) found that pairs or groups of students achieved more than individuals, and that drill effectiveness was greatest in the first few weeks of use, then declined. As with any tool, drill and practice software must be used properly.

TUTORIALS

Tutorials are intended to introduce and present new, unfamiliar material to the student. As the name suggests, they are designed to tutor—to instruct. They are often designed for stand-alone learning, for which other computer-assisted instruction forms are unlikely to be suited. As defined by Alessi and Trollip (1985, p. 52), "Tutorial lessons are computer programs that teach by carrying on a dialogue with the student. They present information, ask the student questions, and make decisions based on the student's comprehension whether to move on to new information or to engage in review and remediation."

Types of Tutorials

There are two general types of tutorials: *linear* and *branching*. Many early CAI programs were linear. Linear tutorials typically present the same information to *all students*. Regardless of any differences in their performance, every student must read and respond to every unit of information. The only real potential for individualization using linear programs is that students work through the material at the pace that suits them best. No student receives instruction different from that of all other students.

In branching tutorials, on the other hand, all students *do not* necessarily work through the same material. Alternate paths are taken based upon responses to the tutorial lesson. If, during a pretest or while actually working through the lesson, a student demonstrates mastery of certain segments of the program, the student may be "branched" or move to more appropriate information in the same lesson or even to a new lesson. Sufficient incorrect responses result in branches to remediation segments. In each case, student response determines the material the student will see next. This type of tutorial, while much more difficult and time-consuming to write, is certainly more in keeping with sound learning theory.

Examples of Tutorials

Many tutorials teach the use of a particular software package. Applications like *WordStar* and *WordPerfect* often include tutorial disks. *Learning DOS* tutors users of the MS-DOS operating system. Keyboarding and typing tutors are also popular.

Hartley Courseware offers tutorials in many subjects. For upper elementary students, each lesson in *Verb Usage* teaches one verb which is often misused. Students must choose its correct form to complete a sentence and can put each option into the sentence to "try it" before committing to their answer. *Analogies Tutorial* teaches the user to identify and solve analogies of all types. The program uses simple vocabulary to build a step-by-step problem-solving method for grades 5 and 6. *Understanding Multiplication* begins with dot counting and patterns. Successive addition leads to addition of patterns, and finally multiplication. Errors invoke remediation sequences.

The Tutorial Debate

Critics of tutorial software contend that, as with drill and practice, many of the programs are poorly written and primarily deal with "trivial" concepts. Tutorials are regarded as nothing more than electronic page-turners that force the student into a limited range of possible responses, thus severely restricting meaningful exploration of the concept.

Advocates of the use of tutorials, however, contend that in some cases tutorials might even teach material better than a teacher. Tutorials provide a one-to-one teaching situation and afford learners an opportunity to proceed with the learning task at their own rate. An additional benefit is that learners respond to *every* question—not just a very few—as is the case in typical classroom instruction.

Perhaps the key question that the teacher must consider is whether the tutorial program is designed to accomplish what the teacher *cannot* do as well or better.

Characteristics of Good Tutorials

When choosing a tutorial for classroom use, the following factors, adapted from Bitter and Camuse (1984, pp. 45–46), should be present:

☐ Concepts developed in a sequence that does not confuse the learner.
☐ Employment of acceptable methodology.
☐ Graphics and sound complement instruction.
☐ Valid pretests and posttests.

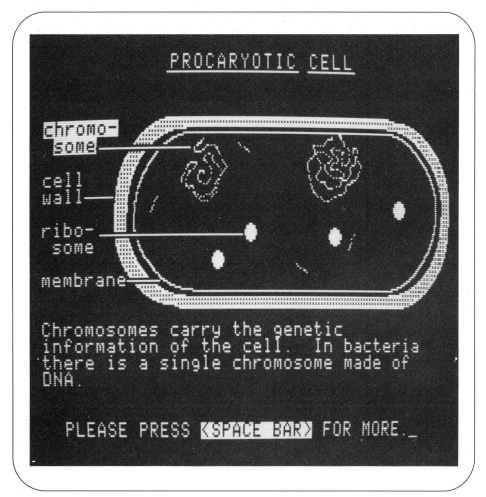

FIGURE 8.2. A tutorial in biology

☐ Tests that actually measure student progress.
☐ Ability to capture and hold the interest of its intended audience.
☐ Student control over the pace of the presentation.
☐ Learner control over frame presentation so that previous material can be reviewed.
☐ And, *ideally*, provision of a way to record student scores automatically so that a teacher can easily access computer records and determine class and individual performance.

Detailed treatment of tutorials may be found in Chapter 7 of Alessi and Trollip (1985).

Applicability in the Curriculum

Tutorial programs have been written for almost all areas of the curriculum and can be used for presenting different types of content, ranging from simple factual information to higher order problem-solving processes. They have been particularly effective in the areas of science and foreign languages, as well as for independent instruction in the use of tool software such as *Lotus 1-2-3*.

Any tutorial being considered for stand-alone classroom use should be carefully checked for congruence with the curriculum and completeness. If the package is inadequate for stand-alone use, the teacher must carefully plan the integration of the package into other learning experiences. According to a review of research by Roblyer (1985), using CAI to supplement the teacher's efforts seems to produce greater effects than seeking to replace the teacher with CAI. Thus, it appears that caution is in order when considering computer-based tutorials as replacement for human instruction.

SIMULATIONS

A simulation is an "analogy of a real situation" with which the learner interacts, (Flake, McClintock, and Turner, 1985, p. 265). Simulations provide students the opportunity to manipulate variables to determine their relationships. Students read or view a scenario, analyze it, make decisions based on the data, and take some course of action based on these decisions. The simulated environment then changes, based upon the student response, creating a new situation with new decisions to make. This type of activity continues until some predetermined solution is attained, the student runs out of time or enthusiasm, or until sufficient inappropriate decisions have been made to terminate the activity.

As should readily be seen, simulations are complex. Designers must anticipate every reasonable response and provide for the effect of that response in the simulation model. Simulations are difficult to conceptualize and require considerable programming skill to implement.

Types of Simulations

Alessi and Trollip (1985, pp. 162–171) distinguish four categories of simulations. While useful, the definitions are not mutually exclusive.

Physical simulations relate to some physical object, which the student may "use" or learn about. Appropriate content for such a simulation ranges from aircraft instruments to experiments in the physical sciences, and includes such subjects as the operation of micrometers in industrial education.

Procedural simulations "teach a sequence of actions that constitute a procedure." The situation presented is not an end in itself (e.g., learning about the instruments in an airplane cockpit), but rather a means for developing the skills and activities needed to function in the situation (e.g., flying the aircraft). This category also includes diagnostic simulations, such as those used in medical education.

Situational simulations place the learner in a role within the scenario presented. Rather than explicitly teaching rules or procedures, situational simulations

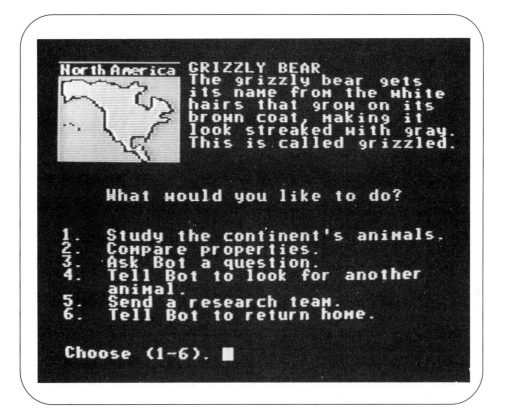

FIGURE 8.3. The user assumes the role of researcher in this simulation.

follow discovery learning principles. The learner explores various responses to a situation and various roles through repetition of the simulation. Other roles in the scenario may be played by the computer or other students.

In *process simulations,* the learner does not play a role, but rather is an external experimenter. Initial decisions are made regarding parameters for one cycle or trial, then the simulation progresses to conclusion without further learner intervention. It is the result of the process that is of primary interest. This form of simulation changes the rate at which the process might occur to one more suited to learning. In the case of economic forecasting or genetic experimentation, time is compressed. In the study of physical phenomena, time may be extended to permit thorough observation of the outcome.

Examples of Simulations

In *Cross-Country California,* students learn state geography by role playing a truck driver who must pick up commodities and deliver them to other locations. Groups can work together to carefully plan routes off-computer, using a map that comes with the package. The goal is to complete the job as quickly and profitably as possible, but without driver fatigue, running out of gas, or losing time due to speeding violations. For a user's view, see *The Computing Teacher*, May 1988, pp. 48–50.

Decisions, Decisions is a simulation series for grades 5–12. Specific titles include *Immigration, Colonization,* and *Television* (media ethics). In *Urbanization,* students begin with a reference book to learn the facts and descriptions of roles they will play. Next they choose priorities relevant to the context. Each of five rounds may take an entire class period and is directly affected by decisions made in the previous round. The teacher is an integral part of the team, serving as a guide and promoting discussion. Teacher support materials are strong and ample. For one user's experience with *Immigration,* see Vlahakis (1987–1988).

Balance of Power is a high-school level geopolitical simulation. In the nuclear age, users assume the role of either the U.S. president or the general secretary of the Soviet Union. Players work to enhance the prestige of their nation while avoiding nuclear war. A unique feature is a 62-nation data base of strategic social, political, historical, and geographic information from which to draw.

Science Literacy: The Lio Project seeks to develop process skills by allowing 6th–9th graders to actually "do" science. A Lio is a one-cell organism which is of economic interest when productive. In a simulated lab, users must determine how to grow their randomly generated Lio to achieve maximum productivity. The task begins with the microscope, then on to a data base for research on similar organisms. Optimal conditions are hypothesized and then applied. Results are observed, hypotheses modified, and so on. The program was developed following the guidelines for science as process of the National Science Teachers Association and the American Association for the Advancement of Science.

In Chapter 4 we introduced the concept of hypermedia. *The Election of 1912* is a *HyperCard* simulation. An initial screen presents ten issues, each a button linked to relevant information. The learner can explore related topics at will. Ultimately, the challenge is to manage Teddy Roosevelt's campaign. Buttons link options and strategy advice. "Bookmarks" allow you to return later to material of possible use. The clock is ticking toward election day all the while. More CAI built from hypermedia seems certain to appear.

The Simulation Debate

Proponents see in simulations considerable promise for teaching problem-solving and decision-making skills for simulations contain the requisite elements: 1) defining the problem, 2) recalling relevant rules previously tried, and 3) regrouping the rules so that a new rule emerges and is learned through appropriate application. They also allow students to explore situations that might be too expensive, too dangerous, too restricted by time problems, or just impossible to attempt in reality.

Simulations provide a nonthreatening learning environment where it is safe for the learner to make an error, to explore complex problems without the fear of being wrong! Students are provided opportunities to make mistakes and safely learn from them. Good simulations are highly motivating to most students because they typically present questions and issues that are truly thought-provoking and not easily answered. Simulations readily evoke higher-order thought processes, including reasoning and logical thinking.

Critics note that when using simulation programs, it is often difficult to assess just what truly has been learned. For example, one popular simulation is *Oregon Trail*, developed by MECC for upper elementary grades. The program simulates a trip from the Midwest to Oregon in a covered wagon. The student makes decisions related to food, ammunition, medicine, clothing, travel, and safety. These decisions affect the survival of the travelers. As part of the simulation, it is sometimes necessary to hunt for food. The animated graphics used in this program are most appealing to children, thus contributing to a decision to hunt even though the situation may not require such action. What have the children learned as a result of this activity?

Another concern is content accuracy. How can one assess the apparent realism of a scenario? What about the accuracy of the model underlying the simulation? Complex mathematical relationships are often involved. Can one be certain of their validity? Teachers need to help students deal with this issue. In terms of desired learning outcomes, perhaps the *process* of working through the simulation is critical, not realism.

Simulations offer many of the best examples available today of applying the power of the computer to the improvement of learning. As with any form of CAI, not every simulation is worth using in the classroom. There will always remain a need to select what one uses with care.

Applicability in the Curriculum

The availability of simulations across the curriculum is uneven. While there are few limits to what the creative software developer might conceive, the greatest concentration is found in the natural and social sciences. It is far more difficult to conceive of scenarios and situations where the content of mathematics or language arts lends itself to simulation activities.

It should also be obvious that simulations require careful background preparation by students for maximum effectiveness. This is not to deny a place for discovery learning, but efficiency of learning will be greater where the basics have first been mastered. What science teacher would consider a pure discovery approach to laboratory experiments? The similarity of simulations and experimentation cannot be overlooked.

Simulations are especially well suited to group work. The McGraw-Hill *Search* series and many products from Tom Snyder Productions were expressly designed for group use in a one-computer classroom. Others can be used readily in this way. Divide the class into teams that must reach consensus on each response. Establish specific tasks for team members to assume, such as recording decisions and their outcomes, researching the next decision, and so on. Class use of a simulation may be greatly enhanced with large-screen projection so that students need not try to follow the activity on a small monitor. Both data projectors and

LCD panels for the overhead projector are well within school budgets today. Woodward, Carnine, and Gersten (1988) offer insights from their research on effective implementation strategies for group simulations.

To help in determining what has been learned as a result of a simulation activity, it may prove extremely beneficial to have teacher-directed "debriefings" after completion of the simulation. The teacher can help the group to focus on the desired learning outcomes and determine what in the simulation "worked" and what did not. Other questions to pose include: What might have been the situation in real life? How might that have differed from the simulated experience?

INSTRUCTIONAL GAMES

Instructional games present content in a game format. The content and the game are integrated and inseparable, in contrast to a game that is a reward for performance within another form of CAI (such as a drill). In the latter, the game may be quite unrelated to the content, serving solely a motivational purpose. Instructional games have been designed to help teach or reinforce a wide range of instructional objectives.

Game Characteristics

Instructional games typically are governed by a clear set of rules, are competitive, and have a winner and a loser at the end. They are designed to be entertaining and make use of the computer's color, sound, and graphics capabilities to capture and hold the student's interest.

In his study of children and their preferences regarding computer games, Malone (1981) reported three characteristics of intrinsically motivating environments: challenge, curiosity, and fantasy. In instructional games, there typically is a goal to achieve (challenge). The player anticipates what will happen (curiosity), but these anticipations are not always fulfilled since chance plays a role. Games rely heavily upon creative mental imagery on the part of the participant (fantasy).

Types of Instructional Games

Instructional games fall into one of two categories on each of two dimensions. First, they may be derived from games already well known in other formats, e.g., hangman, or they may be new creations for the computer. The second dimension is the nature of the competition involved. In some games, individual players complete against themselves, a time limit, or the computer. In others, players complete against each other, or even as teams.

Examples of Instructional Games

Hangman is one of the most ubiquitous of paper and pencil games and has been adapted to the computer in a wide range of subjects. Content is integrated

FIGURE 8.4. United States geography—taught by a mystery game.

with the game in that the player must correctly guess a letter contained in the "secret" word or have a piece added to the "victim." Objections have been raised against hangman games for their inherently morbid theme.

A particularly interesting variation on the hangman theme is found in the program *Raise the Flags*, a language arts game for young children. In place of the traditional blanks to indicate each letter of the word to be guessed, this version displays an empty flagpole for each letter. Beneath the poles, the alphabet is displayed on graphic alphabet blocks. After the player guesses a letter, a small character moves over the correct block and shakes its head yes or no, depending on whether the word contains that letter. If the guess is correct, the block is moved under the appropriate pole(s) and becomes a flag, which then moves to the top of the pole. If the entire word is guessed in the number of tries allowed, the flags then appear to flutter in a breeze and a tune is played.

Geography is the content of *Where in the USA Is Carmen San Diego?* The challenge is to find and stop the criminal Carmen and her gang using reference tools to decipher clues. This popular series includes versions for Europe and the world. *Where in Time Is Carmen San Diego?* treats history.

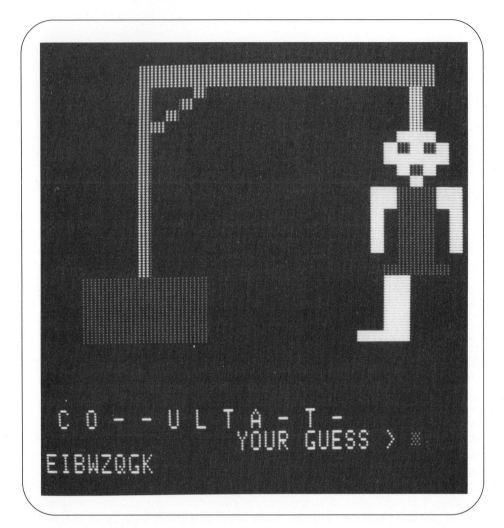

FIGURE 8.5. A typical hangman game

The Game Debate

Proponents of instructional games stress that they provide yet another instructional strategy for the teacher that has been a proven motivator. They have the flexibility to be used effectively with simple drill and practice type activities or may be designed to foster higher-level cognitive processes such as analyzing relationships or synthesizing previous learning when faced with new situations. Such analysis and synthesis can greatly enhance retention of learning.

Opponents focus on the potential for abuse that exists when games are permitted in the classroom. While learning is the desired outcome, play may become the dominant goal for the student. This is especially true in situations where the game is a reward, rather than the essence of the activity, although

FIGURE 8.6. An adaptation of hangman called *Raise the Flags*

we do not classify such programs as instructional games. Clearly, any game should be carefully scrutinized for its likely educational value prior to using it in the classroom.

PROBLEM SOLVING

Problem-solving programs are the final type of CAI. Using this type of software, the student faces a problem and attempts to solve it. Much like a simulation, the emphasis is on higher-level cognitive processes such as reasoning and logical and critical thinking—terms that are used more or less synonymously to refer to a wide variety of complex intellectual processes.

Problem Solving as Procedure

Various writers have defined the steps involved in problem solving, and although there is not complete agreement among them, their descriptions do have elements in common.

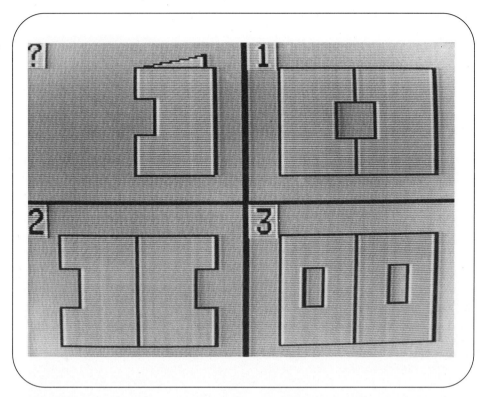

FIGURE 8.7. Problem-solving software aims at higher-order thinking skills.

First is a *motive* or *recognition phase*, where the student senses a problem and the need to do something about it. Second is a *planning stage*, where the individual considers different possible solutions. The third, or *work stage*, consists of gathering as much information about the potential solutions as possible. Finally, in the *action phase* the individual selects one possible solution and actually tries it to satisfy the motive that appeared in the first phase. Note that the process does not always follow a neat, sequential order, but rather steps which may interact at the same time.

Problem Solving as Principles

In opposition to this *procedural* definition of problem solving are those who argue for a *principles* definition. They contend that a process as complex as problem solving cannot be neatly categorized into one set of steps appropriate to all problems. Rather, a core of *principles* will have general applicability and serve as a base from which to depart when meeting unresolved problems.

Role of Motivation

Regardless of which definition one embraces, central to the whole problem-solving process, as in most learning tasks, is the student's motivation. Motivation is an essential element in instruction. Motivation enhances persistence on the part of the learner and contributes to acquisition of essential background, both of which facilitate problem solving. Problem-solving software effectively couples color, sound, and graphics with a high degree of interactivity to create a motivating environment.

Examples of Problem-Solving Software

One highly regarded source of problem-solving software is Sunburst Communications. Let's consider two of their award-winning packages.

The Incredible Laboratory places the learner in a science lab, creating monsters. To a bubbling beaker may be added "chemicals" such as alien oil, yellow rind, slimy rocks, blue goo, and purple links. Each chemical produces a different part of the monster, but all are added to the beaker at once, after which the monster appears in complete form. Five body parts have six variations each. The task is to determine which chemical causes which variation in which body part. At higher difficulty levels, the effects of a chemical change with each run of the program.

The package offers successively more difficult tasks at each of three levels of play. In play mode, students form and test hypotheses to determine the effects of the chemicals. In challenge mode, players alternately add to a beaker chemicals that each hopes the other has not explored. Three monsters appear, only one of which is the product of the chemicals specified. The goal is to guess which monster was the result of their combined choices.

In *The Factory*, students work with squares representing products and three types of machines that perform different operations on them. One punches holes, another rotates the product, and the third paints stripes on it. In one option, students try out the machines to observe their effects on a product. In the second phase, students can combine up to eight machines into an assembly line. Once completed, this factory will produce the product as specified. Other students may be challenged to view a finished product and attempt to reproduce it. Finally, the computer displays a product. Students are challenged on three levels of difficulty to recreate the series of machines and operations required to produce the product.

The Problem-Solving Debate

Problem-solving software exists in significant quantity and variety. As Kinzer, Sherwood, and Bransford (1986, p. 147) note, "The value of improving problem-solving abilities seems clear; we have never met anyone who argued that these abilities are unimportant." You also realize that concern over actual student ability in this area figures prominently in many critiques of American education and in the education reform movement. While certainly no cure-all, problem-solving software appears to many to offer considerable promise.

Advocates of problem-solving software echo the sentiments of Gress (1981), who wrote: "The most significant change in the curriculum of the next ten or twenty years will be to place great emphasis on realistic, non-routine problem solving. . . . In any discipline, the intellectual needs of our time, in light of our technological capabilities, mean developing problem-solving skills" (p. 41).

Critics question whether problem-solving software can deliver on its promise. They note that it is rarely curriculum-specific, leading to difficulties in determining where it fits in. There are also concerns as to whether skills of this sort can be taught in a generalized way that then will transfer to other settings. Is it possible that this whole issue is no more than the current version of the old "mental discipline" justification for teaching Latin?

Characteristics of Problem-Solving Software

Most problem-solving programs are not curriculum-specific. They do not teach specific content as do drill or tutorial programs. While they may have the elements of competition characteristic of instructional games, they may also ignore them. Emphasis is *not* on winning the game but rather on solving the challenge. In that respect, they resemble some simulations but lack the direct tie to the curriculum. *The Incredible Laboratory* is not a science simulation, because it does not deal with actual science content.

As with simulations, you can stress cooperation using these programs by having groups of students work together to arrive at a mutually agreed-upon solution. Our description of *The Factory* explained how one student can develop a product and then challenge others. This need not be an individual challenge; classmates could work together in an attempt to replicate the product. Problem-solving software should be of interest to those concerned that using computer materials individually may decrease student interaction.

An extensive project to develop problem-solving material was undertaken in Rochester, Minnesota. One outcome of this work was a paradigm of problem-solving skills with four categories: memory, cognitive skills, control strategies, and creativity. The memory category includes such elements as sequence, auditory and mnemonic aids, and regrouping. Cognitive skills involve discrimination, attributes, and rules. Among cognitive control strategies are successive scanning, brainstorming, and information gathering. The elements of creativity are fluency, flexibility, originality, and elaboration. Problem-solving software from Sunburst Communications is keyed to specific skills in this paradigm. It offers a useful approach to characterizing problem-solving software.

Applicability in the Curriculum

With the other types of CAI materials, curriculum fit has posed no fundamental problem. The relevant content area is usually obvious. However, problem-solving software is seldom tied to a curriculum area. We have encountered numerous teachers enthusiastic about the prospects but uncertain about implementation. There is no easy answer, but some general observations may help.

The four categories in the paradigm described above imply a sequence in the development of problem-solving skills. Memory is fundamental to learning cognitive skills, which precede control strategies. Creativity depends on the previous three. From this it follows that a decision to emphasize problem solving in a school will necessarily cross grade levels and content areas. These skills do not develop quickly, nor are they limited to one field. To the extent that they can be taught, the task will need to be undertaken on a broad scale throughout the school. The potential from using such software only in fourth-grade language arts cannot be expected to compare to an all-school effort. A school-wide commitment to the task is needed with appropriate cooperative efforts among teachers. A scope and sequence should be developed.

If this is not possible, then individual teachers need to determine their own willingness and ability to incorporate problem-solving software into their teaching. We do not believe this is wasted effort, but it clearly lacks the potential impact of an integrated approach.

NEW CAI DIRECTIONS

MULTIMEDIA CAI

Colvin (1989) identifies linking computer software with other media as one of three major trends in educational software design. Such *multimedia* CAI products are worthy of special consideration. They can heighten interest through variety and may also be more effective through their appeal to additional learning modalities. Any CAI format could be part of such a package. We'll describe a few.

The Voyage of the Mimi is based on a research expedition to study humpback whales off New England. The package contains 26 fifteen-minute video segments—13 adventures of the research party and 13 documentaries of visits to scientists at work. Four software modules deal with ecosystems, maps and navigation, whales and their environment, and basics of computing. There is an overview guide for teachers, teacher and student guides, and even a *Mimi* newsletter for users. Through it all students learn an integrated set of math, science, social studies, and language arts concepts. *Voyage of the Mimi II* is set in Mexico and uses Mayan civilization as its context.

Adventures with Charts and Graphs: Project Zoo for grades 3–5 is three programs, a correlated sound filmstrip, student books, teacher guide with copiable activity sheets, and even library cards. In *Zoo Goer,* students visit a zoo and collect data while learning the basics of charts and graphs. In *Zoo Collector,* they deduce the identities of animals using information in graphs or charts. *Zoo Builder* provides a chance to design a zoo to meet the needs of animals. *The Golden Spike: Building America's First Transcontinental Railroad,* for grades 5–9, includes the same multimedia components. This package requires group work and cooperation, and is well-suited to whole class participation, even if only one computer is available.

Multimedia packages may bring a new level of excitement to the classroom, a recognition of a symbiotic relationship between the computer and other more established media for learning. By combining available resources, teachers should come closer to achieving an optimal learning strategy (Barker, 1989). According to John Scully, CEO of Apple Computer, multimedia learning environments are "tools of a near tomorrow and, like the printing press, they will empower individuals, unlock worlds of knowledge, and forge a new community of ideas" (Ambron and Hooper, 1988, p. 9).

INTERACTIVE VIDEO

Though clearly included within multimedia, interactive video instruction built around laser discs warrants separate attention as the ultimate multimedia tool. Phillipo ("An Educator's Guide," 1988) termed the growth of educational videodiscs "explosive." Military and corporate training applications abound. Still, with the exception of New Hampshire, no state claimed usage in more than 10 percent of its schools in 1988 (Bruder, 1988). Is this technology truly significant for schools?

The impact of television on children has been enormous and its influence discussed for years. The VCR is probably the most ubiquitous device in schools today. Who doesn't enjoy presentations in full color with sound and photographic quality? The VCR has brought them into our homes and schools as never before. Video's key attraction is probably realism.

The power of imagery is clear to software designers as well, as the abundance of graphics in programs shows. Yet, there is a vast difference between photographs and graphics in educational software. Animated graphics usually seem crude compared to animated films, much less a movie. If graphics are valuable parts of learning software now, how much more might real images offer? With videodiscs, we can determine the answer.

Characteristics

Interactive video instruction (IVI) typically uses 12" optical or laser discs as the video medium. A single disc contains 54,000 individual frames, each of which may be a unique image. Unlike videotape, you can display on your screen any single frame for any length of time without damage to the player or wear to the disc. Further, the player can locate and display any single frame at random in just a few seconds. It's a totally flexible "video slide projector." In motion mode, a disc offers about 30 minutes of normal playing time, as well as slow motion. Educational discs often contain a mixture of still and motion segments. Producers can use the dual sound track capability to offer bilingual instruction.

Unlike videotape, videodisc is largely a playback medium. Do-it-yourself recording is not yet economically viable for most users. Production of original discs is costly, although once created, copies are inexpensive.

IVI is described by levels of interactivity. Level one requires only the least-expensive videodisc player. All of the instruction is contained on the disc, much necessarily in motion segments. It is organized in "chapters" which can be accessed randomly from a remote control or built-in keypad. Typically, a motion segment plays, the disc halts on a still image of a multiple choice question, the user keys in an answer, and the player jumps to a segment designed for that response.

Level two IVI is uncommon. The videodisc player must contain a microprocessor and RAM. A level two videodisc stores an instructional program in addition to the video and audio segments. The program loads into the player's RAM and controls the instruction as it executes. The lesson cannot be modified.

Far more versatile is level three IVI in which the videodisc player is connected to and under the control of an external microcomputer. Now all standard CAI approaches can be enhanced with real video and sound. Computer text and graphics may even be superimposed on video images on the same screen. Many level three products employ alternative input devices, especially touch screens, to reduce or remove any difficulties in using the system. See Phillipo ("Videodisc Players", 1988) for more on levels of interactivity.

What educational benefits does one get from IVI? Essentially, all those of CAI with the addition of photo quality images, still or motion, and natural sound with alternate tracks. IVI is an instructional designer's dream come true. The ability to randomly find and display still or motion segments makes videodisc unique. Videotape is a linear medium, but good instruction is not. CAI offers a form of non-linear instruction which IVI pushes closer to the limit. Seal-Wanner (1988) provides an excellent discussion of the potential of IVI.

Applications

Assume that you teach art. How do you expose students to great works of art? Hardly by computer graphics of the Mona Lisa! Rather, extensive slide collections are common. One videodisc holds more than 600 standard slide trays, in the space of one LP. How long would it take to locate one slide in those trays? With a disc, it's only seconds. You can tour the National Gallery of Art and view over 1500 of its treasures with just one disc.

Do you teach German? You may already use foreign language films, but media materials on a beginning language level are scarce. With a videodisc, a visit to Berlin becomes an interactive experience for students. They see a video segment with simplified sound track. At a pause, the computer probes their understanding of what they have just seen. New video segments fit their responses, graphically confirming or contradicting their comprehension. As skill develops, the same video segments are played with a more difficult sound track. When ready for a new site, the user chooses the destination and is whisked there instantly. If the user's language skill is faulty, the arrival location may come as a surprise.

IVI offers sophisticated simulations. Although not particularly educational, you can "play" the great golf courses of the world on videodisc. At each hole, you choose the club and power of the swing. You then see "your shot" and play from there. In science, experiments become possible as never before, including visual portrayal of the outcome of errors. Discovery learning is feasible in chemistry, physics, even driver education.

Resources

What is actually available? *The Videodisc Compendium* (Emerging Technology Consultants, Inc., Box 12444, St. Paul, MN 55112) lists hundreds of existing instructional videodiscs. Science discs range from National Geographic productions on animals and exotic places to episodes from the Nova series to collections of footage and stills from the 20-year travels of the Voyager space craft. There are discs of archival images from aviation history, U.S. history since 1945, and the Statue of Liberty. You can view the growth of the Civil Rights movement and see Martin Luther King's famous "I Have a Dream" speech. All this with inexpensive videodiscs any school can own. Optical Data Corporation created *The Living Textbook,* a visual library of 400 movie clips and 25,000 slides for earth, life, and physical science education. *HyperCard* stacks control some of their products, as well as some from the Voyager Company. CEL Educational Resources is producer of the *Video Encyclopedia of the 20th Century,* a truly unique medium for many parts of the curriculum. Sherwood et al. (1987) even suggest ways to use the disc version of *Raiders of the Lost Ark* as an instructional tool. Such use is known as "repurposing" a disc created for some other purpose.

There are also complete instructional packages which contain both discs and integrated CAI. Biology is the content of the series *Community of Living Things* from SYSCON. Systems Impact offers the *Core Concepts* series in mathematics, including lessons on fractions, ratios, decimals, and percents. Jegi (1987) describes these materials. MECC's emerging technologies group has branched into IVI with *Trigland, Introduction to Economics,* and *Improving Teacher Effectiveness.*

We first saw IVI in 1980. The potential was obvious, and the predictions for an educational revolution were abundant. That revolution has, at best, been slow to take off. Is IVI just another fad embraced by only a few? We think not, although compact disc (CD) may be the final format. As this chapter's reference list demonstrates, IVI has become a common subject in educational publications. A videodisc player suitable for level III costs less than a 16mm projector or most microcomputers. The computers are in the schools now. Excellent discs are available and some complete IVI can be purchased. Disc players are appearing in the schools; critical mass is on the horizon. The microcomputer itself took several years to catch on after becoming viable. Now IVI is reaching the same point. See Appendix D for sources of videodiscs and related products.

INTELLIGENT CAI

Although criticism of CAI has many roots, often it reduces to a desire for materials that are less directly descended from programmed instruction. Until the computer can much more closely resemble a human instructor, some see its power as severely limited. The answer may be intelligent computer-assisted instruction (ICAI).

Knezek (1988) defines ICAI as any program using artificial intelligence techniques to help the user learn. Artificial intelligence (AI) is that branch of computer science concerned with making machines capable of functions which, in humans, require intelligence. These machines would think, reason, and learn from their experiences. Skinner's programmed instruction presaged drill and tutorial CAI. Bruner and Piaget were spiritual fathers of "microworlds" and Logo. AI and information processing theory give us ICAI.

ICAI has several types, of which intelligent tutoring systems (ITS) are of broadest potential for education. An ITS engages the learner in dialogue to identify misconceptions, then remediates to correct them. Rambally (1986) describes an ITS based on modules. The expertise module contains the lesson content, the system's knowledge. It must be able to explain each decision that the system makes. A tutor module contains a repertoire of methodologies for bringing users closer to the ideal represented by the expertise module. The student module tracks student performance, including types of errors and misconceptions. It is that subset of expertise which the student has mastered. In theory, an ITS knows what to teach, to whom, when, and how. It is not constrained by the responses programmed into it, but rather can tailor content and method to the user. When a student errs, rather than just repeating the same presentation as typical tutorials do, an ITS would analyze the cause of the error and remediate accordingly.

Practical applications which truly exemplify ICAI concepts are rare. Rambally (1986) and Kearsley (1987) describe such early systems as *SCHOLAR*, which taught South American geography, *SOPHIE* (electronic troubleshooting), and *BUGGY* (misconceptions in arithmetic). Major constraints on ITS research and development activity include the level of computer power required and the very real limits of our understanding of human learning which make error assessment difficult and imperfect. For example, Martinak, Schneider, and Sleeman (reported in Collis, 1987–88) created an ICAI system to diagnose algebra errors. In a study with ninth and tenth graders the software only anticipated 30 percent of the errors, despite enormous effort in system development.

In addition, development time for ICAI is very great, taking possibly 1000–2000 hours per hour of student material, some ten times that of regular CAI. Knezek (1988) lists over 20 ICAI packages, mostly in science, mathematics, or computer science. He notes that most are not "fully functional." The expertise modules are normally solid, the student module less well-developed, and the tutor module weak, even simple-minded. Capturing expertise is fairly straightforward, tracking performance is feasible, but analyzing it and applying an ideal remediation strategy is much more difficult.

ICAI is easy to appreciate as a theoretical goal. If one believes the claims, progress in artificial intelligence is gaining speed. Software producers already proclaim the presence of AI techniques in products like *RightWriter* (document proofer, writing analyst) and *Mavis Beacon Teaches Typing* (typing tutor). Users of such products may well marvel at their capability. We hesitate, nonetheless, to predict the arrival date of ICAI as it is ultimately envisioned—the learner's personal Socrates.

WHAT THE RESEARCH SHOWS

Computer-assisted instruction has been in use for approximately 30 years. Research findings have become increasingly available and are beginning to show some consistent patterns. However, findings are particularly inconsistent regarding content areas for which CAI has typically been most beneficial.

ACHIEVEMENT

Bracey (1982) cited studies conducted by Educational Testing Service (ETS) over a four-year span with elementary school students. ETS concluded that CAI was an effective learning tool on a long-term as well as a short-term basis. In mathematics, for instance, children who had access to the computer for only ten minutes daily scored significantly higher than those children who did not have any access to the computer. In other curricular areas such as reading and language arts, smaller positive gains were recorded favoring those students taught with the computer.

Somewhat comparable results were obtained by Fisher (1983). His studies showed that student gains were highest in science and foreign languages, followed by mathematics, then reading and language arts. Other studies (Alderman, 1979; Burns and Bozeman, 1981; Magidson, 1978; Splittgerber, 1979; Kulik, Bangert, and Williams, 1983) indicate that the use of CAI either improves learning or shows no significant difference when compared to more traditional classroom approaches.

Goode (1988) reported that fifth and sixth grade students who used CAI in their mathematics instruction scored significantly higher than comparable control groups in both computation and concepts. CAI appeared to have a greater effect on the fifth grade students, however, than on the sixth graders.

In a 1985 overall assessment of the research, Roblyer (1985, p. 20) concluded that "computer-based instruction achieves consistently higher effects than other instructional treatments to which it is compared in experimental situations, but the effects usually range from small to moderate in magnitude." She further noted that the greatest effects appeared to occur at the elementary grade levels, with achievement decreasing as grade level increased. Finally, effects were not uniform across all curricular areas, with mathematics typically benefiting more and reading/language arts less. She did note, however, that newer studies seemed to be yielding greater effects and that much research remained to be done.

More recently, Roblyer, Castine, and King (1988) conducted a meta-analysis of studies dated from 1980 on. Of the content areas reviewed, CAI appeared to have the greatest effect in science. The authors cautioned, however, that this finding was based on only a few studies and must be interpreted cautiously. Consistent with previous findings, mathematics skill learning appeared to profit most from CAI while reading skills continued to profit least. In the area of science, the authors reported that the most effective type of application was simulations for unstructured work. When CAI applications were used for drill in science, much lower effects were determined. In reading, tutorial applications achieved higher effects than any other type while all applications for mathematics were found to be about equally effective.

Findings pertaining to science were supported by Glenn (1988). He reported significant gains in Grades 3–6 after using the WICAT integrated learning system. Results in reading, however, were the most surprising as they showed the greatest increase—as large as two full grade equivalents in Grades 4 and 5. This last finding is particularly surprising since previous research has been quite consistent in finding little effect from the use of CAI in reading and the language arts.

EFFECTIVENESS BY LEVEL OF INSTRUCTION

Kulik, Bangert, and Williams (1983) found that computer-based instructional methods were generally more effective at the elementary grade levels. This finding was contradicted by Roblyer, Castine, and King (1988), who found that while the elementary school level profited more than did the secondary school level, the highest results were obtained at the college/adult level. A word of caution was offered by the authors when they stated "There were only half as many studies at the college level as at the secondary level, and only a quarter of the number for the elementary level. Still the results indicate that, indeed, computer applications can be successful at higher levels, and may be even more effective than at lower levels" (p. 122).

LEARNING RETENTION AND TIME

In addition to positive achievement gains, Kulik et al. (1983) found that CAI improved retention of learning. They reported that four of five studies investigating retention over a period of from two to six months showed greater retention by those students who used CAI. These differences were not, however, large enough to be statistically significant. Roblyer (1985, p. 24) concluded that "data lend little support to the belief that computer-based instruction enhances retention."

CAI has been helpful in decreasing the *time* in which students learn material. Blaschke and Sweeney (1977) compared a simulation application of CAI in Army electronics training with a similar type program in secondary education. They reported a 10 percent reduction in electronics training time resulting from the use of CAI. Dence (1980) cited several studies that suggest students using CAI take less time to learn than do students receiving traditional instruction. Fisher (1983) reported that students successfully completed learning assignments on the computer as much as 40 percent faster than they did when not using the computer. In a study conducted by Lunetta (1972), students reportedly spent 90 minutes on instruction and study when using computers and 745 minutes when taught in the conventional mode. This represents an 88 percent savings in time.

ATTITUDES

In addition to examination of the effects of CAI upon cognitive growth, attention has been directed at its impact upon affective outcomes. Bracey (1984) reported that students react favorably to the use of the computer for instructional purposes. He further noted that students who have worked on computers establish a more positive attitude toward computers than those who have not used computers. One reason given for this is the ability provided by the computer for students to move at their own pace. Perhaps of even greater significance, the computer appears more patient and less likely to be punitive for errors than the teacher.

Kulik et al. (1983) reviewed ten studies related to student attitudes toward subject matter after using CAI. In eight of those studies, student attitudes were more positive in the CAI classrooms. In only three of the studies, however, were the results large enough to be statistically significant. Another four studies reported on student ratings of the quality of instruction received in CAI compared to that received in conventional classes. In each of the four studies, students reacted more favorably toward computer-assisted instruction, but none of the differences were statistically significant.

Attitudes may be positive, but the meta-analysis by Roblyer, Castine, and King (1988) found little evidence to support a belief that good attitudes toward computers result in better attitudes toward school work and academic achievement. While findings were generally positive, the differences were not sufficiently large to support strongly the belief in transfer.

PROBLEM SOLVING

Dudley-Marling and Owston (1988) critically assessed the potential of CAI to teach general thinking and problem-solving skills. The investigators wrote, "In the absence of any significant research literature evaluating the claims of the developers of problem-solving software, the CAI approach . . . can be evaluated only in terms of the general research and theory in problem-solving. Based on this literature, it is highly unlikely that the use of CAI will lead to the development of generalizable problem-solving skills. . . ." They cautioned that this does not mean such software is useless, but rather that there are no simple solutions to developing higher order skills.

Conversely, Yates and Moursund (1988–89) did not claim that research has demonstrated the ability of computers to teach problem solving, but they were able to construct a circumstantial case from research and theory to demonstrate the potential.

PROBLEMS WITH THE RESEARCH

One might expect some relatively definitive results from research on CAI given more than 20 years of experience. This is not, however, exactly true. There are two major problems that trouble many who read existing research.

First, many CAI studies were conducted prior to the availability of microcomputers. While Roblyer (1985) maintained that the similarities in instructional features are great enough to dispel concern, many disagree. Surprisingly few *thorough* studies have been reported based solely on microcomputer environments.

Second is the question of thoroughness or, more broadly, methodology. Roblyer (1985, p. 22) wrote of two 1984 studies, "Descriptions of the study methods do not give sufficient information to determine if methodological flaws are present. And, perhaps because the reports themselves are so brief, the conclusions drawn by the researchers do not always seem supported by the results presented."

In their meta-analysis, Roblyer, Castine, and King (1988) report that of some 200 studies initially reviewed for consideration, 38 studies and 44 dissertations were included in the analysis. The remainder were omitted due to insufficient data or methodological flaws. This is a serious indictment against the quality of research being performed. Our observation is that much of what passes for "research" in CAI is actually anecdotal reports of experiences that in no way resemble experimental research. Clearly, there is a need for more and better research in the outcomes of computer intervention in the instructional process.

SUMMARY

Computer-assisted instruction has been in existence for approximately three decades, but only since the appearance of the microcomputer has CAI become economically feasible to use with large numbers of students. CAI can be used to teach a wide variety of skills and knowledge, ranging from relatively simple stimulus-response learning to complex forms of problem solving.

Typically, drill and practice, tutorials, simulations, instructional games, and problem-solving activities make up CAI software. In the past, drill and practice activities have been the most frequently used. Today, simulations and problem-solving programs are appearing in greater quantity and quality and are finding enthusiastic reception. They are particularly good examples of using the power of the computer and permit instruction previously impractical or impossible.

The potential of CAI is expanding with new approaches. Multimedia CAI links software to more traditional media resources such as filmstrips. Interactive video can enhance CAI with photographic still and motion images—the most sophisticated graphics ever. Artificial intelligence techniques may one day yield a vastly superior "intelligent" CAI.

Research findings suggest that outcomes of computer-assisted instruction depend on many factors and have not been equal at all levels or in all fields, as once widely hoped. Under the right circumstances, CAI has shown positive achievement gains, learning in shorter periods of time than traditional instruction, longer retention of content learned, and a more positive attitude on the part of the student toward the learning process. These results are encouraging and provide support for the use of CAI in our classrooms. Much research is still needed to learn how best to apply the computer to instruction.

The best advice available to those who wish to use CAI in their classrooms is to be cautious about expectations. CAI is not an automatic route to learning; it is not a stand-alone resource. Rather, teachers must devise ways to carefully *integrate* CAI into instruction. Gray (1988) presents concrete ways to enhance learning from CAI. Of critical importance are "debriefing" strategies including role playing, reaction papers, compare and contrast, visual summaries, panel discussions, software evaluation, and non-computer simulation. All are means for integrating computers and instruction. Viewed in this way, as yet another learning tool, CAI can assume a vital role in our schools.

CHAPTER 8 ACTIVITIES

1. For the grade level you teach or plan to teach, select *one* content area such as social studies or science and determine what CAI programs are available in your school. Review them with the intent of determining whether they are drill and practice, tutorials, simulations, games, or problem-solving programs.

2. Review the available drill and practice and tutorial programs using the suggested characteristics of good software presented in this chapter. You may want to set up a data file for each program including such information as name, appropriate grade-level, and strengths and weaknesses of each program.

3. Examine the CAI material available in your school or school district and determine what unit(s) of your curriculum would be most appropriate for the material. You may want to add this information to the files suggested in item 2.

4. Actually try a CAI program with a group of your students. How did it work for the slow learner? How about the gifted child? Discuss the software with the children to determine their feelings about its use. What did *they* see as strengths and weaknesses?

5. Discuss with your students the potential problem of educational game use

in the classroom. Are there ways they see of better ensuring appropriate use as a learning tool as opposed to an entertaining game?

6. Work your way through any available computer simulation. Can you place it into one of the four types presented? How would you rate the simulation for motivation? For entertainment? What would the student minimally have to know before use would be profitable? Design a lesson plan for using a simulation.

7. Examine any available CAI package that claims to teach problem-solving skills. Begin by carefully examining the accompanying documentation. Can you place it within the paradigm presented? Where might the package "fit" in the curriculum? Does the producer encourage use of the package alone, or is there evidence of concern for the total context of problem-solving instruction?

8. How would you envision a school approaching the issue of teaching problem solving? Take and defend a position on the case of individual teacher implementation versus a school-wide plan across levels and areas. Temper idealism with practical concerns.

9. Defend or challenge the view that multimedia CAI offers significant new potential over traditional CAI.

10. Arrange to experience at least one interactive video lesson. What is your personal reaction to it? Research related formats such as CD-I (compact disc interactive) and DVI (digital video interactive).

11. Read more about intelligent CAI and artificial intelligence. What potential do you see in these areas?

REFERENCES

Alderman, D. I. "Evaluation of the TICCIT Computer-Assisted Instruction System in the Community College." *SIGCUE Bulletin*, 13(3), 1979, pp. 5–17.

Alessi, S. M., and Trollip, S. R. *Computer-Based Instruction: Methods and Development.* Englewood Cliffs, NJ: Prentice-Hall, 1985.

Ambron, S., and Hooper, K. *CD Rom 3: Interactive Multimedia.* Redmond, WA: Microsoft Press, 1988.

Barger, R. N. "The Computer as a Humanizing Influence in Ecuation." *T.H.E. Journal,* May 1983, pp. 109–111.

Barker, P. *Multi-Media Computer Assisted Learning.* New York: Nichols Publishing, 1989.

Bitter, G. G., and Camuse, R. A. *Using a Microcomputer in the Classroom.* Reston, VA: Reston Publishing Company, 1984.

Blaschke, C. L., and Sweeney, J. "Implementing Effective Educational Technology: Some Reflections." *Educational Technology,* January 1977, pp. 13–18.

Bracey, G. W. "Issues and Problems in Devising a Research Agenda for Special Education and Technology." Paper presented at Special Education Technology Research and

Development Symposium. Sponsored by U.S. Department of Education, Washington, DC, 1984.

Bracey, G. W. "What the Research Shows." *Electronic Learning*, November/December 1982, pp. 51–54.

Brand, S. *The Media Lab. Inventing the Future at MIT*. New York: Viking, 1987.

Brown, J. S. "Process Versus Product: A Perspective on Tools for Communal and Informal Electronic Learning." *Journal of Educational Computing Research*, 1985, 1(2), pp. 179–202.

Bruder, I. "Electronic Learning's 8th Annual Survey of the States, 1988." *Electronic Learning*, October 1988, pp. 38–45.

Burns, P. K., and Bozeman, W. C. "Computer-Assisted Instruction and Mathematics Achievement: Is There a Relationship?" *Educational Technology*, January 1981, pp. 32–39.

Card, S. K., Moran, T. P., and Newell, A. *Psychology of Human-Computer Interaction*. Hillsdale, NJ: Lawrence Erlbaum Associates, 1983.

Collis, B. "Research Windows." *The Computing Teacher*, December/January 1987–88, p. 6.

Colvin, L. B. "An Overview of U.S. Trends in Educational Software Design." *The Computing Teacher*, February 1989, pp. 24–28.

Crouse-Kemp, S. "Pioneering Computer Graphics in Education." *Video Systems*, November 1988, pp. 30–31.

Davis, B. "Image Learning: Higher Education and Interactive Video Disc." *Teachers College Record*, Spring 1988, 89(3), pp. 352–359.

DeBloois, M. L. *Effectiveness of Interactive Videodisc Training: A Comprehensive Review*, ERIC document ED 278 370.

DeBloois, M. L. *Videodisc-Microcomputer Courseware Design*. Englewood Cliffs, NJ: Educational Technology Publications, 1982.

Dede, C. "Artificial Intelligence Applications to High Technology Training." *Educational Communication and Technology Journal*, Fall 1987, pp. 163–181.

Dede, C. "A Review and Synthesis of Recent Research in Intelligent Computer-Assisted Instruction." *International Journal of Man-Machine Studies*, Vol. 24, 1986, pp. 329–353.

Dede, C., and Swigger, K. "The Evolution of Instructional Design Principles for Intelligent Computer-Assisted Instruction." *Journal of Instructional Development*, 11(1), 1988, pp. 15–22.

Dence, M. "Toward Defining the Role of CAI: A Review." *Educational Technology*, November 1980, pp. 50–54.

Duchastel, P. "Intelligent Computer-Assisted Instruction Systems: The Nature of Learner Control." *Journal of Educational Computing Research*, 2(3), 1986, pp. 379–393.

Dudley-Marling, C., and Owston, R. D. "Using Microcomputers to Teach Problem Solving: A Critical Review." *Educational Technology*, July 1988, pp. 27–33.

Fisher, G. "Where CAI Is Effective: A Summary of the Research." *Electronic Learning*, November/December 1983, pp. 82, 84.

Flake, J. L., McClintock, C. E., and Turner, S. V. *Fundamentals of Computer Education*. Belmont, CA: Wadsworth, 1985.

Glenn, C. "Results of Using CAI to Improve Performance in Basic Skills Areas." *T.H.E. Journal*, June 1988, pp. 61–64.

Goode, M. "Testing CAI Courseware in Fifth- and Sixth-Grade Math." *T.H.E. Journal*, October 1988, pp. 97–100.

Govier, H. "Microcomputers in Primary Education: A Survey of Recent Research." In

Collis, B., "Research Windows." *The Computing Teacher*, December/January 1988–1989, p. 7.

Gray, B. "Enhancing Learning Through Debriefing." *The Computing Teacher*, June 1988, pp. 19–21.

Gress, E. K. "The Future of Computer Education: Invincible Innovation or Transitory Transformation?" *The Computing Teacher*, September 1981, pp. 39–42.

Hajovy, H., and Christensen, D. "Intelligent Computer-Assisted Instruction: The Next Generation." *Educational Technology*, May 1987, pp. 9–14.

Hannafin, M. J. "Empirical Issues in the Study of Computer-Assisted Interactive Video." *Educational Communication and Technology Journal*, 33(4), 1985, pp. 235–247.

Iuppa, N. V. *A Practical Guide to Interactive Video.* White Plains, NY: Knowledge Industry Publications, 1984.

Iuppa, N. V., and Anderson, K. *Advanced Interactive Video Design.* White Plains, NY: Knowledge Industry Publications, 1988.

Jegi, J. "A Math Disc That Offers a New Equation for Learning." *Electronic Learning*, January 1987, pp. 45–46.

Kearsley, G., ed. *Artificial Intelligence and Instruction.* Reading, MA: Addison-Wesley, 1987.

Kinzer, C. K., Sherwood, R. D., and Bransford, J. D. *Computer Strategies for Education.* Columbus, OH: Merrill, 1986.

Knezek, G. A. "Intelligent Tutoring Systems and ICAI." *The Computing Teacher*, March 1988, pp. 11–13.

Kulik, J. A., Bangert, R. L., and Williams, G. W. "Effects of Computer-Based Teaching on Secondary School Students." *Journal of Educational Psychology*, 75(1), 1980, pp. 19–26.

Lambert, S., and Sallis, J. *CD-I and Interactive Videodisc Technology.* Indianapolis: Howard W. Sams & Co., 1987.

Lunetta, V. N. "The Design and Evaluation of a Series of Computer Simulated Experiments for Use in High School Physics." Dissertation, University of Connecticut, 1972. *Dissertation Abstracts International* 33:2785A.

Magidson, E. M. "Trends in Computer-Assisted Instruction." *Educational Technology*, April 1978, pp. 5–63.

Malone, T. W. "Toward a Theory of Intrinsically Motivating Instruction." *Cognitive Science*, Vol. 4, 1981, pp. 333–369.

Manzelli, J. "New Curriculum Soundings on a Voyage of the Mimi." *Computers in the Schools*, Spring 1986, pp. 55–61.

Martin, R. J. "Interactive Video: Easier Than You Think." *The Computing Teacher*, December/January 1987–88, pp. 39–41.

Merrill, M. D. "The Role of Tutorial and Experimental Models in Intelligent Tutoring Systems." *Educational Technology*, July 1988, pp. 7–13.

Merrill, M. D., Schneider, E. W., and Fletcher, K. A. *TICCIT.* Englewood Cliffs, NJ: Educational Technology Publications, 1980.

Nickerson, R. S. "Kinds of Thinking Taught in Current Programs." *Educational Leadership*, 42(1), 1984, pp. 26–36.

Park, O. "Functional Characteristics of Intelligent Computer-Assisted Instruction: Intelligent Features." *Educational Technology*, June 1988, pp. 7–14.

Park, O. and Seidel, R. J. "Conventional CBI Versus Intelligent CAI: Suggestions for the Development of Future Systems." *Educational Technology*, May 1987, pp. 15–20.

Phillipo, J. "An Educator's Guide to Interactive Videodisc Programs." *Electronic Learning,* September 1988, pp. 70–75.

Phillipo, J. "An Educator's Guide to Interfaces and Authoring Systems." *Electronic Learning,* January/February 1989, pp. 42–45.

Phillipo, J. "Videodisc Players: A Multi-Purpose Audiovisual Tool." *Electronic Learning,* November/December 1988, pp. 50–52.

Phillipo, J. "Videodisc Technology and HyperCard: A Combination That Can't Be Beat." *Electronic Learning,* March 1989, pp. 40–41.

Price, R. V., and Frisbie, A. G. "The Videodisc: Past, Present, and Future." *Computers in the Schools,* 1988, 5(1/2), pp. 299–315.

Rambally, G. K. "The AI Approach to CAI." *The Computing Teacher,* April 1986, pp. 39–42.

Reeves, P., and Glyer, S. "Videodisc Applications Bring New Promise to Schools." *T.H.E. Journal,* September 1988, pp. 68–74.

Riedesel, C. A., and Clements, D. H. *Coping with Computers in the Elementary and Middle Schools.* Englewood Cliffs, NJ: Prentice-Hall, 1985.

Robbat, R. J. *Computers and Individualized Learning.* Eugene, OR: International Council for Computers in Education, undated.

Roblyer, M. D. *Measuring the Impact of Computers in Instruction: A Non-Technical Review of Research for Educators.* Washington, DC: Association for Educational Data Systems, 1985.

Roblyer, M. D., Castine, W. H., and King F. J. "Assessing the Impact of Computer Based Instruction: A Review of Recent Research." *Computers in the Schools,* 1988, 5(3/4).

Sales, G. C. "Videodisc Technology: Function and Format." *The Computing Teacher,* February 1989, pp. 34–35, 56. (First of a five-part series.)

Schwartz, E. *The Educator's Handbook to Interactive Video.* Washington, DC: Association for Educational Communications and Technology, 1985.

Schwier, R. (1987). *Interactive Video.* Englewood Cliffs, NJ: Educational Technology Publications.

Seal-Wanner, C. "Interactive Video Systems: Their Promises and Educational Potential." *Teachers College Record,* Spring 1988, 89(3), pp. 373–383.

Sherwood, R. D., Kinzer, C. K., Hasselbring, T. S., Bransford, J. D., Williams, S. M., and Goin, L. I. "New Directions for Videodiscs." *The Computing Teacher,* March 1987, pp. 10–13.

Siegel, M. A., and Davis, D. M. *Understanding Computer-Based Education.* New York: Random House, 1986.

Sleeman, D., and Brown, J. S. *Intelligent Tutoring Systems.* New York: Academic Press, 1982.

Smith, E. E. "Interactive Video: An Examination of Use and Effectiveness." *Journal of Instructional Development,* 10(2), 1987, pp. 2–10.

Splittgerber, F. L. "Computer Based Instruction: A Revolution in the Making?" *Educational Technology,* January 1979, pp. 20–26.

Van Dam, A. "Computer Software for Graphics." *Scientific American,* 1984, 251, pp. 146–161.

Vlahakis, R. "Immigration." *The Computing Teacher,* December/January 1987–88, pp. 26–29.

Woodward, J., Carnine, D., and Gersten, R. "Teaching Problem Solving Through Computer Simulation." *American Educational Research Journal,* 25(1), 1988, pp. 72–86.

Wright, E. B., and Forcier, R. C. *The Computer: A Tool for the Teacher*. Belmont, CA: Wadsworth, 1985.

Yates, B. C., and Moursund, D. "The Computer and Problem Solving: How Theory Can Support Classroom Practice." *The Computing Teacher*, December/January 1988–89, pp. 12–16.

Yazdani, M. "Intelligent Tutoring Systems Survey." *Artificial Intelligence Review*, Vol. 1, 1986, pp. 43–52.

CHAPTER 9

□ Courseware Evaluation □

OBJECTIVES

After completing this chapter, you will be able to:

□ Discuss the issue of courseware quality and suggest possible reasons why complaints about quality have been so common. □
□ Explain why educators need to evaluate courseware for classroom use and who should be involved. □
□ Describe three approaches to courseware evaluation, listing advantages and disadvantages of each. □
□ Select five general evaluation criteria that you believe are most critical and defend your choices. □
□ Select at least four evaluation criteria unique to computer courseware that you find most crucial and defend your position. □
□ Discuss which usability criteria are most significant to you. □
□ List and briefly explain Gagné's nine events of instruction and describe their applicability to computer courseware. □
□ Devise one or more courseware evaluation forms incorporating your most vital criteria. □

Now that you are familiar with the types of computer software for learning, we can turn our attention to evaluating and selecting software for classroom use. This chapter refers to computer packages as *courseware*, a term often used to acknowledge that most materials consist of more than just a diskette. Programs on a diskette are properly called software, but support materials such as documentation, teacher guides, and student manuals are also important.

In this chapter, we will first look at the issue of quality in computer materials. Next, we turn to the need for evaluation and suggest an approach to it. Specific evaluation criteria are examined in several categories—general criteria applicable to all educational materials, criteria unique to computer materials, and factors that make one package more "usable" than another. Finally, we treat the matter of using forms as a basis for courseware evaluation.

THE ISSUE OF QUALITY

The rapid acquisition of computers by schools is well known. Daily newspapers and weekly news periodicals inform us regularly of the latest figures on school computer purchases, figures that change so rapidly as to be outdated in any book. Suffice it to say that for several years now the number of computers in schools has about doubled annually. Bork (1984) noted wryly that "much of this increase . . . occurred when almost no interesting learning materials were available to use with these computers!" (p. 93).

SOFTWARE—THE CRITICAL ELEMENT

Except for programming, to be discussed in the next section of this book, hardware by itself is relatively useless—too large to make a good paperweight, too costly to serve as a boat anchor. A computer may make a nice conversation piece on someone's desk or in a classroom or learning center. Only with the addition of software does the hardware become truly useful.

If software brings "life" to a maze of electronics, then clearly that software is more critical than the hardware. The significance of hardware is its ability to run the software one needs to perform a given task. Thus, it is vital to meeting one's goals to have the best possible software at hand. Mediocre software can only hide the potential of the machine.

QUALITY TRAILS QUANTITY

Anyone following developments in the computer industry knows that improvements in hardware are an all but daily phenomenon. Regrettably, the same cannot be said of courseware. Virtually any gathering of educators with computer interests will at some point prompt discussion of the appalling quality of courseware on the market. This concern, which borders on a cry for help, is

FIGURE 9.1. Software brings ''life'' to a computer.

not a reflection of naivete on the part of educators with limited computer experience. Alfred Bork, a major figure in educational computing virtually since the beginning, commented on the rapid increase in software *quantity*, but not *quality* (1984). He stated:

> We know how to produce decent computer-based learning material at the present time. But most of the available programs have not been produced by any careful process, and few have undergone careful evaluative study. Our increased capabilities in producing materials have largely gone unused (p. 93).

His are among the more tactfully worded comments on this topic.

WHY QUALITY IS PROBLEMATIC

There appear to be several possible explanations for problems of courseware quality.

Lack of a Theoretical Base
The field of learning theory offers many views concerning how we learn. Yet little educational courseware refelects an effort to apply *any* theory. Courseware

developers seem to require little more than a vague notion of content to begin production of a new package. Would it not be wiser to consider what we know about learning and include that in the design?

Technical Concerns Dominate

In the early days of educational software, errors in programming were common, even in commercial materials. Developers were still exploring the capabilities of the new micros and lacked sophistication. Complaints of amateurish results were common. Today, this has changed dramatically. Most commercial materials are technically sound. Graphics are slick, sound may be quite varied, and concern for visual appearance is evident. Actual programming flaws are rare. However, nothing resembling comparable attention to the methodology of the program exists in most cases. Jaeger (1988) and Trollip (1987) both address these concerns and offer evidence concerning the real value of popular "features." We have reached a level of technical excellence and continue to ignore educational soundness. One can only wonder whether experienced educators have played a role in developing many of the materials on the market.

Applying Old Models to a New Medium

Someone once observed that the railroads sealed their doom by failing to realize that their business was transportation, not trains. The history of motion pictures contains something of a parallel. Early film makers viewed the new medium as a means of recording stage plays for posterity. Only after considerable time did the adventurous begin to break out of old patterns and seek to determine the limits of the new medium itself.

Much educational courseware appears to suffer a similar problem. We are still in the infancy of this medium, and few have yet approached it free of the preconceived notions of the past. A classic example is the creation of a program that merely duplicates existing print materials on the screen. One can only ask, Why bother? Computers do not threaten to make print materials obsolete. They must go beyond what print does very well and create their own niche. Courseware developers could do worse than to read Marshall McLuhan and consider the notion of medium as message.

Educators Have Not Demanded Quality

Courseware production and sales are big business. Success is measured in gross sales and net profits. With hardware springing up like mushrooms and software necessary to make it useful, there was a rush to get products on the market. In the very early days, educators were desperate for anything to use with their new tools. One could hardly be fussy about quality or the equipment might sit unused.

Regrettably, the situation has not changed as much as one might hope. Many educators remain fascinated with the technology and fail to look carefully at outcomes. Courseware is accepted based on the producer's claim of value in too many cases. A catchy title, flashy graphics, and bold claims of applicability

FIGURE 9.2. Much attention is paid to graphics in commercial software.

tend to be adequate to sell materials to uncritical consumers. Only when educators demand accountability from producers is this likely to change.

THE NEED FOR EVALUATION

Computers in the schools may ultimately join other early technological devices in dusty storerooms if results are not demonstrated. Courseware is the critical element in this, and a more serious approach to courseware selection will be required. Consider the elaborate efforts undertaken in most schools for textbook selection. It is common for teacher committees to devote much time and effort to assessing and comparing the latest offerings of publishers before adoption. Filmstrips and other media under consideration for purchase are similarly evaluated. Snap decisions are uncommon; too much is at stake. Does computer courseware deserve less attention?

Evaluating courseware is significantly different from examining other educational materials. Teachers involved in selecting textbooks and media tend to have years of experience teaching and learning from such materials. Few educators have such an experience base to draw on for courseware evaluation. We believe educators are well aware of the need to evaluate courseware. However, many are perplexed about procedures, and we shall attempt to provide assistance.

WHO SHOULD EVALUATE COURSEWARE?

There is no magic answer to the question of who should be involved in courseware evaluation. In most cases, the best approach is probably to begin in the same manner used to select textbooks. Clearly, the teacher(s) who will use the materials must be involved. If these individuals have no role in selection, the likelihood of their using the materials declines rapidly.

Because of the technical aspects of courseware, it seems likely that the school's computer "expert" should also be involved. This may be a designated coordinator, a resource specialist, or even an administrator. It should be someone with a greater understanding of computer materials than a typical classroom user is apt to have or need. This person's role might be to conduct a workshop for the actual working committee on the intricacies of courseware evaluation, rather than to be actively involved in the entire process.

If school policy includes administrators and/or parents in selection of other materials, the same should be true of computer materials. It may, in fact, be quite advantageous to include parents in the process. Even those who are highly and vocally committed to bringing computers into the schools may have little knowledge themselves of the whys and wherefores. We can ill afford a repeat of the new math situation of some years ago. That curriculum development failed in part because parents had not learned in such a manner in their school days and were unable to cope with what their children were doing. Parental support of computers in the schools is vital to the success of a program. Efforts to involve and inform parents about these tools can only help.

APPROACHES TO COURSEWARE EVALUATION

There are at least three distinct but not mutually exclusive approaches to courseware evaluation. First, one may turn to other educators in the area to determine what packages they have used and their experience with them. Second, reviews of courseware products can be found in various sources and may offer valuable insight. Third, hands-on evaluation of the product will yield the best assessment for any specific situation.

ADVICE OR RECOMMENDATIONS

Clearly, one approach to selecting courseware is to talk with colleagues in other buildings or districts to see what they are using and how satisfied they are.

This can be a valuable *start* in identifying courseware worthy of more detailed evaluation. To actually select software based solely on recommendations is satisfactory only if you pursue in detail the strengths and weaknesses of a package. The key element must be effectiveness in promoting learning, but that hinges upon the curriculum. To what degree is your curriculum comparable to that of the advisor? If that person's satisfaction is criterion based, are your course objectives similar enough to assure your own satisfaction? Did you probe for weaknesses in the materials, problems in using them, and difficulties with the producer?

In general, it may well be safer to use the advice of more experienced persons primarily as a method of eliminating poor products from further consideration rather than for making a final determination to buy.

PROFESSIONAL REVIEWS

What about that wonderful-sounding new package for which a flyer just crossed your desk? If it is new, you'll have trouble locating an experienced user. Perhaps you do not know anyone using courseware in your field at all, or possibly none of your contacts has yet identified the kind of product you are seeking. It may be necessary to turn to reviews to learn about such materials.

Locating Reviews

Where do you find software reviews? You have probably seen many already. Initially, one had to turn to specialized computer magazines for such information. Part of the impetus for such periodicals was the lack of broad interest in computer materials on the part of professional organizations. Today, teachers find much computer information in the professional journals of most fields. By looking first to journals in your field, you should find reviews covering only packages of potential interest.

Additional reviews can be found in every issue of computer magazines. Education-oriented publications such as *Electronic Learning, The Computing Teacher*, and *Classroom Computer Learning* concentrate their reviews on educational materials. However, even the "consumer" publications sold at newsstands and in computer stores review educational courseware. The reviews may be less thorough from an educator's view, and you may have difficulty finding any in your subject area. On the other hand, such publications are excellent sources of information about general-purpose software such as word processing programs.

There are also specialized publications to which educators can turn. *Only the Best: The Discriminating Software Guide for Preschool–Grade 12* includes products based on the conclusions of 30 evaluation services in the U.S. and Canada. A negative rating from any one eliminates the software. This is a product of Education News Service, P.O. Box 1789, Carmichael, CA 95609 (916-483-6159).

Another resource of excellent quality is MicroSIFT (Microcomputer Software and Information for Teachers), a clearinghouse for microcomputer-based courseware. MicroSIFT was created by the Northwest Regional Educational Laboratory in 1979 and is well-known for its courseware reviews. For current information on services and resources, including their Resources in Computer Education (RICE) data base, contact: Northwest Regional Educational Laboratory, 101 SW Main St., Suite 500, Portland, OR 97204.

Anyone involved in the identification and selection of courseware should become acquainted with the Educational Products Information Exchange (EPIE). Perhaps the most complete and up-to-date software resource is *TESS—The Educational Software Selector*—from the EPIE Institute. *TESS* is published biennially in four volumes, each covering different subject areas. *TESS* contains brief program descriptions, including title, subject area, type, grade level, producer, required hardware, and so on. It also lists published reviews and EPIE's own rating. *PC-TESS* is the *TESS* data base on diskette for local automated searching. In between editions of *TESS*, supplements are published. For the most up-to-date information, obtain a subscription to *MICROgram*, EPIE's monthly coverage of about 200 new software products entering the *TESS* data base. Finally, EPIE also publishes the *Parent's Guide to Highly Rated Educational Software*, a subset of the total data base. For more information about the work and services of EPIE, write to EPIE Institute, Box 839, Watermill, NY 11976. EPIE reviews are regarded by many as the finest available.

For Apple computer users, contact your Apple education representative for Apple's *Curriculum Software Guides*. Available in various curriculum areas, these resources include highly rated programs indexed through a Curriculum Skills Matrix. This allows you to locate software to fit your objectives. *Technology in the Curriculum* not only covers software but also video, both matched to curriculum objectives. Model lesson plans for integrating materials into instruction are provided. *TEC* is available from the California State Department of Education, Box 271, Sacramento, CA 95802-0271.

The annual *Educational Software Preview Guide* from the International Society for Technology in Education is a compilation of views from North American nonprofit evaluation agencies. The Canadian Council of Ministers of Education established in 1987 the *Database for Educational Software*, a bilingual directory, including extensive listings of software evaluations by Canadian educators. Contact: Council of Ministers of Education, 252 Bloor West, Suite 5-200, Toronto, Ontario, Canada M5S 1V5. Finally, if you want information on business, communications, games, and other personal software in addition to educational products, try *Software Reviews on File*. This is a monthly publication by subscription only. Contact: Facts on File, Inc., 460 Park Avenue, New York, NY 10016.

Problems with Reviews
It would be unfortunate to have to base a purchase solely on published reviews. They seldom provide the kind of information needed for wise selection. They may not even be a totally reliable screening device for selecting items for hands-on examination.

One problem is objectivity in reviews. Are they true pictures of some measure of quality in a product? You may want to look at several issues of the same periodical. Are there any negative reviews? If not, is there any way to determine whether this publication "likes everything," or if only products receiving genuinely good reviews are mentioned out of space considerations? Either is possible. In addition, as Jolicoeur and Berger (1986) demonstrated, published reviews may differ completely on the same product. Evaluation is hardly a science.

Another problem is the inevitable time lag between release of new courseware and the appearance of reviews in publications. Because of the long lead time involved in getting material into print, one rarely sees reviews of the very latest products.

Finally, any courseware product is of value only as it fits the need for which it is being considered. Effective evaluation requires assessment in light of the intended use for the package. Reviews tend to be one person's impression of the software and related materials, with no indication of how the product was used or what results were achieved. It is less common by far to find reviews reporting on actual classroom testing or reviews based on the experiences of several individuals with the package. Even the qualifications of the reviewers may not be given or may be impossible to assess. Thus, many reviews are best characterized as superficial and grossly inadequate as a basis for purchase decisions.

HANDS-ON EVALUATION

Once courseware of interest has been identified, educators should actually try out the materials. There are several aspects to this task.

Obtaining Materials to Evaluate

Computer users wishing to purchase a new word processing package can usually go to the nearest computer store for a "test drive." Even more widely available are microcomputer versions of arcade and other games. However, educational courseware will appear more rarely on some retailers' shelves. The reason is, no doubt, relative demand. Only those packages that appeal to families for home educational use are apt to be found, and these cluster in the preschool and lower grades groups (e.g., the *Stickeybear* series, *Reader Rabbit*, Sesame Street spinoffs).

Direct from Producers. Educators discovered early on that, unlike films and other media being considered for adoption, courseware distributors seldom offered a preview opportunity, with the right to return the product if it was not suitable. This reluctance stemmed from the relative ease with which a computer diskette can be duplicated. Publishers do not fear that teachers will photocopy sample texts because the cost would be higher than purchase. However, the same is not true of software, where a $0.50 blank disk may become a copy of a $50-program in a few minutes. Unfortunately, teachers have been notorious violators of copyright law, and software producers' fears are not unfounded.

With advances in diskette anticopy protection schemes and growing resistance from educators to "buying a pig in a poke," most reputable software houses now allow school preview of materials. In an effort to spend limited funds most wisely, educators must insist on preview privileges. In turn, they must also scrupulously resist any temptation to illegally duplicate software on loan. (Software piracy is addressed in the last section of this book.)

Specialty Stores. While most software retailers do not carry a wide selection of educational materials, there are specialists in the business who do. Many educators have come to rely on firms catering to the needs of teachers for everything from bulletin board materials to resource books and fancy chalks. Such firms often operate both mail order and retail store businesses and have computer materials in their product lines. If you have access to such a store, be sure to visit it to explore the possibilities.

Colleagues. Another possible resource for viewing materials prior to purchase is other educational institutions in your area. We have also suggested talking with colleagues as a source of information. If you know someone who uses a particular courseware package, ask to visit to see it in use or try it out yourself. Local community colleges, colleges, or universities may have courseware collections available for examination. In some states, regional media or computer consortia maintain courseware collections for teacher perusal. It may take some legwork, but the persistent educator today has a much greater chance of hands-on evaluation than was true in the past.

A Unique Source. Would you like to be able to preview a host of software right in your own school without any of the bother the preceding methods involve? Some rural teachers in Oklahoma can do so, as can teachers in the Los Angeles Unified School District and in Nassau County, New York (Foster, 1987). The key is ESDS, the Electronic Software Delivery System from Rainbow Telecommunications (6814 Kenosha Pass, Austin, TX, 78749: 512-288-5460). ESDS is actually a whole telecommunications network, but a key feature is software delivery. Sophisticated system software enables authorized users to download public domain materials, preview copies of commercial materials for local assessment, and class or lab copies with automatic billing. Preview copies are protected from piracy to the extent that major software producers have no objection to a central office installing their products on ESDS. Contact Rainbow for full details about this system. This could be a sound reason for getting into networking.

Standardizing the Evaluation

When a product has been obtained for review, a common approach to evaluation is needed so that multiple reviewers can later reach consensus. An evaluation form is normally used to guide all reviewers to consider the same basic points. Even if review is the province of a single individual, some form of "objective" documentation is at least desirable, showing that decisions were not based solely on a cursory "love it or leave it" reaction.

Teacher or Committee Review

Within the structure employed by a school, it commonly becomes a committee task to review courseware and make purchase recommendations. Few initiates into this process are prepared for the time demands that follow. This is a result of both the number of criteria one needs to consider and the fundamental differences between courseware and those materials we are more accustomed to evaluating.

Why is the process of evaluating courseware so different from other materials? One answer is the lack of an experience base with the medium, as mentioned previously. Beyond that, the answer can be summed up in the word *interactivity*. No other popular medium of instruction offers this element. When teachers evaluate a new text, they seldom read it page by page, beginning to end. It is possible to look at the table of contents, index, or selected parts of special concern and reach a reasoned conclusion. There is no such "skimming" potential with courseware. Evaluators will need to study student and teacher guides, workbooks, activity sheets or booklets, *and* the computer programs. The programs are the most difficult part. Generally, a three-phase assessment of a program is necessary.

A Three-Step Approach. First, one should go through the entire program as a better student would; that is, give relatively few incorrect responses along the way. This will demonstrate what the sharpest students will experience with the program and clearly show the program's treatment of correct responses. It is desirable to keep track of the time spent completing the program, to have an approximation of the minimal time a student will require to use the material.

Second, go through the program again as a weaker student might. Only in this way can you determine the extent of branching offered by the program. How much remediation is provided to the user having difficulty? Is it just a repeat of previous screens, or does the program offer several different looks at the same content? Is there a "help" function for the person who gets stuck? What is the nature of such help? Again, record the time required to use the program in this manner, which will typically be much longer than in step one.

Third, run the program again, this time testing for its ability to handle inappropriate responses. For instance, if a numeric response is required, try entering letters or symbols and vice versa. No program worth owning will come to a halt under such circumstances. Also observe what happens if you press only the return or enter key without typing an actual answer. This should produce either no response at all or a message to give a real answer. It should never be counted as a wrong response. What happens if you "accidentally" press the reset or break key? The program should not "crash." It may seem trivial or absurd to test a program in this manner, but you will find that students soon discover any deficiencies of this type, as they delight in outwitting the machine. The programmer should have anticipated all such accidental or malicious possibilities and guarded against their upsetting the learning process.

Student Field Tests

The ultimate proof of courseware value is in the learning outcomes produced. Courseware evaluation should, if at all possible, occur during the school year, not the summer, so that materials can actually be "field tested" with real learners. Teacher review can assure that a product is appropriate to the curriculum, but even experienced computer educators cannot always determine the actual learning value. For this, a real live test is needed.

Where a supplier offers preview privileges, the most common period allowed is 30 days. This should be ample time for a test with at least a limited number of students. As the cost of the package increases, the need for certainty of its value grows as well. Dudley-Marling, Owston, and Searle (1988) and Callison and Haycock (1988) describe thorough approaches to student field testing.

EVALUATION CONSIDERATIONS

INTENDED USE

The fundamental starting point in evaluating courseware is to clearly define the learning objectives for a lesson. Only then does one have a basis for assessing the value of a coursware product in one's teaching. Ideally, the teacher will determine what needs to be learned and seek supporting courseware. The intended purpose for which a package is to be considered must play a major role in assessing its suitability. While the same courseware may potentially serve multiple goals, its suitability may not be equal for each. It is quite possible for two teachers to arrive at very different assessments of a package based on different learning objectives.

The producer of courseware had some intended use in mind for the product. This may or may not have led to the specification of objectives for the product. Where objectives exist, they should be considered a guide to appropriate use of the materials. However, they should not be viewed as prescriptive, precluding other uses envisioned by creative teachers. Hopefully, teachers will not allow published objectives for courseware to determine their own curricular goals. Careful assessment against established goals is the ultimate criterion for courseware selection and use.

LEARNING THEORY

In discussing issues of quality, we made the point that courseware seldom seems to reflect application of any common theory of learning. Evaluation can be approached by starting with a theory and scrutinizing a package against it. Such an approach will not necessarily lead to all criteria given above, although some will clearly surface. However, theory may also raise further issues to consider. See Bell (1985) for a full discussion of theory and evaluation. Jonassen (1988) provides a very detailed look at many theories and their application to coursework.

For purposes of illustration, let's take a well-known theory and apply it to courseware. Gagné and Briggs (1974) posited nine events of instruction as components of effective lessons. Figure 9.3 adapts the nine events into a flow chart, showing how a learner might progress through a lesson. Not all nine events will necessarily be found in every courseware product, nor need they be. One must keep the overall requirements of the lesson content and instructional format in mind when considering these criteria. Furthermore, some of the nine components may be intentionally left to the teacher to develop with students before or after the computer lesson, rather than being explicit elements of the courseware.

Let's consider the nine events of instruction individually.

Gain Attention/Provide Motivation

Before learning can occur, the learner must be motivated by the lesson. Much educational courseware seeks to gain attention through colorful, even animated, graphics that appear at the beginning of the program. Such an approach tends to be effective initially but has little carry-over into the program. Motivation throughout will be better maintained by other features. Critical to motivation is a clearly defined goal toward which the user works.

Timing. Though not always appropriate, a program that requires the student to compete against the clock can be highly motivating. Usually some visual cue as to available time is provided on screen—a clock face, a digital display, or an hourglass slowly emptying.

Competition. A package may provide for competition between the computer and the user. Other packages allow for two students or teams to compete. Simple scorekeeping on the user's performance provides competition with oneself or against a criterion. The result may be a reward—a certificate, a short game, or a graphic display that grows like a puzzle with each correct response.

Difficulty. Motivation quickly dies if the demands are inappropriate, either too easy or too difficult. Motivation is enhanced by challenge, but only if effort is required and the goal seems attainable. Programs may offer user-selected difficulty levels or may be self-adjusting based on response patterns. If self-selected, the user should be able to leave the current level at any time to choose a more or less difficult one.

Present the Objective

A fundamental principle of performance objectives is that the learner must know what is expected and what the result of the lesson will be. Preparation of objectives occurs before design of a lesson and guides that design. At delivery time, the learner must be informed of the objectives. We see no compelling

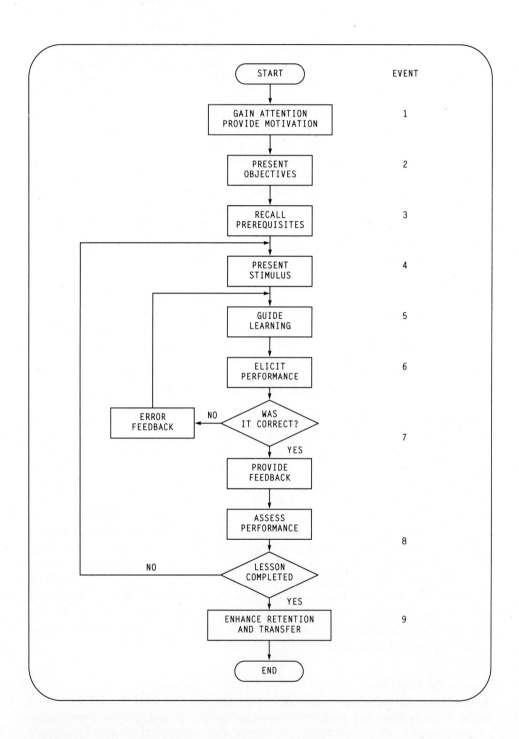

FIGURE 9.3. The nine events of instruction

argument to prefer on-screen over written objectives, although many teachers prefer to avoid ancillary materials by having the program "do it all."

Recall Prerequisites
Except for one's very first exposure to a field of study, new learning usually builds upon past learning. Whatever prior knowledge or skills are required to benefit from courseware should be reviewed with the student. This may be done as a class activity prior to assigning work with the courseware. It may be achieved with support materials such as study guides or worksheets provided by the package producer or created by the teacher. Naturally, there could also be an on-screen review. If the computer is used for this purpose, a pretest may be given that either directs the learner back to earlier materials or determines placement into the current lesson based on mastery of components.

Present Stimulus
This is the beginning of the lesson itself. In a tutorial, the material presented will be new to the learner; in a drill, it will be familiar. For a simulation, the scenario must be presented. A strategy appropriate to the lesson format and content must also be established and followed.

Guide Learning
Stimulus presentation alone may be inadequate for learning to occur. Guidance in the form of examples that illustrate the rule is often needed. Questions that probe the learner's understanding may be employed; hints or clues may be available on request or provided automatically at certain points.

Elicit Performance
This is the essence of interactivity in a computer package. Books are excellent conveyors of information but can do no more than suggest that the learner complete some activity based on the learning. The computer must pose questions that the learner is required to answer and do so frequently. As noted in the previous chapter, one great advantage of computer courseware is that each learner must answer each question, as opposed to the occasional opportunity to respond in most classrooms. If a high level of interactivity is missing, the package may not represent a worthwhile use of the computer.

Provide Feedback
Closely tied to performance is knowledge of results. A major problem of typical homework assignments is that the student could complete all items incorrectly and not know of the errors until the next school day. Most computer programs provide feedback on every question posed. The quality of the feedback must be carefully examined. Related to this is whether multiple tries are allowed for questions and, if so, whether the number permitted is appropriate and defensible. Programs that "trap" the learner until a correct response is given are likely to destroy the motivation of a person having difficulty.

Reinforcement. Closely allied to feedback, but not specifically identified in the model, is reinforcement. Feedback entails knowledge that a response was correct or incorrect. Reinforcement takes two forms. One is to provide the correct answer for the student. This should occur whether the correct answer was given or the learner has exhausted the allowed number of tries. Feedback and reinforcement are often combined in a form like, "That's correct. You knew the answer was _____."

The other side of reinforcement is praise for a job well done and/or encouragement to continue. Psychologists have conducted much research on various levels and frequency of reinforcement, which seem generally to be ignored by courseware developers. By and large, such reinforcement is either absent, or it occurs on every item.

Assess Performance

As learners work through a lesson, they need to know of their progress toward the criterion. This provides a feeling of accomplishment, possibly the light at the end of the tunnel. If the exercise is timed, a timing device on the screen can serve at least part of this purpose. A performance "scoreboard" showing the number of correct responses also works. To stress achievement, it may be best to report only the number of correct responses and omit reference to percentage correct or number of errors until a final summation.

Clearly, there is an element of reinforcement in this instructional event, not of the content, but of the individual. Other methods include a special display when the halfway mark in the lesson has been reached, or a periodic report on the number of items remaining. Few programs count down toward zero, but for many students it is more encouraging to know there are only two more items to go than to be told that 18 have been finished.

Promote Retention and Transfer

Clearly, the goal of learning is retention and, in many cases, transfer to new situations. Neither should be assumed to be an automatic outcome of CAI. Instead, explicit provision should exist for enhancing both. This may occur within the context of the program, such as provision for the user to elect enrichment activities after mastering the basic content or to ask for more practice on similar items.

Some courseware, especially simulations, provides for concurrent on- and off-computer activities. One possibility is data recording forms that help students organize data, analyze results, and determine appropriate actions for the next computer session. One good example of this is the multimedia package *Voyage of the Mimi* from Sunburst. Manzelli (1986) provides a introduction to this intriguing product. Of course, if your courseware does not include such materials, consider developing them locally.

In addition, one should not overlook the need to promote retention and transfer after the computer activity is completed. Many courseware packages now contain suggestions for follow-up activities. If yours does not or the suggestions are inappropriate or too few, consider how you will extend the experience. This is an essential element in integrating the computer into the curriculum, one sadly lacking in many schools today.

SPECIFIC CRITERIA

Before considering forms for evaluating educational courseware, let's examine a wide range of factors that can and should be considered. There are no "standard" lists of points to consider, but we shall divide ours into four major categories: demographics, general criteria, CAI-specific criteria, and usability factors. Within each category, the evaluator must refrain from rejecting a package based solely on concerns with one or a few items. Rather, omissions or weaknesses must be viewed in the total context of what the materials do provide and how well they fit the intended use. For the criteria of one prominent evaluation group, see Bitter and Wighton (1987).

Demographics
Demographics are those basic pieces of information about a courseware product that fully identify it and indicate its compatibility with available hardware.

Identification. This consists of the following items:
1. Name of the program and curriculum area, if not obvious.
2. Manufacturer, including address and phone, if available.

Getting Started

To use WHAT WILL HAPPEN, you will need an Apple //, Apple //+, Apple //e, or Apple //c microcomputer with at least 64K memory, one disk drive, and a video monitor. (*Apple* is a registered trademark of Apple Computer, Inc.)

To begin, decide whether you want to use Side 1 or Side 2 of the disk. (See pages 5–7 of this manual for an explanation of the contents of each side.) Then insert the disk into the drive (Drive 1) with the appropriate side facing up. The edge that contains the oval cutout should be inserted first. Close the door on the disk drive and turn on the computer and the video monitor. The title and credit screens will appear.

FIGURE 9.4. Software manuals usually detail hardware requirements.

3. Source of review copy if different from item 2.
4. Program type (drill, simulation, etc.).
5. Producer's claim of grade level suitability. (You may disagree!)
6. Producer's licensing, backup, and replacement policies. (All affect total cost.)

Compatibility
1. *Computer brands for which product is available.* This may seem needless for a school that owns only one brand but could save time in the future if another make is acquired and the same package is desired for it.
2. *Required hardware configuration,* including:
    □ Specific model, e.g., Apple IIe, IBM PC–AT, MacII.
    □ Memory required. Packages are rapidly growing in size. Wonderful reviews and great enthusiasm for the product are of no value if your equipment has insufficient memory to run it.
    □ Number of disk drives required; need for hard disk drive.
3. *Format options,* including:
    □ Disk size (5 1/4-inch is most common; 3 1/2-inch is growing in popularity).
    □ Transferability to a hard disk or availability of a network version. If you want to avoid handling diskettes by using a network and hard disk, be sure your software can be used within it.
    □ Availability and contents of multi-disk lab packs.
4. *Other software required to use it.* For instance, when considering classroom data bases as described in Chapter 4, what filing system is requried?

Acquisition Data. If you record all ordering information at this point, you may speed up the actual purchase of selected products later.

General Criteria
This category covers broad concerns for *all* educational materials, whether print, traditional media, or computer format.

1. *Is the content accurate?* Obviously, errors in fact are unacceptable. However, content accuracy may be relative. For example, a simulation such as *Oregon Trail* or any of several based on elections may be difficult to assess in terms of accuracy. The purpose of such programs is less to convey content than to provoke analysis of the context presented, to raise questions for discussion, and to allow testing of strategies. Adherence to "reality" is not crucial to these goals. Likewise, a business simulation like *Lemonade Stand* may not be "accurate" enough for older students but will suffice as an introduction to business principles for young children. Accuracy depends on the learning objectives and student level in some cases.
2. *Is the instructional strategy sound?*
3. *Is the material free of violent or aggressive behavior and all bias, including gender and race?*
4. *Are the objectives clearly stated?* When one looks at computer materials, it is

remarkable how often no objectives are specified at all. If they exist, they tend to be very general and low-level. This may result from claims that some packages suit a range of potential users from preschool through adult!

5. *Are the objectives important components of the curriculum?* There is a tendency to allow curriculum to be dictated by publishers and materials producers, rather than to be the reasoned decisions of professional educators. If a computer product does not fit the current curriculum, is it of such great potential as to justify a curriculum change?

6. *Is the readability level appropriate for the intended audience?* This becomes crucial in the face of claims of very broad audiences. Do not rely on producer's claims; check readability yourself.

7. *Is the material free of grammatical errors, typos, and misspellings?* The infallible image of the computer might well reinforce language errors as correct usage.

8. *Are instructions clear and correct?* One should never wonder what to do next.

9. *Is the overall difficulty level appropriate for your learners?*

10. *Will the material help to motivate the learners?*

11. *Does the package appear to offer good value for the price?* Important here may be the versatility of a given product. In how many different courses or grades could it be used? Will it fit only a brief period of instruction in one grade? Are there both remedial and enrichment applications that extend usability? A costly graphing program may find wider usage in mathematics than an inexpensive tutorial on a specific topic, for example. Price alone is an inadequate criterion.

CAI-Specific Criteria

The unique qualities of computer materials yield certain criteria not applicable to most educational products.

1. *Does the package take advantage of the capabilities of the computer?* For instance, are questions, problems, or situations presented in varying order, or does the same sequence occur on each program run? This can be a major distinction from noncomputer materials.

2. *Is this a more effective and/or efficient approach to the content than any other?* Or is it really a case of print materials converted to the computer screen?

3. *Is the sequence of the presentation appropriate?* Is it compatible with your approach to the topic or are you willing to change? Remember, with a book or set of slides you can alter the sequence if you wish. There is much less potential, if any, to do so with computer materials.

4. *Does the learner control the pace and/or sequence of the presentation?* Is there a menu of choices or does the computer adjust the sequence to fit user response patterns? Can the user back up in the program to review? Are displays changed by user action or are they timed? The programmer should not presume to know how long an individual needs to read any screen.

5. *Is the program "bombproof"?* Or can the user make responses that will cause

the program to crash? Students often delight in bringing a program to its knees.

6. *Do responses require more than minimal typing?* If so, typing skill or spelling may be as much a key to success as knowledge or analytic thinking.

7. *Do all responses require pressing the RETURN key?* If not, the learner may be easily confused on how to respond.

8. *Is feedback to responses appropriate?* Is the learner assisted in understanding the cause of errors or merely told that an answer was wrong? Is the feedback demeaning? In earlier years, it was popular to write programs with "smart" responses such as "Wake up, dummy, and try again." This is inappropriate.

9. *Is feedback effective?* Many programs unintentionally provide more attractive feedback for wrong answers than correct ones, especially in graphics. This may encourage students to give wrong answers just to see what happens.

10. *Are graphics, if used, supportive of the learning process?* Or are they merely window dressing? Graphics, including animation, can readily enhance the appeal of a program, but they should also provide visual learning.

11. *If sound is used, does it serve a useful purpose?* Auditory cues when a user has made an error can be very helpful, but musical tunes can become a nuisance in a classroom or a lab. Can the sound be turned off? Some computers contain internal speakers with no volume control; others output sound through the monitor so that volume can be controlled.

12. *What is the level of interaction?* How much must the student read before making a more meaningful response than pressing the space bar to continue? Do not accept "electronic page turners." One rule of thumb is that there should be no more than three screens of instructional text before the user is queried on the material.

13. *Can the student exit the program before the end is reached?* If so, are the directions for exiting clear and easy to remember? Better yet, are they given on the screen whenever it is possible to exit? Can the student later reenter the program at the point of exit, or is it necessary to start all over again?

14. *Is the program designed for only one student at a time or does it encourage group activities?* Many persons are concerned that the computer could decrease student socialization, if all activities are individual.

15. *If there are pretests and posttests, do they appear to be valid?* Do all "tests" actually measure learner progress?

Usability Factors

This category treats factors that make one package easier to use than another. Both student and teacher concerns should be considered.

Teacher Concerns

1. *Can the program easily be integrated into your instruction?* What support materials are provided? How appropriate and useful do they appear to be? Are both teacher and student manuals available, if appropriate? Are there worksheets or study guides? Are suggested activities and references to related materials

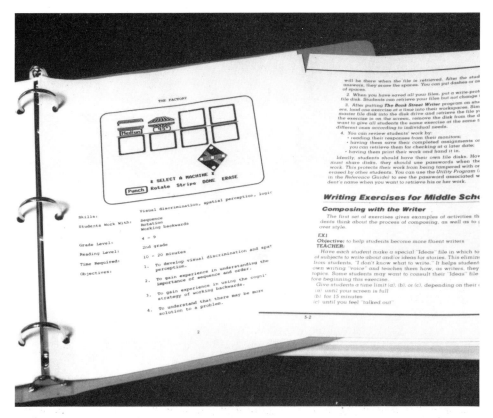

FIGURE 9.5. Educational courseware should include ample support material.

included? The more assistance provided, the easier the package will be to incorporate into instruction and the more likely you are to be using it in the manner intended. That is the difference between courseware and just software.

2. *Is there a recordkeeping or management component?* If so, what does it provide, and how complex is it to use? The next chapter will examine the potentials and pitfalls of computer-managed instruction.

3. *Can the program be modified?* Most teachers lack the time and knowledge to tamper with a program and make major changes. However, drill programs become more versatile if the teacher is allowed to enter or change the content of the drill, say a weekly spelling list. This is usually achieved through a utility program provided with the package. If this option exists, how difficult is it to enter your material?

Student Concerns

1. *Can the package be used with little or no teacher intervention?* Does the program run automatically when the disk is booted? Are all directions presented on

screen or must the user keep a manual at hand for guidance? Manuals are not necessarily less effective, just more cumbersome. On the other hand, printed manuals allow skimming or by-passing information for quick access to what one is seeking. In classroom settings, wall charts of directions can also be very effective. Preparing them could be a worthwhile student project.

2. *How difficult is it for a student to get started on a lesson?* Some packages with management components require fairly elaborate "log on" procedures that can be problematic.

3. *Does the package require much disk handling or swapping?* Especially with younger students, it is desirable to avoid student contact with diskettes as much as possible.

4. *Is there provision for use of alternative input devices* such as light pens, joy sticks, or touch screens that could make the package more usable for special needs populations?

5. *Is there a "HELP" function available?* If so, what does it provide?

EVALUATION OF SPECIFIC CAI TYPES

Some authors suggest that one should divide the task of courseware evaluation according to the type of program involved (Bitter and Camuse, 1984; Wright and Forcier, 1985). They maintain that significant differences exist among the types that require separate approaches. Rather than provide separate lists for each type, large portions of which would be redundant, we have tried to provide one comprehensive set of criteria, not all of which apply to every form of CAI. (Even with Gagné's theoretical model, not all elements will be present in every package, nor must they be.) Ultimately, the most important aids in evaluating courseware become personal experience in working with CAI and a broad understanding of factors that lead to effectiveness. There is a holistic element to evaluation that cannot be reflected in narrow prescriptions of absolutely mandatory components. Common sense, after all, has not been rendered obsolete by computer technology.

PULLING IT ALL TOGETHER

It should now be abundantly clear that courseware evaluation is a multifaceted and complex task. As suggested earlier in this chapter, the time required to simply work through a given package as a user can be significant. Any approach may fail to reveal some aspects of a program, especially a tutorial or simulation with complex branching schemes. The more sophisticated the program, the less certainty there is that any evaluation approach will uncover all the possibilities.

EVALUATION FORMS

There is an obvious need for some method of getting a handle on the task. The usual approach is to create an evaluation form to be completed by each reviewer during and after an evaluation session. Forms for such a task abound, with new variations appearing frequently in the periodical literature. Each has its own predilections, of course, and may or may not suit one's needs.

The goal of an evaluation form is to organize the plethora of factors and concerns in some coherent and manageable way. Otherwise, the task quickly overwhelms. At the same time, there is a tendency to view the result as some relatively simple, highly quantifiable, and totally accurate wonder. Just make checks where a quality is observed, leave blank all others, tally the checks, and voilà—a good or bad product has been found. Would that it were so simple!

Creating an Evaluation Form

Recognizing the complexity of the task and the undeniable need to organize it, we offer in Figure 9.6 a rather sketchy evaluation instrument in comparison to most. Our experience is that the most useful form for evaluating courseware is the one that speaks directly to the primary concerns of the evaluator, be that an individual or team. Therefore, we recommend that anyone setting out to evaluate courseware begin by developing a personal, school, or district form for the purpose. As the figure suggests, some elements of each of the four broad categories will be needed. Exactly which may be highly varied depending on your own needs and views, as well as the type of courseware to be evaluated. Thus, we offer only the outline and leave it to you, the user, to fill in as many elements as you choose from the suggestions given in the chapter.

Adding a Rating Scale

Once you have chosen your criteria, you may find it desirable to have more than just a check list, because the final significance of the evaluation may be hard to determine from only a series of checks. To quantify your findings in some way, we suggest that you evaluate each item on your list using some scale. You may wish to rate each element as Outstanding, Acceptable, or Unacceptable, assigning 3, 2, or 1 point, respectively. Devise another scale if you prefer. You will then be able to sum the ratings in each category to produce an assessment of the product.

Adding Weights

Going a step further, it is unlikely that all chosen criteria are of equal importance to you. This suggests weighting each in some manner. In most cases, assigning a weight from 3 (most important) to 1 (least important) will probably suffice. Adding a numerical value to your rating categories and multiplying your assessment by the weight for that item yields a potential score of 9 (outstanding and most important) to 1 (unacceptable and least important). A final sum of these values would probably yield a more complete picture of the package's merits for your context.

Using Your Form

If you adopt a point-based scheme, you may wish to apply it only to the last three categories, omitting the demographic details that are more for information

```
DATE OF REVIEW _____   NAME OF REVIEWER _____

DEMOGRAPHICS

IDENTIFICATION

PACKAGE NAME: _____      TYPE: _____

CURRICULUM AREA: _____   LEVEL CLAIMED: _____

PRODUCER: _____

BACK-UP POLICY: _____


COMPATIBILITY

_____

_____


ACQUISITION DATA

AVAILABLE FROM (FULL ADDRESS) _____

COST _____   REFERENCE SOURCE _____


GENERAL CRITERIA


CRITERION                RATING  ×   WEIGHT  =  TOTAL PTS.

_____  _____ × _____ = _____

_____  _____ × _____ = _____

_____  _____ × _____ = _____

_____  _____ × _____ = _____

_____  _____ × _____ = _____

_____  _____ × _____ = _____
```

FIGURE 9.6. Courseware evaluation form

CAI SPECIFIC CRITERIA

CRITERION	RATING	×	WEIGHT	=	TOTAL PTS.
_____	_____	×	_____	=	_____
_____	_____	×	_____	=	_____
_____	_____	×	_____	=	_____
_____	_____	×	_____	=	_____

USABILITY FACTORS

CRITERION	RATING	×	WEIGHT	=	TOTAL PTS.
_____	_____	×	_____	=	_____
_____	_____	×	_____	=	_____
_____	_____	×	_____	=	_____
_____	_____	×	_____	=	_____

OVERALL ASSESSMENT

SUMMARY REACTION TO THIS PACKAGE

RECOMMENDATION:

_____ EXCELLENT-DEFINITE PURCHASE

_____ GOOD-SECOND PRIORITY PURCHASE

_____ FAIR-PROBABLY USABLE BUT WOULD PREFER BETTER

_____ POOR-INSUFFICIENT VALUE TO CONSIDER PURCHASE

FIGURE 9.6. *continued*

and basic determination of suitability to one's hardware. We also caution against overreliance on the quantifiable data. Your final subjective assessment should be made *before* the numbers are tallied. This should represent your holistic reaction to the package, which can then be compared to and may even overrule the "hard data" from the form. The more experience one has in examining and actually using software, the more valid the subjective view is apt to be. Experience is also the best guide to developing a usable evaluation form, so expect that yours will undergo many revisions as your expertise grows.

Other Approaches

If you wish to examine more prescriptive approaches to evaluation, complete forms can be found in Wright and Forcier (1985, pp. 158–161); Hofmeister (1984, pp. 7–8 to 7–12); Flake, McClintock, and Turner (1985, pp. 326–327); Bozeman (1985, pp. 160–164); or Bitter and Camuse (1984, Chapter 6). Each approaches the matter differently but defensibly.

Examples of other approaches to evaluation can be found in Reed and Judkins (1986) and Zohar and Tamir (1986). Although geared to science, the concepts may be adapted to other areas. A very extensive treatment of evaluation based on the York Educational Software Evaluation Scales developed in Canada is found in Owston (1987).

In addition, many professional organizations such as the National Council of Teachers of Mathematics (1906 Association Drive, Reston, VA 22091) have developed evaluation instruments that you may wish to examine. The Northwest Regional Educational Laboratory is responsible for the MicroSIFT software evaluation clearinghouse cited earlier. Their evaluation form and procedures have been published by the International Society for Technology in Education as *Evaluator's Guide for Microcomputer-Based Instructional Packages,* an inexpensive paperback booklet. Contact the ISTE at 1787 Agate St., University of Oregon, Eugene, OR 97403-9905.

SUMMARY

With appropriate and effective courseware, the computer can become an integral part of the learning process. It can assume a portion of the teaching responsibility, becoming a student's private tutor. In turn, this may free the teacher to spend more time with individual students. However, to achieve such a goal assumes the availability of excellent courseware.

After identifying courseware of potential interest, a review or evaluation process is critical prior to purchase. The ideal approach is to begin with advice or recommendations from experienced users of a given product. Next, other reviews of the package may be helpful. Finally, a hands-on evaluation is required, unless it is absolutely impossible to obtain the materials.

The criteria against which a package could be evaluated are so numerous as to appear impossible to manage. However, as one gains experience in courseware evaluation, the most critical elements will come to mind readily, minimizing the effort. It is advisable for even the very experienced to have some sort of evaluation form to work from, to assure that no vital point is overlooked and to standardize to some extent the work of multiple reviewers. It seems best for individuals, schools, or districts to develop a form that addresses their own major concerns, rather than to adopt one that seeks to serve all.

Despite all efforts to streamline the process, courseware evaluation, if done conscientiously, will always be a time-consuming task, much more so than teachers are accustomed to in selecting other materials. However, if the computer is to live up to its potential as an aid to learning, this task cannot be ignored or minimized. The quality of materials and curriculum fit will determine whether the computer achieves its potential as an indispensable element in the educational process or joins earlier technological marvels in the school basement.

CHAPTER 9 ACTIVITIES

1. Starting with the outline model of an evaluation form in Figure 9.6, complete the form by adding the criteria most important to you, your school, or district. (Expand the space devoted to categories as you wish.) Try to balance a desire for thoroughness with concern for the time it will take to complete your instrument.

2. Compare your evaluation form with those of your colleagues. Discuss the reasons for selection of different elements to include.

3. In groups of at least three, try to create a common form acceptable to all, much as a school or district committee would. What did you have to give up from your list of important elements to reach consensus while avoiding a ten-page instrument? Did your negotiations cause you to rethink the merits of certain possible items?

4. Using your instrument, critically evaluate at least one courseware product in each of as many different categories (e.g., simulation) as you have access to.

5. Using your instrument, evaluate three or more courseware products intended for the same or similar instructional use. Does your "objective" assessment agree with your holistic view of these packages? If not, why? Does your form require modification?

6. Select a package that looks especially good to you. Contact the producer to request field test data for the materials, if none are provided in the documentation. If there has been no field testing, ask the producer why products are not thoroughly tested before release. An entire class might undertake this activity, being certain not to duplicate producers. When answers have been received, compare the approaches of various companies to this issue. What does this tell you about the courseware industry? See Smith (1988) for guidance in evaluating producer performance claims.

7. Try to find several published reviews of a product to which you have access.

Without first reading the reviews, conduct your own evaluation of the package. Compare your findings with the reviews. What does this tell you about relying on "professional" reviews?

8. Evaluate at least one courseware package solely on the basis of Gagné's events of instruction. From this theoretical perspective, does the package appear to be effective? If you could find no evidence of one or more events, is the omission justifiable in this case?

REFERENCES

Bell, M. E. "The Role of Instructional Theories in the Evaluation of Microcomputer Courseware." *Educational Technology*, March 1985, pp. 36–40.

Bitter, G. G., and Camuse, R. A. *Using a Microcomputer in the Classroom.* Reston, VA: Reston Publishing, 1984.

Bitter, G. G., and Wighton, D. "The Most Important Criteria Used by the Educational Software Evaluation Consortium." *The Computing Teacher*, March 1987, pp. 7–9.

Bork, A. "Education and Computers: The Situation Today and Some Possible Futures." *T.H.E. Journal*, October 1984, pp. 92–97.

Bozeman, W. C. *Computers and Computing in Education.* Scottsdale, AZ: Gorsuch Scarisbrick, 1985.

Callison, D., and Haycock, G. "A Methodology for Student Evaluation of Educational Microcomputer Software." *Educational Technology*, January 1988, pp. 25–32.

Dudley-Marling, C., Owston, R. G., and Searle, D. "A Field-Testing Approach to Software Evaluation." *Computers in the Schools*, 1988, 5(1/2), pp. 241–249.

Flake, J. L., McClintock, C. E., and Turner, S. V. *Fundamentals of Computer Education.* Belmont, CA: Wadsworth, 1985.

Foster, D. L. "A Computer Network for Oklahoma's Rural, Small Schools." *Educational Technology UPDATE*, September 1987.

Gagné, R. M., and Briggs, L. J. *Principles of Instructional Design.* New York: Holt, Rinehart and Winston, 1974.

Hofmeister, A. *Microcomputer Applications in the Classroom.* New York: Holt, Rinehart and Winston, 1984.

Jaeger, M. "Zaps, Booms, & Whistles in Educational Software." *The Computing Teacher*, March 1988, pp. 20–22.

Jolicoeur, K., and Berger, D. E. "Do We Really Know What Makes Educational Software Effective? A Call for Empirical Research on Effectiveness." *Educational Technology*, December 1986, pp. 7–11.

Jonassen, D. H. *Instructional Designs for Microcomputer Courseware.* Hillsdale, NJ: Lawrence Erlbaum Associates, 1988.

Manzelli, J. A. "New Curriculum Soundings on a Voyage of the Mimi." *Computers in the Schools*, Spring 1986, pp. 55–61.

Owston, R. G. *Software Evaluation. A Criterion-Based Approach.* Scarborough, Ontario: Prentice-Hall Canada Inc., 1987.

Reed, J. H., and Judkins, J. "Evaluation of a Holistic CAI System in Introductory Chemistry." *Journal of Computers in Mathematics and Science Teaching*, 1986, 6(1), pp. 21–27.

Smith, R. A. "Claims of Improved Academic Performance—The Questions You Should Ask." *The Computing Teacher*, May 1988, pp. 42–44, 61.

Trollip, S. "Four Computer Features to Avoid." *The Computing Teacher*, May 1987, pp. 33–35.

Wright, E. B., and Forcier, R. C. *The Computer: A Tool for the Teacher*. Belmont, CA: Wadsworth, 1985.

Zohar, A., and Tamir, P. "A New Instrument to Assess the Inquiry Characteristics of Science Computer Software." *Journal of Computers in Mathematics and Science Teaching*, 1986, *6*(1), pp. 44–46.

CHAPTER 10

□ Computer–Managed Instruction □

OBJECTIVES

After completing this chapter, you will be able to:

- □ *Define computer-managed instruction and explain its use.* □
- □ *Describe several ways of facilitating classroom management tasks with a computer.* □
- □ *Explain the role of the computer in individualizing instruction.* □
- □ *Discuss the use of the computer in testing.* □
- □ *Explain the scope and nature of integrated learning systems.* □
- □ *Criticize or defend computer-managed instruction.* □

We conclude this section with a look at another facet of educational computing, computer-managed instruction (CMI). While superficially similar in some ways to programs presented in Chapter 6, the scope is sufficiently different to warrant distinct treatment. CMI refers to software that aids the teacher in performance assessment and monitoring, evaluation, and record-keeping. CMI is often intimately linked to implementation of computer-assisted instruction as in integrated learning systems. Thus, it is appropriate to consider CMI at this point.

AN OVERVIEW OF COMPUTER-MANAGED INSTRUCTION

BACKGROUND CONCEPTS

The Teacher as Manager

When teachers prepare résumés of their professional experience, comparatively few identify management skills among their achievements. Yet many management activities are part of daily life in the classroom. Teachers organize and direct a complex array of activities, learning resources, and even auxiliary personnel such as aides. There are countless records to keep: attendance, grades, text distribution, classroom inventory, and so forth. The end of a marking period brings with it the calculation of grades and preparation of grade reports. Parents may desire, or demand, more thorough information about their children's progress.

Teachers often complain about the proportion of their time that these activities consume. A microcomputer in the classroom can help the teacher dig out from under the paperwork avalanche and reclaim time for working with students. This is, after all, a teacher's primary function.

Using software to aid in classroom management is often referred to as *computer-managed instruction*, or CMI. The primary purpose of CMI is to help track and document student learning. The forms that CMI takes are as diverse as the needs that led to creation of such software. Early efforts in this direction predate microcomputers by some years. They were an outgrowth of the concepts of mastery learning and individualized instruction.

Mastery Learning

Very simply put, mastery learning contends that all students can achieve at a very high level under the right conditions. To implement mastery learning, the curriculum is defined as a series of objectives stated in observable, measurable form. Students progress to new objectives by demonstrating mastery of logically preceding ones. These concepts are fundamental to the teaching/learning models of Benjamin Bloom, Madeline Hunter, Ronald Edmonds, and the Outcomes Based Education movement, according to Hall (1988). The teacher must identify the proper starting point on the objectives continuum for each student, provide instruction appropriate to each selected objective, and monitor performance.

Teachers attempting to implement mastery learning quickly find themselves facing enormous management tasks.

Individualized Instruction

Because mastery learning aims for performance at a high level, implementation all but necessitates some form of individualization of instruction as well. Not all students will "master" the content in the same time, so a lock-step approach to instruction is inappropriate. Individualization acknowledges differences in learning needs and rates and adds the idea that students have differing learning styles or modalities. The basis of mastery learning, as well as other effective learning experiences, is individualization.

Prescription of learning activities results from individual diagnosis of needs. As Becker (undated) notes, "Research suggests that using tests to individualize instruction targeted to each student's identified skill deficiencies is a practice that has merit" (p. 31). The teacher now faces a group of students progressing at different rates through diverse sets of objectives using varied materials and forms of learning. Assuming a satisfactory method of handling diagnosis and prescription, the teacher must next find a way to gain time to work with students individually.

Problems in Implementation

Many efforts at individualization and mastery learning have foundered on problems of management. The Chicago Public Schools abandoned a mastery learning reading program after four years because it was "just so demanding" and the record keeping was "overwhelming" (Banas, 1985). The teacher's role can quickly default into one of recordkeeper just to keep up with the flow. In fact, implementation has tended to be minimal because of management problems.

Clearly, a solution had to be found if these promising ideas were ever to succeed. As Dennis and Kansky (1984) pointed out, "Instructional management is a means to an end. The end which it serves is the utilization of the learning environment in a manner that best serves the individual needs, talents, and interests of both students and teachers" (p. 139). If we are to espouse individualization as a goal, we must also recognize the enormity of the task of implementation.

AN EARLY CMI SYSTEM—PROJECT PLAN

One early effort at CMI was Westinghouse Learning Corporation's Project PLAN. PLAN was conceptualized as a method of returning the teacher to the most productive role possible, largely small group instruction and individual student assistance. A large computer at a remote location took over the tasks of assessment, progress monitoring, and prescription of student work.

How PLAN Worked

Once a student was entered into the system, objectives were selected. Based on available data, the computer prescribed learning activities for the student, with objectives matched to a wide variety of text series and other resources. Each "unit" concluded with a test, which was completed in machine-readable form.

Overnight, the computer would evaluate the tests, update progress records, and provide the next day's work assignments for the student. The teacher received daily printouts on student achievement, progress through the objectives, and future study plans. Mostly individualized work was entailed, so teacher preparation for class was significantly reduced. Time became available for working directly with learners.

Problems with PLAN

For some teachers, PLAN was a great success. It clearly supported mastery learning, allowed individualization to work, and relieved many management problems. However, for others, it also removed the sense of purpose and control. Teachers sometimes felt like laborers, carrying out the orders of the great boss machine.

PLAN meshed well with the concepts of individualized instruction, but ultimately foundered like most early computer projects on high cost. Schools with which the authors worked directly were generally impressed by the achievement gains of their students under PLAN, but few could afford to continue the experiment.

MICROCOMPUTERS AND COMPUTER-MANAGED INSTRUCTION

CMI AS PERFORMANCE MONITORING AND ANALYSIS

Some aspects of PLAN and other attempts at CMI reappeared with the spread of microcomputers in schools. Inexpensive computer power became available to diagnose, deliver instruction (which PLAN never did), process learner responses, and analyze and store results. PLAN had been a traffic director for the learning system, not an integrated part of it. With the addition of delivery of instruction to the computer's task, it was quite natural to build a record-keeping management component into software for computer-assisted learning.

Typically, management programs are included on a diskette along with student lessons and are ostensibly accessible only to the teacher. A special command and password allow the teacher access to the CMI portion of the disk.

Setting Up a CMI System

To use CMI software, the teacher usually must establish a class roster on the disk, following the guidance of menus on the screen. A rudimentary sequence of events might be:

☐ Load the software and access the management program.
☐ Enter teacher's name.
☐ Enter name or other designation for the class.
☐ Enter student names.

How It Works

From the data base created by the teacher, the software controls student access through "sign on" procedures. Any student not found on the roster for the requested class and teacher is prevented from using the program. Those who successfully sign on proceed through the program, with the computer recording their performance as they go. The teacher returns to the diskette at a convenient time to examine or print out the information recorded on each user's performance.

Differences in Implementations

CMI software is highly variable in sophistication. The retained information may be as minimal as total correct and incorrect responses, or as complex as each individual response to all questions throughout the program. Provision may exist for analysis of student responses individually, across the entire group, or even across multiple classes.

If the software involves multiple lessons, the teacher may need to assign a starting point for each student during setup. The program will then not require the student to repeat work already mastered and can remind students at each work session of what they have already completed. In some systems, the teacher may also specify the order in which the student is to receive the instruction, how long each student may spend on a given lesson, acceptable performance levels, minimum and maximum numbers of items to be presented, and other individual parameters.

As an example, *MECC Management Master* allows the user to integrate lesson plans with popular textbook series, student performance records, and MECC software. The computer is not the total instructional system, nor must a school purchase all new materials to use it. The teacher remains in control of the scope, sequence, and format of instructional units or lessons. After the teacher presents a lesson, students use the computer network to supplement the instruction. The system collects progress data and prevents students from moving on if they are having difficulty. Students move on to a new set of lessons only when the teacher approves.

TenCORE Computer Managed Instruction for PCs and compatibles automates student testing, lesson assignments, and gradebook management. *Data Warehouse* is a modular system from which one may purchase instructional management and IEP modules, *Skills Bank* basic skills software, and school administration modules.

The most sophisticated CMI pretests the student on the content of the lesson(s). From this diagnosis, the computer begins the instruction at the most appropriate point for that student. As the learner progresses, the computer monitors achievement and moves the student forward as rapidly as possible and backward whenever errors warrant. Such an approach is highly efficient; the student need never linger on previously mastered material, yet is never frustrated by material that is too advanced.

Benefits of Performance Monitoring

One common criticism of computer-based learning is that one may have little sense of what the student has learned until one gives a written or oral exam. Unlike homework assignments, individual work on separate computers cannot be monitored easily, and there is seldom any paper record of the student's work.

Even a rudimentary scorekeeping approach to CMI can help to minimize these concerns. Just a retrievable record of questions attempted and number correct, such as nearly all programs provide on screen, may help to guide student study and minimize the need for some other forms of testing. Furthermore, evaluation may require less time because fewer questions (randomly selected by the computer) may yield student performance data comparable to that obtained from more lengthy paper and pencil assessments in the past.

CMI AS TEST-SCORING AND TESTING DEVICE

The term *computer-managed instruction* is also applied to the use of the computer for testing purposes, even apart from computer-based learning materials.

Automated Test Scoring

One form of CMI uses the computer as a test-scoring device only. Most microcomputers can be interfaced to small electronic optical scanners. These scanners read the ubiquitous answer sheets carefully marked within the boxes using a No. 2 lead pencil. Here the computer is divorced from the learning/teaching process and merely performs a clerical service. In addition to the requisite hardware, corresponding software will determine just what information one gets from such machine-scored tests. It may be as simple as individual student scores or as complex as analyses of all tests scored as a batch. An example is *Testworks,* software which translates scanner output into *AppleWorks* or ProDOS text files.

On-Line Testing

Testing may also occur directly on the computer, apart from computer-based instruction. The teacher prepares a bank of test items for each objective and unit of instruction. Students take their tests on the machine when they feel ready. Each completes a different test since the computer selects items for each student at random from the item bank.

The teacher is freed from the burden of producing alternate forms of each test, as well as from scoring them. Testing need not occur at only one time for the entire class. Students benefit from immediate feedback about their performance. The computer stores the records, which the teacher retrieves and examines when convenient. Such testing has great potential, as described by Feuer (1986), but also raises many issues regarding interpretation of results which are discussed by Sarvela and Noonan (1988).

Test Item Analysis

For teachers seeking to improve their objective tests over time, computerized test scoring often provides for an item analysis. *Item analysis* is a valuable procedure for determining which test items are sound and which should be eliminated or improved. The key is whether individual items are measuring the same thing as the total test.

For instance, a question that is typically answered correctly by students with high total scores but missed by those with low total scores is contributing to the overall assessment properly. If the reverse is true, the item is not contributing to the overall assessment and is in need of revision or replacement. Further, item analysis will reveal patterns of responses, such as showing that of five alternatives, one or more are rarely chosen by students. Such alternatives are ineffective and should be improved.

While item analysis can be carried out manually, few teachers are likely to devote the necessary time to it. With the aid of the computer, item analysis can become a regular contributor to better evaluation procedures.

STUDENT USERS OF CMI

Thus far, our discussion has focused on teacher use of CMI tools. Since this is a book for teachers, we intentionally omit discussion of administrative applications such as budgeting, attendance, and equipment inventory. These, too, may be legitimately classified as CMI but are outside our scope.

Riedesel and Clements (1985, pp. 84–85) offer an interesting scenario of students directly involved with CMI software. They describe students eagerly awaiting their turns to take daily attendance with an appropriate program. Student access to a limited number of computers is scheduled using a computer, of course. A quick check of the schedule on screen will resolve conflicts over turns.

Students routinely learn from computer programs, which diagnose problems based on response patterns and suggest off-computer remediation materials. The teacher checks the prescriptions and suggests alternatives when warranted. Beyond this, the hypothetical teacher employs CMI in all the ways suggested previously.

The significance of this scenario is the suggestion that perhaps students can be involved in using certain forms of CMI, thereby gaining further exposure to the computer as a tool in daily living.

INTEGRATED LEARNING SYSTEMS

The Rolls Royce of CMI is the *integrated learning system* (ILS). The name reflects the total integration of CAI and management in a single system. Some systems can be installed on existing microcomputers; others require their own hardware, sometimes a minicomputer.

Among the best-known systems are PLATO and WICAT, both with very extensive curriculum offerings. Computer Curriculum Corporation (CCC) pioneered mainframe drill and practice systems as mentioned in Chapter 8. CCC's Microhost Instructional System uses microcomputers to deliver and manage basic skills courseware from kindergarten level through adult literacy. ESC integrated learning systems can run on Apple IIs, Macs, and MS–DOS computers, and include nearly 2000 lessons in basic skills for grades K–8.

An ILS is a complete system in the sense that users need not shop around for other computer products with comparable curriculum goals. It offers a single-source solution to instructional needs. The quantity of software is enormous compared to what most schools now have in CAI. Naturally, there is a price for this. According to Bruder (1988), a 30-station lab of hardware and CCC Microhost software costs about $100,000. Her article provides further details on ten ILS suppliers. See Appendix B for a list of selected ILS suppliers.

CONCERNS REGARDING CMI

Complexity of Set-Up

The most common complaint about software with a management component is difficulty in setting up the system for student use. Considerable time has to be spent entering the student rosters, defining task sequences for each student, and so on. Most such complaints stem from unrealistic expectations as to how much the computer should be able to do on its own. Further, work that would normally occur over an extended period of time for a teacher suddenly has to be completed all at once before students are given access to the programs. Thus, the task looks larger than it may when pieces are scattered over time. Hall (1988) described the use of paraprofessionals to operate a CMI system.

Today's software is constantly becoming more "user-friendly," meaning it's easier to use with less need to digest and depend on written documentation. However, the day when the computer can act based on a teacher's intentions, rather than explicit instructions, is a long way in the future. The best one can expect is increased ease of operation.

Student/Teacher Interaction

Coburn, Kelman, Roberts, Snyder, Watt, and Weiner (1982, p. 48) suggested other problems with CMI. First, they noted that some educators perceive CMI as decreasing student/teacher interaction. Our previous discussion of the role of CMI in the individualization of instruction speaks to the exact opposite as the proper outcome. Where interaction decreases, it can only be a result of the method of implementation, not something inherent in the concept.

Software Quality

Another criticism of CMI, according to Coburn et al., is the eternal question of software quality. This requires separation of CMI from programs for learning, and management assistance from actual instruction. To the extent that the system includes CAI, the concern is the same one raised in previous chapters. However, when looking only at the management component, you must assess whether the kinds of records and analyses provided are, indeed, what you need and want. Only to the extent that they are will the program prove useful to you, the classroom teacher.

You may determine that for your needs the diagnosis and prescription capabilities of the software are too simplistic. The data collected may not be retrievable in the most useful ways, thereby lessening the labor-saving potential of the system. Perhaps you could achieve the same net results manually in less time. In such situations, the software is clearly not of interest to you.

Teacher and Student Evaluation

Hall (1988) suggested resistance to CMI may stem from concerns that only lower-level skills will be tested since computer-based testing is largely limited to multiple-choice, true-false, and matching formats. What is the curricular impact of this? Further, if a computer is maintaining extensive records on student "achievement," this could become the basis for evaluation of teachers.

Our response is identical to both concerns. What the computer does is only *one* part of the educational process. Its limits must be clearly understood and respected.

Cost

When CMI is simply a feature of a CAI package, it has no separate cost, so there is no issue. However, integrated learning systems can easily cost large sums. To justify such expense requires a strong commitment to both CAI and the benefits expected from the CMI dimension. On a cost per hour of student-use basis, an ILS may well be the least expensive approach to computer-based learning. However, schools without such a system are far less likely to even attempt such extensive computer use. Cost comparisons are, therefore, difficult to make.

Effectiveness

Given the responsibility delegated to a CMI system, especially in the ILS context, one may ask whether the computer is competent to assess student performance and provide appropriate prescriptions. Clements (1985, pp. 39–41) noted that CMI has been sparsely studied, with results more suggestive of benefit than conclusive. One newer study raises particular concern. Hativa (1988) studied 300 students who used the CCC mathematics curriculum. The researchers created paper-and-pencil tests clustered around the level indicated by the CMI, but with problems both above and below that level. Most of the subjects went further than their recommended level on the paper test—on average over seven levels higher! Those classified as lowest-achieving based on their computer work averaged thirteen levels higher on paper than on computer. Possible reasons for the differences are carefully assessed, focusing on software design and instructional considerations. The point is that, even with extensively researched materials like CCC's, we seem not to have reached the desired level of sophistication in computer analysis of student achievement.

EVALUATING A CMI SYSTEM

Hall (1988) notes that the benefits of CMI vary with the product selected. She suggests that a desirable system must:

1. Be able to reflect and support the district's curriculum and philosophy, not dictate it.
2. Support any instructional mode, large group to one-on-one.
3. Be building-based, so that decisions are made at the most knowledgable level.
4. Provide useful data at the district level.
5. Be easy to use and provide clear reports.
6. Be constantly updated and upgraded by the vendor.
7. Handle continuous monitoring and testing with ease and flexibility.
8. Provide data on any subgroup desired, not just by class or grade.
9. Truly save time and reduce or eliminate manual record keeping.
10. Provide for extensive item analysis.

Flake, McClintock, and Turner (1985, pp. 305–306) add the important question of how teachers will perceive their role. Some may perceive a loss of control and responsibility. Others may fear assessment, a concern addressed already.

SUMMARY

Computer-managed instruction is yet another potential use of the computer in the classroom, one that cannot be totally separated from direct instruction via computer. Teachers perform many management functions with which the computer may assist. The foundations of CMI are the concepts of mastery learning and individualized instruction. Project PLAN demonstrated some of the potential of CMI, but only the advent of microcomputers permitted combining instruction and management in one system at reasonable cost. Beyond CMI as a component of computer-assisted learning, the computer can also be helpful in test administration and analysis. There are even potential student uses for some aspects of CMI. Integrated learning systems offer a complete CAI curriculum and management system from a single supplier.

Critics of CMI software have raised concerns over its difficulty of use, the quality of software, evaluation issues, cost, and effectiveness. Clearly, any CMI system under consideration requires careful assessment. Many computer-using educators see considerable merit in CMI. As Wright and Forcier (1985) stated, "The most significant benefits to students resulting from the use of CMI are the increased time for the teacher to interact with students and the increased effectiveness brought about by rapid analysis of performance and prescription of learning activities" (p. 101).

CHAPTER 10 ACTIVITIES

1. Examine an available software package with a management component. What are its capabilities? What are its limitations? If possible, actually set up a hypothetical class using the program. How easy is it to do so? Does the benefit appear to justify the work?
2. Visit a school using CMI and discuss its advantages and disadvantages with an experienced user.
3. What is your view of the computer as a test-giver?
4. Contact several sources of integrated learning systems for their literature. (See Appendix B.) Compare their features. Which do you find most appealing? Why?
5. Justify or refute the concerns raised over student and teacher evaluation with CMI.

REFERENCES

Banas, C. "Mastery Learning Demoted." *Chicago Tribune,* August 15, 1985.

Becker, H. J. *Microcomputers in the Classroom. Dreams and Realities.* Eugene, OR: International Council for Computers in Education, undated.

Bitter, G. G., and Camuse, R. A. *Using a Microcomputer in the Classroom.* Reston, VA: Reston Publishing Company, 1984.

Bruder, I. "Integrated Learning Systems: An Overview of What's Available." *Electronic Learning,* November/December 1988, pp. 54–57.

Clements, D. H. *Managing the Classroom with Computers.* Englewood Cliffs, NJ: Prentice-Hall, 1985.

Coburn, P., Kelman, P., Roberts, N., Snyder, T. F. F., Watt, D. H., and Weiner, C. *Practical Guide to Computers in Education.* Reading, MA: Addison-Wesley, 1982.

Dennis, J. R., and Kansky, R. J. *Instructional Computing: An Action Guide for Educators.* Glenview, IL: Scott, Foresman, 1984.

Feuer, D. "Computerized Testing: A Revolution in the Making." *Training,* May 1986, pp. 80–86.

Flake, J. L., McClintock, C. E., and Turner, S. V. *Fundamentals of Computer Education.* Belmont, CA: Wadsworth, 1985.

Hall, M. "The Case for Computerized Instructional Management." *Educational Technology,* June 1988, pp. 34–37.

Hativa, N. "CAI Versus Paper and Pencil: Discrepancies in Students' Performance." *Instructional Science,* Vol. 17, 1988, pp. 77–9.

Riedesel, C. A., and Clements, D. H. *Coping with Computers in the Elementary and Middle Schools*. Englewood Cliffs, NJ: Prentice-Hall, 1985.

Sarvela, P. D., and Noonan, J. V. "Testing and Computer-Based Instruction: Psychometric Considerations." *Educational Technology*, May 1988, pp. 17–20.

Wright, E. B., and Forcier, R. C. *The Computer: A Tool for the Teacher*. Belmont, CA: Wadsworth, 1985.

□ PART 4 □

The Computer as Learner

CHAPTER 11

□ The Concepts of Programming □

OBJECTIVES

After completing this chapter, you will be able to:

- □ Give an example of your own of directing a person to do some task. □
- □ Explain what a computer program is. □
- □ Discuss the importance of planning in developing a computer program. □
- □ Explain the three major elements of problem analysis. □
- □ Describe what a flowchart is and why flowcharts are valuable. □
- □ Identify the four basic flowcharting symbols. □
- □ Discuss the concepts of structured programming. □
- □ Differentiate coding from programming. □
- □ Differentiate low-level from high-level languages. □
- □ Explain the difference between machine language and assembler language. □
- □ Explain the difference between an interpreter and a compiler. □

This book introduced you initially to the computer as a tool in everyday life. We then turned to the computer as a personal tutor, providing direct instruction in a variety of ways. In this chapter and the remainder of this section, you will look at the final major aspect of microcomputer usage—the computer as learner or "tutee."

The previous sections of this book have focused on making use of available programs. This is the most common way that microcomputers are used in schools today. But it is not the only way. The programs that we use had to be written by someone. An understanding of programming concepts provides the user with an appreciation of how computers are actually controlled, how they are "taught" to perform their tasks.

Lest we create an erroneous initial impression, we do not want to teach you to program. The time and effort required to develop programs from scratch are seldom available within an introductory computer education course. Rather, you will learn the fundamental concepts of computer programming in this chapter. In succeeding chapters you will explore common implementation languages. This is a sufficient introduction to programming to enable an informed decision regarding further study of programming.

Our conceptual overview begins with a rationale for the study of programming. Next, we present the fundamental concepts of programming: control, planning, structure, coding, and testing and revision. In the final section of this chapter, you will learn about the various levels of programming languages and the different modes of language execution.

A RATIONALE FOR PROGRAMMING

Programming is perhaps the most controversial element of computer education today. Some view it as the key ingredient in "computer literacy." For others, tool and tutoring uses are vastly more important, even to the extent of ignoring programming entirely. Our organization of this book indicates our position. We do not believe educators should be ignorant of programming, but we prioritize it behind tool and direct instructional applications.

PROGRAMMING AND TEACHERS

There are several possible reasons for a teacher to be exposed to computer programming. While many teachers are literally afraid to learn to program, others are genuinely curious about it and welcome the challenge that it provides. Some have all but been forced to learn something about programming to be able to answer student inquiries. We have found this especially among elementary grade teachers.

In some schools, teachers have been drafted into a computer program based upon programming. They actually teach some minimal level of programming to their students. Programming classes or parts of classes can be found at all levels of schooling. This is often a result of schools acquiring computers but little or no software suitable for other purposes, leaving programming as the primary use for the computers. The higher the grade level, the more knowledge is usually required of the programming teacher.

In addition, understanding programming concepts provides teachers with a starting point for possibly writing their own programs. This may be a necessity in the absence of ready-to-use programs in a school. It may also stem from a teacher's desire to use computers in areas or applications for which either no programs are commercially available or where available programs do not meet specific teacher needs.

PROGRAMMING AND STUDENTS

Several reasons are commonly expressed for teaching students to program. One is that it is the best way to show students that computers are under human control, not vice versa. In addition, computer programs seldom have only one correct solution. Thus, programming offers one of few opportunities for students to experience success other than in a right/wrong context.

Many students want to learn programming to satisfy their curiosity about the computer. They have seen many intriguing examples of what the machine can do and want to know how it does them. This has often led to pressure on the school to teach programming, even as an after-school activity. In some schools, the computer whiz may acquire stature comparable to athletes.

Some educators support programming as a viable approach to teaching problem solving. Clearly, one cannot plan and develop a computer program without application of logical thinking, problem analysis, organization, and other higher order thought processes. We know of little research, however, that supports the direct transfer of problem-solving skills from programming to other applications. (See chapter references.)

For some, programming is an excellent means of fostering meaningful communication among students. When a group of students is working on a programming problem, there are many opportunities for mutual assistance and cooperation. This may be an antidote to the perception that computer activities tend to isolate students. Programming may lead to student collegiality.

Numerous students today have access to a computer in the home and have begun to learn programming on their own with the help of books. They have found it to be fun, something many teachers find hard to comprehend. Perhaps it is appropriate that the school provide opportunities for development of these skills, giving form to what has been self-taught and taking students beyond their present level of understanding.

Finally, the extensive programming curricula of some secondary schools suggests that programming is taught either as preparation for postsecondary data processing study or some other prevocational purpose.

Each teacher and school will respond to these justifications for programming in their own way. The most critical factor is that a school have a well-developed rationale for what it does with programming, and then assure that its activities support that goal. Several chapter references offer guidance.

FUNDAMENTAL PROGRAMMING CONCEPTS

Most books purporting to teach programming actually concentrate on specific languages. Yet learning a language is quite different from learning to program. In learning a language, you must master the *statements* that are the vocabulary of the language and all that the computer can understand. You must also learn the *syntax* of the statements; that is, exactly how they are written to be intelligible to the machine.

Programming can be conceptually separated from any language. Most critical is the ability to develop the logic needed to solve a programming problem. This is far more difficult to master than the mechanics of a language. Required are an understanding of the concept of control and skills in the process of planning a solution. Further, one should apply the best contemporary approaches in programming methodology to the solution. We turn now to these fundamental concepts.

CONTROL

In and of themselves, computers are mazes of electronics awaiting direction. The goal of using a computer is to perform some task. To do so, the machine must be directed in its work, that is, controlled.

In order to understand how a computer is controlled, it may be instructive to consider first how a person could be directed to do something and then to apply the same reasoning to a microcomputer. Control is fundamental to a conceptual understanding of programming and critical to eventually learning how to program.

Individual Control
When an individual does something, that "something" is usually a series of steps, although they may not be conscious ones. When you get up in the morning, your series of steps might well include the following:

1. Open eyes.
2. Look for clock.
3. Shut off alarm.
4. Read time.
5. Decide on 40 more winks.
6. Close eyes.
7. Open eyes again.
8. Throw off covers.
9. Swing body around.

10. Hunt for slippers.

11. Stand up.

12. Stretch.

    *A **Detailed Example.*** Another example of functioning in steps might be completion of a homework assignment in mathematics to calculate the squares of 25 numbers on a list. The answers must be written and will be collected the next day. Most students will go home, work the problem for each number, and write down the answers. However, suppose one of the students in the class is lazy, but has a little brother who is good at numbers and even knows how to square them. Little Brother is cooperative, but unfortunately has no ability to organize and, what is worse, forgets what he has done as soon as he has done it.

    Lazy Student decides there must be some way of getting Little Brother to do the assignment, since he has other plans for the evening. It occurs to him that if he breaks the assignment into many simple steps, writes these steps down, and gives them to Little Brother, then Little Brother might complete the assignment. Lazy Student would then be free to go out.

    Even though the preparation might be time consuming, Lazy Student decides that it is worth the trouble. To begin with, he must thoroughly understand the problem, after which he may outline the solution, and finally write the individual steps to accomplish the solution. Each step must be one operation. When Little Brother has completed one step, he will go on to the next. In addition, the numbers to be squared must be provided as part of the step-by-step procedure.

    Now Lazy Student can turn his attention to writing the steps necessary to do the homework assignment.

STEP 1. Read a number on the sheet from the teacher.

STEP 2. Square the number just read.
        (This presents no problem since Little Brother does know how to find the square of a number. How he does it is not important.)

STEP 3. Write the answer down.
        (It would not help Lazy Student if Little Brother did not record the obtained square of the number.)

STEP 4. See if there are more numbers on the list.
        (This is a simple step, but crucial if the entire assignment is to be finished. The answer to this is either YES or NO. If the answer is YES, then Little Brother can be instructed to go to STEP 5. If the answer is NO, then Little Brother can be instructed to skip STEP 5 and go directly to STEP 6.)

STEP 5. If there are more numbers, go back and start again with STEP 1.
        (Little Brother would do this if the answer to STEP 4 was YES. The squaring procedure would then continue with the next number on the list.)

STEP 6. Stop. The assignment is complete. Put the work away and do whatever you want.

(Little Brother would do this if the answer to STEP 4 was NO—when he has squared all the numbers on the list.)

Although he does not know the terminology, Lazy Student has developed an *algorithm,* a carefully planned series of steps that define a solution to a problem. Algorithm development is fundamental to problem solving.

This series of six steps directs Little Brother to complete the assignment, but Lazy Student must *verify* that this is the desired procedure. Little Brother is not able to figure out what to do if there are any errors in the steps, nor can he do any steps that are not on the instruction list. If Lazy Student forgets to tell Little Brother to write down the answer, Lazy Student will return home to find the task "completed," but no answers on the sheet. Thus, it is important to carefully reexamine the steps to the solution to determine completeness and accuracy. For a simple problem like this, Lazy Student might even work through the steps with a list of, say, just two numbers to verify his algorithm.

Later that evening, Lazy Student calls Little Brother, gives him the instruction list and the list of numbers to be squared, and leaves. If all goes well, when he returns, his homework will be finished.

Computer Control

Three factors were involved in the homework problem: Lazy Student, the directions he wrote, and Little Brother. This example parallels computer control, which also has three factors: 1) the programmer (Lazy Student), 2) the program (the directions), and 3) the computer system (Little Brother). The computer system and Little Brother are problem solvers with particular characteristics that cannot be changed but that must be accommodated as they are. The programmer, or Lazy Student, has to develop a program or set of instructions for the computer system to do a desired job. This means that he must describe in the program each individual step that the computer must do *in a way the computer can understand.* These instructions must be accurate and complete to get the job done.

Through an input device, the programmer gives the instructions (program) to the computer, which stores them in memory. Next, the system executes the steps sequentially, one at a time, until the program directs it to stop. If the steps were correctly written, the desired result is obtained. If not, the program must be carefully reexamined and "debugged."

A series of instructions that direct the computer is called a *program,* which is written by a *programmer* to accomplish a specific task. The whole procedure is called *programming.*

As long as the instructions are correct and complete, there is no limitation to the jobs a computer can do. Any number of programs can be written, each to do a different job. Programs may be short or long, simple or complicated, depending upon the task to be performed. There is no necessity for continuity across job runs. One job might be to calculate the squares of a series of numbers, the next might be to add groups of numbers together and compute averages. The program for each job is written to do just that job, and the computer executes each program individually.

In the "program" written by Lazy Student for Little Brother, only six steps were needed to direct Little Brother to do the assignment. Little Brother's list of numbers might contain 10 or 80 items, and the same six steps would still accomplish the job of squaring them all. Further, the same six steps could be used over and over again with new sets of numbers.

The directions allowed Little Brother to make some limited decisions. He was told to see if there were more numbers on the list, and the answer to the question resulted in one of two alternatives. If the answer was yes, he was told to go back to the beginning of the procedure and do it again. If the answer was no, he was told to stop.

Just like Little Brother, the computer is capable of handling its own program. The programmer loads instructions into the computer's memory, and, upon command, the computer executes them one instruction at a time. Most programs are written to process whatever volume of data is available and are capable of processing any other comparable sets of data. Based upon decisions, the program directs the system to go back and repeat some of the earlier instructions or to proceed to another set of instructions entirely.

PLANNING

Now that you understand the control concept, we turn to the most critical factor in programming—planning. The more carefully, thoroughly, and accurately one plans a program, the less time the remaining steps in the program development cycle will require. The total time spent creating a program will also be minimized. We will look at planning as two major steps—problem analysis and algorithm development.

Problem Analysis

Applying sound principles of problem analysis is a complex task that varies from one problem to another, one programmer to another, and one problem-solving situation to another. Skills in problem analysis develop slowly from experience. Do not expect to have everything fall into place quickly and easily. However, a few basic points will serve as a start.

First, as a programmer, you must understand the problem. What *exactly* is the program to do? Never attempt to solve a problem until you are certain that you understand the problem completely. You will avoid much frustration and many failures just by following this advice.

Second, you must know what the input data will be. If you are also in charge of preparing the data, you must have control over the accuracy of data preparation. If data are already prepared, you must be familiar with exactly

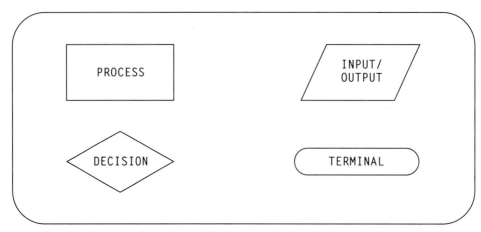

FIGURE 11.1. Common flowchart symbols

what is available, what form it is in, and whether more information may be required.

Third, you must know what is required as output from the computer and what its form must be.

A programmer must determine precisely what has to be done to the input to produce the desired output. (In our example, input numbers had to be squared to produce the desired output.) It is the responsibility of the programmer to analyze the requirements of a specific problem, to determine how these requirements can be met by the computer, and then to proceed with planning and writing a program that will produce the required result.

The importance of problem analysis cannot be overemphasized. Incomplete understanding of information and poor or faulty planning will only result in having to alter constantly what has been done already as additional facts become available. Even worse, you may never really get off the ground with a solution. It is both easier and more efficient to begin program planning with the initial understanding gained from problem analysis, then proceed to algorithm development.

Algorithm Development (Flowcharting)

Flowcharting is one of several techniques that allow a programmer to graphically represent proposed solutions to a problem. We belive it is the simplest technique for the beginner. A flowchart is a *visual* algorithm, which can be extremely helpful in locating errors in one's planning. Flowcharting is a very useful and powerful procedure. It is strongly recommended as a vital step in the programming cycle, prior to any attempt to actually write the instructions in a specific language.

Flowcharting Symbols. After careful problem analysis, the steps required to solve the problem are diagrammed using standardized symbols. Specific symbols represent each function of processing. Although there are many such symbols, our needs will be met with the use of just four: PROCESS, INPUT/OUTPUT, DECISION, and TERMINAL. Figure 11.1 illustrates these symbols.

For each step in an algorithm, the developer selects the correct symbol and places it on the chart. Within the symbol, a concise statement of the function is written. The symbols are connected by arrows to show the flow of execution.

An Example Flowchart. Our previous example will serve to illustrate flow-charting. The original problem was to square all the numbers on a provided list. Problem analysis yields these steps: obtain a number from the list, square that number, write down the answer, and repeat the process until all the numbers on the list have been squared. A flowchart of these steps is presented in Figure 11.2 on page 254.

A TERMINAL symbol shows where the flowchart begins and contains the word "Start." "Get a Number" is an INPUT operation and is written in an INPUT/OUTPUT (I/O) symbol. The PROCESS rectangle is used for "Calculate Square." "Write Answer" is an OUTPUT operation and is also represented by an INPUT/OUTPUT symbol. The determination of whether there are more numbers is a yes/no decision and the question "More Numbers?" is written inside a diamond-shaped DECISION symbol. Decisions always lead to one of two actions. Here, if the answer is Yes, processing resumes at the "Get a Number" I/O symbol, and the cycle is repeated. If the answer is No, processing continues with the next sequential step, a TERMINAL symbol that directs the system to halt. This outlines the entire program and gives, in graphic or schematic form, the general steps necessary to accomplish the task.

The writer of this flowchart can now examine it in detail to see if it will accomplish the desired task. The programmer may discover that additional processing might be necessary under certain conditions, that steps have been omitted, or that there may be ways to simplify the entire procedure. Experienced programmers know that time spent at this stage will greatly facilitate and speed up the more mechanical steps of coding and debugging.

Discussion of Flowcharting. After a problem has been analyzed, a programmer may construct several flowcharts, each illustrating a somewhat different approach to the same problem. Beyond the simplest problems, there is seldom only *one* correct solution. As a flowchart is being drawn, a programmer must consider various alternatives that may be encountered during the course of problem solution. A flowchart provides an efficient way to see if any steps have been omitted and if the overall logic of the solution appears to be correct. If errors are later discovered or modifications must be made to achieve the goal, one can return to the flowchart to find and correct them.

Beginning programmers are often more interested in actually writing the computer instructions (coding) than in problem analysis and flowcharting. It seems more useful to be actually writing instructions than to be drawing diagrams. However, the importance of problem analysis and flowcharting is quickly realized by a programmer working on full-scale problems. To analyze the method of attack on any problem is as important as writing the actual

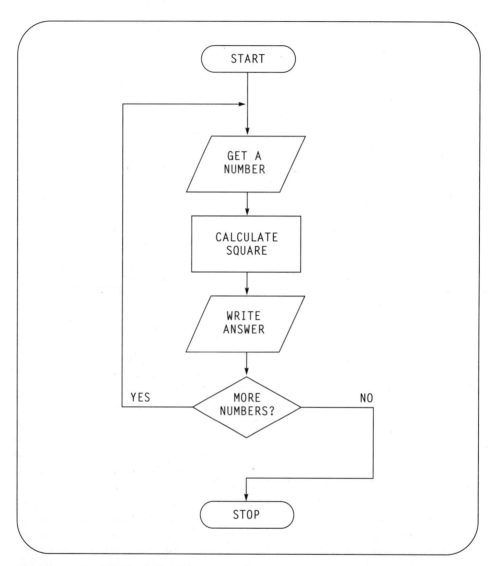

FIGURE 11.2. An example flowchart

instructions, perhaps more important. If the structure of the solution is not fully and accurately understood, no combination of instructions will produce useful output.

In fairness, it should be noted that some programmers rarely flowchart their problems and still write sound and efficient programs. The ability to do so is a direct result of extensive programming experience. Flowcharting is a step one may eventually abandon or, more likely, replace with other techniques not presented here. We question that anyone other than a professional will reach that level and strongly recommended flowcharting as the easiest approach for the beginner.

STRUCTURED PROGRAMMING

According to Dijkstra, "the art of programming is the art of organizing complexity, of mastering multitude and avoiding its bastard chaos as effectively as possible" (Dahl, Dijkstra, and Hoare, 1972, p. 6). The most widely accepted approach to meeting this challenge is called *structured programming*.

Origin and Nature

In the early days of computers, getting the machine to produce the desired output was very difficult. Any means of doing so was considered acceptable. Programmers were virtually a priesthood of miracle workers who individually developed ways of achieving results. There were no general standards for how programs should be written.

As the field of data processing evolved, it became necessary to develop common approaches so that programs written by one person would be easily understood by others. Early programs truly demonstrated a level of "operational chaos" in that they worked, but how and why was difficult to tell. Even programmers were often unable to comprehend their products shortly after completing them. As computers became more common and the number of programs in existence exploded, the old ways no longer sufficed.

Today, a standard for programming exists and is almost universally accepted in the data processing industry—structured programming. According to Schnake (1985, p. 357), structured programming "is a set of techniques designed to improve the organization of the program, to facilitate solving a problem, and to make the code easier to write and read. . . ."

For our purposes, we will consider four basic components of structured programming: top-down design, modularity, use of a well-defined set of logical constructs, and documentation.

Top-Down Design

Early programmers attacked their problems in a manner somewhat similar to putting together a jigsaw puzzle with no guarantee that all of the pieces are for the same puzzle and without an illustration of what the completed picture should be. The method has been called *bottom-up design*. The smallest details of a program were attacked first. If they could be solved, then work progressed up a level, putting more pieces together, hoping ultimately to have a total product that still worked.

It seems that this approach developed because of the newness of programming and the inexperience of many practitioners. They had little confidence in their ultimate ability to solve the entire problem and wished to begin with what they thought would be the most difficult parts. Major problems in making all the pieces work together were very common.

Top-down design, in contrast, seems intuitively correct to most people today. It begins with the big picture, not the minutiae. From an overall understanding of the problem, the major components are identified at a relatively abstract level. Each major component is then refined into subtasks required for it to work. The process is carried on through as many levels of refinement as required to reach a point where only a relatively trivial programming task remains. The technique, also referred to as "step-wise refinement," is illustrated in Figure 11.3.

Modularity

Modularity is a logical extension of top-down design. When a programming problem has been refined into minor steps that together meet the requirements, it is only reasonable to actually prepare the instructions to the computer as a series of *modules.* Each module fulfills one of the well-defined tasks described in the design and therefore has a limited function.

Because planning began at the top, there is little likelihood that the parts will not fit together and work properly as a whole. In fact, each module will have a high degree of independence from others. This makes it possible to reuse modules from one program to the next, so long as the processing need is the same and only the specific data vary. Over many programming projects, this adds greatly to programming efficiency.

Limited Constructs

Within modules, structured programming makes the work of one programmer readily understandable to others by limiting the techniques used to achieve the

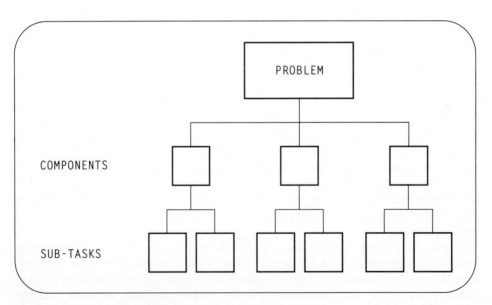

FIGURE 11.3. Top-down design

desired result. These techniques are known as *logical constructs.* They lend a distinctive style to programs, which is known to be efficient and effective, and which reduces the chaos of idiosyncratic programming to a widely accepted standard. One might say that structured constructs produce "educated, literate programming."

Boehm and Jacopini (1966) proved mathematically that all programming requirements can be met by only three logical constructs. They are sequence, selection, and iteration or repetition. Figure 11.4 on page 258 shows minimal flowcharts for these constructs.

Sequence. *Sequence* entails one or more instructions carried out by the computer in the exact order in which written. This is the most fundamental of the constructs. Only process and I/O symbols are needed to flowchart a sequence. In fact, every program can begin as a sequence of one process box, as shown in Figure 11.4. This one box is then replaced with a series of symbols in a longer sequence and/or other constructs as the overall program is refined into subtasks.

Selection. The *selection* construct involves a question, the answer to which determines what happens next. Only two answers are possible for each question, yes or no. Either answer may cause specific processing to occur, or one may produce no result at all, simply by-passing the processing required in the other case.

Iteration. The final allowable construct is *iteration* or repetition. This entails repeating a series of processing operations until some specified condition is met. Another common term for this construct is *looping.*

An iteration construct also involves a *decision symbol.* Rather than leading to two alternate forward paths as selection does, one path of an iteration continues, the other goes back to repeat steps. If the decision is made *before* any processing, the loop is referred to as a "Do While." If processing occurs first and then the need for repetition is determined, it is known as a "Repeat Until."

Code Documentation

The goal of code documentation is to enable a programmer to read a printed listing of the instructions comprising a program and to understand *what* it does and *how.* This is essential where several programmers work jointly on one program. It is also helpful in program maintenance and modification at a later date. Even the creator of a program can easily forget how it works over time. In fact, if the documentation is thorough, a nonprogrammer may be able to at least understand the essence of the program.

Each language has its own means for placing documentation within a program. The methodology is language specific, but the need for documentation is universal.

CODING

We have now described the programming process in terms of procedures and principles. There has been no reference to a specific programming language,

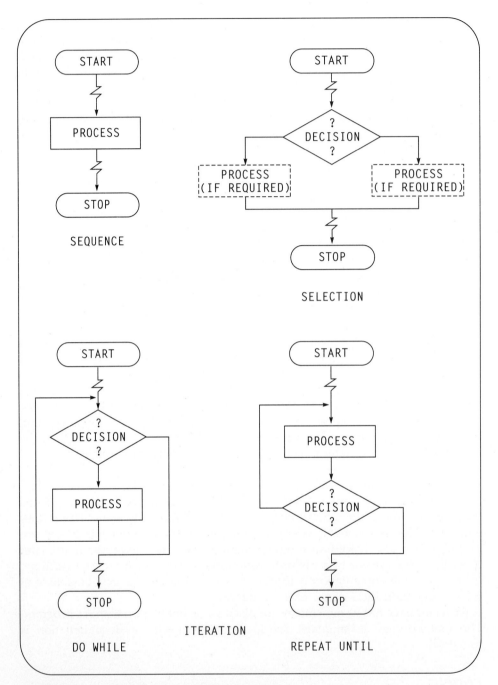

FIGURE 11.4. Structured programming constructs

because all of the earlier steps are language independent. By this we mean that one can and should plan the attack, devise an algorithm, and express that algorithm as a flowchart using structured constructs quite apart from any concern over which language will ultimately be used.

While most beginning programmers are justifiably concerned over details of a specific language, its vocabulary and syntax, these concerns become important only after the preceding steps are completed. Writing the actual instructions in some language is known as *coding*. It is quite possible to become technically proficient at coding in one or more languages without ever developing the far more critical analytical skills we have described.

Learning to code in any language tends to be a time-consuming task. It may reasonably be likened to learning a foreign language. For some it is far more difficult than for others. You will see modest examples of code in several languages in the chapters that follow.

For now, it should be clear to you that programming is *not* synonymous with coding. Coding is only one part of the entire process. Our point in making this distinction is that in many school settings, emphasis is placed on teaching students a language, that is, coding. We agree with Luehrmann (1983) who wrote, "the powerful ideas of computing . . . are vastly more important than the details of the programming language used." For a more detailed discussion of what should be taught in a school programming curriculum, see Lockard (1985–1986) and Anderson, Bennett, and Walling (1987).

TESTING AND REVISION

Without further concern over coding, we move on to the last phase of the program development cycle, *testing* and *revision*. Following the principles of structured programming, the product under development will be modular in design. In turn, it is both possible and desirable to code the program module by module. Each can be tested for proper operation upon completion.

Especially in the early stages of learning to program, it is only reasonable to expect errors in both logic and coding when one begins to test a module. Errors must be corrected before further work is undertaken, a process known as *debugging*. Debugging is the bane of the programmer and can be very time-consuming.

While there is little likelihood of ever becoming so skilled as to have only flawless initial test runs, the time spent on debugging generally decreases significantly with experience. Errors in logic are more difficult to resolve than errors in coding. Meticulous attention to the precoding stages can dramatically reduce logical errors. That is a major reason for structured programming. Coding errors will also diminish as fluency in the language increases.

PROGRAMMING AND LANGUAGES

When you write instructions for a computer, they cannot be the instructions you would give to another person. Computers have very limited capacity to understand, with none of the human ability to compensate for poor communication. Essentially, we humans must conform to the limits of the machine; it cannot adjust to us. Computer languages are the means for human-machine communication.

Computer languages are a vast topic, which we must restrict in our context. The focus will be on categorical distinctions for now, looking at various levels of computer languages as well as two methods of implementation.

LOW-LEVEL LANGUAGES

Shelly and Cashman (1980) defined low-level languages as languages closely related to a particular computer. There are two basic categories of such languages, *machine* and *assembler*. Actual implementations of either vary drastically from one computer to another.

Machine Language

The most fundamental language that a computer can understand is referred to as *machine language*. When a computer is designed and built, a specific functional language is provided in its processing circuits. Instructions in machine language can be understood directly and executed by the computer system. In fact, a computer system always executes machine language instructions because they are all that it actually understands.

Machine language is a very intricate and complicated language that would be difficult to use for writing programs. Since a computer is just a massive set of electrical switches, which can be set either on or off, its native language consists exclusively of binary digits. It is patterns of zeros and 1's that really cause the computer to function. If the only language available to a user to control a computer system were binary machine language, computers would be far less popular than they are today.

Assembler Language

The very first stored program computers could be programmed only in machine language. It quickly became apparent that a language more suited to humans was needed. An assembler language is machine-oriented, structured closely around the actual machine language. However, instead of programming in binary digits, machine language instructions are represented by symbolic instructions. For instance, the programmer uses mnemonic instructions like LDA (LoaD Accumulator) or CLI (Compare Logical Immediate), which an assembler program translates into the corresponding binary representation.

Assembler languages represent an attempt to make writing programs easier. They are the lowest level at which one can program most computers today. However, assembler languages remain close enough to machine language to still be comparatively difficult to use. We would probably not be teaching programming in the schools today if only assembler were available. The computer had to come closer to accommodating human needs.

HIGH-LEVEL LANGUAGES

High-level programming languages have been designed to meet human needs rather than to accommodate the computer. They are not languages to which a computer can directly respond, and they are *not* closely linked to the internal characteristics of the computer. In fact, most common high-level languages are available for virtually any computer.

In order for a computer to understand and execute high-level language instructions, they must first be translated into equivalent machine language by a "translator" program. Each high-level instruction typically yields several machine language instructions. Most high-level language instructions are common words, such as PRINT or WRITE, which are much easier for humans to learn to use correctly.

High-level language execution can be thought of as a two-step process. In Step 1, the translator program converts high-level instructions into machine code. In Step 2, the system executes the machine language instructions. In this manner, the program in the higher level language is actually executed by the computer in machine language.

High-level languages make computer language learning and programming accessible to most interested persons, the vast majority of whom would never attempt to learn a machine or assembler language. Such languages require less time to master and make programming far easier. Programmers tend to make fewer coding mistakes, and errors are easier to find and correct.

Succeeding chapters will present the two most common high-level languages used in education, Logo and BASIC. Brief illustrations of several other languages will also be provided.

Implementation Methods

Within high-level languages, there are two differing approaches to implementation. Both interpreters and compilers translate instructions into machine code.

Interpreters. An *interpreter* is a program that reads another program in some high-level language, one statement at a time. The interpreter translates this "source statement" into the corresponding machine code, which executes immediately. A language interpreter may be a program on a disk, which is loaded into RAM memory for use. In microcomputers, language interpreters are often provided on ROM chips.

When the interpreter finds an error in the coding, it cannot translate the statement, so the program halts at that point. This makes it relatively easy to identify the problem and correct it. In fact, an interpreted language is interactive, meaning that the user enters the instructions, runs the program, and is told of errors as they are found. The programmer can correct the error and rerun the program immediately. This makes interpreted languages ideal for beginners. Logo and many microcomputer versions of BASIC are interpreted languages.

Compilers. *Compiler* languages add another step to the process of moving from code in a high-level language to execution of the code. The programmer creates an entire program in the source language, say, FORTRAN. The compiler program attempts to translate the entire source program into machine instructions, noting errors as it goes, but generally not stopping until the end. The machine instructions are called *object code*.

If errors were found, the programmer must correct them and compile the program again. When there are no language errors, the object code is executed. Logic errors may be revealed that must then be corrected.

Thus, an interpreter translates source code instructions into machine instructions one by one and executes them. A compiler translates the entire source program into object code and executes it only when no coding errors remain. This is a somewhat more cumbersome process altogether, but has the advantage of faster execution of the program. Languages like FORTRAN, COBOL, and Pascal are usually implemented as compiled languages. Because the process is somewhat more complicated, compiled languages are less suitable to young and beginning programmers.

SUMMARY

A program is a set of instructions to a computer that cause it to carry out some clearly defined task. Programming is essentially a matter of controlling the computer, a process that parallels telling another person how to do something. The most important aspects of programming are understanding the problem and planning a logical approach to solving it, not the actual writing of specific language instructions to do the job.

Structured programming is a set of guidelines for writing programs in an efficient and effective manner. Following the principles of top-down design, modularity, use of only a limited number of logical constructs, and program documentation, a programmer can create programs that are easy to read and modify. Structured programming provides a widely understood and accepted approach to programming with proven benefits.

Programming should not be confused with coding, which is merely the conversion of careful plans into corresponding instructions in a chosen language. Beginning programmers must guard against moving too quickly into the coding phase. Careful planning can prevent many errors. Regardless of one's skill as a programmer, all programs require extensive testing to be certain that they truly perform as specified under all conditions. Errors are likely, either in coding or in logic. Correcting such errors is called debugging.

Programming languages are divided into low-level languages (machine and assembler languages) and high-level languages, such as BASIC or Pascal. Most programmers today use one of the numerous high-level languages that have been created to make programming easier and less error-prone. Low-level languages are very closely linked to specific computers and therefore differ widely. High-level languages exist for most computers in forms that are similar, regardless of the specific computer.

High-level languages may be implemented as interpreters or compilers. An interpreter is a program that converts high-level language instructions into their corresponding machine instructions one at a time and executes them immediately. A compiler translates an entire program into machine or object code, which executes only when no language errors remain. Interpreted languages are better suited to any beginning programmer, especially children.

REFERENCES

Anderson, R., Bennett, H., and Walling, D. "Structured Programming Constructs in BASIC: Tried and Tested." *Computers in the Schools,* Summer 1987, pp. 135–139.

Boehm, C., and Jacopini, G. "Flow Diagrams, Turing Machines, and Languages with Only Two Formulation Rules." *Communications of the Association for Computing Machinery,* May 1966, pp. 366–371.

Burton, J. K., and Magliaro, S. "Computer Programming and Generalized Problem-Solving Skills: In Search of Direction." *Computers in the Schools,* Fall/Winter 1987/88, pp. 63–90.

Dahl, O., Dijkstra, E., and Hoare, C. *Structured Programming.* New York: Academic Press, 1972.

Lockard, J. "Programming in the Schools: What Should Be Taught?" *Computers in the Schools,* Winter 1985–1986, pp. 105–114.

Luehrmann, A. "Slicing through Spaghetti Code." *The Computing Teacher,* April 1983, pp. 9–15.

Mayer, R. E., Dyck, J. L., and Vilberg, W. "Learning to Program and Learning to Think: What's the Connection?" *Communications of the ACM,* 29(7), pp. 605–610.

McCoy, L. P., and Orey, M. A., III. "Computer Programming and General Problem Solving by Secondary Students." *Computers in the Schools,* Fall/Winter 1987–1988, pp. 151–158.

Ohler, J. "The Many Myths of Programming." *The Computing Teacher,* May 1987, pp. 22–23.

Reed, W. M. "A Philosophical Case for Teaching Programming Languages." *Computers in the Schools,* Fall/Winter 1987–1988, pp. 55–58.

Schnake, M. *The World of Computers and Data Processing.* St. Paul: West Publishing, 1985.

Shelly, G., and Cashman, T. *Introduction to Computers and Data Processing.* Brea, CA: Anaheim Publishing, 1980.

Walton, R. E., and Balestri, D. "Writing as a Design Discipline: Exploring the Relationship between Composition and Programming." *Machine-Mediated Learning,* 2(1&2), 1987, pp. 47–65.

CHAPTER 12

□ Logo □

OBJECTIVES

After completing this chapter, you will be able to:

□ *Briefly describe the origins of Logo.* □
□ *Describe the philosophical and psychological bases of Logo.* □
□ *Define the terms* primitive, procedure, and recursion. □
□ *List the essential characteristics of Logo and its derivatives.* □
□ *Discuss reasons why Logo is taught.* □
□ *Present appropriate strategies for the teaching of Logo.* □
□ *Discuss Logo research findings.* □

Computer programming languages have been developed to help people communicate with their computers. Without such languages, the use of computers would be tremendously limited. The search for a computer language that is simple yet efficient and flexible has involved considerable time and expense. Perhaps one day in the not-too-distant future, speech will afford us the optimum communication tool, enabling us to "speak" to the computer. Until that time comes, however, programming languages will remain essential.

One such language is Logo, a computer language developed at the Massachusetts Institute of Technology in the late 1960s. Supporters of the use of Logo contend that it is *more* than a programming language since Logo is based upon a philosophy of learning guided by important learning principles. It is the intent of this chapter to introduce you to the Logo language and its underlying philosophical and psychological tenets.

WHAT IS LOGO?

Logo is unquestionably a programming language, but it is viewed by its developers as much more than that. According to Abelson (1982):

> Logo is the name for a philosophy of education and for a continually evolving family of computer languages that aid its realization. Its learning environments articulate the principle that giving people personal control over powerful computational resources can enable them to establish intimate contact with profound ideas from science, from mathematics, and from the art of intellectual model building. Its computer languages are designed to transform computers into flexible tools to aid in learning, in playing, and in exploring (p. ix).

Logo is a unique blend of a programming language, learning theory, and educational philosophy. It is intended to be both powerful and simple to use. Indeed, it is this simplicity and power that have made Logo so appealing to educators and students alike.

PHILOSOPHICAL AND PSYCHOLOGICAL FOUNDATIONS

The principal credit for the development of Logo is attributed to Seymour Papert, a mathematician at the Artificial Intelligence Laboratory of the Massachusetts Institute of Technology. Papert had studied for five years with the Swiss developmental psychologist Jean Piaget and was unquestionably influenced by Piaget's views about learning.

Piaget's Influence
According to Mouly (1973), Piaget's cognitive-developmental position is based on the premise that basic mental structure is the result of the interaction between certain structuring tendencies of the organism and the environment. As a result

of this interaction, the child's intellectual development systematically proceeds through different hierarchical stages that become more complex and integrated as the child matures.

To help facilitate this development, children should be allowed a great deal of activity on their own, directed by the use of materials that permit these activities to be cognitively beneficial. Children must become builders of their own intellectual structures. In the area of mathematics, Piaget contended that children gain *real* understanding only from that which they themselves invent. Furthermore, when we try to teach children something for which they are not ready, we keep them from learning it themselves. Thus there is little sense in trying to accelerate learning too much, since such teaching is largely a waste of time.

Cognitive development proceeds through several stages, becoming more complex as the child matures. To facilitate this development, the child needs an opportunity to explore. Instruction occurs as children initiate some action in the context of their environment rather than in response to imposed actions by instructors. As Piaget (1971) stated, "It is clear that an education which is an active discovery of reality is superior to one that consists merely in providing the young with ready-made wills to will with and ready-made truths to know with."

Papert's Beliefs

Papert appears to have strongly agreed with the majority of Piaget's teachings but departs somewhat from that portion dealing with accelerating learning. It is Papert's contention that the materials so essential to the intellectual growth of the child are, in fact, the responsibility of the culture in which the child resides. One major reason that children are slower in their intellectual development than they might be is the "relative poverty of the culture in those materials that would make the concept simple and concrete" (Papert, 1980, p. 7).

The need for the child to be in an environment that encourages free exploration and provides an abundance of materials that facilitate this exploration is central to the philosophical and psychological foundations of Logo. Removal of either of these two key ingredients greatly diminishes the intent of its developers.

Papert's work has emphasized the use of computers and computer programming to create a totally new type of learning environment for the child. Emphasis is upon discovery, exploration, manipulation, and serendipitous learning. The intent is clearly to provide a rich learning environment where the child can use the computer in ways that best facilitate meaningful learning.

IMPLEMENTATION

Papert and his colleagues believed that the computer was the key to providing the kind of learning environment envisioned. The problem was how to provide children easy access to the power of the computer. In addition to what we might today call "user friendliness," the product they dreamed of had to provide immediate, visual reinforcement of what the student had directed the computer to do. In their pre-microcomputer world, they developed Logo as a mainframe language based on a vocabulary of common command words such as FORWARD, BACK, LEFT, and RIGHT. In turn, such instructions caused a small robot to move about on the floor in response. In addition, the robot, which they dubbed a "turtle," was equipped with drawing pens that could be raised or lowered to selectively leave a trail on paper of its movements.

Since the drawn results of the turtle's movements were graphic images, the concept of "turtlegraphics" was born. As with so many other aspects of educational computing, the impact of Logo was minimal until microcomputers made it widely accessible. Furthermore, to have held only to the idea of a physical robot to manipulate would have raised the cost of implementing Logo beyond reason for many schools. Instead, the physical "turtle" became a graphic figure on the screen in microcomputer versions of Logo. The physical pens and paper were traded for the ability to leave or not leave visible trails on the screen—in varied colors in some versions of Logo.

Aside from the actual cost of physical robots, one may reasonably speculate that far fewer teachers might have been willing to experiment with Logo had they also needed to contend with yet another piece of equipment. For many elementary school teachers, just dealing with a computer for the first time was quite enough of a challenge. Although the Logo robots of today are quite reasonable in price, the vast bulk of Logo work is done solely with the screen turtle.

CHARACTERISTICS OF LOGO

The previous discussion was intended to provide an understanding of the major philosophical and psychological tenets upon which Logo is based. Using these as a foundation, Papert and his colleagues were able to develop a unique computer language offering considerable problem-solving potential, yet appropriate for use with elementary school children as well as adults. What are the major characteristics of Logo that contribute to this uniqueness?

LOGO OFFERS MANY PRIMITIVES

A *primitive* is a basic word that the computer is capable of understanding. Since Logo was initially written for use with large mainframe computers, its vocabulary made use of large amounts of RAM. Other languages written for the limited RAM capacity of early microcomputers had to be kept small in scope to fit. Logo was not implemented on micros until substantial memory became standard. As a consequence, Logo retains a large primitive vocabulary affording the user simpler and greater communication potential. Is it not easier to speak more effectively with a large vocabulary than a limited one? While it is beyond our scope to present *all* of Logo's primitives, an example will illustrate the concept.

Logo's graphic primitives are used to cause the turtle to draw on the screen. Beginning with an empty screen, the turtle is located at the center, heading up. All moves are relative to the turtle's heading. To draw a box, we use the primitives FORWARD (FD) and RIGHT (RT). The turtle must be told how many "steps" forward to move and how much to turn. The following sequence of instructions illustrates these points.

FD 50 RT 90 FD 50 RT 90 FD 50 RT 90 FD 50 RT 90

The image left on the screen by the turtle is shown below, with labels added to clarify the movements. The turtle moved from point A to B, turned right 90 degrees, moved to C, and so on back to point A. The final RT 90 returns the turtle to its original heading.

A second box can be added to the first using the primitives BACK (BK) and LEFT (LT).

BK 50 LT 90 BK 50 LT 90 BK 50 LT 90 BK 50 RT 90

This produces the figure below as the turtle moves backward from A to E to F to D to A, again facing up at the end. You may want to trace these movements yourself using some small object to visualize the outcome. There are many other combinations of moves and turns that would provide the same image.

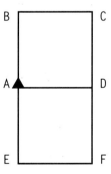

LOGO IS PROCEDURAL

A procedure is "a short set of instructions that can be named and defined by the user and then used as if it were a primitive" (Flake, McClintock, and Turner,

1985, p. 390). Using Logo, students can teach the computer new words by defining procedures. In effect, they create their own programming language by extending Logo's original vocabulary. Let's look at an example.

Our goal is to cause the turtle to draw a rectangle. To create a procedure, you must give it a name, preceded by the word TO. Next, the required directions are given. A procedure concludes with the word END. Once the procedure is defined, you can simply type the word RECTANGLE to produce the shape. The turtle will respond to RECTANGLE just as it does to a primitive like FORWARD. One possible solution is given in Figure 12.1, along with the output produced.

A procedural language encourages the user first to look at the overall problem and then to break this large problem into smaller subsets. A procedure is then written for each smaller piece. This is a direct application of the concepts of top-down design and modularity presented in the previous chapter. Students learning Logo come to use these concepts naturally without formal definitions or instruction concerning them. In other words, they can "do" top-down design and modular program building without knowing the terms or being able to define the concepts. This is Papert's key idea of appropriating knowledge. It demonstrates how the Logo environment can give children access to concepts too abstract for their level of cognitive development. Here is another illustration.

Suppose you wished to have the turtle draw the outline of a house. Even a mental image of the house shows two components, a box for the shell and a triangle for the roof. We can now write a procedure for HOUSE.

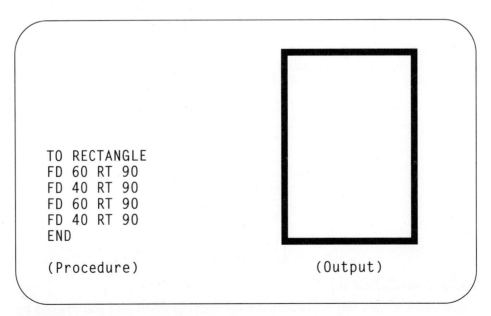

```
TO RECTANGLE
FD 60 RT 90
FD 40 RT 90
FD 60 RT 90
FD 40 RT 90
END

(Procedure)                    (Output)
```

FIGURE 12.1. Drawing a rectangle in Logo

```
TO HOUSE
BOX
ROOF
END
```

Of course, this procedure would not yet work, because Logo does not have a definition for BOX or ROOF. We must create procedures with those names that HOUSE will then use as primitives. We can also test our procedures one by one to determine if they do what they are supposed to. In this way, we can be sure the HOUSE procedure will work correctly.

The box procedure could be just like our earlier example of Logo primitives. However, if we make the height and width the same number of steps, we can simplify the procedure by using the REPEAT command to make the same move and turn four times.

```
TO BOX
REPEAT 4 [FD 60 RT 90]
END
```

This is one way of achieving iteration or looping in Logo, although the concept would not be described to children. Any sequence of instructions may be given in square brackets and repeated as many times as required in this manner.

When we test this procedure by typing BOX, a problem appears. It leaves the turtle at the lower left corner of the box, when it needs to be at the upper left to add the roof. We can solve the problem by adding a final FD 60 to the procedure. (Can you think of another way of achieving the same result?)

```
TO BOX
REPEAT 4 [FD 60 RT 90] FD 60
END
```

To create the roof, we need to draw a triangle. This is conceptually more difficult and requires a good deal of trial and error for most beginners. There are many possible approaches, of course. We settled on this one:

```
TO ROOF
RT 45 FD 43 RT 90 FD 43 RT 135 FD 60
END
```

For this specific example, the final FD 60 is not necessary, as it merely retraces the top line of the box. We include it so that ROOF alone does indeed produce a complete triangle.

Now it is possible to draw a house by typing only the word HOUSE. HOUSE will in turn execute BOX and ROOF to produce the completed drawing. The

```
TO HOUSE
BOX
ROOF
END


TO BOX
REPEAT 4 [FD 60 RT 90] FD 60
END


TO ROOF
RT 45 FD 43 RT 90 FD 43
RT 135 FD 60
END

(Procedures)                              (Output)
```

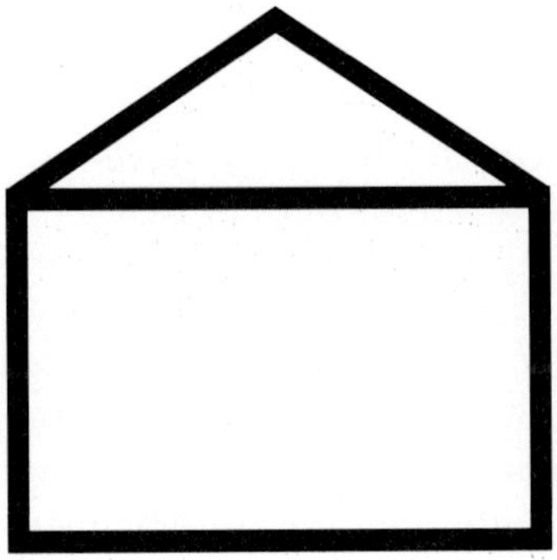

FIGURE 12.2. Drawing a house in Logo

three procedures and the turtle's drawing are shown in Figure 12.2. Additional procedures could be developed to add windows, a chimney, and so on.

LOGO IS RECURSIVE

Among the most powerful and least understood of Logo's features is *recursion*. When working with a procedural language, one procedure can use another as a *subprocedure*. In our HOUSE example, the definition of HOUSE uses BOX and ROOF as subprocedures. The next step beyond this concept is recursion.

Recursion occurs when a procedure calls *itself* as a subprocedure. Thus, recursion is nothing more than the ability to use a procedure as part of its own definition. As Harvey (1982) suggested, recursion allows a rather complex problem to be described in terms of simpler versions of itself. Because Logo is recursive, it is possible to build more complex programs by using simpler subprocedures and structurally adding to them.

Perhaps an example at this point will help. An appropriate procedure for drawing a box would be:

```
TO BOX
REPEAT 4 [FD 40 RT 90]
END
```

To illustrate recursion, let's use the box just defined to create a "spinning" box design. The procedure for this will be SPINBOX.

```
TO SPINBOX
BOX
RT 45
SPINBOX
END
```

When we type SPINBOX, one box is drawn, then the turtle turns 45 degrees to the right. The procedure "calls" itself, and the cycle repeats endlessly, eventually drawing over itself. This procedure must finally be stopped by the user. The output is shown in Figure 12.3.

LOGO IS INTERACTIVE

Abelson (1982) wrote:

> Logo is an interactive programming language. Any Logo command, whether built into the language or defined as a procedure, can be executed by simply typing the command at the keyboard (p. ix).

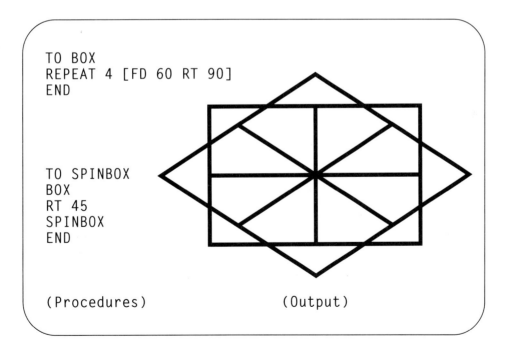

```
TO BOX
REPEAT 4 [FD 60 RT 90]
END



TO SPINBOX
BOX
RT 45
SPINBOX
END


(Procedures)                    (Output)
```

FIGURE 12.3. Drawing a complex pattern with recursion

When using Logo, all one must do is type a command (FD 40) or procedure name (SQUARE) to see the result immediately. Logo requires the student and computer to communicate *actively* with one another. This interactivity provides students immediate feedback as to the progress being made in their programming efforts—a desirable learning outcome.

According to Harvey (1982), whether or not a programming language is interactive has a profound effect upon its efficiency of use. Generally, writing programs is faster with an interactive language, since it affords the opportunity to "debug" or make necessary corrections at the point of error—it is easier to find and fix mistakes. You no doubt realized that Logo enthusiasts use the term interactive to mean that the language is *interpreted*.

LOGO USES EASILY UNDERSTOOD WORDS

Another desirable feature of Logo is its use of common words, such as LEFT and BACK. This contributes to its usability with young children. They can relate body movement directly to the turtle. In addition, students can create procedures with names that are meaningful to them. If a face is being developed as a procedure, the child can appropriately name the top level procedure FACE. FACE may require procedures called EYES, NOSE, and MOUTH, all appropriate and easily understood names. Essentially, Logo involves controlling the computer by using primitives to develop new commands in small, manageable blocks, rather than creating one long, complicated set of instructions in sequential order.

In addition to allowing the programmer to develop procedures using common, easily understood words, Logo also provides easily understood error messages. For example, two error messages provided in Terrapin Logo are FORWARD NEEDS MORE INPUTS (e.g., you typed just FD, not FD 50) and THERE IS NO PROCEDURE NAMED (whatever name you typed).

LOGO IS EASY TO USE

One of the most compelling characteristics of Logo for use in our schools is the ease and speed of getting started. Once a child has mastered a few basic concepts such as left and right, forward and back, meaningful, interesting, sometimes unexpected and rewarding results begin to appear on the screen. The learner can actually *do* something in just minutes after being introduced to Logo. The basic Logo commands have simple visible effects affording the child a wide range of creative activities and possibilities.

Furthermore, once choices are made in the procedures written, they can be seen immediately and provide vital reinforcement to the learner. Finally, if the results are not what was anticipated or desired, it is a simple matter to alter any given procedure so that it is more in keeping with the wishes of the programmer.

OTHER CAPABILITIES OF LOGO

Although for our purposes we have shown only graphics examples, you should not assume that this is the extent of Logo's capabilities. Logo is a full-featured programming language, offering arithmetic, text manipulation, and even music creation. It is possible to use Logo for a wide range of programming needs. However, since Logo has been used largely with younger students, the primary focus tends to be on graphics. For further details about Logo, we suggest the following Logo texts: Harper (1989), Lukas and Lukas (1986), Sharp (1984), and Babbie (1984).

Since we began this section of the book with detailed treatment of the concepts of programming, some comments about Logo and structured programming are also in order. We did not present Logo in the context of these concepts because of the nature and typical application of Logo. Logo is most often used with children. It would be inappropriate and antithetical to the intentions of its creators to actually "teach" programming. Rather, concepts are developed through use, not by instruction. Many programming concepts are abstract and beyond the developmental readiness of the intended audience. Just as children "learn" geometric concepts like angles and degrees by using Logo, even though they may be unable to articulate them, so will they also "learn" programming concepts.

The procedural nature of Logo leads naturally into top-down design. Planning will occur, but much will also be trial and error. The sequence construct is inherent in writing any procedure, and iteration is learned easily with the REPEAT command. The selection construct is readily available also but is less likely to be used in exploring graphics. Anyone who has first learned Logo should, at an appropriate age, be able to grasp programming concepts easily in another context.

LOGO DERIVATIVES

LOGOWRITER

Dubbed as a "second-tier" successor to the concept of word processing by Papert (1986), *LogoWriter* from Logo Computer Systems, Inc. greatly increases the flexibility of Logo. The program not only extends the "turtle graphics" capabilities by incorporating four different turtles and multiple turtle shapes with which to work but also adds the dimension of word processing, including the ability to copy, search, replace, and cut and paste text. Another positive feature of the program is that it provides for integration of text and graphics both on the screen and when printing—even providing opportunities for animation and music. *LogoWriter* can be a "customized" text editor. It is possible to write a *LogoWriter* procedure that will carry out some editing function that is not initially included and then identify this procedure with a control key just like those already built into the program.

Students learn to use *LogoWriter* by doing projects presented in booklets and activity cards that accompany the program. Themes in the booklets are intended to cover all curriculum areas. Newman (1988) cautioned that these aids have the potential, when not used properly, of contributing to rote activity on the part of the children and not the discovery learning so emphasized by Logo developers where students are encouraged to experiment with their own ideas. Adams and Hamm (1987) further cautioned that *LogoWriter* may prove somewhat difficult to use—particularly with students new to computing.

Keeping these possible pitfalls in mind, *LogoWriter* still appears to offer an exciting potential for fostering a tremendous diversity of ideas and projects across many curriculum areas.

LEGO® TC logo

Combining the programming language Logo and the familiar Lego building blocks provides opportunities for students to build, invent, and create. In some ways *LEGO TC logo* revisits earlier days when a cybernetic turtle was moved by Logo procedures written by children. Essentially *LEGO TC logo* is a specialized version of *LogoWriter* that lets students program machines they build from Lego pieces (including gears, motors, and sensors). Rosen (1988) contended that a major advantage of the program is that it requires children to employ the scientific method as they invent. When problems are encountered with a machine, students have to develop strategies for determining the cause. Hypotheses are developed and tested, and many times data are gathered and recorded. The emphasis is on "hands-on" experiences with real scientific and mathematical problems—an approach to learning that offers considerable merit.

Lough and Harris (1988) reported that in their examination of students' responses to *LEGO TC logo,* girls accomplished more than boys and were better organized about their work. There appeared to be some reversal of traditional sex roles; girls worked with gears while boys studied kitchen appliances—an interesting outcome.

LOGO PLUS

Terrapin has introduced an upgraded version of Logo that combines all previous features with over 40 additional commands. *Logo Plus* allows the user to add text to the graphics screen using various colors, fonts, and styles. In addition, a built-in shape editor permits the design of new shapes for the turtle. Other features include the ability to print graphics, using an ImageWriter printer, to type commands in upper or lower case, and to debug programs more quickly and easily than previously.

Note that these three spin-offs of Logo represent only a few of the numerous options available. *Logo Probability, Logo Innovations,* and *Kinderlogo* are three additional programs that may prove of interest. Information regarding these and other Logo programs can be obtained by contacting Terrapin, Inc.,

400 Riverside Street, Portland, Maine 04103 or Logo Computer Systems, Inc. (LCSI), 330 West 58th Street, New York, New York 10019.

WHY TEACH LOGO?

Now that you are familiar with some of Logo's features and program enhancements, let's consider why Logo is taught in schools. Many of the general reasons given in the previous chapter for teaching programming are also used to justify teaching Logo. However, because Logo is so different in its origins and nature from other computer languages, some reasons for using it also differ.

LOGO IS UNIQUE

Logo is not just a language, but also a philosophical approach to learning. While you may wish to read *Mindstorms* (Papert, 1980) for an in-depth presentation, the following represent major points taken from an interview with Papert (Reinhold, 1986).

Logo exists to allow students to appropriate other knowledge; that is, to make it their own. This implies a use of knowledge that goes beyond our typical educational emphasis on content. Of greater concern is how children relate to their knowledge. This is an outgrowth of Piaget's constructivism, emphasizing the importance of the individual as an active learner. The role of the teacher changes from conveyor of knowledge to facilitator of a positive learning environment. Papert stated, "If students could learn topics in a way they could enjoy, they would learn them like anyone else; they wouldn't need remediation" (p. 36).

The computer becomes an "object to think with" when learners can readily interact with it. Logo affords such an opportunity to even the youngest school children. The computer is a vehicle for important conceptual learning, not the focus of interest itself. Further, the key outcome is not a working program, as is true with most languages. Logo is not taught from the programming frame of reference provided in the last chapter. Rather, the emphasis in Logo is upon process in a learning environment that safely provides opportunity for exploration. Free exploration produces not errors, but unexpected outcomes and serendipitous learning.

PROBLEM-SOLVING POTENTIAL

From Logo's process emphasis, it follows that the primary reason for teaching Logo is not programming itself, but to enable learners to use the computer as a problem-solving tool. Many educators are paying increased attention to the need to teach students higher-order thought processes. Paul (1984) suggested that our schools are lacking in those types of learning activities that require children to think in a serious, logical, and analytical way. Logo offers one such activity.

It should be stressed that teaching effective problem solving requires more than one activity, however. Other opportunities for the application of problem-solving skills must be provided in all areas of the curriculum. Teachers may be sadly disappointed in the development of these skills in their students if they rely only on Logo or any other single approach. Effective transfer of learning will require a teaching strategy that calls upon the use of skills in other contexts.

RELATIONSHIP TO BLOOM'S HIERARCHY

In her article "Logo Builds Thinking Skills," Dale (1986) referred to Benjamin Bloom's six levels of intellectual activity: (1) knowledge, (2) comprehension, (3) application, (4) analysis, (5) synthesis, and (6) evaluation. She then went on to suggest that Logo has the potential to elicit use of each of these six levels—a rare achievement in our schools.

Knowledge and Comprehension
For children to use Logo, they must have knowledge of direction and distance and must comprehend or understand such knowledge. Body movement, experienced very early in a child's life, contributes to this knowledge and comprehension.

Application
Since Logo uses familiar knowledge and comprehension in a meaningful way, it is not difficult for the student to apply or use that information in an appropriate situation by quickly learning simple programming skills.

Analysis
Analysis, defined as the recognition of elements, relationships, and organizational structure of selected information or a problem, is very much involved in the construction of procedures that allow for the building of a problem-solving program.

Synthesis
At the synthesis level, children reorganize or recombine previously existing procedures into new ones.

Evaluation
Evaluation, the highest level of Bloom's taxonomy, is applied in several ways. Perhaps the most pronounced use of evaluation comes in the "debugging" process, where it is necessary to find and fix errors and revise procedures in an effort to improve the program. Dale contended that evaluation is an integral step in the development of Logo projects.

ESTABLISHING THE LOGO ENVIRONMENT

Papert (1980, p. 129) described microworlds as "explorable and manipulable environments." Logo is itself such a microworld and can be used to create further microworlds. In a microworld, subject matter and the approach to it are interwoven in a living laboratory. The Logo environment is obviously intended to be different from the traditional classroom. Papert (1980, p. 6) described the contrast between learning a foreign language artificially in the classroom and learning it naturally by living where it is spoken. Logo is meant to offer such natural learning opportunities.

To establish the type of learning environment espoused by Piaget and Papert will require some significant changes in the way teachers interact with students.

ROLE OF THE TEACHER

At the heart of the Logo environment for Papert is discovery learning. Students are expected to learn through their own investigations rather than being "taught" as most teachers presently teach. The role of the teacher changes drastically from disseminator of knowledge to a learning facilitator. The teacher is not expected to know the answer to all questions posed by the students but rather to know the *process* of investigation—how to go about finding the answers. Appropriate questioning skills are vital.

The teacher becomes essential in establishing an environment where children are comfortable in posing their own problems and working toward solutions. Right or wrong responses are not the end goal; the goal is, rather, reflective thinking and the analysis of what has happened and what might happen under certain circumstances. Dale (1984) described the teacher's role with Logo:

> You are not meant to direct learning from a podium and the security of a carefully mapped curriculum. Instead, you are meant to be in the thick of things, sometimes taking an active part in the learning process, sometimes suggesting new ideas, sometimes stepping back and letting explorations continue under student control (p. 183).

DIFFICULTY WITH TEACHER'S ROLE

To assume this type of role is difficult for many teachers. It is contrary to how we were taught and probably even how we were taught to teach. It is troublesome not merely to provide the answers to questions posed by students. It may prove much more time-consuming to afford the learner the necessary time to "discover" what could be so easily shown or told to them by the teacher. This presents a genuine dilemma to teachers who want to work with Logo but find the facilitative role foreign.

What is perhaps the cause of the dilemma is erroneously assuming that because the teacher's role is changed, the teacher is not expected to do anything but stand out of the way and let children "do their thing." The teacher *is* an active participant, one who questions, one who works *with* children in the solution of problems. He or she *must* be knowledgeable about the learning process. Learning this different active role may take time—may take some "easing into." Teachers need to move toward the type of interactive learning environment suggested by Papert, but it is essential that they be qualified and feel comfortable with this environment if the desired outcomes are to be obtained.

TEACHING STRATEGIES

Papert (1985) has suggested that there is no "right way" of using Logo:

> But by definition, there isn't any one way of "using it right." That implies that some particular correct way exists—and *that* would be against the spirit of what Logo is all about. It's like asking, "Did Shakespeare and Hemingway 'use English right?' "

While there is substance to Papert's contention, several techniques or strategies have proven helpful in the acquisition of certain skills important to the Logo user.

USING ONE'S BODY AS "TURTLE"

Fundamental to the use of turtlegraphics is an understanding of directionality (forward, backward, right, and left). In order for students to move the turtle and develop a graphic design, it is imperative that they know in which direction the turtle is facing and then what direction to move the turtle to accomplish their program goals.

Younger children may have difficulty with directionality concepts. Older students, even adults, may not easily translate directionality into correct instructions to the turtle. Learners can be assisted by having them actually walk through a design just as the turtle would. In this way, students gain a sense of direction and distance that can prove beneficial when developing instructions for the turtle. Working in pairs or in small groups is recommended. Having one student recording the movements of another will help establish the movement pattern and commands needed to accomplish a design. Reviewing the recorded movements can help the students consider what was done, what worked, and what didn't.

TRANSPARENCY MAZES

To help students master controlling the turtle's movements in terms of direction and distance, mazes can be produced as transparencies and temporarily taped to the monitor. One such maze shows streets that a student might take to get to school. The student attempts to move the turtle from the home starting point to school in as few movements as possible. Another maze useful with older students to achieve the same objectives is a golf course transparency. Emphasis is placed upon playing the course in the fewest possible movements or shots.

DISPLAYING STUDENT WORK

Flake et al. (1985, p. 26) suggested that it is just as important to display student progress in learning Logo as it is in mathematics, science, or social studies. It is possible to print graphic designs developed by students and display them. Along with the actual design, print out the corresponding procedures developed by the student and attach them to the actual graphic output. This will help motivate students to develop new images and share ideas. Such recognition can help foster the proper Logo learning environment.

EMPHASIZE PEER QUESTIONING

Papert (1985) recounted a classroom in Pittsburgh where the teacher established the rule, "Ask three before you ask me." In other words, it was her expectation that children would ask each other when they encountered questions. The students became teachers and learned from one another. Furthermore, this freed the classroom teacher from responding to often trivial questions and provided time to deal with more substantive matters.

WHAT THE RESEARCH SHOWS

Logo has been on the scene for approximately 20 years. Much has been written about its virtues, but relatively little empirical research has been conducted to examine the effects of using Logo. Maddux (1985) stated, "A casual scanning of the literature on the effects of teaching Logo to children is enough to reveal that much has been written, but little has been said on this topic."

While this is largely true, studies are beginning to appear which examine the effects of Logo upon children's learning. This is an encouraging sign, for it is only through the acquisition of such evidence that the many claims made concerning Logo will be verified.

METACOGNITIVE AND COGNITIVE DEVELOPMENT

Clements (January 1985) investigated the effects of learning to program in Logo on a small group (N = 18) of first grade students. Students were assigned to either a Logo programming group or a control group that used computers for CAI. The Logo group showed significant gains from pre- to post-test scores in fluency, originality, and overall creativity based on the Torrance Test of Creative Thinking. The CAI group showed no significant differences.

On the Matching Familiar Figures Test, "the Logo group made significantly fewer errors on the posttest and significantly increased their latency time." On two metacognitive tasks, the Logo group required significantly fewer prompting questions than did the CAI group. Finally, on a describing directions test, the Logo group gave a significantly higher percentage of correct responses.

No significant differences were found between the two groups in the areas of cognitive development, logical thinking, and other aspects measured by the McCarthy Screening Test.

In conclusion, Clements stated, "Thus, there was no evidence that 12 weeks of Logo programming affects cognitive development as compared to 12 weeks of CAI. Rather it may affect the way in which children use the cognitive abilities they possess" (p. 74).

Horton and Ryba (1986), using a method for assessing learning with Logo developed by Nolan and Ryba, attempted to systematically examine the effects of Logo programming on junior high school students' thinking skills. Logo and non-Logo groups were established randomly from volunteers. The Logo group received instruction after school two times a week for seven weeks while the non-Logo group received no treatment. The Logo group outperformed the non-Logo group on measures of exploration, analysis and design, and prediction and creativity. Unexpectedly, the non-Logo group excelled in debugging.

PROBLEM SOLVING

Kinzer, Littlefield, Delclos, and Bransford (1985, p. 34) reported on studies by Pea and Kurland in which "students who received training in Logo failed to show any transfer to tasks involving planning and other problem solving." They did note, however, that most studies of this type have failed to measure the actual extent of Logo learning that occurred or have found it to be far less than expected. Clearly, one cannot expect the transfer of what was never learned.

Horner and Maddux (1985) summarized six other studies. They reported that these studies failed clearly to support claims that Logo enhances either academic performance or problem-solving skills. In their own study involving junior high school students, Logo instruction during mathematics class provided the experimental treatment. Similarly, they found no significant differences between experimental and control groups on measures of problem solving, locus of control, math attitudes, and selected geometric abilities.

Ginther and Williamson (1985) cited a 1973 Logo study conducted by Statz, which involved students aged 9 to 11 learning Logo in a mainframe environment. Of four problem-solving tasks used as dependent measures, the Logo group performed significantly higher on two. The control group never outperformed the experimental (Logo) group. Thus, modest support for Logo as a facilitator of problem-solving ability was obtained.

In their study examining the effects of instruction in BASIC and Logo at the university level, Reed, Palumbo, and Stolar (1987–1988) found that both Logo instruction and BASIC instruction resulted in statistically significant gains in problem-solving skills as measured by subtests from the Ross Test of Higher Cognitive Processes (Analysis of Relevant and Irrelevant Information and Analysis of Attributes) and the Watson-Glaser Thinking Appraisal (Deduction and Interpretation). They further determined that while both treatments enhanced problem-solving skill development, there was no significant difference between the gains of the two approaches, leading to the conclusion that although both languages resulted in an increase in problem-solving skills, neither was superior to the other in promoting such an increase.

Roblyer, Castine, and King (1988) completed a meta-analysis of research pertaining to microcomputers and computer-based instruction. Thirty-eight studies and forty-four dissertations were included in the analysis. One finding reported that Logo showed promise as a means of improving various cognitive skills and appeared particularly promising when compared to the learning outcomes obtained from unstructured, discovery-learning approaches.

REASONING ABILITY

Another higher-order thought process is reasoning ability. To investigate the relationship between Logo instruction and reasoning ability, Many, Lockard, Abrams, and Friker (1988) used the New Jersey Test of Reasoning Skills as the dependent measure. Scores obtained by seventh and eighth grade students who had received nine weeks of Logo instruction were compared to those of similar students who had received no such instruction. Significant differences were found in favor of the Logo students. In addition, "collapsing" across grades, males in the Logo group outperformed their counterparts significantly, but females did not. Thus, the benefit of Logo appeared to accrue mostly to males.

SOCIAL-EMOTIONAL DEVELOPMENT

Clements and Nastasi (1985) investigated the effects of Logo programming versus CAI experience on social-emotional development. Subjects were first and third grade children. Contrary to some prior research, they found no evidence of "increased initiation of, and participation in, social interactions" for computer environments over others (p. 24).

Results supported previous research showing that students played less and worked cooperatively more in the computer environment than in the noncomputer environment. Working on the computer led to more potential conflict situations, hence more resolution. Children in the Logo groups resolved conflicts more successfully than those in the CAI groups.

Computer situations appeared to encourage helping behavior among third grade students, but there were no significant differences between the Logo and CAI groups. According to Clements and Nastasi (p. 25), "Based on increases in rule-making, self-direction, and pleasure at discovery, a strong case can be made that Logo experience develops effectance motivation." CAI was found to generate dependence behaviors, especially in first grade children.

RESEARCH SUMMARY

In discussing the state of Logo research, Ginther and Williamson (1985) reiterated the fact that some 20 years experience remains just that—experience, with precious little hard evidence of value. With this caution in mind, however, it may prove beneficial to present certain of the summarizing statements offered by Clements (Summer/Fall 1985).

1. It appears that Logo can encourage social interaction, positive self-concepts, positive attitudes toward learning, and independent work habits.
2. Working in pairs while programming in Logo appears to be most advantageous.
3. Only selected areas of achievement may be affected by Logo. Research findings appear conflicting, and even those that support Logo tend to be somewhat unimpressive.
4. Programming in Logo does appear to promote specific problem-solving behaviors.
5. It appears that Logo may enhance certain metacognitive abilities and enhance creativity.
6. Such skills as classifying, seriating, and conserving may be positively affected by the use of Logo.
7. The issue of transfer of learning resulting from the use of Logo is still largely unresolved.

In conclusion, it appears that the research reviewed justifies the statement that Logo is unlikely to be equally effective with students of all ages or for all learning skills. While it may prove successful at various grade levels, it will be the *specific* application of Logo that is or is not effective. Out of context, the language will accomplish little.

It is encouraging that there is beginning to appear a body of knowledge regarding the effects of Logo in the learning environment. The word *beginning*, however, points to the need for considerably more carefully controlled empirical investigation. Only time and attention to this will provide that information needed to fully evaluate the impact of Logo.

SUMMARY

Logo is a programming language, but it is more than that. It represents the application to computers of Piaget's theories of learning as they relate to cognitive development. Emphasis is placed upon the establishment of an appropriate learning environment, rich with materials, and freedom to explore, using the computer as the explorative tool. Logo is easily learned, yet powerful. It is flexible and affords children a quickly learned vehicle for problem-solving activities. The use of "turtlegraphics" allows the child to apply familiar direction and distance concepts to build procedures. These procedures are modular and when combined can be used to develop sophisticated programs.

The teacher's role is one of facilitator or guide in the learning process. This role may be a difficult one for teachers to assume, for it rather drastically changes the traditional role—that of information disseminator. It must be emphasized that the changed role does *not* suggest that teachers have no responsibility in the learning process. They must have good questioning skills, be able to identify difficulties when encountered by the student, and be able to provide cooperative assistance in working toward a solution of these difficulties.

While there is no one *best* way to teach Logo, using appropriate questioning skills and providing an environment that encourages "freedom to try" without evaluation are important to successful program implementation.

Research studies have increased in number but remain largely inconclusive. The research that we have does afford encouragement that the intended outcomes of Logo are plausible and attainable. There continues, however, to be a need for additional research to provide further evidence as to the justification for many of the claims made by Logo proponents.

CHAPTER 12 ACTIVITIES

1. Briefly discuss the philosophical and psychological bases upon which Logo is founded.
2. Do you agree with Papert that cognitive development can be accelerated with the establishment of a proper cultural environment? Discuss your response in terms of learning implications.
3. What do you see as the crucial factors necessary for the establishment of a learning environment appropriate for the teaching of Logo?
4. How would you feel about assuming the role suggested for the teaching of Logo? What would be your biggest concern about assuming such a role? What type of training do you see as essential for the Logo teacher?
5. Several activities were presented in the chapter as appropriate for the teaching of Logo. See if you can suggest at least three other activities that you believe would contribute to learning Logo.
6. If possible, secure a Logo program disk and a book written for the purpose of teaching Logo. Work through at least those portions dealing with the use of the REPEAT command and the writing of simple procedures.
7. Try your hand at developing a graphics procedure. When done, review in your mind the types of cognitive decisions you made in the preparation of your procedure. What did you learn during the process?
8. It has been suggested that Logo was not meant to be taught and furthermore

that the type of learning achieved was not intended to be evaluated like other school learning. What is your reaction to this statement?

9. Teaming two students on a computer while working with Logo appears to have several advantages. Discuss what you see as potential benefits derived from such a practice.

10. The suggestion has been made that it is possible for educators to teach programming when they themselves don't know how. What is your reaction to this statement?

REFERENCES

Abelson, H. *Apple Logo*. Peterborough, NH: Byte/McGraw-Hill, 1982.

Adams, D., and Hamm, M. " 'LogoWriter'. Stretching the Boundaries of Educational Computing: A Review." *British Journal of Educational Technology*, May 1987, pp. 93–96.

Babbie, E. *Apple Logo for Teachers*. Belmont, CA: Wadsworth, 1984.

Clements, D. "Logo Programming: Can It Change How Children Think?" *Electronic Learning*, January 1985, p. 28, 74.

Clements, D. "Research on Logo in Education: Is the Turtle Slow but Steady, or Not Even in the Race?" *Computers in the Schools*, Summer/Fall 1985, pp. 55–71.

Clements, D., and Nastasi, B. "Effects of Computer Environments on Social-Emotional Development: Logo and Computer-Assisted Instruction." *Computers in the Schools*, Summer/Fall 1985, pp. 11–31.

Dale, E. "Logo Builds Thinking Skills." In D.O. Harper and J.H. Stewart, eds. *Run: Computer Education*. 2d ed. Monterey, CA: Brooks/Cole Publishing Co., 1986, pp. 173–176.

Dale, L. "Teaching Thinking with Logo." *School Microcomputing Bulletin*, January 1984, pp. 183–184.

Flake, J., McClintock, C., and Turner, S. *Fundamentals of Computer Education*. Belmont, CA: Wadsworth Publishing Company, 1985.

Ginther, D., and Williamson, J. "Learning Logo: What Is Really Learned?" *Computers in the Schools*, Summer/Fall 1985, pp. 45–54.

Harper, D. *Logo Theory & Practice*. Pacific Grove, CA: Brooks/Cole, 1989.

Harvey, B. "Why Logo?" *Byte*, August 1982, pp. 163–165, 170–182, 186, 188, 191–192.

Horner, C., and Maddux, C. "The Effect of Logo on Attributions toward Success." *Computers in the Schools*, Summer/Fall 1985, pp. 45–54.

Horton, J., and Ryba, K. "Assessing Learning with Logo: A Pilot Study." *The Computing Teacher*, October 1986, pp. 24–28.

Kinzer, C., Littlefield, J., Delclos, V., and Bransford, J. "Different Logo Learning Environments and Mastery: Relationships between Engagement and Learning." *Computers in the Schools*, Summer/Fall 1985, pp. 33–43.

Lough, T., and Harris, J. "A Computerized LEGO Kit Has Students Building LOGO-Motives." *Electronic Learning*, March 1988, pp. 38–39.

Lukas, G., and Lukas, J. *Logo: Principles, Programming, and Projects*. Monterey, CA: Brooks/Cole, 1986.

Maddux, C. "The Need for Science Versus Passion in Educational Computing." *Computers in the Schools*, Summer/Fall 1985, pp. 9–10.

Many, W., Lockard, J., Abrams, P., and Friker, W. "The Effect of Learning to Program in Logo on Reasoning Skills of Junior High School Students." *Journal of Educational Computing Research,* 4(2), 1988, pp. 203–213.

Mouly, G. *Psychology for Effective Teaching.* 3d ed. New York: Holt-Rinehart and Winston, Inc., 1973.

Newman, J. "Online: Logo and the Language Arts." *Language Arts,* October 1988, pp. 598–605.

Papert, S. "Different Visions of Logo." *Computers in the School,* Summer/Fall 1985, pp. 3–8.

Papert, S. *Mindstorms: Children, Computers and Powerful Ideas.* New York: Basic Books Inc., 1980.

Papert, S. "The Next Step: LogoWriter." *Classroom Computer Learning,* April 1986, pp. 38–40.

Paul, R. "Critical Thinking: Fundamental to Education for a Free Society." *Educational Leadership,* Vol. 42, 1984, pp. 4–14.

Piaget, J. *The Science of Education and the Psychology of the Child.* New York: The Viking Press, 1971.

Reed, W., Palumbo, D., and Stolar, A. "The Comparative Effects of BASIC and Logo Instruction on Problem-Solving Skills." *Computers in the Schools,* Fall/Winter 1987/ 1988, pp. 105–117.

Reinhold, F. "An Interview with Seymour Papert." *Electronic Learning,* April 1986, pp. 35–36, 63.

Roblyer, M., Castine, W., and King, F. "Assessing the Impact of Computer Based Instruction." *Computers in the Schools,* 5 (3/4), 1988, pp. 1–149.

Rosen, M., "Lego Meets Logo." *Classroom Computer Learning,* April 1988, pp. 50–58.

Sharp, P. *Turtlesteps.* Bowie, MD: Brady Communications Company, 1984.

CHAPTER 13

□ BASIC □

OBJECTIVES

After completing this chapter, you will be able to:

□ *Explain why BASIC was developed.* □
□ *Explain the key features of BASIC and contrast them with Logo.* □
□ *Describe the steps in developing a program in BASIC.* □
□ *Prepare a top-down design for a simple program.* □
□ *Make small changes in a simple BASIC program.* □
□ *Give advantages and disadvantages of BASIC as a programming language.* □
□ *Read a well-written simple BASIC program.* □

Computer programming is a skill that requires a great deal of time and effort to master. Further, it is an activity for which one must have a clear need to justify the effort involved. Within the context for which this book was written, proficiency in programming is unlikely to be the issue. Rather, computer literate educators should be familiar with the concepts of programming and their implementation in the languages most common in schools.

This chapter provides an overview of the BASIC language. We present BASIC because it is the most widely available and used language for teaching programming on microcomputers. There is even a magazine just for teachers of BASIC (*BASIC Teacher*, Box 7627, Menlo Park, CA 94026). While Logo is also a language, it was presented in the preceding chapter as more than just that; it is less commonly taught for the sake of programming per se.

Our treatment of BASIC will *not* teach you to program in this language. Rather, we focus on the development of BASIC, its key features, and modest examples of problems solved in BASIC. We will also present the advantages and disadvantages of this language. This introduction will serve as a basis for further work with the language, should you decide to pursue the matter.

DEVELOPMENT OF BASIC

COMPUTERS AND STUDENTS

Although computer availability in education developed slowly at first, by the early 1960s educators were looking for ways to make computers accessible to students. In the absence of software of the types covered in the first parts of this book, educational computing had to focus on programming. However, programming requires a computer language, and existing languages had been developed to meet the needs of science and business. For students, a different approach was required.

BASIC (*Beginner's All-purpose Symbolic Instruction Code*) was developed in 1965 at Dartmouth College expressly for education. The language and its operating environment were designed with ease of *learning* as the primary concern, not to serve the needs of professionals in data processing. In contrast to Logo, BASIC was not designed to implement a particular educational philosophy or psychology.

THE SPREAD OF BASIC

From its beginnings at Dartmouth, BASIC became popular as a student programming language in higher education. However, it might well have touched very limited numbers of persons even then, were it not for the development of microcomputers.

BASIC became the primary language of early micros because it was easy enough for anyone to learn and required minimal memory. It could be supplied on a ROM chip built into the machine, thereby creating a computer system that was ready to go at a touch of the power switch. Because of microcomputers, there are undoubtedly more people today who "know" BASIC than any other computer language. The spread of microcomputers has brought BASIC to all levels of education. Today, many different dialects of BASIC exist.

KEY FEATURES OF BASIC

Before we approach the language itself, let's look at the most fundamental aspects of common dialects of BASIC, such as *Applesoft* and *GW–BASIC.*

LINE NUMBERS

A major difference between BASIC and other languages is its use of line numbers to determine the order in which instructions are carried out. You previously learned that a Logo procedure consists of "primitives" like FORWARD and the names of other procedures that you create, such as HOUSE. Each primitive is executed in sequence. A procedure name begins execution of that procedure, which itself consists of more primitives in a carefully planned sequence. A language of this type is called a *block-structured language,* because instructions must be written in well-defined blocks.

BASIC, in contrast, is a line number oriented language. Each BASIC statement or group of statements must be preceded by a number. Execution proceeds in line number sequence, lowest to highest, unless a statement that alters the flow is encountered. Changes in flow are based on jumps to specified line numbers, rather than to names as in Logo.

MODEST VOCABULARY

BASIC has a relatively limited number of statements analogous to Logo's primitives. The exact number depends on the additions to the version in question, such as graphics or sound. Most BASIC statements are familiar English words, although their meaning may not be totally obvious and the syntax of their use can become complex. There is no provision for extending the language as new procedures do in Logo.

INTERACTIVE

BASIC was designed from the start to be a language for learning. It is most commonly implemented as an interpreted language, making it interactive and therefore comparatively easy to use. One can focus on BASIC itself, rather than the environment within which it functions. This is similar to Logo.

STRUCTURED BASIC

Your introduction to BASIC will rest on the structured principles that were given in Chapter 11. However, we treat documentation and modularity only minimally to keep the examples modest. For the sake of generality, we selected examples requiring only features of BASIC common to virtually all dialects. This precludes paralleling our Logo graphics examples, since differences in graphics are substantial from one BASIC to another.

Recall that the allowable constructs in structured programming are sequence, selection, and iteration. Each construct will be illustrated in BASIC with a problem to solve. We will follow each problem through its developmental steps, from planning through flowcharting to coding a solution in BASIC.

To get a feel for using BASIC, you may wish to enter our sample solutions on your computer, run them, correct any typos, and save them on disk when they work correctly. Do not assume that you will be a BASIC programmer as a result. Keep in mind, you will see only a portion of the vocabulary and syntax of BASIC in the process.

THE SEQUENCE CONSTRUCT

Our first problem is to develop a program that calculates and displays the mean of two fixed values.

The Planning Step

The description of the problem provides the highest level of a top-down design of the program. Presented in diagram form, it is:

```
┌─────────────────────┐
│   CALCULATE MEAN    │
│    OF 2 NUMBERS     │
└─────────────────────┘
```

Now refine this broad problem statement into its elements at the next level. What data must the computer have to perform this task? Obviously, two numbers, so we must provide them. Since the problem statement says the values are fixed, we build them into the program rather than having the user enter them at the keyboard. Our design now becomes:

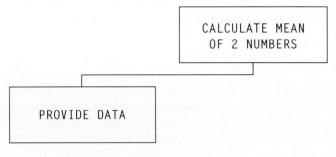

Once the computer has the values, it is ready to do the necessary arithmetic. That becomes step 2, and the diagram adds another block.

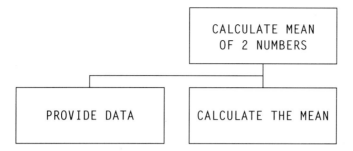

All that remains is to display the result, which completes the top-down design at the second level of refinement. Since each of the three steps is a trivial task, there is no need for further refinement. Each will become a separate module in our solution.

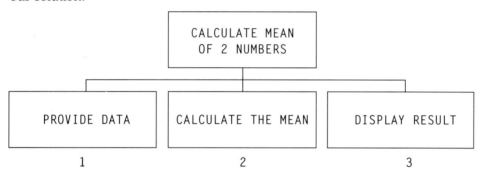

Unfortunately, the mechanics of creating true modules in BASIC are not so obvious as Logo procedures and are often not treated until well into a BASIC programming course. We will develop these three components within the *spirit* of modularity, but for the sake of simplicity, not as BASIC's counterpart to Logo procedures.

The Flowchart Step

Our design diagram represents a partial algorithm for the solution to our problem. Missing is clear depiction of the program's logic and flow, the interrelationships of the three modules. A flowchart of the program will provide a picture of these factors.

To the first module, we add one small item not apparent in the design diagram. It is customary to begin a program by clearing the screen of other information. We include this step as part of the flowchart for the first module. Clearing the screen is an input/output operation. Providing two fixed values is a process. The appropriate symbols yield the following flowchart for this module:

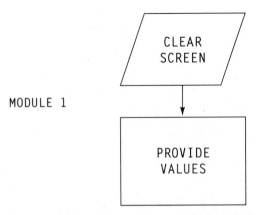

MODULE 1

The second module has only one purpose, to carry out the required calculation, a process. However, since the values involved are provided within the program, we will embellish the program slightly by displaying them on screen. This is another I/O operation. The resulting flowchart for Module 2 is:

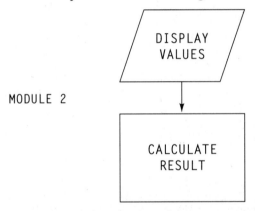

MODULE 2

The final module consists of only one I/O operation, displaying the result:

MODULE 3

Each of the modules is a straight *sequence* of actions. Combine them *in order* to produce Figure 13.1, the complete flowchart of our program. We need only add the beginning and ending symbols, plus arrows to show the flow.

The Coding Step

From the flowchart, we proceed to code the solution in BASIC. Since this is our first look at the language, we'll provide more detail here than in later examples.

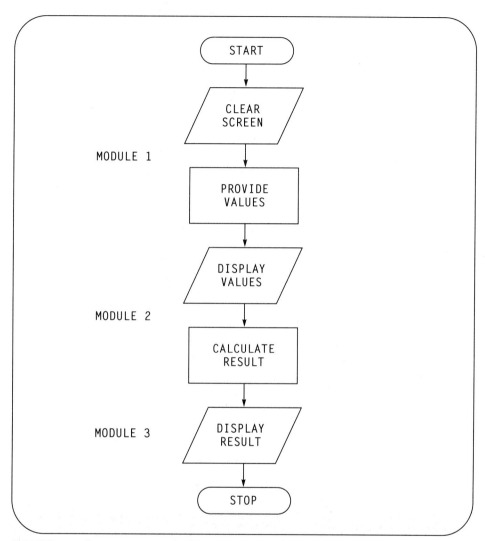

FIGURE 13.1. Sequence example flowchart

Line Number Usage. Recall from the discussion of the essential features of BASIC that this language requires line numbers. Our program will then consist of instructions to the computer, each preceded by a number. It is common practice to number lines by 10, leaving numbers unused in case the process of debugging uncovers a need to add new lines. We elect to begin Module 1 with line number 100, Module 2 with 200, and Module 3 with 300. Other choices would be equally valid. Just remember to number by 10.

Coding Module 1. Every module will begin with minimal documentation. BASIC provides for inclusion of comments to the programmer or anyone reading a program with the REMark statement. REM may be followed on a program line by virtually anything useful in documenting the program. Just identifying the module is adequate. Place the REMark at the start of the module as line 100.

```
100 REM MODULE 1
```

Module 1 consists of two subtasks, clearing the screen and providing the data that the program is to manipulate. Clearing the screen requires only a single command. In most Microsoft versions of BASIC (IBM and others), the required statement is CLS. In Applesoft BASIC, it is HOME. Using CLS, the next line becomes:

```
110 CLS
```

Providing data within a program is conceptually more complex, but quite simple to do. The data must be stored in a way that the computer can access and manipulate. This involves the use of *variables*. A variable is simply a place to store data by label or name, much like a post office box stores mail. Variable names in BASIC consist of one letter followed by additional letters or numbers if desired. Our program requires two different values, so two variables are needed. For our purposes, the traditional mathematical X and Y will work well. Each designates a *numeric* variable.

Having selected variables, the data must be placed in them. This is called *assignment* and, at its simplest, is accomplished with what appears to be an equation. Thus, if our respective values are 50 and 10, we can write:

```
120 X=50
130 Y=10
```

The complete module is:

```
100 REM    MODULE 1
110 CLS
120 X=50
130 Y=10
```

Coding Module 2. The second module also consists of two subtasks, displaying the values to be used in the calculations and the actual calculation. We previously determined that this module would begin at line number 200. (It is perfectly permissable to skip blocks of line numbers, as we will do here, since Module 1 ended with line 130.) Line 200 is our documentation line:

```
200 REM    MODULE 2
```

To display anything on the computer's screen in BASIC requires the PRINT statement. To display specific information, enclose it in quotation marks after PRINT. To leave a blank line on the screen, which greatly enhances readability, use just PRINT. In this example, exactly what we display is arbitrary, so here is our version. (Can you rewrite these lines to do the same job using different words?)

```
210 PRINT "THIS PROGRAM CALCULATES THE MEAN OF TWO NUMBERS."
220 PRINT
230 PRINT "CURRENT VALUES ARE:"
240 PRINT
```

Beyond this message, we still need to display the actual values of X and Y. While we could follow the pattern for print statements in lines 210–240—e.g., PRINT "X=50"—it is better to display the values placed into variables X and Y in lines 120–130. By doing so, we could change the values in those two lines and have no other changes to make in the entire program. To do this, we need to display specific text plus the contents of a variable, all with one PRINT statement. To display the contents of a variable, one need only give the variable's name following PRINT; e.g., PRINT X. To combine the PRINT " " and PRINT X formats, separate the elements to be printed with a semicolon. The result is:

```
250 PRINT"    X=";X
260 PRINT"    Y=";Y
270 PRINT
```

The blank spaces within the quote marks simply indent the text from the left edge of the screen.

Study lines 250–260 carefully to be sure you understand how two different approaches to displaying information were combined in a single PRINT statement.

The second subtask is to calculate the mean of our two values. This requires that we add them together and divide by two. The result must be stored somewhere, so we create a third variable. Since it will contain the mean, let's just name it MEAN. This is a case where a longer variable name seems like a sensible idea; it provides additional documentation within the program. The final outcome is again something resembling arithmetic:

```
280 MEAN=(X+Y)/2
```

This is a combination of the assignment statement MEAN = and the required arithmetic. This completes Module 2 as follows:

```
200 REM    MODULE 2
210 PRINT "THIS PROGRAM CALCULATES THE MEAN OF TWO NUMBERS."
220 PRINT
230 PRINT "CURRENT VALUES ARE:"
240 PRINT
250 PRINT "    X=";X
260 PRINT "    Y=";Y
270 PRINT
280 MEAN=(X+Y)/2
```

Coding Module 3. We have now done the real work of the program, but at this point the user would not know the outcome. Simply calculating something is not enough; we must display that result with another PRINT statement. Of course, we also need to document the final module.

```
300 REM   MODULE 3
310 PRINT "THEIR MEAN IS";MEAN;"."
```

That final PRINT statement may seem quite odd at first glance, but it is just a slight extension of the principle demonstrated in lines 250–260, combining literal printing of text in quotes with variable information and separating the elements by semicolons. Of course, we could have stopped after the variable MEAN in line 310, and the correct information would be displayed, but in a sentence lacking final punctuation. We strongly believe that any screen display must be grammatically correct; hence, the final quote marks containing a period.

The Complete Program
The complete program consists of putting the three modules together. Figure 13.2 shows the final listing and the output of the program as a user would see it. You should be able to trace the flow of the program line by line, from beginning to end. If anything remains unclear, reread the description of the appropriate module before going on.

Entering the Program
If you wish, you can enter this program on your computer and run it. Pay careful attention to your typing. A few observations should help.

You may have wondered why all of our code is written in capital letters. Most computers permit the text of PRINT statements (the characters inside the quote marks) to be upper or lower case. Older Apples, however, do not display lower-case letters. In addition, many versions of BASIC require that all BASIC statements be in caps and all versions will accept caps. Thus, using all caps is the most general form, but not the only one your computer may allow.

To enter this program, be sure your computer is in BASIC. Then simply type each line exactly as shown. At the end of each line, press the RETURN or ENTER key. Continue until all lines have been entered. If you make an error in a line, simply retype it using the same line number. Only the last version will be saved.

For further details, consult your BASIC manual.

THE SELECTION CONSTRUCT

Our second problem is to create a simple computer-user "conversation." The computer will ask users to enter their first name. For one female name of our choice, the computer will claim to have the same name; otherwise it will call itself HAL.

```
100 REM          MODULE 1
110 CLS
120 X=50
130 Y=10
200 REM          MODULE 2
210 PRINT "THIS PROGRAM CALCULATES THE MEAN OF TWO NUMBERS."
220 PRINT
230 PRINT "CURRENT VALUES ARE:"
240 PRINT
250 PRINT"    X=";X
260 PRINT"    Y=";Y
270 PRINT
280 MEAN=(X+Y)/2
300 REM          MODULE 3
310 PRINT "THEIR MEAN IS";MEAN;"."
```

```
THIS PROGRAM CALCULATES THE MEAN OF TWO NUMBERS.

CURRENT VALUES ARE:

    X=50

    Y=10

THEIR MEAN IS 30.
```

FIGURE 13.2. Listing and output of sequence example

The Planning Step

First, we briefly state the problem as a single top-level diagram entry.

```
COMPUTER-USER
CONVERSATION
```

Two elements of the problem are apparent for the next level. First, the computer must initiate the conversation and request the user's name. Second, the computer must respond based on the entered name. This gives us level 2 refinement.

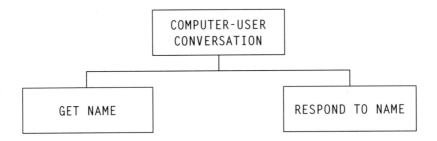

This is already sufficient in terms of the problem specification. However, it might produce a rather brusque conversation. We can avoid this by adding some initial and final comments from the computer. Since these are not actually required by the problem, they could just be added at level 2. Instead, we will treat them as refinements of the level 2 blocks and create level 3. Either way is justifiable and results in four modules.

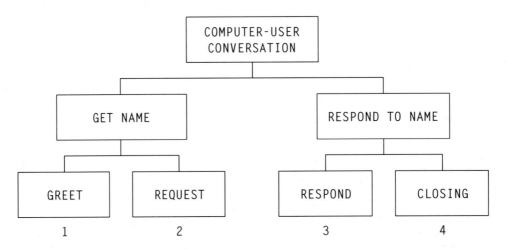

The Flowchart Step
In this example, the ability of a flowchart to show the logic of a problem will become clear. Our design diagram merely shows four modules. Modules 1, 2, and 4 can be envisioned as straight sequences of instructions. However, the third module—"Respond"—will involve assessing the name entered by the user and selecting one of two responses to it. The computer must make a decision. Let's look at this alone, before we create the entire flowchart.

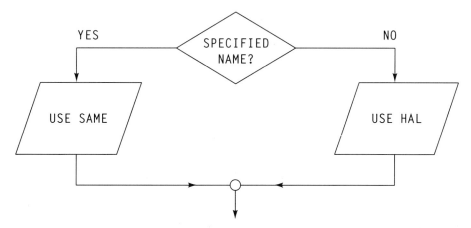

This flowchart segment clearly shows that a decision leads to one of two different actions, beyond which the program continues again on one path. Figure 13.3 shows the complete flowchart.

The Coding Step

Except for new BASIC statements, few comments will be made about the code. Refer back to the sequence example if something is not clear and not explained here. Since none of our modules is very long, we can use lines 100, 200, 300, and 400, respectively, to begin them.

Coding Module 1. After our documentation line and clearing the screen, how we choose to greet the user is arbitrary. Here is one version.

```
100 REM    MODULE 1
110 CLS
120 PRINT "HI, I'M YOUR FRIENDLY MICROCOMPUTER."
130 PRINT
140 PRINT "I'D LIKE TO GET BETTER ACQUAINTED WITH YOU."
150 PRINT
```

Coding Module 2. First we must tell the user what to do, then allow entry of the user's name. The latter requires a new BASIC statement—INPUT. INPUT causes the computer to wait until the user types something and presses the RETURN key. The user input must be stored in a variable. An *alphanumeric* or *"string"* variable is required to hold alphabetic data. String variable names end with a dollar sign. We will use FIRST$ as the variable name, and add blank lines for readability on screen.

```
200 REM    MODULE 2
210 PRINT "PLEASE TELL ME YOUR FIRST NAME."
220 PRINT
230 INPUT FIRST$
240 PRINT
```

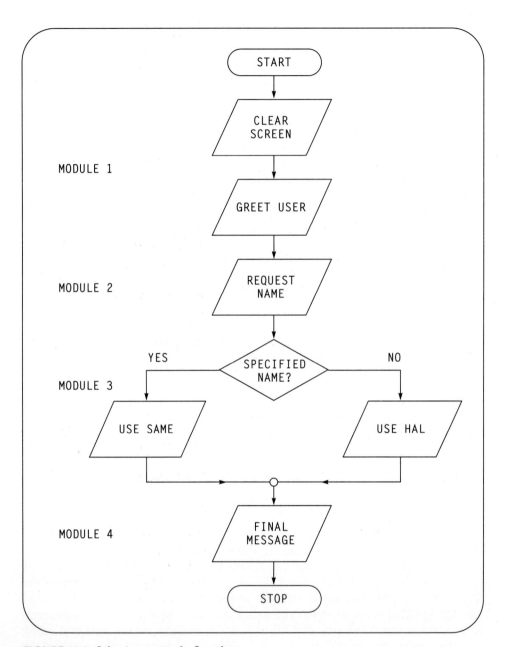

FIGURE 13.3. Selection example flowchart

Coding Module 3. The third module is the most complex because it rests on the selection construct. The concept is similar to an English description of what must happen. If a specified name is entered, respond in one manner. If not, use a different response. BASIC uses the statements IF . . . THEN to achieve this selection. We have chosen MARY as the name to watch for.

```
300 REM    MODULE 3
310 IF FIRST$<>"MARY" THEN 340
320 PRINT "HOW INTERESTING. MY NAME IS ALSO MARY."
330 GOTO 370
340 PRINT "I AM VERY PLEASED TO MEET YOU, ";FIRST$;"."
350 PRINT
360 PRINT "MY NAME IS HAL."
370 PRINT
```

Since a lot is new here, a more detailed explanation is in order. In line 310, we determine if the user entered the name MARY, which is stored in the variable FIRST$. If not (the symbol <> means not equal or does not contain), program flow jumps to line 340. Lines 340–360 provide the response to any other name, repeating the name entered by the user. If the user entered the name MARY, the computer stops executing line 310 at the word THEN and moves on to line 320, the appropriate response to MARY. Since lines 340–360 are appropriate only for other names, we must skip over them for anyone named Mary. Line 330 directs the program flow around those lines by telling it to GOTO line 370. In either case, we end up at line 370. Here is the code again with lines drawn to show how the flow varies depending on the user's entry.

```
300 REM    MODULE 3
310 IF FIRST$<>"MARY" THEN 340
320 PRINT "HOW INTERESTING. MY NAME IS ALSO MARY."
330 GOTO 370
340 PRINT "I AM VERY PLEASED TO MEET YOU, ";FIRST$;"."
350 PRINT
360 PRINT "MY NAME IS HAL."
370 PRINT
```

Study this example carefully to be sure you understand how it works.

Coding Module 4. The final module is merely to close the conversation in some manner. We propose the following:

```
400 REM    MODULE 4
410 PRINT "I'M SURE WE WILL BECOME GOOD FRIENDS."
```

The Complete Program

Putting the four modules together into one complete program gives us Figure 13.4. Two different versions of the output are included, showing the result of

```
100 REM          MODULE 1
110 CLS
120 PRINT "HI, I'M YOUR FRIENDLY MICROCOMPUTER."
130 PRINT
140 PRINT "I'D LIKE TO GET BETTER ACQUAINTED WITH YOU."
150 PRINT
200 REM          MODULE 2
210 PRINT "PLEASE TELL ME YOUR FIRST NAME."
220 PRINT
230 INPUT FIRST$
240 PRINT
300 REM          MODULE 3
310 IF FIRST$ <> "MARY" THEN 340
320 PRINT "HOW INTERESTING. MY NAME IS ALSO MARY."
330 GO TO 370
340 PRINT "I'M VERY PLEASED TO MEET YOU, ";FIRST$;"."
350 PRINT
360 PRINT "MY NAME IS HAL."
370 PRINT
400 REM          MODULE 4
410 PRINT "I'M SURE WE WILL BECOME GOOD FRIENDS."
```

```
HI, I'M YOUR FRIENDLY MICROCOMPUTER.
I'D LIKE TO GET BETTER ACQUAINTED WITH YOU.
PLEASE TELL ME YOUR FIRST NAME.
? (MARY)——— USER INPUT
HOW INTERESTING. MY NAME IS ALSO MARY.
I'M SURE WE WILL BECOME GOOD FRIENDS.
```

```
HI, I'M YOUR FRIENDLY MICROCOMPUTER.
I'D LIKE TO GET BETTER ACQUAINTED WITH YOU.
PLEASE TELL ME YOUR FIRST NAME.
? (JOHN)——— USER INPUT
I AM VERY PLEASED TO MEET YOU, JOHN.
MY NAME IS HAL.
I'M SURE WE WILL BECOME GOOD FRIENDS.
```

FIGURE 13.4. Listing and output of selection example

entering different names. Any screen line beginning with a question mark is the result of an INPUT statement; what follows it was entered by the user.

THE ITERATION CONSTRUCT (LOOPING)

For our final problem, HAL, your computer, wants to demonstrate its prowess with numbers. It will count for you from a starting value to an ending value by some increment, all of which you specify. We assume that you will enter only reasonable values; e.g., ending is greater than starting and the increment is less than the difference. These restrictions are necessary only to keep the example fairly simple.

The Planning Step

A concise statement of the problem again constitutes level one. We use simple math notation for the numbers.

```
COUNT FROM X
 TO Y BY Z
```

Two components can be envisioned easily at level two.

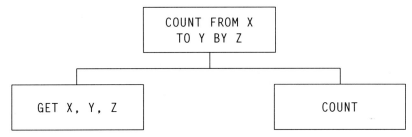

Our final refinement, which would not have to be a third level, provides the context for the user and closure.

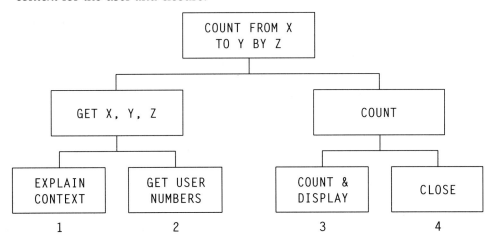

The Flowchart Step

You may already realize that Modules 1 and 4 will likely require only some PRINT statements and Module 2 will use INPUT. They should be fairly obvious by now and require no discussion.

Module 3 contains the new concepts. The task will be to compare the starting number (call it X) to the ending number (call it Y). If the first is less, as it should be, then display it. Next, add to it the specified amount (call it Z). Compare this new value of X to the ending value. If X is still less than Y, display X and add the increment again. This is the cycle that will be repeated over and over (a loop) until X exceeds Y. Here is the flowchart for this module, which again displays the logic not apparent in our design diagram.

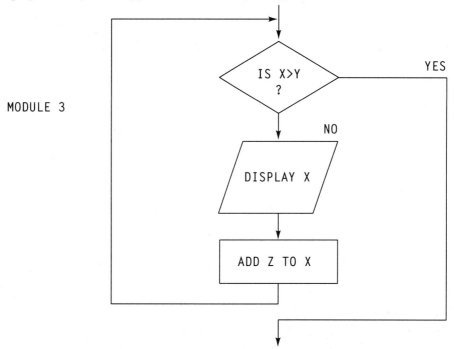

MODULE 3

Since the other modules contain no new concepts, we do not present them individually. The complete flowchart is Figure 13.5.

The Coding Step

Although a new construct is used in this example, no new BASIC statements are required. Rather, iteration uses IF . . . THEN in a slightly different manner than selection. Multiple INPUTs are also needed to allow for three entered values. All of this is just an extension of earlier ideas, so minimal explanation is required. We can still use 100, 200, 300, and 400 as our starting line numbers for the four modules, since none seems likely to be too long.

Coding Module 1. How one introduces the user to the program is a matter of choice. The following possibility should be self-explanatory in the coding.

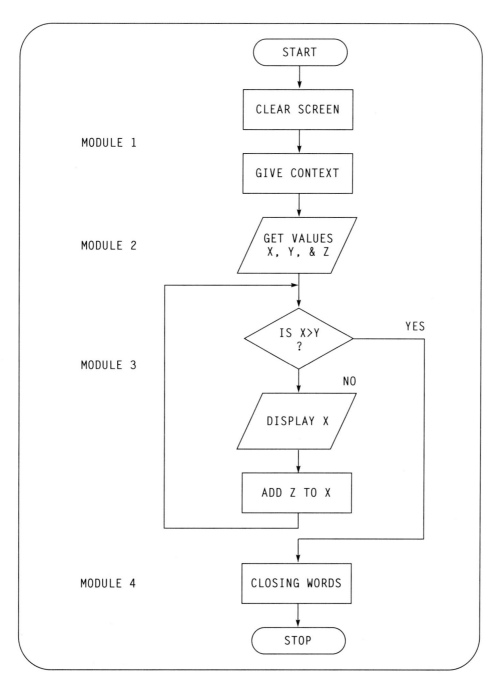

FIGURE 13.5. Iteration example flowchart

```
100 REM    MODULE 1
110 CLS
120 PRINT "HI! I'M HAL, YOUR FRIENDLY COMPUTER."
130 PRINT
140 PRINT "I'D LIKE TO SHOW YOU SOME NUMBER FUN."
150 PRINT
160 PRINT "I'LL ASK YOU FOR THREE NUMBERS, WHICH I WILL"
170 PRINT
180 PRINT "USE TO DEMONSTRATE MY COUNTING ABILITY."
190 PRINT
```

Coding Module 2. Now we can ask for the three numbers and give a little more explanation. You might have preferred to explain the program more fully in module 1, which would be fine. We are asking for three numbers from the user, so numeric variables are needed. The only new idea here is combining the features of separate PRINT and INPUT statements into a single statement. As line 210 shows, you can specify your "prompting" message in quotes after INPUT, then use a semicolon to separate the message from the variable.

```
200 REM    MODULE 2
210 INPUT "WHAT NUMBER SHALL I START COUNTING FROM";X
220 PRINT
230 INPUT "WHAT NUMBER SHALL I COUNT TO";Y
240 PRINT
250 INPUT "HOW MUCH SHOULD I ADD EACH TIME";Z
260 PRINT
270 PRINT "THANK YOU. NOW WATCH ME GO!"
280 PRINT
```

We now have all the required information stored in variables X, Y, and Z.

Coding Module 3. Look back at the flowchart of module 3. The logic of the iteration construct is to compare two things, then take action depending on the outcome. Does that sound like a decision? It should, and that means we can use IF . . . THEN. However, in the selection example, the decision led to alternate *forward* paths. With a loop, one path goes ahead, the other returns to an earlier point to repeat some set of instructions. Here's how this module looks in BASIC.

```
300 REM    MODULE 3
310 IF X>Y THEN 350
320 PRINT X
330 X=X+Z
340 GOTO 310
350 PRINT
```

Remember what we set out to do. The program should count from X to Y by Z. To do so, we compare the values of X and Y (line 310). As long as X is less than Y, we display its current value (line 320) and add the increment (line 330). We then return to the check point (line 310) to see if we are finished or should go through the loop again. Once X exceeds Y, the task is finished. We conclude the module with a blank line (350) for screen readability.

Coding Module 4. The final module provides only a friendly farewell to the user, so its exact content is arbitrary.

```
400 REM    MODULE 4
410 PRINT "THAT WAS FUN! LET'S DO IT AGAIN SOMETIME."
```

The Complete Program

Pulling all four modules together gives us the finished program in Figure 13.6. Included is the output of the program for a very short example.

THE GREAT BASIC DEBATE

In the world of computing, 1965 is ancient history. Developments since then have occurred at an incredible rate. New computer languages have been created; it is estimated that over 200 now exist. It should be no great surprise that continued widespread use of an "old" language would spark debate. BASIC has indeed come under a lot of fire. Now that you have some familiarity with the language, let's look at the controversy surrounding BASIC and try to put into perspective the question, Why BASIC?

It is important to note that the significance of the debate depends on one's purpose for teaching BASIC. Many aspects of the controversy seem relevant primarily to secondary schools that teach programming as college preparation or for some vocational purpose. The arguments presented must be viewed in the context of one's goals and grade level.

ADVANTAGES OF BASIC

Proponents of BASIC are quick to point out its advantages *within its intended sphere*, i.e., students in schools.

First, BASIC remains one of the easier languages to learn, although the learning curve is broad between enough knowledge to program the computer to perform some small task like our examples and actual mastery of the language.

Second, BASIC already exists in the majority of computers in use in schools today. It is on a chip in the microcomputers most schools have purchased or is available on disk free with the system or at very low cost. Thus, schools wishing to teach programming to students will have little or no additional investment.

Third, BASIC will run on any microcomputer without additional hardware. Many other languages require more than minimal RAM.

Fourth, the versions of BASIC found on most school micros have been enhanced beyond Dartmouth's original in ways significant to educators. For

```
100 REM        MODULE 1
110 CLS
120 PRINT "I'M HAL, YOUR FRIENDLY COMPUTER."
130 PRINT
140 PRINT "I'D LIKE TO SHOW YOU SOME NUMBER FUN."
150 PRINT
160 PRINT "I'LL ASK YOU FOR THREE NUMBERS, WHICH I WILL"
170 PRINT
180 PRINT "USE TO DEMONSTRATE MY COUNTING ABILITY."
190 PRINT
200 REM        MODULE 2
210 INPUT "WHAT NUMBER SHALL I START COUNTING FROM";X
220 PRINT
230 INPUT "WHAT NUMBER SHALL I COUNT TO";Y
240 PRINT
250 INPUT "HOW MUCH SHOULD I ADD EACH TIME";Z
260 PRINT
270 PRINT "THANK YOU. NOW WATCH ME GO."
280 PRINT
300 REM        MODULE 3
310 IF X>Y THEN 350
320 PRINT X
330 X=X+Z
340 GO TO 310
350 PRINT
400 REM        MODULE 4
410 PRINT "THAT WAS FUN! LET'S DO IT AGAIN SOMETIME."
```

```
HI! I'M HAL, YOUR FRENDLY COMPUTER.
I'D LIKE TO SHOW YOU SOME NUMBER FUN.
I'LL ASK YOU FOR THREE NUMBERS, WHICH I WILL
USE TO DEMOSTRATE MY COUNTING ABILITY.
WHAT NUMBER SHALL I START COUNTING FROM? (100)
WHAT NUMBER SHALL I COUNT TO? (102)
HOW MUCH SHOULD I ADD EACH TIME? (1)  ──►USER INPUT
THANK YOU. NOW WATCH ME GO.
100
101
102
THAT WAS FUN! LET'S DO IT AGAIN SOMETIME.
```

FIGURE 13.6. Listing and output of iteration example

instance, most have had graphics added, usually with color capabilities. Many can also produce sound. Text display capabilities are generally as good as any other language.

Fifth, BASIC is already well-entrenched in the schools. Teachers are now available to provide programming instruction, and more are learning the language at all times. No other language has such a ready-to-go cadre of teachers.

DISADVANTAGES OF BASIC

Vocal groups of computer educators routinely condemn BASIC for a variety of reasons. Such concerns usually center on perceived advantages of Pascal or C and, to a lesser extent, Logo.

First, although BASIC is relatively easy to learn, it may not be well-suited to younger students. An introduction to programming often focuses on graphics, which many find too complex in BASIC for young children. Logo is superior for this purpose.

Some might argue that Logo can be and is taught as preparation for later exposure to BASIC. Although problem-solving skills developed through learning Logo may help a student to program in another language, there is little similarity between Logo and BASIC. Thus, a change to BASIC at a later age will be esentially a fresh start. Furthermore, if one waits until an appropriate age, say junior high level, to introduce BASIC, students should be able to learn a "better" language like Pascal just as readily.

Second, commonly available versions of BASIC are based on early implementations of the language. Dartmouth's creation predates the development of structured programming principles, which are now all but universally accepted as the basis for proper programming. Many believe that BASIC serves only to develop very bad programming habits and styles, which a student seriously pursuing programming later in life will have to unlearn. They argue that it is better to begin with proper techniques because old habits are often very difficult to change. We have personally observed the difficulties many students face when attempting to learn structured programming concepts in any language after developing initial skills in BASIC.

Third, while BASIC can be used in a manner compatible with modern programming theory and style, few books on the market adequately present BASIC in this fashion. Even those purporting to teach "structured" BASIC generally begin with a traditional approach and introduce structure only much later. In effect, they first present "bad" BASIC, then try to undo their own damage.

Fourth, the existence of BASIC in current computers is no more a justification for its use than the presence of a cigarette lighter in most automobiles requires the driver to smoke. Pascal is readily available for school computers today, it has become easier to use (especially in interpreted versions), and cost is no longer prohibitive. Not all versions of Pascal support graphics, but that is also irrelevant because Logo provides all the graphics experience a student will likely need.

Fifth, the existing pool of BASIC teachers is not a valuable resource, but a problem. For all the reasons cited above, BASIC is not worth teaching, so the pool is irrelevant. Further, the majority of current teachers are self-taught from materials that make no attempt to treat BASIC in a modern fashion. If they at least knew and presented BASIC from a structured perspective, their skills would have more value. Since this may involve substantial relearning, why not just learn a better language instead?

Sixth, the addition of graphics, sound, and other extensions to BASIC has led to many differing versions or dialects in wide use. Even dialects produced for different computers by one company (such as MicroSoft) vary considerably. Thus, a program written for an IBM-PC will require modification to run on an Apple, even though both use a MicroSoft BASIC. This needlessly complicates the inevitable moves from one machine to another and may be avoided with other languages.

OUR RESPONSE TO THE DEBATE

We stated previously that this language debate is most relevant when the goal is teaching programming as a specific skill. For other goals, such as creating a problem-solving environment, the critical issue is which language best serves the goal. In our view, Logo has far more to offer than BASIC for problem solving, especially for younger pupils. Still, many teachers have developed interesting uses of BASIC to teach other content, for instance in physics (Crull, 1987) and eighth grade mathematics (Johnson and Gilda, 1987). The continued appearance of such articles in prominent computer publications is evidence of the staying power of BASIC.

When programming is taught for its own sake, the arguments over BASIC extend into vociferous disagreements on language choice in general. Purists who argue for "modern" languages such as Pascal are as apt to dismiss Logo as irrelevant as they are to support it. Fuel was added to the fire by the decision of Educational Testing Service (ETS) to base the Advanced Placement (AP) Exam in Computer Science on Pascal rather than BASIC. Many educators looked on this as the death knell for BASIC at the high school level.

However, ETS took this approach not to condemn BASIC, but for pragmatic reasons. AP exams serve to sanction high school learning with college credit. Structured programming is so ingrained in higher education that few institutions would grant credit in computer science for BASIC. Pascal, on the other hand, is widely accepted. Further, ETS did not expect huge numbers of schools to ever offer an AP course in computer science, any more than is true in other AP areas (Benderson, 1983, p. 11).

Our only intent in the foregoing is to inform you of the issues. The debate has quieted in recent years. This is due in part to decreased emphasis on programming as the heart of computer literacy. Fewer students are being taught programming solely because it is the only possible computer activity. Furthermore, newer versions of BASIC such as *True BASIC*, *Quick BASIC*, and *Turbo BASIC* have been enhanced in ways that meet many of the objections. For advanced discussion of superior structured BASIC programming using newer versions of the language for Apple II, see Abernathy (1989).

In the end we believe the issue reduces to simply good programming and bad programming, essentially structured versus unstructured style. To that end, we are comfortable with BASIC taught as a structured language, a structured version of the language such as True BASIC, or some other structured language like Pascal. We do not expect BASIC to disappear and believe that teachers can profit from some rudimentary familiarity with it, properly structured, of course.

SUMMARY

Learning to program in BASIC or any other language is a major undertaking. Within the context of an introductory computer education experience, it is appropriate for teachers and future teachers to gain some exposure to the most common microcomputer language. This chapter has sought only to provide a frame of reference regarding BASIC, on which other experiences may be built. There are countless BASIC programming books available, although few follow solid structured programming principles.

The need for an instructional language led to creation of BASIC at Dartmouth College. The key concepts in BASIC are use of line numbers, modest number of statements to be learned, and interactivity in interpreted versions. Actual consideration of BASIC as a language focused on three problems to solve, which utilize the three structured programming constructs of sequence, selection, and iteration. Each problem was developed from planning through flowcharting and finally to BASIC code.

Because BASIC is an old language in computer time frames, it has many adherents as well as vocal critics. We suggest that the language itself is not the real issue, but rather whether one adheres to structured programming principles in using it. There no doubt are "better" languages available, but properly used, BASIC remains a viable language in education.

CHAPTER 13 ACTIVITIES

1. Compare and contrast BASIC and Logo. When would you choose to teach one versus the other? Do you find them equally usable for all grades? As problem-solving environments?
2. Take a position for or against BASIC as a language to be taught in the schools. Defend your position.
3. Look briefly at some available BASIC texts. Do they teach programming or just the mechanics of the language? Do the examples given illustrate even

the minimal levels of documentation and modularity shown here? Compare the examples in this chapter to any other simple BASIC programs you can find. Do you find documentation and modularity helpful in understanding a program?

4. Make the following changes to our first example (Figure 13.2).
   a. Change the two values to 200 and 100.
   b. Have the program use three values, not two.
   c. Make the program flexible by allowing the user to give the values.
5. Modify example two (Figure 13.4) to look for a name other than Mary. Change the computer's name as well.
6. Change the third example (Figure 13.6) to count *down* from one number to another by a specified step.
7. Using the examples provided for guidance, *design* a program that calculates the average of three fixed values. Modify your design to allow the user to enter the values from the keyboard.
8. *Design* a program that carries on some kind of conversation with the user. Include at least one point where the user's input determines the computer's response.
9. As a challenge, try to develop the code for the programs you designed for activities 7 and 8.

REFERENCES

Abernathy, J. "Launching into BASIC." *Call -A.P.P.L.E.*, March 1989, pp. 27–35.

Benderson, A., ed. *Focus 11*. Princeton, NJ: Educational Testing Service, 1983.

Castek, J. E. *Structured BASIC Programming on IBM Personal Computers*. New York: John Wiley and Sons, 1988.

Crull, J. L. "The Speed of Sound." *The Computing Teacher*, March 1987, pp. 29–32, 56.

Hallenbeck, M. J., and Boetel, D. F. *Teacher Friendly*. Belmont, CA: David S. Lake Publishers, 1985.

Heimler, C., Cunningham, J., and Nevard, M. *BASIC for Teachers*. Santa Cruz, CA: Mitchell Publishing, 1987.

Johnson, J., and Gilda, B. "The Chocolate Chip Cookie Caper—Part I." *The Computing Teacher*, March 1987, pp. 33–35.

Poirot, J. L., and Adams, R. C. *40 Easy Steps to Programming in BASIC and LOGO*. Austin, TX: Sterling Swift Publishing Co., 1983.

Ross, S. M. *BASIC Programming for Educators*. Englewood Cliffs, NJ: Prentice-Hall, 1986.

CHAPTER 14

□ Beyond Logo and BASIC □

O B J E C T I V E S

After completing this chapter, you will be able to:

□ *Explain the potential significance to teachers of each language presented.* □
□ *Give the primary use of each language presented.* □
□ *List advantages and disadvantages of each language presented.* □
□ *Compare algorithmic and logic programming.* □
□ *Explain the differences between authoring languages and authoring systems.* □
□ *Identify any languages you feel you might wish to study further and explain why.* □
□ *Describe HyperCard as an authoring tool.* □
□ *Place expert systems within the artificial intelligence framework and explain their nature.* □
□ *Discuss possible educational applications of expert system shells.* □

With this chapter, we conclude our treatment of computer languages and programming. You have already considered the fundamental principles of algorithmic programming and taken a careful look at the languages most commonly taught in schools today: Logo and BASIC.

No doubt you realize that there are many more languages in existence than those two. Since the 1950s, over 200 different programming languages have been developed (Shelly and Cashman, 1980, p. 12.1). Most never came into common use; many were developed for narrowly specialized purposes.

This chapter has two major parts. In the first, you will take a brief look at Pascal, the remaining language most likely to be of interest to educators, and C, a language used to develop many software applications. Because so many have at least heard of them, we also offer a glimpse of FORTRAN and COBOL, which are taught in some secondary data-processing curricula. Non-algorithmic programming and PROLOG conclude this part.

The second section will introduce you to "authoring" software, which offers rather different means of creating your own programs. Authoring software is highly specialized and not intended for general programming purposes. However, for the teacher wishing to create CAI for the classroom, authoring tools deserve careful consideration. We will examine authoring languages, authoring systems, *HyperCard*, and expert systems shells.

PROGRAMMING LANGUAGES

Beyond Logo and BASIC, other languages have had minimal impact on K–12 educational computing for several reasons. Many are not as readily available and are less generally applicable, although each was created for a very specific purpose. There is little justification for teaching these languages to large numbers of students. Comparatively few schools have chosen to purchase these extra languages, which rarely come with a computer system. They may also require additional memory and disk capacity, which may not be available. Still, your exposure to computer languages would be incomplete without a brief look at them.

To provide a basis for comparison, we will use a common problem throughout and show a possible solution in each algorithmic language. The problem is to write a program that allows the user to specify the number of values to be entered at the keyboard. The computer will then request the values one by one, compute their mean, and display the result.

PASCAL

Pascal is the source of a great deal of interest in the educational world today, as well as considerable confusion and misunderstanding. Like BASIC, Pascal was developed to be a teaching language. Its originator was Niklaus Wirth, a Swiss computer scientist, who sought to implement the structured programming concepts of Dijkstra in a new language for beginners. He named his creation after the seventeenth century mathematician Blaise Pascal. Working versions of Pascal became available in the early 1970s.

Pascal quickly became popular with postsecondary computer science departments because it solved the problem of trying to teach structured programming with unstructured languages. The idea was to introduce programming to students via Pascal, so that sound programming habits would develop naturally through the language. These habits should extend quite readily to other languages.

Figure 14.1 provides a Pascal solution to the problem we stated and may give some feel for the nature of the language. Notice particularly that variables are identified at the very beginning and that segments of Pascal code are blocked with BEGIN and END statements, allowing considerable flexibility compared with BASIC.

Discussion of Pascal

Interest in Pascal stems largely from its strict adherence to the principles of structured programming. While it is still possible to write a "poor" program in Pascal, it almost requires an effort to do so. The requirement that variables be clearly specified and identified by data type before they can be used is considered a related advantage. It fosters clear thinking about the needs of your program.

```
PROGRAM MEAN;
{DOCUMENTATION IS GIVEN IN CURLY BRACES}
{FIRST, IDENTIFY ALL VARIABLES BY NAME AND TYPE}
VAR
      NUMITEMS, CYCLE : INTEGER;
      ITEM, MEAN, SUM : REAL;
BEGIN
      {GET THE NUMBER OF ITEMS FROM THE USER}
      WRITELN ('ENTER NUMBER OF ITEMS  TO AVERAGE');
      READ (NUMITEMS);
      {SET UP A LOOP FOR THAT NUMBER OF ITEMS}
      SUM := 0.0
      FOR CYCLE = 1 TO NUMITEMS DO
          BEGIN
               {GET ONE VALUE AND ADD IT TO SUM}
               READ (ITEM);
               SUM := SUM + ITEM;
          END; {THIS FINISHES THE LOOP}
      {CALCULATE AND DISPLAY THE MEAN}
      MEAN := SUM / NUMITEMS;
      WRITELN ('THE MEAN IS',MEAN);
END.
```

FIGURE 14.1. Problem solution in Pascal

Some versions of Pascal have been enhanced to include turtlegraphics, which can help provide a smooth transition from Logo. Other sophisticated graphics enhancements may also be included.

As a final advantage, study of Pascal at the high school level is more likely to be directly relevant to later college study in computer science than is study of BASIC.

Several disadvantages of Pascal are often noted. Pascal has been available primarily as a compiled language. Thus, students are faced not only with the task of mastering the language, but must also master an editor to enter and alter their programs. The program development process may be slower as explained previously regarding compiled versus interpreted languages. Interpreted versions such as *Instant Pascal* for the Apple IIe and *MacPascal* for the Macintosh address this concern.

Another concern is that far fewer teachers are prepared to teach Pascal than either Logo or BASIC. While the latter have often been learned independently, Pascal is a more difficult language to learn, and comparatively few self-teaching materials have appeared. Generally, teachers have had to seek somewhat scarce opportunities at a college or university to learn Pascal.

As a final concern, although Pascal was intended to be a student's first language, the student envisioned by Wirth was of college age. Some question the suitability of Pascal for younger students. Where it is taught, the audience tends to be the very best students, whereas a broader audience is being served by Logo and BASIC.

Pascal was something of a curiosity among public schools until Educational Testing Service announced its Advanced Placement exam for computer science based on Pascal. Suddenly, interest in Pascal grew enormously. We presented the issues surrounding BASIC and Pascal in Chapter 13 and need not repeat them here. We primarily urge that schools choose the languages they will teach with a clear understanding of why programming is being taught and how the languages chosen meet their specified goals.

In considering possible teaching of Pascal, do not forget that it will rarely be the first language a student learns, which was Wirth's intention. By the time a student reaches the level where Pascal is taught, prior experience with Logo or BASIC is likely. Thus, some of the rationale for Pascal is negated by common practice. Schools need to look carefully at the entire sequence of language instruction and analyze the potential and pitfalls of what has become a fairly common pattern: Logo, followed by BASIC in junior high, then Pascal in high school. The ramifications of this progression have yet to be thoroughly explored.

THE C LANGUAGE

Many application programs for microcomputers are written in C (Computer language), which was developed in the 1970s. This language is an adaptation of the C language that was implemented as part of the programming environment within the UNIX operating system. In turn, UNIX C was an outgrowth of an older language called BCPL (still in use in Europe) which influenced a language called B, the forerunner of the current C.

C is referred to as a *middle-level language;* that is, in concept it lies between assembler languages and high-level languages such as BASIC, PASCAL, FORTRAN, and COBOL. As a middle-level language, C allows the manipulation of bits, bytes, and addresses, thus making control over processing very direct and fast (similar to the advantages of assembler languages). On the other hand, its program code is *portable;* that is, C can be run on a wide variety of computers, such as different microcomputer families, minicomputers, and even mainframe computers (similar to the advantages of compiler languages). Thus, C incorporates many of the advantages of assembler languages and of high-level languages without their limitations. It is easy to understand why the C language is finding widespread use.

In addition, C has other important characteristics. First, C is *modular.* Each specific implementation includes files of definitions and functions which enable the basic C language to take full advantage of the specific features of a particular

```
/* C Documentation is given between slash-star pairs */
/*
/* program mean */
main ( )
{
/* IDENTIFY ALL VARIABLES BY TYPE AND NAME */
int    numitems, cycle;
float item,mean,sum;

/* GET NUMBER OF ITEMS FROM USER */
printf ("ENTER NUMBER OF ITEMS TO AVERAGE", \n);
scanf ("%d", &numitems);

/* INITIALIZE VALUE OF SUM */
sum = 0.0;

/* SET UP A LOOP FOR THAT NUMBER OF ITEMS */
for (cycle = 1; cycle <= numitems; cycle ++)
    /* GET ONE VALUE AND ADD TO SUM */
    {
    scanf ("%f", &item);
    sum = sum + item;
    }    /* THIS FINISHES THE LOOP */

/* CALCULATE THE MEAN AND DISPLAY IT */
mean = sum / numitems;
printf ("THE MEAN IS %4.2f \n", mean);
}
```

FIGURE 14.2. Problem solution in C

computer. This increases its power. A specific C version may be used to control drop-down menus, windows, and sophisticated help screens on the monitor, as well as to make better use of various RAM memory configurations which contribute to optimal program execution.

Second, C is *extensible*. This means the programmer can write "library" routines to meet a particular need and then reuse them in other programs, thus making programming tasks considerably more efficient.

Third, C is *structured*, which also makes programming easier and more efficient. Finally, C is *concise*. This makes the actual physical inputting of code quicker, easier, more accurate. It is easy to understand why programmers like this language.

For all of these reasons, the C language will continue to find considerable use as the language of choice for professional developers of general applications programs (as discussed in earlier chapters of this book), as well as an all-purpose programming language for more specific applications.

FORTRAN

FORTRAN is one of the oldest of the high-level languages. It was developed by IBM and released in 1957. The essence of FORTRAN is revealed in its name, *FOR*mula *TRAN*slator. IBM designed this language for use by persons with need for complex mathematical calculations requiring great precision, notably engineers, scientists, and mathematicians. FORTRAN spread quickly among computer manufacturers and came into very wide usage. There were few options at the time.

While FORTRAN was developed for mainframe computers, its lingering familiarity has brought microcomputer versions into existence. Although there are still many FORTRAN users in the world, the language has primarily vocational applicability. In today's schools there may be little reason to teach it.

A possible FORTRAN solution to our general problem is given in Figure 14.3.

Discussion of FORTRAN

The primary advantages of FORTRAN lie in the characteristics around which it was designed. It remains popular in heavy mathematical applications settings. The language allows easy formulation of complex functions and produces results with decimal place accuracy beyond many other languages, at least in mainframe versions.

A second advantage of FORTRAN is that standards have been set for those features that should exist in all versions of the language. These standards are widely adhered to, enabling a high degree of "transportability" of programs from one computer to another. Differences among computers are accounted for in their respective compilers, while to the user, the language remains constant.

On the negative side, FORTRAN was created to be a "number cruncher." As a result, only limited capacity to process nonnumeric data was provided, precisely the data of most interest in education. FORTRAN also lacks sophis-

```
C       FORTRAN EXAMPLE PROGRAM
C       LINES BEGINNING WITH C ARE DOCUMENTATION COMMENTS.
C       FIRST IDENTIFY ALL VARIABLES BY TYPE AND NAME.
        INTEGER N
        REAL VAL,SUM,MEAN
C       SET THE SUM VARIABLE TO ZERO.
        SUM=0.0
C       PROMPT USER FOR NUMBER OF ITEMS USING FORMAT
C       STATEMENT 101.
C       DISPLAY STATEMENT ON SCREEN.
        WRITE (1,101)
C       GET USER INPUT IN VARIABLE N USING FORMAT
C       STATEMENT 102.
        READ (1,102)N
C       SET UP A LOOP TO INPUT ALL N VALUES.
        DO 10 I=1,N
C       GET ONE ITEM AT A TIME AND ADD IT TO SUM.
        READ (1,103)VAL
        SUM=SUM+VAL
10      CONTINUE
C       CALCULATE MEAN AND DISPLAY RESULT USING FORMAT
C       104.
        MEAN=SUM/N
        WRITE (1,104)MEAN
        STOP
101     FORMAT ('ENTER NUMBER OF ITEMS TO AVERAGE:')
102     FORMAT(I2)
103     FORMAT (F2.0)
104     FORMAT ('THE MEAN IS',F5.2)
        END
```

FIGURE 14.3. Problem solution in FORTRAN

ticated file processing capabilities and is quite limited in its controls over the format of output, a major concern in both education and business applications.

FORTRAN predates modern concepts of structured programming. As with BASIC, many FORTRAN programmers now attempt to apply structured principles to their programs, but it is something akin to putting the proverbial square peg in a round hole. FORTRAN programs must be heavily documented to be read easily by other than the original programmer; the language does not promote clarity of expression.

COBOL

COBOL is among the most widely used languages in data processing. It is slightly newer than FORTRAN, having appeared in 1960. COBOL was developed by committee, rather than by a single manufacturer, specifically for the needs of the business community. This is apparent in the name, COmmon Business Oriented Language. COBOL was carefully designed to provide the kinds of numeric processing required in business applications, as well as extensive, flexible control over output formatting. The vocabulary of COBOL is much like English, providing a degree of self-documentation in a program. The language was also designed to be transportable across computers.

COBOL owes its broad acceptance to two factors. First, it had no peers for business applications when it was released. Second, the federal government was very interested in a standard language for business applications. The COBOL development team was, in fact, led by a naval officer, Grace Hopper, one of the major figures in modern computing (See Mace, 1984). When the government specified that COBOL had to be available for all computers it purchased, many manufacturers quickly released versions of COBOL for their machines.

COBOL is most commonly used on mainframes, although microcomputer versions are available. These are somewhat scaled-down implementations because full COBOL requires very large memory. Like FORTRAN, COBOL is of interest primarily for vocational reasons.

There are many syntactical requirements in COBOL, such as dividing the program into *divisions*. The Identification Division provides for some rudimentary documentation. The Environment Division contributes to transportability across machines and may be the only part of the program requiring changes if the program is moved. In the Data Division, explicit provision must be made for the types of data to be processed. Finally, the actual "working code" is gathered in the Procedure Division. The solution to our problem is given in Figure 14.4. Notice the English base of COBOL and its heavy reliance on verbs to specify functions to be executed.

Discussion of COBOL

Despite being more than 30 years old, COBOL is still going strong in the data processing world. It is a very practical language for persons interested in data processing careers and has some notable strengths.

On a rudimentary level, the syntax of COBOL is quite easy to learn. The ability to go fairly directly from an English verbal explanation of what is to be done to COBOL syntax is appealing.

COBOL contains many special features to ease data processing tasks in business, including a special Report Writer option. It is especially strong in file-handling capabilities so vital to business. Studying COBOL can be an experience in business data processing.

The formal structure of a COBOL program into the four required divisions illustrated in our example is a strength of the language. Programmers are required to give thought to many aspects of their task as they approach it.

There are also several disadvantages to COBOL. For the school world, it is not as widely available on microcomputers as many other languages. Typical

```
IDENTIFICATION DIVISION.
PROGRAM-ID.MEANCALC.
DATE-WRITTEN.2-NOV-1990.
DATE-COMPILED.2-NOV-1990.

ENVIRONMENT DIVISION.

CONFIGURATION SECTION.
SOURCE-COMPUTER. CPM-80.
OBJECT-COMPUTER. CPM-80.

DATA DIVISION.

FILE SECTION.
* NONE USED

WORKING-STORAGE SECTION.

    01 NUMBER-OF-ITEMS          PIC S9(1) COMP.
    01 ITEM-COUNT               PIC S9(2) COMP.
    01 ONE-ITEM                 PIC S9(4) COMP.
    01 SUM                      PIC S9(4) COMP VALUE 0.
    01 MEAN                     RIC S9(4) COMP.
    01 SHOW-MEAN                PIC S9(3).

PROCEDURE DIVISION.

100-MAIN-PROGRAM.

    PERFORM 200-INPUT-MODULE THROUGH 200-INPUT-END.
    PERFORM 300-OUTPUT-MODULE THROUGH 300-OUTPUT-END.
    STOP. RUN.

200-INPUT-MODULE.

    DISPLAY "ENTER NUMBER OF ITEMS TO AVERAGE" UPON TERMINAL.
    ACCEPT NUMBER-OF-ITEMS FROM TERMINAL.
    DISPLAY "ENTER YOUR ITEMS ONE AT A TIME." UPON TERMINAL.
    DISPLAY "PRESS RETURN AFTER EACH." UPON TERMINAL.

    MOVE 1 TO ITEM-COUNT.
    PERFORM 250-GET-ITEMS THROUGH 250-GET-END UNTIL ITEM-COUNT >
        NUMBER-OF-ITEMS.
200-INPUT-END.

250-GET-ITEMS.
    DISPLAY "ENTER A NUMBER" UPON TERMINAL.
    ACCEPT ONE-ITEM FROM TERMINAL
    ADD ONE-ITEM TO SUM.
    ADD 1 TO ITEM-COUNT.

250-GET-END.

300-OUTPUT-MODULE.

    DIVIDE SUM BY NUMBER-OF-ITEMS GIVING MEAN.
    MOVE MEAN TO SHOW-MEAN.
    DISPLAY "THE MEAN OF YOUR" NUMBER-OF-ITEMS "ENTRIES IS"
        SHOW-MEAN"." UPON TERMINAL.
300-OUTPUT-END.
```

FIGURE 14.4. Problem solution in COBOL

COBOL applications require greater power and storage capacity than microcomputers have had, so there has been little demand for COBOL on micros.

If you looked carefully at the COBOL example, you may have noticed a certain "verbosity" to the language. While it is easy to understand DIVIDE FIRST BY SECOND GIVING THIRD, persons familiar with other languages tend to prefer the more concise Z = X/Y format.

Finally, COBOL also predates concepts of structured programming and must be forced into the mold by the programmer. However, our experience is that this is less difficult to achieve in COBOL than in most other unstructured languages.

AI, PROLOG AND LOGIC PROGRAMMING

Until now we have presented languages and their applications in terms of algorithms. Our conceptual approach to programming in Chapter 11 was totally procedural—problems with solutions that are a sequence of precise steps that must be planned in advance. This yields the classic data processing input—process—output cycle.

However, the types of problems we solve most frequently in our lives are not algorithmic. When deciding what to fix for dinner, we draw on our knowledge of what is in the pantry and refrigerator, the tastes and preferences of others attending the meal, and judgments concerning cost and time to prepare each possible dish. Such decisions rest on past experiences and judgment, not algorithmic steps. Life's decisions rest on rules of thumb called *heuristics*. Perhaps it is this discrepancy between our common experiences and the demands of most programming that makes programming so foreign to many individuals.

The quest for ways to apply computers to daily human problems is the basis for the computer science speciality of *artificial intelligence* (AI). AI researchers are searching for ways to implement programs which can perform tasks associated with intelligence in humans. AI can be highly theoretical or practical, strictly an R&D activity, or a solution to a concrete problem. The languages used in AI have many different names: logic, declarative, descriptive, symbolic, nonalgorithmic. They are fifth-generation languages and differ radically from the languages you have met previously.

The two major AI languages in use world-wide are LISP and PROLOG. LISP (LISt Processing) was developed at MIT in 1959 and has been favored in the United States. PROLOG (PROgramming in LOGic) was developed in France in 1972 and has been dominant in European AI work. PROLOG received a major boost when the Japanese selected it as the basis for their massive fifth-generation computing project, an effort to develop intelligent machines (Poirot and Norris, 1988).

The structure of PROLOG is derived from predicate calculus. A PROLOG program begins with a declaration of facts and their arguments, that is, the objects to which they refer or apply. For instance, to state that Mary likes John, you might write:

```
likes(mary,john)
```

Other facts might be defined as:

```
drinks(baby,milk)
likes(john,sportscar)
nice(susan)
adult(john)
sportscar(porsche)
big_money(john)
```

Using facts, a PROLOG program seeks the answer to a GOAL. From the simple examples above, PROLOG could answer queries such as: Who drinks milk? Does Mary like John? Does John like Porsches?

More complex goals can be answered via rules, such as:

```
drives(X,Y) := adult(X), likes(X,Y), big_money(X)
```

which might tell us that John drives a Porsche.

In general, a PROLOG programmer describes the domain of a "problem" using facts and rules, and then asks the computer to find *all* possible solutions to the problem. Given *what* to compute, "the PROLOG system itself organizes *how* the computation is carried out" (*Turbo PROLOG*, p. 3). Algorithmic programming normally leads to a single right answer based on precise specification of how to find it.

Our examples are not given as exact PROLOG code, but rather serve to illustrate the nature of logic programming. Logic programming is altogether different from algorithmic programming and requires a very different approach. While it may be true that knowing one algorithmic language makes it easier to learn another, the cross-over to logic languages is far from a clear step. The languages differ greatly, and the problems to be solved with them are very dissimilar. There is some evidence of a trend away from Pascal toward AI languages as initial programming languages, both in higher education and earlier (Nichol, Briggs, and Dean, 1988; Poirot and Norris, 1987, 1988). In fact, the Logo language is a derivative of LISP and has extensive list processing capabilities, yet is used primarily in a largely algorithmic fashion for graphics. Logo could be used to introduce logic programming.

Educators should be alert to developments in the fifth generation of languages and machines. Many references are included at the end of the chapter for further study.

AUTHORING SOFTWARE

Thus far, you have viewed programming languages from the perspective of broad uses. All are languages that students may learn at various levels as tools for solving data processing problems, presuming a very broad definition of data processing. Each has its own vocal adherents and specific reasons for being. Most could be used to solve virtually any problem facing the user.

Now turn your attention to a very specific programming need—the creation of educational software. Although many of the languages previously described are used for this purpose, especially BASIC, assembler, and Pascal, you will now meet other tools specifically suited to this task.

WHY TEACHERS CREATE SOFTWARE

In earlier chapters, we explored the various types of CAI and approaches to evaluating them. With literally thousands of courseware packages on the market and more appearing each week, it might seem that any teacher wishing to use the computer as classroom tutor would need only to survey the marketplace, select seemingly appropriate packages, evaluate them, and purchase the best. The situation is not that simple.

Inability to Find Appropriate Packages

In Chapter 9 we described several approaches to obtaining courseware to evaluate. All presume that the teacher has successfully identified potential packages of interest. In itself, this may be much more difficult than it seems. There are countless producers of educational software today. Teachers often lack access to a broad range of their catalogs from which to select items.

Because of the rapid development and introduction of new products, most efforts to prepare complete guides to available software have been less than successful. By definition, they are out of data before they are ever published. The most successful effort to date, in part due to continual updating, appears to be *TESS* from the Educational Products Information Exchange (EPIE), described in Chapter 9.

More significant even than just identifying potentially useful software is *curriculum fit.* Few software products are identified by their producers as correlated to specific texts or other curriculum materials. EPIE has created *IIIR*, the Integrated Instructional Information Resource. *IIIR* is a data base devoted to matching materials of all kinds, including software, to curriculum objectives. We will discuss it more in Chapter 16 in the context of implementation.

Even a resource like IIIR can only guide you to materials contained in its data base. Not every instructional need can necessarily be addressed by commercial software. Production costs are very high, and producers expect to earn a profit. Modest retail price, say under $100, is critical to most educational buyers. Producers must count on volume to succeed, which means only those parts of curriculum common to most schools are even candidates for commercial software development. Many topics of interest to individual teachers will never become commercial products. Even those that are produced often appear in such generic forms that they are not well-suited to specific needs.

Budgetary Considerations
Let's assume that a teacher has found exactly what suits the need at hand. The package has been evaluated favorably, and the curriculum fit is right. The very real problem of budget remains.

Few schools today have the kind of budget for materials acquisition teachers wish for. No matter what the dollar amount may be, it is rarely, if ever, enough. In fact, many schools have allocated so much of the available budget to computer hardware that little or nothing remains for software. Even in the best of situations, it is not uncommon for the software budget to decline over the years because schools fail to recognize the need for ongoing purchases rather than a one-time expenditure.

Personal Preference
Teacher education programs generally prepare teachers to create many of their own teaching materials. Most teachers are quite accustomed to generating worksheets, producing overhead transparencies, creating slide sets, and so on. It becomes a natural extension to develop one's own computer programs. In fact, some teachers all but reach a point of feeling that materials which they did not develop personally are simply not up to their own standards and needs. Just as they had to learn to produce other forms of student materials, they will accept the challenge to do so in this new medium.

Problems in Developing Software
For all of the reasons described, teachers often wish they could develop their own materials in house. Many do so, with varying degrees of success. Clearly, teachers know best what their students need and may well be able to conceptualize a better product than can be bought. However, there are two major problems in developing software.

First, few teachers have any training in the design of computer-based learning materials. Without an understanding of underlying principles, the result is apt to be an electronic version of some other approach to meeting the need, rather than sound CAI.

If the teacher has the requisite design skills, the program envisioned must be developed. For most "home authors," work is done in BASIC. To be able to write anything but a very simple program may require an investment of a year or more in just learning the language. If the teacher has no other reason to learn to program, the effort may be hard to justify.

Once the skill requirements are met, the teacher faces a second problem—the time actually required to design and develop a software product. A common rule of thumb among experienced software developers is that one hour of student use will require as many as 200 hours of design and programming time! Anyone who completes a one-semester programming course will appreciate the time required to write even a simple program.

Can the most energetic teacher realistically expect to develop software for the classroom? We believe the answer is no in any broad sense. At best, the teacher should contemplate developing some very specific items that simply can't be handled any other way, but never envision creating all the software needed for any subject or grade.

To meet even a scaled-down goal, the language skill requirements remain. Authoring tools can reduce the learning task to a more acceptable level. These tools make software development viable for a larger number of educators.

AUTHORING LANGUAGES

Authoring languages began as responses to the belief that programming with a high-level language like BASIC is difficult because of the number of available commands and the complexity of their syntax. A language with fewer commands, each of which might be equivalent to a series of instructions in another language, would have to be much simpler to learn. Authoring languages generally have relatively few commands and a simplified syntax.

Just as one command in a high-level language causes the computer to carry out many machine-level instructions, a single command in an authoring language causes even more instructions to be executed. The command structure is geared specifically to the needs of software developers. Such a language may not be ideal for general programming needs, although some authors suggest that an authoring language can be used to introduce students to programming (Maddux and Cummings, 1985).

PILOT—An Authoring Language

Although there are numerous authoring languages on the market today, many are available for only one computer or a limited group of machines. For the sake of commonality, we consider PILOT, which is available in some form for nearly all computers.

PILOT (*Programmed Inquiry, Learning, or Training*) was introduced in 1969, making it one of the oldest authoring languages. It was created by John Starkweather and associates at the University of California, San Francisco, to make it easy for teachers to prepare computer-based lessons.

As originally implemented, PILOT consists of only eight commands, which provide those capabilities minimally necessary for creation of drill or tutorial CAI. To keep things very simple, most commands consist of only one letter followed by a colon as the basic syntax. Here are the critical commands and their meanings:

T: (display text)
A: (accept user answer)

M: (match user answer to listed alternatives)
C: (calculate)
J: (jump to a specified place in the program)
E: (end)

In addition, a section of a program can be marked or identified by the use of a label, which consists of an asterisk followed by a name, e.g., *LOOP.

The short PILOT program in Figure 14.5 illustrates use of the basic commands of the language in a very simple drill on synonyms.

In this example, each T: causes the words following it to be displayed on the screen. Just T: will produce a blank line on the screen. Each A: causes an answer to be accepted from the keyboard. The match command (M:) compares the user answer with one or more acceptable responses. Once the comparison has been made, an internal "flag" is set to either Yes or No. Subsequent commands are then "conditioned" to be executed only if the flag is Y (TY: and CY:) or N (TN: and JN:). This permits flexibility in responding, tallying correct responses, and branching to desired portions of the program.

What sets PILOT apart from other languages is the MATCH command (M:).

```
        T: IN THIS PROGRAM YOU WILL BE SHOWN A SERIES OF WORDS.
        T: YOU ARE TO GIVE A SYNONYM FOR EACH ONE.
        T:
        T: PRESS 'RETURN' WHEN YOU ARE READY TO BEGIN.
        A:
 *A     T:
        T: GIVE ME A SYNONYM FOR SMALL.
        A:
        M: TINY, LITTLE
        TY: VERY GOOD. THAT IS A CORRECT ANSWER
        CY: C=C+1
        TN: SORRY, THAT IS NOT ONE OF MY SYNONYMS. TRY
        TN: AGAIN.
        JN: *A
        T:
 *B     T:
        T: GIVE ME A SYNONYM FOR BIG.
        A:
        M: LARGE, HUGE, ENORMOUS
        TY: EXCELLENT. A GOOD CHOICE.
        CY: C=C+1
        TN: PLEASE TRY AGAIN. I HAD OTHER WORDS IN MIND.
        JN: *B
           [REMAINDER OF PROGRAM]
        E:
```

FIGURE 14.5. A program example in PILOT

A major requirement of interactive programs is to allow for alternate responses to questions, whether because of different correct answers as in this example, or just variations in a single answer. For instance, one might wish to allow for such possibilities as WASHINGTON, GEORGE WASHINGTON, or G WASHINGTON. Allowance for common spelling errors could also be made. Errors in case and even extraneous blank spaces in an answer can also be ignored.

In most languages, such response processing is complex to program. Even many commercial programs are very "intolerant" of possible alternatives. With PILOT it is easy to achieve this important goal. MATCH is an excellent example of how one simple command in an authoring language is the equivalent of much more complicated code in other languages.

Advantages of Authoring Languages

From the preceding discussion of PILOT, it should be obvious that authoring languages benefit from the simplicity of their command structure. This normally means much less time to learn enough to begin to write lessons. Further, the actual coding of a lesson will generally require far less time than would be true with a general-purpose language. Authoring languages are designed to foster interactivity in lessons.

Authoring languages also contain features of special interest to the CAI developer. PILOT's MATCH command is a good example. Many such languages also include comparatively easy-to-use graphics and sound commands, as well as commands to control optical and videodisc players. Some make provision for rudimentary recordkeeping, a mini-version of CMI.

Disadvantages of Authoring Languages

To achieve the advantages just described, trade-offs necessary in the design of authoring languages may become liabilities.

First, in simplifying the structure of the language, capabilities may also be sacrificed. It is impossible to achieve the same level of sophistication in a program using some authoring languages that could be achieved with a general-purpose language. One example is the absence of graphics capabilities of any kind in some authoring languages.

Second, the original goal of creating a very easy to learn and use language is somewhat compromised by the addition of such desirable features as graphics and sound. Without them, the capabilities of the language are quite limited. With them, the user has that much more to master to utilize the language fully. Some contend that many versions of PILOT have been so "enhanced" as to be minimally easier to work with than, say, BASIC (Maddux and Cummings, 1985).

Third, authoring languages are still languages, however simplified. They do little or nothing to assist the software developer with the logic or structure of a program. Thus, concepts of branching and looping must still be mastered in order to design a lesson, even though the coding will be simplified.

Finally, one is unlikely to find any written guidance on the use of a language like PILOT except what is provided as documentation. If the documentation is less than one needs, as if often true, there may be no place to turn. Student texts are virtually nonexistent.

AUTHORING SYSTEMS

The second major tool for the teacher who wishes to develop CAI is an authoring system, which seeks to eliminate entirely the programming aspect of development. Authoring systems present to the developer an "instructional framework" within which the lesson is constructed. While the entire design of a lesson is in the hands of the developer using a general-purpose language or an authoring language, an authoring system inherently dictates the overall design. The developer essentially creates the lesson on paper as a series of screens, then follows the guidance of the system to turn the material into a lesson. There is neither syntax nor vocabulary to learn, at least for a text-only lesson.

A General Authoring System

A typical authoring system is menu-driven. With content and organization carefully planned, the developer boots the authoring system and sees the opening menu. Typical choices include:

1. Create a new lesson.
2. Edit an existing lesson.
3. Run (or test) a lesson.

Creating a Lesson. If option 1 were chosen, a new menu would appear. The fundamental criterion differentiating one lesson from another in many systems is simply the format of the questions posed to the learner. The system asks whether questions will be multiple choice, true-false, matching, single word, or short answer. Following that decision, the system prompts the developer to enter the lesson. Here's a typical sequence of events.

First, the system prompts for a segment of text, which the student will read. This will become a "text screen." Some systems have limits on the amount of text permitted; others allow for multiple screens before a question is posed. The developer simply enters the text. It may also be possible to specify where on the screen the text is to appear, but in many cases there is little or no control over screen design.

Second, systems that support graphics may prompt for a graphic to accompany the text, either as part of the same screen or separately. While graphics are often highly desirable in CAI, creating them can be a considerable task. Even if the authoring system has some form of graphics editor, the work will not be trivial. In some cases, the system is only capable of displaying graphics previously created outside the system. Less sophisticated users are unlikely to want to deal with graphics.

Third, the system prompts for one or more questions related to the text and/

or graphics. The prompts will vary depending on the format chosen initially. For instance, for multiple choice, separate prompts would appear for the question and each alternative answer. Many systems specify the number of alternatives required for all questions; some permit the developer to create one lesson using, say, four alternatives, another using five.

Fourth, except for matching format, the developer next indicates the correct response(s). (In matching, the system would accept items in pairs, then scramble one column automatically for presentation.) As described with PILOT, for single word or short answers, many systems allow for alternate correct responses, misspellings, and so on.

Finally, the developer enters feedback messages for both right and wrong answers. In a multiple-choice format, it may be possible to provide different feedback for each wrong answer.

Beyond these basics, systems may offer such capabilities as:

☐ Providing the student a hint on demand or after a specified
  number of incorrect responses to an item.
☐ Varying the number of tries allowed per item.
☐ Branching to remedial segments.
☐ Tracking student performance.
☐ Allowing only a specified amount of time for a response.

In each case, the system prompts the user for the information it needs to construct the final lesson.

Other Primary Functions. Lesson editing is necessary when lesson development was started but not completed at one sitting, or when errors appear in testing or use. The process may involve going through the entire lesson from the start, pausing to make changes wherever necessary. Some systems keep track of lesson components as numbered "frames," allowing fast access to any part of the program.

Once a lesson has been entered, it must be tested for correct operation and content. Unless there are bugs in the authoring system itself, the new lesson should "run" without a problem. However, it may not do what the designer intended; perhaps errors were made in sequence, specifying correct answers, answer processing, feedback, or branching. Such problems take the developer back to the edit stage.

Actual lesson presentation to the student often occurs through a "presentation" disk or module, which permits storage of more lessons on the disk in space otherwise used by the lesson development modules. Most systems have presentation capability on the development disk for testing purposes.

Advantages of Authoring Systems

Clearly, the primary advantage of an authoring system is the hand-holding, step-by-step approach to lesson development. The prompting provided by the system makes creating a lesson a very straightforward, fast process. Bramble and Mason (1985) claimed that courseware can be generated 10 to 50 times faster with an authoring system than with a general-purpose language.

Second, there is no need to learn a language or to have much knowledge of programming considerations. The lesson developer can focus on content, with virtually no concern for the mechanics.

Third, there is often a level of sophistication possible that only skilled programmers could duplicate with a general-purpose language. This is most apparent in answer matching and recordkeeping functions.

Fourth, many systems include provision for controlling videotape or videodisc players, allowing creation of highly visual and realistic interactive lessons.

Disadvantages of Authoring Systems

While the "fill in the blanks" approach to lesson creation is simple and fast, it also is quite limiting. For ease of use one sacrifices flexibility. Only those presentation styles, techniques, and formats designed into the system are available to the developer. Lessons tend to look much alike, and content must be forced into the established mold. Creativity in presentation can be severely restricted.

Furthermore, complexity does increase within an authoring system when one wishes to include graphics and/or sound. Even in the best of systems, these may not be trivial additions for most novices.

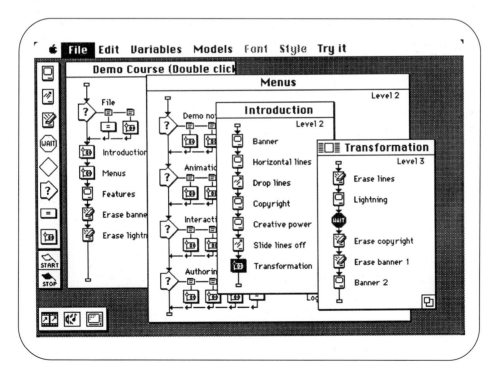

FIGURE 14.6. An icon-based authoring system

Finally, sophisticated authoring systems are expensive. The more the system can do or allows, the higher the price is likely to be. Prices in excess of $1,000 are not uncommon, placing them out of reach of many K-12 educators.

For overviews and directories of authoring languages and systems covering Apple II, MS-DOS, and Macintosh products, we refer you to Tyre (1988) and Staff (1989). In 1988, Apple Computer Inc. published *The Apple Guide to Courseware Authoring*. Although aimed at higher education, this booklet features case studies of novices developing complex software using the Macintosh. It also profiles leading authoring software for the Macintosh. Contact a local Macintosh dealer or the company directly to determine availability of this informative booklet.

HYPERCARD

In Chapter 4 you briefly met *HyperCard* as a non-linear data base. More accurately, *HyperCard* is a software development tool, a software erector set (Camp and Cogan, 1988), a toolkit (*HyperCard*, 1988) for manipulating dissimilar elements. It clearly merits discussion in the context of software authoring tools.

The basic unit of information in *HyperCard* is a card, somewhat like a data record. Cards contain fields for graphics or text. Similar to files, groups of cards are "stacks," which led to the term "stackware" for *HyperCard* products. Whereas

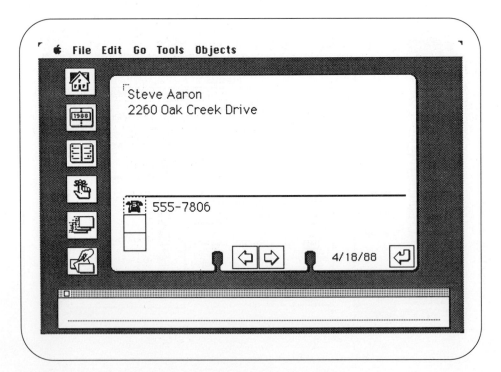

FIGURE 14.7. This *HyperCard* stack simulates Rolodex cards.

all records in a data base file contain the same fields, cards in a stack can vary greatly. Cards may contain text, graphics, instructions to control a videodisc or CD–ROM player, animation sequences, music generating code, and so on. Virtually any item on any card can be linked through "buttons" to any item on any card in any stack on the system.

One of the major attractions of *HyperCard* is the claim that its capabilities are manageable by the non-programmer, making it a software development tool for all. Phillipo (1989) described the five levels of user interaction with *HyperCard*. A user can *browse* through existing cards and stacks. *Type* permits the user to add or change text within a field on a card. Graphics tools are available in *paint* mode, while *author* permits creation of buttons and fields. The most sophisticated use is *scripting*, using the *HyperTalk* language to create new stacks, program the action of buttons, create music, and so on.

HyperCard is so unlike other approaches to software creation that it is very difficult to describe. Rather, you must experience it for yourself—something we urge you to do. The instructional potential of *HyperCard* is clear and impressive, but we caution against unwarranted expectations. As with all authoring tools, the benefits are mixed blessings. *HyperCard* can permit the non-programmer to create useful instruction. This presumes the existence of a modifiable model, a stack useful as a shell or template. Ragan (1988) described

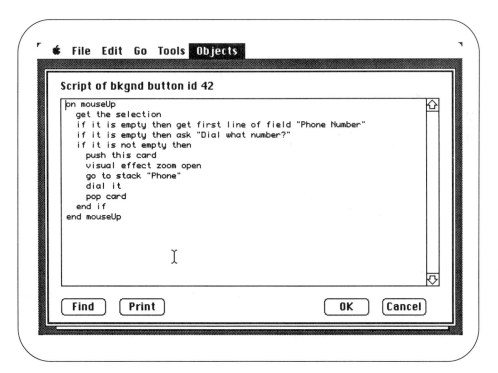

FIGURE 14.8. *HyperTalk* instructions for a button.

these non-programming capabilities of *HyperCard* as "limited," since one cannot go beyond basic linking of cards. Further, as Camp and Cogan (1988) pointed out, even creating and linking cards requires planning the flow and creating its control, clearly programming tasks. Advanced applications require mastery of the unique language *HyperTalk*. There is no free lunch, even with *HyperCard*.

With all its potential and wonder, *HyperCard* is a product specific to Macintosh computers and thus of limited applicability for the majority of K–12 educators. Perhaps it will further advance the place of the Macintosh. Despite far less publicity, you should note that similar products are available for other, more common computers. *Tutor-Tech* is a mouse-oriented authoring tool for Apple II. Buttons are the link among pages, and control of a videodisc player is supported. This product actually predates *HyperCard* by some two years and received very favorable review in *Electronic Learning*, March 1989.

For the MS–DOS user, *Black Magic* is low-cost hypertext software. *Guide* is a hypertext product which can link data in more than three dimensions, compared to *HyperCard*'s two dimension limit. *Opus I* includes graphic support and permits up to 10,000 records of information per graphic! IBM's own product is *LinkWay*, which is mouse-based and uses icons to indicate availability of related information. Videodisc players and CD–ROM drives are supported. *MacWeek* reports on such programs periodically (for example, see 6 December 1988).

Finally, just as there are imitators of *HyperCard*, there are also products designed to improve upon the theme. One that claims to be superior is *HyperStudio* for the Apple IIgs. *HyperStudio* is especially strong in sound capabilities, coming as a package with an external, amplified speaker, microphone, and sound digitizer board. If a *HyperCard* application uses the same information on separate cards, each must store a complete copy of those data. *HyperStudio* can remember where to find the information, and so requires only one copy. The program also takes full advantage of the color graphics capacity of the IIgs.

Where will it all lead? We are just at the beginning of hypermedia in education, so directions are speculative. Jones (1988) and Chignell and Lacy (1988) point to some of them. However, given that hypermedia represent a move toward machines that act more like humans and therefore, demand fewer accommodations from the user, we anticipate a bright future. Sparks (1989, p. 10), obviously a great enthusiast, put it this way:

> Our society will spend the next ten years learning how to produce and distribute high-quality hypermedia. Whole careers and new companies will emerge around it. But it will not be confined to computer professionals. This will be to the 1990s what hobbyist programming was to the late 70s, what word processing and spreadsheets were to the 80s. The difference will be that hypermedia will attract many, many more people who need to get their thoughts and ideas into better circulation.

EXPERT SYSTEMS SHELLS

In presenting the PROLOG language, we briefly mentioned the goal of artificial intelligence (AI) research—machines that imitate human intellectual capacity.

Elements of this goal are present in the quest for intelligent CAI (Chapter 8). Several practical applications of theoretical AI have become widely known. *Robotics* depends heavily on AI in areas such as machine vision. *Natural language processing* will one day allow us to communicate with computers in everyday language. Among the most concrete applications is the realm of captured expertise—*expert systems.*

An expert system is a computer program which performs some task at the level of an expert. Expert systems emulate the problem-solving methods of experts to diagnose medical or automotive maladies, assess insurance risks and loan applications, prescribe an appropriate wine for dinner, recommend purchase versus lease of equipment, or classify learning objectives according to a taxonomy. Like a colleague, an expert system is also able to explain its reasoning. As we often must do, a system can reach a conclusion even in the absence of complete data. Conventional data processing is concerned with the *correct* answer to a problem. Expert systems yield *usable answers.*

A classic example is MYCIN, the first large system to perform at truly expert level. MYCIN's expertise concerns meningitis and bacteremia infections (Harmon and King, 1985, p. 15). Both are conditions which can be fatal and which require swift diagnosis and treatment. In fact, treatment must begin before conclusive diagnosis from tests is possible. The "knowledge base" of MYCIN pools the expertise of medical specialists to perform at par with the best of them.

In addition to a knowledge base of facts and rules defining their relationships, an expert system requires information about the current problem. For instance, a knowledge base may contain countless facts about cheeses or wines, but they are of use only when your specific meal plans and preferences are also known. Expert systems are interactive and request such needed information from the

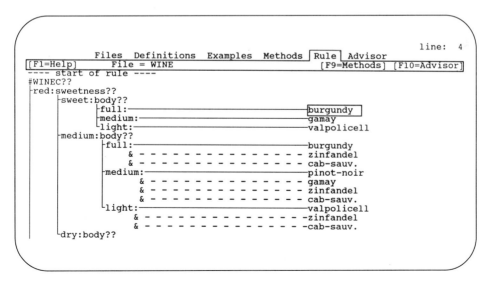

FIGURE 14.9. Part of an Expert System Rule

user. Finally, an expert system must have an "inference engine," the logic component that "reasons" from the knowledge base and current information to a conclusion.

Until the mid-1980s, expert systems were developed on large computer systems using an AI language, usually LISP. Some even required computers expressly designed to perform under LISP. Both hardware and software development costs were extremely high, and the technology was virtually unavailable to educators. However, the MYCIN team recognized early that the specific content of their system could be separated from the inference engine and the user interface, leaving a development shell analogous to spreadsheet software, the worksheet shell. While expert system development in PROLOG, for instance, is quite possible on microcomputers, shells offer a much more expedient approach, one which anyone can learn to employ. Expert system shells are available for MS–DOS and Macintosh computers at affordable prices. They constitute a new software authoring environment. You will find reviews of shell software in many popular publications including *The Computing Teacher* (Knox-Quinn, November 1988), *InfoWorld, PC Magazine,* and *PC AI* (Rasmus, 1988). We have used several shells and particularly like *1st Class* and *VP–Expert* for education use.

Expert systems are in use or under development in a large proportion of America's largest corporations, as well as throughout the world. Applications to education are being proposed, and more will surely follow. Knox-Quinn (1988), Wideman and Owston (1988), and Trollip and Lippert (1987) have suggested teaching students to develop expert systems as a means of enhancing problem-solving skills. Lippert (1988) concurred and suggested that such use of the technology had the potential to unite all three computer roles (tool, tutor, tutee) in a single application. The need to understand a problem domain fully to be able to develop an expert system demands a high level of learning.

Martindale and Hofmeister (1988) described "Written Language Consultant," an expert system designed to help teachers teach mildly and moderately handicapped students to write business letters. Ragan and McFarland (1987) suggested four distinct ways in which expert systems may benefit educators: knowledge clarification, accessible consultant for instructional problems, decision support, and intelligent tutoring systems. Juell and Wasson (1988) discussed a system for diagnosing learning problems in mathematics. Lockard and McHugh (1989) described a system that assists residence hall advisors in performing their duties within the requirements of a university's judicial system. The system combines tutorial CAI with expert system technology.

Brady (1986), Poirot and Norris (1987), Lawler and Yazdani (1987), and Romiszowski (1987) merit reading by anyone interested in educational applications of artificial intelligence and expert systems.

SUMMARY

In this chapter, we have given you brief background information about four programming languages: Pascal, C, FORTRAN, and COBOL. Each was used to implement a solution to the problem of creating a simple interactive program. The strengths and weaknesses of each language were also presented.

For educators, Pascal is clearly the most significant of the languages. It has found popularity in secondary schools as well as among computer science departments. Pascal is a modern, structured language, which was designed for educational use. However, it is not a particularly easy language to learn. We believe Pascal is an excellent language to teach and learn, but only if it fits the curriculum goals of the school. C illustrates a language suitable and popular for developing commercial applications.

FORTRAN and COBOL were presented because they are so well-known. Neither is commonly taught on microcomputers, and both are "serious" data processing languages with no particular qualities to recommend them for general study. They merit very brief attention as part of the evolution of computing.

PROLOG introduced you to a radically different view of programming. Like LISP, the other major language of artificial intelligence, PROLOG permits solution of problems which are not algorithmic, but rather rely on rules of logic. It's impact on educational computing is not yet clear.

In the second section of the chapter, we turned to ways of creating educational software without learning a general purpose language at all. Authoring languages offer a somewhat easier approach, especially to programming drills and tutorials. Most have rather limited vocabularies and much simplified syntax, making them quicker and easier to learn than BASIC. An example was provided in PILOT.

Authoring systems go another step beyond languages by also providing a framework within which the lesson is developed. They are normally menu-driven and allow the user to create a lesson by designing a series of screens. Lessons can be developed very quickly and easily, even with features like recordkeeping. However, there is little flexibility in designing a lesson. There is apt to be an assembly-line look to the lessons from most authoring systems.

We presented *HyperCard* for the Macintosh within the authoring context, for authoring is clearly the purpose envisioned for it by Apple and its developer. Although *HyperCard* is the best-known product, hypermedia software exists for MS–DOS and Apple II computers also. Hypermedia presents many new possibilities to the software developer.

Finally, we suggested that artificial intelligence may play a role in education now through its application in expert systems. Few expert systems for education can be purchased at this time, but their development is as feasible as any other form of educational software. The key is to use an expert system shell, software very similar in concept to a spreadsheet or data base program.

CHAPTER 14 ACTIVITIES

1. Check other sources for comparisons of programming languages. How do others rate the relevance of each to schools?

2. Define and defend a position on appropriate languages for teaching in schools.
3. Locate additional resources on any language of particular interest to you.
4. Select one of the languages discussed and try to get access to it. Using available documentation, modify our example program to run on your system.
5. Do you find authoring software appealing? If so, how can you envision using it personally?
6. Most authoring software includes step-by-step instructions for its use. Develop a minimal lesson using any available language or system.
7. Explore *HyperCard* or any other hypermedia to which you have access. If possible, go beyond the execution of available stackware, beyond the browse level. Learn to modify cards and link them into new stacks.
8. Consult any accessible expert systems. Literature on the subject is exploding in volume. Read several current articles on education and artificial intelligence.
9. If you have access to an easy-to-use shell like *1st Class,* develop a simple expert system. Think of possible applications for student development of systems.

REFERENCES

Anzovin, S. *Exploring HyperCard.* Greensboro, NC: COMPUTE! Books, Inc., 1988.

Baer, J. "Artificial Intelligence. Making Machines that Think." *The Futurist,* January-February 1988, pp. 8–13.

Barker, P. *Author Languages for CAL.* New York: Elsevier, 1987.

Boddie, J. "A Tour of Babel." *The Computing Teacher,* December/January 1984–1985, pp. 8–11.

Bork, A. "Production of Technology-Based Learning Material Tools vs. Authoring Systems." *Instruction Delivery Systems,* March/April 1989, pp. 22–24.

Brady, H. "Artificial Intelligence: What's in It for Educators?" *Classroom Computer Learning,* January 1986, pp. 26–29.

Bramble, W. J., and Mason, E. J. *Computers in Schools.* New York: McGraw-Hill, 1985.

Brough, J. "Problem Solving Using Logic Programming." In Ramsden, E., ed. *Microcomputers in Education 2.* Chichester (UK): Ellis Horwood Limited, 1984, pp. 33–38.

Brynjolfsson, E., and Loofbourrow, T. "PC Tools. An Overview of Expert System Building Tools for PCs." *PC AI,* September/October 1988, pp. 31–35.

Camp, J., and Cogan, M. "HyperCard: A Milestone in Educational Computing." *Electronic Learning,* March 1988, pp. 46–51.

Carr, C. "Hypertext: A New Training Tool." *Educational Technology,* August 1988, pp. 7–11.

Chignell, M. H., and Lacy, R. M. "Project Jefferson: Integrating Research and Instruction." *Academic Computing,* September 1988, pp. 12–17, 40–45.

Crowell, P. "Authoring Systems: Genesis through Revelations." *Instruction Delivery Systems,* March/April 1989, pp. 19–21.

Davis, D. B. "Artificial Intelligence Enters the Mainstream." *High Technology,* July 1986, pp. 16–24.

Gery, G. J. "The Learner Can Now Be in Control." *Instruction Delivery Systems,* March/April 1989, pp. 6–9.

Goodman, D. *The Complete HyperCard Handbook.* New York: Bantam, 1987.

Harmon, P., and King, D. *Expert Systems.* New York: John Wiley and Sons, 1985.

Harmon, P., Maus, R., and Morrisey, W. *Expert Systems: Tools and Applications.* New York: John Wiley and Sons, 1988.

"HyperCard in Higher Education." *TechTrends,* November/December 1988, pp. 13–15.

Jones, R. A. "Building a Multi-Media Laboratory." *Academic Computing,* October 1988, pp. 24–29, 43–44.

Juell, P., and Wasson, J. "A Comparison of Input and Output for a Knowledge Based System for Educational Diagnosis." *Educational Technology,* March 1988, pp. 19–23.

Kaehler, C. *HyperCard Power: Techniques and Scripts.* Reading, MA: Addison-Wesley, 1988.

Kahn, K. "A Grammar Kit in PROLOG." In Yazdani, M., ed. *New Horizons in Educational Computing.* Chichester (UK): Ellis Horwood Limited, 1984, pp. 178–189.

Kearsley, G. "Instructional Design and Authoring Software." *Journal of Instructional Development,* 1984, 7(3), pp. 11–16.

Knox-Quinn, C. "A Simple Application and a Powerful Idea: Using Expert System Shells in the Classroom." *The Computing Teacher,* November 1988, pp. 12–15.

Knox-Quinn, C. "Expert System Shells." *The Computing Teacher,* November 1988, pp. 44–47.

Kowalski, B. "Logic as a Computer Language for Children." In Yazdani, M., ed. *New Horizons in Educational Computing.* Chichester (UK): Ellis Horwood Limited, 1984, pp. 121–144.

Latham, J. "PROLOG and English Teaching." In Ramsden, E., ed. *Microcomputers in Education 2.* Chichester (UK): Ellis Horwood Limited, 1984, pp. 50–55.

Lawler, R. W., and Yazdani, M., eds. *Artificial Intelligence and Education, Volume One.* Norwood, NJ: Ablex, 1987.

Leonard-Barton, D., and Sviokla, J. J. "Putting Expert Systems to Work." *Harvard Business Review,* March-April 1988, pp. 91–98.

Levine, R., Drang, D., and Edelson, B. *A Comprehensive Guide to AI and Expert Systems.* New York: McGraw-Hill, 1988.

Linden, E. "Putting Knowledge to Work." *Time,* 28 March 1988, pp. 60–63.

Lipkin, R. "Making Machines in Mind's Image." *Insight,* 15 February 1988, pp. 8–12.

Lippert, R. C. "An Expert System Shell to Teach Problem Solving." *TechTrends,* March 1988, pp. 22–26.

Lockard, J., and McHugh, B. "CBT and Expert Systems for Training University Residence Hall Staff." *Proceedings of the Seventh Conference on Interactive Instruction Delivery.* Warrenton, VA: Society for Applied Learning Technology, 1989.

Mace, S. "Mother of COBOL—Still Thinkin', Still Workin'." In Craighead, D., and Bitter, G. G., eds. *The Best of the Proceedings 1982–1984 Microcomputers in Education Conference.* Rockville, MD: Computer Science Press, 1984.

Maddux, C., and Cummings, R. "BASIC, Logo, and PILOT: A Comparison of Three Computer Languages." *Computers in the Schools,* Summer/Fall 1985, pp. 139–164.

Maran, R. *HyperCard Quickstart.* Carmel, IN: Que Corporation, 1988.

Martindale, E. S., and Hofmeister, A. M. "An Expert System for On-Site Instructional Advice." *Educational Technology,* July 1988, pp. 18–20.

Merritt, D. "Rule-Based vs. Procedural Programming." *PC AI,* September/October 1988, pp. 51–53.

Michael, S. L. *HyperCard: The Complete Reference*. Berkley, CA; Osborne McGraw-Hill, 1989.

Miller, B. H. "Expert Systems. An Introduction." *PC AI*, September/October 1988, pp. 26–28.

Moursund, D. "HyperWhat??" *The Computing Teacher*, March 1988, p. 4.

"Multimedia Gets It Together in MS–DOS." *Electronic Learning*, Special Supplement, January/February 1989, pp. 22–23.

Nichol, J., Briggs, J., and Dean, J., eds. *Fifth Generational Computing in Education I: PROLOG, Children and Students*. New York: Nichols Publishing, 1988.

Nichol, J. "Computing for Everyman or Computer Applications in Micro-PROLOG." In Ramsden, E., ed. *Microcomputers in Education 2*. Chichester (UK): Ellis Horwood Limited, 1984, pp. 56–66.

Phillipo, J. "Videodisc Technology and HyperCard: A Combination that Can't Be Beat." *Electronic Learning*, March 1989, pp. 40–41.

Poirot, J. L., and Norris, C. A. "AI Programming Languages." *The Computing Teacher*, December/January 1987–88, pp. 17–19.

Poirot, J. L., and Norris, C. A. "Artificial Intelligence Applications in Education." *The Computing Teacher*, August/September 1987, pp. 8–10.

Poirot, J. L., and Norris, C. A. "Logic Programming." *The Computing Teacher*, February 1988, pp. 28–30.

Quinlan, R., ed. *Applications of Expert Systems*. Reading, MA: Addison-Wesley, 1987.

Ragan, L.C. "HyperCard—A User's Description." *TechTrends*, September 1988, pp. 38–39.

Ragan, S. W., and McFarland, T. D. "Applications of Expert Systems in Education: A Technology for Decision-Makers." *Educational Technology*, May 1987, pp. 33–36.

Rasmus, D. W. "Playing the Shell Game. Expert System Shells for the Macintosh." *PC AI*, September/October 1988, pp. 36–43.

Rasmus, D. W. "Speaking of the Macintosh. An Exploration of AI Development Languages." *PC AI*, January/February 1989, pp. 34–37, 58–60.

Richards, J. "Expert Systems and the Next Generation of Tools." *Computers in the Schools*, Spring 1986, pp. 89–99.

Ricks, J. "Fourth-Generation Computer Languages: An Overview." *T.H.E. Journal*, October 1988, pp. 101–104.

Rohm, C. E. T., Jr., and Stewart, W. T., Jr. *Essentials of Information Systems*. Santa Cruz, CA: Mitchell, 1988.

Romiszowski, A. J. "Expert Systems in Education and Training: Automated Job Aids or Sophisticated Instructional Media?" *Educational Technology*, October 1987, pp. 22–29.

Sanders, W. B. *HyperCard Made Easy. 2nd Edition*. Glenview, IL: Scott, Foresman, 1989.

Seyer, P. "Performance Improvement with Hypertext." *Performance and Instruction*, February 1989, pp. 22–28.

Shalvoy, M. L. "HyperCard: Apple's New Mac Product May Revolutionize Microcomputing." *Electronic Learning*, February 1988, p. 10.

Shapiro, S. *Encyclopedia of Artificial Intelligence*. New York: John Wiley and Sons, 1987.

Sheftic, C., and Wood, G. D. "Student-Teacher: The Learning Machine as an Instructional Device." *Journal of Educational Research*, 4(1), 1988, pp. 57–70.

Shell, B. *Running HyperCard with HyperTalk*. Portland, OR: MIS Press, 1988.

Sparks, D. G. "HyperStudio." *Call -A.P.P.L.E.*, March 1989, pp. 8–10.

Staff. "Authoring Systems, Programs, Languages." *Instruction Delivery Systems*, March/April 1989, pp. 10–18.

Trollip, S., and Lippert, R. C. "Constructing Knowledge Bases: A Promising Instructional Tool." *Journal of Computer-Based Instruction,* Spring 1987, *14*(2), pp. 44–48.

Turbo Prolog. Owner's Handbook. Scotts Valley, CA: Borland International, Inc., 1986.

Tyre, T. "Authoring Systems Help a Teacher Offer More Personalized Education." *T.H.E. Journal,* August 1988, pp. 14–24.

VanHorn, M. *Understanding Expert Systems.* New York: Bantam, 1986.

Vaughan, T. *Using HyperCard: From Home to Hypertalk.* Carmel, IN: Que Corporation, 1988.

Walker, L. L., and Gerkey, P. "The Seven Veils of Expert Systems. The First Veil." *PC AI,* September/October 1988, pp. 29–30.

Wideman, H. H., and Owston, R. D. "Student Development of an Expert System: A Case Study." *Journal of Computer-Based Instruction, 15*(3), 1988, pp. 88–94.

Yazdani, M., ed. *New Horizons in Educational Computing.* Chichester (UK): Ellis Horwood Limited, 1984.

Zachmann, W. F. "Trying to Choose a Programming Language? Climb Aboard the C Train." *InfoWorld,* 28 September 1987, p. 82.

PART 5

Microcomputers in Education

CHAPTER 15

□ *Computer Literacy and Beyond: Curriculum Integration* □

O B J E C T I V E S

At the end of this chapter, you will be able to:

□ *Briefly trace common computer literacy models.* □
□ *Differentiate infusion from integration.* □
□ *Discuss computer integration concepts.* □
□ *Discuss trends among the states regarding computer literacy.* □
□ *Assess issues involved in considering significant curricular changes.* □
□ *Persuasively argue your own view concerning the proper model for computers in education.* □

The growth and acceptance of microcomputers in education has been little short of spectacular. It is both a cause and an effect; a result of new ideas for application, and in many cases, a stimulus for new ideas, as well as a prod to educators to find ways to use these devices. This is the Information Age, where computer technology pervades our lives, and the schools alone may be responsible for preventing generations of "technopeasants" (Collis, 1988).

You have learned about major uses of computers in earlier chapters. Now you will focus on the question, How can we actually deal with microcomputers in our schools? Roblyer, Castine, and King (1988) stated, "[Research] findings have also made it clear that computer applications have an undeniable value and an important instructional role to play in classrooms in the future. Defining that role is the task of the next decade." We place efforts at definition in two categories—*computer literacy* and *curriculum integration*. Let's see what they mean.

COMPUTER LITERACY

Computer literacy became a buzzword in computer education around 1980, but has also been a topic of controversy. Inherent in the idea is that there exists some body of fundamental knowledge and skill regarding computers that *all* members of society should possess. A literate citizenry has long been an unquestioned goal; the computer is merely a new component. As Luehrmann (1983) stated, "The ability to use computers is as basic and necessary to a person's formal education as reading, writing, and arithmetic." Disagreement about the meaning of "use" is the major concern, not whether there is a need for such literacy.

Central to the arguments is the issue of computer programming. At one end of a continuum are those who have argued strongly that some programming skill is essential if an individual is to be considered computer literate. At the other end are those who view programming as completely unnecessary. Rather, one must be able to *use* computers and application software. In between come various compromises, and some definitions are all-encompassing. Regardless of position on the continuum, we classify as computer literacy those approaches which focus on the computer rather than the curriculum.

THE PROGRAMMING MODEL

When the first microcomputers entered the schools, there was virtually no software available for them. Usually a science or math teacher was the first to attempt to use the new device, probably because those teachers were the most likely to have had some contact with computers during their teacher preparation. That contact nearly always meant programming. With such a background and no software, naturally the microcomputer was used for programming instruction.

Arthur Luehrmann, often regarded as the father of computer literacy, was a vocal advocate of programming as the heart of computer literacy. Luehrmann (1982, p. 20) wrote, "To tell a computer what you want to do, you must be able to communicate with it. To do that, you will need to learn a language for writing your ideas down so that you can review them, show them to others, and improve them." He stressed that computer literacy meant the ability to do something constructive with a computer, not just possess a general awareness gleaned from what one is told about computers. Luehrmann suggested that a computer-literate person can write and interpret a computer program, can select and operate software written by others, and knows from personal experience what a computer is and is not capable of doing.

The ability to control and program a computer was also part of an earlier definition of computer literacy by Watt (1980). For many educators, literacy and programming were synonymous, a view that probably contributed to teacher technophobia.

THE LITERACY CURRICULUM MODEL

Warren Jones and colleagues (1983) defined literacy in terms of appreciation of principles underlying hardware, software, and applications across the curriculum. Hunter (1983, p. 9) defined it as "whatever a person needs to be able to do with computers and know about computers in order to function in an information-based society." She viewed this as context- or discipline-dependent, not totally universal, and as vital preparation for later life tasks. Programming is no more than a part of a literacy curriculum.

Literacy Topics
Riedesel and Clements (1985) categorized literacy topics under four general headings:

1. What is a computer?
2. How does a computer work?
3. What can a computer do? (Awareness Level)
4. What can a computer do? (Abilities/Skills Level)

Bitter and Camuse (1984) offered an extensive scope and sequence design. Under the broad headings of computer awareness and programming, topic suggestions and specific activities were given for grades K–12.

In general, a computer literacy curriculum includes the following: survival skills, computer awareness, application skills, and programming. Let's consider each area briefly.

Survival skills are skills that students must possess if they are to work effectively on the computer. For example, it is important that students know how to properly handle disks, how to insert and remove a disk from the disk drive, how to "boot up" a program, and how to use the keyboard appropriately. Certainly, these basic skills are important for *all* students who use the computer.

Perhaps they are analogous to inserting the key into the ignition, turning the key, and properly placing the gearshift into reverse before backing a car out of a garage. They are low-level skills, but important ones.

Computer awareness pertains to knowledge and skills that help us better understand what a computer can and cannot do. Awareness of how computers are used in our society, the misuses of the computer, and computer ethics are topics that would receive attention. Future trends and developments of the computer could also be dealt with under this category.

Application skills include word processing, the use of data base management programs, and spreadsheets. This category emphasizes the use of *existing* programs that enable students to accomplish some desired task and provides considerable carry-over value into later life needs.

Programming. Within the context of computer literacy, programming experience is not intended to prepare programmers for future employment. Rather, it provides an opportunity to learn a skill that may enhance a student's ability to function intellectually, as a problem solver. It can also develop an understanding of the components of a computer communication language and some appreciation for the efforts behind the programs we buy and use. Increasingly, Logo is being used as the language introducing students to problem solving through programming. The level of introduction varies considerably, however, ranging from primary grades to middle school. Instruction may follow in later years using BASIC or Pascal.

How Literacy Is Taught

A computer literacy curriculum may be approached in two ways—across the existing curriculum or as separate courses.

Scope and sequence advocates seek to diffuse computer instruction throughout the curriculum. Literacy should be a total commitment throughout the school system, beginning in kindergarten and continuing through high school. Teachers at all levels and in all fields can and should become "computer teachers." At the very least, one teacher must be responsible for teaching the literacy units at each grade level.

Such diffusion is appealing because the computer is encountered within regular class contexts throughout the school years. In the lower grades, students learn about computers from the individual who knows them best—their regular classroom teacher. This approach also demands a strong district-wide commitment.

Problems arise when one considers diffusion carefully. Assuming that only some teachers will participate, which seems most likely, who will it be? If volunteers, what about the holes in that K–12 sequence that are almost certain to be left? If a teacher is "drafted" for duty, what about preparation for the new demands? More significantly, given the demands of an already crowded curriculum, will many teachers, much less poorly prepared ones, find the time or inclination to squeeze more into the day, week, or year? A plan on paper does not guarantee that effective implementation follows.

Separate computer literacy courses, also called "pull-out programs," have been strongly advocated by Luehrmann (1984). He suggested that a class be established somewhere around grades 7–9, designed so that *all* students are able to achieve selected computer literacy goals. It is his contention that such a class has the potential for careful monitoring in terms of outcomes and also establishes a learning climate where a well-trained teacher has the responsibility for instruction. He writes, "In short, put all your eggs in one basket, and then watch that basket very, very closely" (p. 40).

Luehrmann recognized that certain computer skills just cannot wait until the middle school years. Those "survival skills" previously mentioned need to be taught at an early grade level so that children can use the computer in computer-based activities. Certainly, keyboarding skills need attention early in the child's education.

Separate courses, then, offer the prospect of well-trained, specialist teachers delivering carefully constructed and sequenced content. Accountability should be greatly enhanced over a diffused approach. Still, separate courses have been criticized for creating a new content area apart from the rest of the curriculum. The computer becomes yet another subject to be learned, then forgotten as the student moves on to other unrelated subjects. Further, teachers may view the computer as "the other person's problem" because it is removed from their domains, a "special subject" like art, music, or physical education in lower grades. In addition, a separate course usually necessitates a lab facility, which may increase costs or preclude access to computers in individual classrooms.

THE PROBLEM SOLVING MODEL

Norton (1988) identified problem solving as another model of computer literacy. Problem-solving ability is a universally accepted objective. Concerns parallel those discussed for the literacy curriculum. Software aimed at problem solving tends to be general, making it difficult to link to the curriculum. Although Logo is firmly rooted in mathematics, it is frequently used as a change of pace, as a way to make pretty patterns, as something separate and unto itself. In either case, time for these activities comes at the expense of something else. Unless a teacher is firmly convinced of the value of the activity, *and* comfortable in presenting it, there is little likelihood that the teacher will voluntarily do so. If coerced, however gently, effectiveness is almost certain to fall.

THE TOOLS/APPLICATIONS MODEL

By the mid-1980s, even though computers were still new to many educators, the tide had begun to turn against programming as literacy. Literacy curricula proved more difficult to implement than anticipated, Logo's impact was suspect, and the question of where to find time for problem-solving software was not fully answered. Educators were still seeking ways for computers to make an impact. They turned in many cases to the applications software we discussed in Chapters 3 through 7. In 1988 Collis declared that applications had replaced programming as the most common definition of computer literacy (1988, August/September).

The reasoning was sound. Computers are a part of our lives that will not go away. Schools prepare children for productive lives in society. The "real world" has embraced computer applications wholeheartedly. Therefore, students need to learn to use these tools in school.

In many cases, the approach was to revamp existing computer literacy courses. Out went programming, computer history, non-critical terminology, and other marginal topics. Survival skills became the precursors of word processing, data bases, spreadsheets, and more. Students got excited, and so did many teachers. The computer had become relevant.

Norton (1988) criticized the tool approach from two perspectives. First, tool courses tend to emphasize mechanics. Assignments are contrived to meet the needs of a stand-alone course. "Tool applications are worthwhile only when students are prepared to use them to solve problems which have meaning and applicability to their needs." Second, tools are typically treated as neutral, which they never are. Students must study the *effects* of the computer on themselves and society, not just how to use them effectively.

CONCLUSION

A major problem in dealing with computer literacy is that it is not a single concept. Rather, there have been and still are distinct definitions and approaches to it. They may even represent a developmental hierarchy stretching from the programming model through applications. Each model has had its proponents and defenders—all have their critics. The common thread through the criticism is that these models all basically treat the computer as subject matter, an end in itself (Hill et al., 1988).

Where does one turn next? How can we capitalize on what we have learned from our experiences? The next section offers a response.

CURRICULUM INTEGRATION

Beyond computer literacy is the computer as an integral part of the process of education at all levels. Judah Schwartz of Harvard's Educational Technology Center, spoke of "... a clear sense of wanting to integrate the computer across the curriculum into the classroom, and a clear move away from what was very common four years ago, the computer literacy movement. The sterility of computer literacy is something that we find being increasingly recognized" (Johnson, Maddux, and O'Hair, 1988). Integration replaces literacy as the buzzword.

To begin, let's distinguish between infusion and integration. *Infusion* means simply that computers are physically present in our schools. Collis (1988, p. 3) reminds us that for all the talk of a computer revolution, hardware proliferation should not be taken as a sign of it. When we read statistics about the number of microcomputers in schools, the ratio of computers to students or teachers, and so on, we see growing infusion. The hardware is there. Now it is time to make it a vital part of the instructional process. *Electronic Learning* (Staff, 1988) defined *integration* as "the process of totally integrating the use of computers into the existing curriculum through learning activities that address the subject-area objectives. To date, the technology has been infused into the schools but not integrated into the curriculum."

Komoski (1987) spoke of "systemic" integration of technologies by which he sought to avoid the linear connotation of "systematic" (fix A, then B, etc.) and focus on the complex ecology of educational systems. He wrote, "(T)he true pioneers . . . are dealing systemically with all aspects of the curriculum in order to create well integrated systems designed (1) to meet the needs of the students and (2) to be improved on the basis of feedback from those students" (p. 22).

In fairness, note that Bitter and Camuse's (1984) literacy curriculum included elements attainable within the existing curriculum, as did Hunter's (1983). With some updating to focus more on the curriculum as it exists, those models still may offer sound guidance.

WHAT IS THE SCOPE?

What, then, is an integrated approach to computers in education? It means capitalizing on the best of what has preceded it, starting with education, with curriculum, not with the computer. It means identifying those places in the curriculum where the computer can contribute, either as a way to improve effectiveness, to do what could not be done at all or as well, or to teach life skills. An integrated approach is all-inclusive, but more importantly, all-pervasive. Let's be more specific and return to the computer literacy models.

Is programming precluded from an integrated approach? Not at all. Programming is appropriate whenever it affects a specific curricular need, clearly a vital part of the content of a data-processing curriculum. In other subjects programming can be an appropriate technique for mastering some particular component (Norton, 1988).

What about the literacy curriculum? It would be difficult to imagine any published scope and sequence being more than a very rough guide, since curriculum is a local concern in this country. However, one could well begin with such a model, strip away the parts that do not clearly support curriculum objectives, and find a usable core.

Problem solving may be more difficult. Its "flaw" from the start has been its inherent lack of a curricular home. Everybody wants the result, no one claims responsibility for it, nor wants to give up time to it. The issue is not whether it fits within an integration model, but rather how to treat it at all. Research suggests that approaches to problem solving may have been too simplistic. Logo advocates seldom distinguish just what its benefits are, preferring to discuss general gains. Specific software usually aims at some principle deemed basic to problem solving, something of presumed generalizability.

Dudley-Marling and Owston (1988) reviewed a vast range of research and concluded that "while problem-solving skills within any particular domain can be taught, . . . transfer . . . across domains is very difficult to achieve. . . . Therefore, it is likely that no single problem-solving program, Logo or CAI, will develop the wide range of problem-solving skills students need to survive in and out of school." However, they were quick to note that they in no way suggest that one should abandon the quest entirely. Again, begin with the curriculum, then carefully examine the potential of any approach to problem solving to effect curricular goals. The result may be worthwhile. Just be reasonable and realistic in your expectations.

Finally, there is the applications model. We have tried to make clear from the start that we are biased in this direction. We believe the potential is eminently practical to begin with, and that tool software offers very powerful ways to improve student learning. Chapters 3 through 7 were devoted to those views. An integrated approach simply means using tools throughout the curriculum *wherever appropriate*, rather than relegating them just to an applications course. November (1989) reported that Wellesley (MA) Public Schools dropped their middle-school applications course "to the shock and dismay of staff who taught the course, but to the benefit of all students, who will now learn how to use word processors in their English courses and spreadsheets in their math courses." Turner and Land (1988) mentioned using telecommunications to gather material for a research paper to be written with a word processor, creating data bases in any content area, learning about graphs with graphing software. Throughout this book, we have tried to present applications which fit an integrated model.

ADVANTAGES

Why is such an approach "better" than its predecessors? First, integration puts the emphasis squarely where it belongs—on the curriculum, not on the computer. Second, there is no need to add new objectives to the school's curriculum to deal with computers. Instead, existing objectives are enhanced with computer applications. This minimizes, but may not totally dispel, the problem of "How do we make room for it?" Third, the computer becomes a partner, not a competitor. Any lingering fears that teachers may be displaced by computers can be vanquished. Fourth, it treats the computer in a natural way, as one fundamental tool for learning and living. Was there ever a course in pencil? Perhaps for those who aspire to manufacture them. Does there need to be a course in computer? Outside of data processing, we think not. Fifth, integration fosters invisibility. Someone once said, technology *essential* to a process becomes invisible; technology is visible *inversely* to its necessity. Computer technology is here for the duration and will, one day, be as invisible as pencil or calculator technology. By *not* separating it from current routine, education can help computers become invisible.

THE NATIONAL VIEW

One barometer of educational change is state-level involvement reflected by legislative action. To get a clearer picture of present conditions, we first glance backward. According to *Electronic Learning*'s 1985 survey of the states (Reinhold and Corkett, 1985), 26 had some form of computer literacy requirement. Nine required students to take a literacy course, six others required that one be offered as an elective. Some states were beginning to require students to demonstrate minimal "competence," usually about grade 7 or 8. Only eleven states reported teacher certification requirements in computing.

In 1987 ("Educational Technology 1987"), the survey determined that nearly 80 percent of the states officially recommended exposure to computers in schools. Eleven states plus the District of Columbia required all students to take a course. More often the recommendation was to integrate computers into the curriculum. Five states required competence. As for teacher preparation, thirteen states plus the District of Columbia required all persons seeking teaching certification to take a computer course.

The 1988 survey (Bruder, 1988) found that courses were required in nine states plus D.C. and that only 22 of 47 reporting states officially recommended that schools offer computer courses. However, twelve states required demonstrated competence. (Four of the twelve are among the nine with required courses.) Eleven states plus D.C. required computer integration, five more strongly recommended it. At least some students were required to take computer courses to gain certification in 23 states plus D.C. Wisconsin even required integration of computers throughout the teacher education curriculum.

What does this mean in terms of our discussion? Regrettably, the reports on these studies are not totally compatible from year to year, making comparisons more difficult. It appears that the concept of competency is on the rise, the popularity of requirements on the decline. More states are demanding that future teachers know about computers. It seems that increasingly the concept of computer integration is being mandated at state level. We applaud the goal, despite reservations about the ultimate effectiveness of such state directives.

BEYOND INTEGRATION

Is integration by itself enough? Obviously, there are many issues surrounding implementation of any plan for computers in education. We examine some of them in the next chapter. However, even an integrated approach does not go far enough for some observers. Norton (1988) saw significant gains in the integration approach, but found it insufficient nonetheless. "[I]ntegration carries with it a set of unspoken assumptions which fail to recognize the unique potentials of the computer. . . . [It] defines learning and education as content specific and content oriented and presupposes an existing curriculum that is best left unchallenged" (p. 10). Norton argued it is not enough to bolster the current curriculum; rather the curriculum must change.

The report of the National Assessment of Educational Progress released in early 1989 noted that "most students' school experiences are dominated by memorization of content presented by teacher or textbook, and by the practicing of skills in workbook or ditto exercises. . . Students are given limited opportunities to apply knowledge and procedures for new purposes" (Banas, 1989). The report calls for educators to find ways to make students more active learners and to move away from traditional authoritarian roles. Computers are included in the recommended approaches.

The issues involved in significant curricular change are numerous and complex. Norton begins by reassessing what society requires of education. The critical factors are higher-order thinking skills, adaptability to change, and creativity. Next she presents a view of learning appropriate to a computer curriculum. The third step is to identify the unique potentials of the computer in the curriculum. "Using computers in education, therefore, permits curriculum designers to expand their concepts of the curriculum—to emphasize processes for acquiring experiences and applying knowledge (doing) as well as content to be mastered" (p. 11). In short, Norton views content as a reason to teach process, not as an end unto itself. There is no need for a computer curriculum, just one fully in tune with society, the technology, and its capabilities. She concludes with specific examples and new curriculum objectives.

We believe Norton's views have merit and deserve careful consideration. You should consider reading the original article to fully understand her arguments. At the same time, we realize education tends to move slowly. (Who once said that changing education is the only task more difficult than moving a cemetery?) In this last decade of the 20th century, some educators are still at the programming as literacy stage, many have adopted the applications model, and some are well on the road to integration. All deserve recognition for their efforts and assistance as they evolve. We accept Norton's challenge to make more of the computer than integration necessarily does. This is a long-term goal that requires several steps before it can be achieved.

SUMMARY

Agreement is widespread that knowledge and understanding of computers and those skills essential for using a computer are legitimate goals of education. Approaches to meeting such goals can be divided into categories of computer literacy and integration. Within literacy, at least four approaches have been tried: programming, a literacy curriculum, problem solving, and applications or tools. The essential characteristic of literacy approaches is treating the computer largely as something unique, special. One might call it a "museum" approach.

Integration, on the other hand, can incorporate all of the previous ideas, but in the context of very directly supporting the curriculum. Problems with finding time for computers largely vanish because there are no new curriculum objectives. Rather, the computer is a teacher's colleague and on the way to becoming as invisible as the pencil. Students learn what they need to know when and where they need it—much closer to real world computer usage.

Surveys of the states over several years suggest changes in the direction of integration. However, for some observers, integration does not go far enough. They call for changes in the curriculum itself, changes which capitalize on the unique potential of the computer. To merely support what already is, may retard the inevitable evolution of education which must occur to keep abreast of changes in society.

CHAPTER 15 ACTIVITIES

1. Which model of computer literacy appears to be most acceptable to you? Justify your position.
2. In your opinion, is programming skill essential for an individual to be truly computer literate? Why?
3. Discuss the respective merits of the separate class and the K–12 scope and sequence approaches to the literacy curriculum. Which is preferable? Why?
4. Is computer literacy a meaningful term? How can it assist or hinder the implementation of computers in our schools?
5. Define computer integration in contrast to computer literacy and infusion. Outline its essential characteristics.
6. Analyze literacy versus integration, setting forth strengths and weaknesses of each.
7. Determine the position of your state education authority on computers in education, both for K–12 students and for teachers. How has this changed? What further changes would you support, if any?
8. Evaluate the view that integration is itself insufficient unless curriculum change also occurs.
9. What is the legitimate role of the schools relative to computers? What is the historical, philosophical, and/or sociological basis for this role?

REFERENCES

Banas, C. "Study: Students Not Using Knowledge." *Chicago Tribune*, 15 February 1989, Section 1, p. 5.
Bitter, G., and Camuse, R. *Using a Microcomputer in the Classroom*. Reston, VA: Reston Publishing Co., 1984.
Bruder, I. "*Electronic Learning's* 8th Annual Survey of the States, 1988." *Electronic Learning*, October 1988, pp. 38–45.
Collis, B. *Computers, Curriculum, and Whole-Class Instruction*. Belmont, CA: Wadsworth, 1988.

Collis, B. "Research Windows." *The Computing Teacher*, August/September 1988, pp. 6–7.

Dudley-Marling, C., and Owston, R. D. "Using Microcomputers to Teach Problem Solving: A Critical Review." *Educational Technology*, July 1988, pp. 27–33.

"Educational Technology 1987." *Electronic Learning*, October 1987, pp. 39–44, 53–57, 83.

Hill, M., Manzo, F., Liberman, D., York, J., Nichols, C., and Morgan, P. "A Plea for Computer Integration: Let's Bring Computers into the Classroom." *Educational Technology*, May 1988, pp. 46–48.

Hunter, B. *My Students Use Computers.* Reston, VA: Reston Publishing Company, 1983.

Johnson, D. L., Maddux, C. D., and O'Hair, M. M. "Are We Making Progress? An Interview with Judah L. Schwartz of ETC." *Computers in the Schools*, 1988, 5(1/2), pp. 5–22.

Jones, W., Jones B., Bowyer, K., and Ray, M. *Computer Literacy: Programming, Problem Solving, Projects on the Apple.* Reston, VA: Reston Publishing Co., 1983.

Komoski, P. K. "Beyond Innovation: The Systemic Integration of Technology into the Curriculum." *Educational Technology*, September 1987, pp. 21–25.

Luehrmann, A. "Computer Literacy: What It Is; Why It Is Important." *Electronic Learning*, May/June 1982, pp. 20, 22.

Luehrmann, A. "Computer Illiteracy—A National Crisis and a Solution for It." In D. O. Harper and J. H. Stewart, eds. *Run: Computer Education.* Monterey, CA: Brooks/Cole Publishing Co., 1983, pp. 29–32.

Luehrmann, A. "The Best Way to Teach Computer Literacy." *Electronic Learning*, April 1984, pp. 37–44.

Norton, P. "In Search of a Computer Curriculum." *Educational Technology*, March 1988, pp. 7–14.

November, A. "Pioneers and Settlers." *Update*, February 1989, pp. 1–2.

Reinhold, F., and Corkett, K. "EL's Fifth Annual Survey of the States." *Electronic Learning*, October 1985, pp. 25–31.

Riedesel, C. A., and Clements, D. H. *Coping with Computers in the Elementary and Middle Schools.* Englewood Cliffs, NJ: Prentice-Hall, Inc., 1985.

Roblyer, M. D., Castine, W. H., and King, F. J. "Assessing the Impact of Computer-Based Instruction." *Computers in the Schools*, 1988, 5(3/4). (This is a special topic volume.)

Staff. "One Hundred and One Things You Want to Know About Educational Technology." *Electronic Learning*, May/June 1988, pp. 32–48.

Turner, S., and Land, M. *Tools for Schools.* Belmont, CA: Wadsworth, 1988.

Watt, D. H. "Computer Literacy: What Should Schools Be Doing about It?" *Classroom Computer News*, November/December 1980, pp. 26–27.

CHAPTER 16

□ Implementation: How Do We Do It? □

OBJECTIVES

After completing this chapter, you will be able to:

□ Outline the implementation goals and methods of the early 80s. □
□ Analyze reasons why the computer "revolution" has had limited impact. □
□ Explain the importance of a plan for computers in education. □
□ Analyze several reasons commonly given for why teachers do not use computers. □
□ Assess possible ways to implement an integrated program for computers in education. □
□ Assess possible approaches to staff development. □
□ Discuss the three major microcomputer types and their relative merits in K–12 education. □
□ Analyze the merits of a lab, classroom computers, and mobile computers. □
□ Outline applications for a one-computer classroom. □
□ Propose and justify distribution of budget funds into major categories. □
□ Outline approaches to stretching the budget for hardware and software. □

> It took education more than 300 years to fully take advantage of the technological
> revolution in movable type. And it was almost 100 years between the invention
of the pencil and its wide use in schools. This is not so with microcomputers. Change
has come quickly. Our challenge is to manage that change, and to put the new technology
into the service of quality education (Lengel, 1983, p. 18).

> Revolutions have a way of mandating change while glossing over logistical details. . . .
(Roblyer, Castine, and King, 1988).

One could debate whether microcomputers in education constitute a revolution. Evolution is perhaps more accurate, a change in a direction with profound possibilities if we properly capitalize on it.

In this chapter you will consider one view of the brief history of implementing computers in education. You will learn of problems with our efforts and consider that perhaps a different approach to computer implementation is required. Logistical details will require much attention as you develop and implement any plan. What should be done? Who will be involved? Where will the computers be located? What about money? Articulation? Where can I turn for more help?

ONE VIEW OF IMPLEMENTATION HISTORY

Schools have embraced microcomputers at an unprecedented rate by educational standards. No other episode in the history of American education allowed so much money to be spent for anything with so few questions asked, so little known about the implications, so little thought given to implementation, and ultimately so little expected in return. In many cases, computers entered the schools with less consideration than was given to the year's order for paper towels for the washrooms. There were pockets of coherence, of course, but the general picture was chaotic.

THE EARLY 80s—GETTING STARTED

Idealists arose and proclaimed the need for *planning* (*see* Fisher, 1983; Klein and Strother, 1983–1984; Lengel, 1983; Norwood, 1983; Poirot and Heidt, 1983; *Computer Applications Planning,* 1984). The process could be neat and tidy. First, establish a planning committee to draft a school (district, state) philosophy concerning computers and get the appropriate authorities to endorse it. Extend the philosophy into policy statements. Develop a curriculum plan, even a scope and sequence, with clear objectives for all grade levels. Establish a computer budget, determine hardware and software to purchase and plan staff development activities. Draw up a facilities plan for placement of the computers; order hardware and software. Implement staff development. All teachers will be inspired and will eagerly utilize computers throughout the schools. Magic will occur; learning will flower.

However inaccurate this synopsis for any specific case, as with many generalizations, there is a thread of truth running through it. There is also evidence that the magic has not occurred. Although aimed more broadly than at just computers, Komoski (1987, p. 21) put it this way: "Despite more than a half century during which almost every type of technological innovation has been introduced into U.S. schools, most classroom teachers still rely primarily on the textbook and the chalkboard for their day-to-day teaching." According to the Federal Office of Technology Assessment (OTA), "Today's classrooms typically resemble their ancestors of 50 years ago more closely than operating rooms or business offices resemble their 1938 counterparts (U.S. Congress, 1988, p. 3). McCarthy (1988) claimed that fewer than 15 percent of teachers use computers in their teaching. Is that what we thought would happen?

THE LATE 80s—ASSESSMENT AND REFLECTION

One significant explanation for lack of greater change is that we put all our faith in the technology and gave, at best, lip service to teacher training. Preskill (1988), McCarthy (1988), and Knupfer (1988) all cited lack of training as a major concern of teachers. The Office of Technology Assessment found that only one-third of K–12 teachers had even 10 hours of in-service (U.S. Congress, 1988, p. 18). Knupfer (1988) reported a median of three hours of in-service for sixth grade teachers in Wisconsin, with the large majority having none at all!

Is the issue only lack of training opportunity? Stieglitz and Costa (1988) surveyed teachers to assess the impact of Rhode Island's three-year Technology in Education Initiative, which made six 12-hour workshops available to teachers. The overwhelming majority of teachers opted *not* to go beyond the introductory workshop and less than half reported any actual classroom use of computers, despite positive attitudes. Friedman (1985) claimed that resistance to computers was much greater than most believed and needed to be countered directly. Balajthy (1988) concluded that significant effort would be required to substantially increase the motivation of teachers to incorporate computers into classroom instruction.

Some teachers faced shortages of hardware which were difficult to cope with. Other found that the physical placement of computers in their school discouraged use (Knupfer, 1988). Preskill (1988) reported that teachers found computers too difficult to incorporate into their teaching. This may reflect the in-service problem or a growing realization that it takes *more* time to teach with computers than without (Collis, 1988).

Mathinos and Woodward (1987) studied one school considered to be exemplary in its use of computers. There were plenty of computers (both in rooms and a lab) and software, a building computer coordinator and aide, extensive in-service, and a five-year district plan in its final year. Over 13 weeks, 60 percent of the students never used a computer at all, and half of those who did had only one such experience in that quarter. Computer use was rarely integrated, but rather a reward for finishing work early with students free to select software to use. Teachers complained that equipment was scarce, but the researchers found at least five computers unused at all hours of the day. Plomp, Steerneman, and Pelgrum (1988) found much the same thing in a study of "exemplary" schools in the Netherlands.

What can we learn from such findings? The Ontario Ministry of Education concluded that most proponents of new educational technologies (NETs) "vastly underestimate how difficult it will be for teachers to implement the changes NETs will require in practices, materials, beliefs, and skills" (Fullan, Miles, and Anderson, 1987, p. 141).

Collis (1988) synthesized two primary lessons from the lack of progress toward broad computer impact. First, efforts to evoke change must take current reality into account, especially that computers go counter to established teaching styles. In another source she attributed the problems partially to the fact that teachers lack role models during their own training of strategies for implementing and managing computers in the classroom (Collis, August/September 1988). This reflects the common perception that teachers generally teach as they were themselves taught, not as they may have been taught to teach. Second, the ways teachers tried to use computers were inappropriate because they were not tightly linked to the curriculum.

The critical theme underlying these conclusions emphasizes the importance of the individual teacher. In general, achievements rise and fall on the individual level. The one thing you can count on in your school is what you are yourself ready and willing to do. This book is our attempt to provide you with the motivation and skills to make a difference.

IMPLEMENTATION FOR THE 90s

One might take the foregoing discussion as an invitation to toss in the towel. The problems could seem beyond solution. If you have come this far with us and accept that view, then we have failed to get our message across. By now you should be so convinced of the potential of the microcomputer that you will not permit difficulties to stand in your way. Good for you! Read on as we sketch some directions and offer resources for additional help.

THE GOAL

You considered the proper goal for computers in education in Chapter 15. In short, it is to see the computer play an essential, invisible role in daily classroom activity. We call this *integration*. To achieve integration requires recognition of existing reality. Start where teachers are; start with the curriculum as it is (Collis, 1988). Find places where the computer has the potential to make a difference. Implement at those points and make implementation compatible with the "existing rhythms of school life. . . ." Knupfer (1988).

Eventually this will have an impact on the curriculum itself. Norton (1988) argued that integrating the computer into the existing curriculum is insufficient. We do not wish to limit the technology by forcing it into an existing mold.

However, we believe that change cannot be *imposed* successfully. Instead, provide the conditions for it to evolve.

To work toward a goal of curriculum integration, a carefully developed plan is important for many reasons. It articulates the vision of the school or district in a general way and sets a tone for budget issues. A district plan commands support at the building level and signals commitment. We favor something more general than early scope and sequence efforts produced, something that provides a framework without excessive specificity. Numerous planning resources are listed in the chapter references.

Early in planning, schools must address the issue of a *computer coordinator*. Successful change in an educational setting requires effective leadership. Computers represent a change that is qualitatively different from the influx of VCRs, for example. The task of integrating computers throughout the curriculum for effective learning is enormous. As you will soon learn, there are many issues to consider, many decisions to make. Someone has to be in charge. Collis (1988, p. 302) quoted Robert Schuller as saying, "If you fail to plan, you plan to fail." To that we add, plans must be carried out. Results do not just happen.

Questions to answer about coordination include operating level (district, building, both), extent (full- or part-time), and staff level (administrator, teacher, or both). Collis (1988) ascribed a vital leadership role to the principal, but also advocated district and building coordinators. Becker (undated) strongly advocated at least district level coordinators. We concur and note that the specifics of coordination depend on the individual situation.

TEACHER INVOLVEMENT

Classroom teachers will ultimately develop and implement actual plans on the curriculum, class, or unit level. Perhaps some day a large share of teachers will be computer users, but consider current reality. Teachers fall into two groups—those ready to go now and others. Those in the first group have self-selected themselves to participate, and clearly should. For the others, we favor a casual proactive approach.

McCarthy (1988) advocated working in a few areas which are most problematic—don't fix what is not broken. Pogrow (May/June 1988) argued that resources should be focused on narrow areas to maximize the benefit. Do more in less of the curriculum. Given our goal of invisible integration into the curriculum, proactive hinges on "appropriate and feasible." Ask teachers what they find difficult, then consider possible computer interventions. If there is an acknowledged problem, the teacher is probably willing to consider possible solutions. If not, try again next year.

Is such an approach equitable? Perhaps not, but prior efforts have achieved no more. Let's focus on teachers who are already eager to use computers and those who will give it a try if it helps them solve a problem. Mandatory in-service and cajoling are unlikely to motivate others. We can at least hope that seeing excitement in some classes will pique their interest. Perhaps students will expect more as they advance through the grades until teachers feel pressure to incorporate computers. Efforts to impose change rarely succeed. Broad involvement of teachers is a long-term goal.

Staff Development

Komoski (1987) equated the level of support a school puts into training teachers to use technology effectively with the likelihood that technology will have an educational impact. Achieving impact is the highest concern. Of immediate importance is support for those teachers ready to implement computers. Staff development cannot mean the same thing for everyone. There may be a small group in need of training to use a common software product, perhaps a word processor, or data base. There may be enthusiastic teachers with minimal basic knowledge or with experience with a different computer than the type the school owns. The areas in which to offer development activity are those identified by the users.

"Institute days" with one speaker are not the answer. Collis (1988) offered many suggestions for staff development built upon "levels of use of an innovation" research. She advocated exchanges among teachers who are doing things (e.g., computer support groups); some form of incentive for the time and effort invested; setting an annual school target and working toward it; and more.

How does one work toward broader involvement? We must show teachers conclusively how computers can help them. Demonstrations of methods and materials, perhaps in an institute setting, may help, but must be kept free of sermonizing. Done well, they should evoke a response. Fullan et al. (1987) stressed the importance of modeling—demonstrating actual strategies that are or may be effective. Even videotapes will do. (Sunburst Communications loans tapes on use of its software to educators at no cost.) Stimulate individual "Ahah's" and requests for assistance should follow.

We can also look at what has enhanced computer use elsewhere. In the *Sloane Report* (September/October 1987) a Rand Corporation study of 155 districts showed the most significant factor was *increased technical support,* help when it was needed. Rand also found that usage increased when teachers who used microcomputers were paid more. The report suggested master teacher programs and summer curriculum development jobs.

The Office of Technology Assessment (OTA) found that hands-on experience and credible instructors were critical to effective staff development (U.S. Congress, 1988). The best instructors were other teachers who focused on usable applications that each participant could customize. The OTA report supported incentives like pay for technical expertise, release time during the school day, computer access at home and school, grants to purchase software, summer employment to develop applications, support to attend conferences, and master or lead teacher status and salary.

McCarthy (1988) reported that a district in Washington gave computers to teachers willing to take some in-service training. Classroom usage increased dramatically, labs overflowed, one week brought more software requests than the previous year. Pogrow (May/June 1988) advocated using computers as reward or incentive for those who improve conventional instruction most.

We join Moursund (August/September, 1988), Collis (1988), and Bitter (1985) to urge sending computers home on weekends and breaks, as well as for the summer. No one likes the embarassment of making mistakes. The privacy of one's home is an ideal place to learn to use a computer, a necessary step toward effective use in the classroom.

We offer no clear answer to staff development from all of these ideas. Those related to financial incentives would be controversial. Whatever the methods, the goals should be clear—the fullest possible support for those ready to move, and gentle encouragement of others to join in. We also urge schools to demand computer skills of candidates for open positions.

HARDWARE AND FACILITIES

Specific issues of hardware selection are beyond our scope. However, let's address the issue of the major competing hardware types, namely Apple versus MS–DOS, as well as many issues surrounding placement of computers and special needs resources.

Apple II, IBM–PC, or Macintosh?

Since the early days of microcomputers in schools, there has always been the question of which brand to buy. Almost from the beginning, the question has pitted Apple against "the others." While "the others" have changed over time, the question remains. There has never been a clear-cut answer.

The Apple II series dominates the K–12 scene. Advantages of the Apple II include the vast number of educators knowledgeable about them, sustained support for education which translated into a massive volume of CAI software, and excellent reliability. Disadvantages today include technical obsolescence of 8-bit technology, limited memory and diskette capacity which restrict software sophistication, relatively high cost, comparatively low graphic resolution, and high cost of desirable peripherals like hard disks. Some of these problems are overcome with the IIgs model, but at a still higher cost for the computer system and some loss of software compatibility.

The most serious challenge to Apple II comes from the IBM–PC standard known most generically as MS–DOS computers. These computers feature speedy microprocessors, large amounts of RAM, and numerous ways to configure a single system—types of disk drives, monitors, auxiliary input devices, and so on. Sophisticated software is readily available. Prices range from competitive to considerably less than an Apple II for a more powerful machine.

Disadvantages of MS–DOS computers include a more complex operating system to cope with, less CAI software, and far fewer experienced users in education.

For K–12 education, we view the Macintosh as a third-place contender. It continues to point the way to the future with its ease of use, graphic interface, virtually invisible operating system, and high-resolution displays. Its influence is obvious in current software for both the Apple II and MS–DOS. However, we find it hard to justify the price. The Mac is not the machine for elementary CAI—there is very little such software. It offers little or no gain for Logo or BASIC. Excellent tool software is available, but little is truly better than the best in MS–DOS. We cannot find a compelling argument for the Mac at this level beyond limited special applications such as desk-top publishing.

As long as existing Apple II computers continue to work and repairs are possible, we believe they will remain common. We also realize that few schools are prepared simply to replace what they have with something different. It is in the purchase of new computers that one faces a decision.

In general, we believe that MS–DOS computers are a better, more cost-effective choice for most tool application uses (Chapters 3 through 7). The greater power and sophistication of these computers is hard to deny. For CAI, Apple leads in sheer volume of available products, but over time much of the best CAI software has been converted to MS–DOS. Products like *Writer Rabbit,* the *Carmen San Diego* series, and *Print Shop* are often even better in their MS–DOS versions. The catalog may be smaller, but many schools could satisfy their CAI needs under MS–DOS.

But what of the existing inventory of Apple software? It would cost a fortune to replace. That is also not necessary. Schools could switch to MS–DOS versions as purchases are made. Furthermore, it really isn't strictly an Apple or IBM decision. Cordata produced the WPC Bridge computer which runs both Apple and MS–DOS software. MS–DOS and Apple computers can be outfitted with plug-in boards to allow them to use each other's software. You really can have two computers in one case. Perhaps all formats will one day be available in a single computer, or the formats will themselves merge into one. Such standardization would benefit us all.

Hardware selection is a very difficult decision. Start with what you are really using computers for and what you envision in the next few years in your school. Then find the most cost-effective way to meet those needs. It may well be the Apple II, but it also might not be.

Peripherals

Beyond brand of computer, there is also the issue of peripherals. With the trend toward more tool uses, printers become more important than is typical in a CAI environment. Many schools would be better off with fewer computers and more printers. Liquid crystal display (LCD) projectors and panels have made group viewing economically possible. Every school should have at least one of these devices, even if it means cutting a computer or two from the purchase plan.

Facilities

Another major question is how to arrange computers physically. Collis (1988) gives detailed pros and cons of computers in classrooms, in labs, as mobile stations, in libraries, and in "learning assistance centers." Each possibility has its own merits. We present selected points in Table 16.1.

TABLE 16.1 Characteristics of Three Possible Computer Placement Patterns

Factors	Fixed Lab	Mobile	Individual Classroom
Usage	Individual or group	Individual or group	Individual unless with video projection
	Requires scheduling, decreasing flexibility	Requires scheduling, decreasing flexibility	Readily available
	Curricular integration only if routinely accessible, e.g. daily	May encourage integration	Encourages integration
	Tool, tutor, learner roles	Same potential as a lab with enough computers	Mostly tutor for enrichment and remediation
	Can include specialized hardware interfacing		
Personnel	Should have staff (own or from LRC)	Personnel to transport	No new personnel
	May require and justify a computer specialist who lacks content expertise for students sent there	Draws primarily on content expertise	Draws primarily on content expertise
	Teachers need mostly software skills	Necessitates teacher training on hardware as well as software	Necessitates teacher training on hardware as well as software
Cost	Based on number of systems	Number of systems plus carts, etc.	Could involve more or fewer machines
	Potential economy of networking	Movement may increase repair costs	May require most copies of software
	Highest security	Moderate security outside school hours	Least secure
Most common building level	High school or junior high	Any	Elementary schools

Physical arrangement should arise again from our goal, to integrate computers into instruction. In many cases, that suggests one or more computers in a classroom. Where better to integrate them into the flow? Bitter (1985) suggested that educators consider the probable use of other media, including books, if they were available *only* in a lab setting versus on-demand in a classroom. He recommended that computers be available to those who want them like a checkout system—for a day or all year—rather than automatically being placed in rooms, which may threaten some teachers.

Labs are important for vocational skills classes, word processing, and programming instruction. Data-base research, tutorials, and drill and practice will benefit from many machines, but can often be managed on a rotating basis, just like other forms of small group work.

Each approach carries hardware implications. Labs probably require the most computers. With mobile computers one may need fewer than one per room until demand grows. In all likelihood, the ideal is both lab and classroom computers. Beaver (1988) looked at 51 high-quality school computer programs and found that most had both.

Cooperative versus Individual Learning

The dream of a computer for each student has been common. However, the financial implications are staggering. Furthermore, evidence suggests it is not necessary, that cooperative learning with computers is beneficial.

Bracey (1988) reported two studies showing advantages of cooperative learning with computers. Competitive environments showed gender differences disadvantageous to females that did not exist in cooperative environments. Allen (1988) offered modest research evidence to support group work and counter concerns over desocialization from individual use. Collis (December/January 1988–89) reported one U.S. and one U.K. study showing superior gains from group work compared to individual work.

Glasser (1989) strongly recommended group work because it meets a basic human need. He found that students usually said they felt important only in extracurricular activities. Glasser attributed this positive self-image to the group or team nature of such activities.

Cooperative learning means much more than just putting students together at a computer. One will surely get or take more than a fair share of the time. For maximum effectiveness, always have two sets of exercises and designate pair members as A and B. Each must complete one exercise. When skill levels and nature of the activity permit, have pairs give each other assignments or tasks to perform. This can increase practicality of the work. Consider designating groups of two or three computers for mutual help. Students can seek answers from one another before asking the teacher (Staff, 1988).

The One Computer Classroom

A common lament is, "But I have 25 students and one computer in my room. What can I possibly use it for?" Clearly, requiring that all writing assignments be done with a word processor is not viable. A single computer cannot support such intensive use by a group. However, what other tools do you have just one of? Chalkboard? Overhead? VCR? You make do with those, don't you? Why is the computer different? (Dockterman and Snyder, 1988).

One answer has been problems of visibility. How many can really see a typical monitor screen at once? With the dramatic decline in the cost of data projectors and the arrival of even less expensive LCD projection panels, large-screen projection is now viable. As previously stated, most schools would be well-advised to reduce the computer purchase order by one or two units and get several LCD panels instead. Classroom computer use will almost certainly rise.

Another problem is that much software has been designed with individual work in mind. But must it be used that way? Do you invariably use a book in its physical sequence? Do you watch the commercials in the programs you videotape when away from home, or pass over them as quickly as possible? Just because a program seems to be for one learner is no cause to use it only as such. Given their purposes, drill and tutorial software are not well-suited to group use. Games may also be difficult. However, simulations and problem-solving software can be adapted easily to small-group or even whole-class instruction. Some software producers, such as Tom Snyder Productions, emphasize group applications for many products.

How about the computer as a demonstration tool? Graphing programs could be used to show the effects of changes in data. With a spreadsheet, the whole group can observe what happens if an assumption changes. Consider the potential of a simulation like *Operation: Frog.* The ideal may still be real dissection, but if that is not possible, or as instruction prior to a lab dissection, demonstrate by projecting the software for the group. How many really were able to see your live demonstration in the past?

Presentation graphics (Chapter 6) are explicitly meant for one computer before a group. Think of this as an electronic overhead or slide projector without the physical media. Your lecture presentations can be kept up to date easily. Clip art and graphing power may enhance what you otherwise have done.

Lab Monitoring and Networking

Using computers in a lab means many students and a significant number of computers. Two problems arise immediately. The first is being able efficiently to monitor student work and to help each student as needed. Anyone who has ever taught in a lab knows how difficult this can be. The second is coping in any orderly fashion with all the necessary software. Each has a solution.

Suppose you could see any student's screen at your own computer in the lab. You can with the Video Branch, a hardware device that creates a master teacher's console. From this console, you can also show your screen to students, or let them view the work of any other student. Instead of moving to the student needing help, you can view the same screen and diagnose from the console. (Video Branch is available from Chuck Lewis, Box 495, Ottumwa, IA 52501; 515-683-1636.)

Even more versatile are systems which can also distribute signals from a VCR or videodisc. Two such products are *IVAN* (PC Learning Systems, 7754 Harwood Avenue, Milwaukee, WI 53213. 414-774-4644, 800-251-IVAN out-of-state) and *LINK* (Applied Computer Systems, Inc., 3060 Johnstown-Utica Rd, Johnstown, OH 43031. 614-892-2100, 800-237-LINK out-of-state). Such systems greatly enhance a lab as a teaching environment. For one teacher's experience with data projection and an *IVAN*-type viewing network, see Barile (1985). Blankenberger (1986–87) described her experiences with LINK and IVAN systems. She found them valuable for gaining and holding student attention, demonstrating concepts, sharing student work, and for group composition editing.

Solutions to the software problem come in two forms. First, assuming that the lab supports a wide range of software, one could equip all the computers with hard disk drives and load software onto each. Users could easily access whatever was needed, using floppies only for personal files. This can be a great leap forward, but still requires the care and maintenance of some number of copies of software. In case of a new version, all systems must be upgraded.

The second solution is to electrically interconnect all of the computers into a network, usually called a *Local Area Network* (LAN). In a typical LAN, all software is stored on a central microcomputer called a *server*. Each individual computer is a *work station* and can download needed software from the server. No modems are involved; the computers are connected by cables. There is only one copy of the software to maintain. Usually you must obtain a network version of your software, which costs several times what an individual copy would, but still much less than the 20 or 30 copies you legally would need otherwise.

LANs also offer the potential for electronic mail among the work stations and for sharing peripherals, most notably expensive printers. If all 20 computers in a lab can share a single laser printer, that printer becomes very cost effective compared to one printer for even every two computers otherwise.

On the negative side, LANs are complex and somewhat prone to malfunction. They require expertise to maintain. In some LANs, if the server fails, the entire lab is down—a very serious situation. Furthermore, not all educational software is available in a network version.

Business has rushed into LANs, but can also afford the expertise to keep them running. Schools need to consider such a move very carefully. A LAN of scattered computers may be advisable for administrative purposes. A LAN in a lab for instructional purposes is very nice, but may not be essential.

Adaptive Hardware

Computers offer many potential benefits to handicapped individuals. To obtain these benefits, adaptive devices are often required—speech synthesizers, specialized software such as products to enlarge text on the screen, special input devices ranging from simple touch screens to complex apparatus for overcoming motor impairments, braille printers, and so on.

This is too large a subject for significant treatment here. If you are interested in computers and special needs users, refer to books on the subject such as Lindsey (1987) or *Ideas for Integrating the Microcomputer with Special Education* from the Northwest Regional Educational Laboratory. You may also find an article by Bates and Trumbull (1987) useful, as the authors describe effective uses of software not specifically aimed at the handicapped. In addition, the Fall/Winter 1986 issue of *Computers in the Schools* is devoted to special education, to say nothing of specific special education publications. We also provide a resource list for specialized products and services at the end of this chapter.

Beyond Classroom and Lab

Teachers, especially those not yet committed to computers, need to have ample opportunity just to explore the computer, to become comfortable with it, privately or at least non-threateningly. Moursund (August/September, 1988) recommended taking one computer from student use and putting it at the exclusive disposal of teachers. Presumably, this would be in a teachers lounge or work room. We support this idea in the hope that as teachers see their colleagues using a computer to prepare class materials or preview software, it may stimulate interest. However, this is not an answer to motivating the timid. It offers insufficient opportunity and privacy.

Although previously mentioned, we again stress sending computers home with teachers, as have Coburn et al. (1982), Ruthen (1985), and others before us. A computer sitting in the school, unused, achieves nothing. That same computer with software sitting in a teacher's home overnight, on a weekend, or over the summer just might enlist a new recruit into the technology army. We recommend that the availability of "loaners" be made known, but that requests to borrow a computer be kept confidential. Anything which can allay embarrassment is worthwhile. The borrowers will themselves share their experiences as they see fit.

BUDGETARY POTPOURRI

The ugly subject of money rears its head. Of course, there is never enough of it. So what can you do?

Allocating the Funds

The budget should be driven by the plan for computers in a given school. It is important to avoid common errors of the past. In the absence of a plan, the computer budget has often been like personal savings—whatever is left over. This is likely to be an inadequate approach even for a short term and is clearly harmful to any long-term vision.

However the budget has been set, often virtually all of the money is spent on hardware. This is a serious error as it ignores the real need for software, staff development, maintenance, supplies, and materials such as books and relevant journals.

Even a first-year budget should allocate *no more than 50 percent to hardware*, perhaps *20 percent to software* and at least *20 percent for staff development*. The remaining 10 percent may cover other items, excluding salaries. If there are major hardware purchases one year, other categories could well increase in the next. These are hardly absolutes, but rather suggestions to emphasize the significance of non-hardware components.

Levin (1987) found that over two or three years, hardware was typically 11 percent of the total cost of computer use. Software was more and personnel was 40 percent. We believe personnel should not be considered within the computing budget, unless the school also includes library and media center personnel in the book and videotape budgets and allocates amounts accordingly.

Another common error has been to view the computer budget as a one-time or short-term allocation. In fact, to bring computers into the curriculum means serious financial commitments each year. Proportions may change, but there will be ongoing needs for repair, replacement, software updating and replacement, new peripherals, and so on. To plan otherwise can doom the effort. Moursund (April 1987) cited failure to provide long-term funding as a serious and common problem in computer implementation.

Stretching the Hardware Budget

Since all budgets are inadequate by definition, how can you get the most out of what you do have? Smart shopping is the answer, though aspects of it may be politically impossible in some cases.

First, look for significant educational discounts. Many major companies, including Apple, IBM, and Zenith, offer products at significant savings to schools, individual educators, and students. No school should ever pay list price for a microcomputer.

Second, consider dual purpose machines. The cost of an MS–DOS clone with an Apple emulation board may be enough less than one of each to warrant consideration.

Third, whatever your choice of hardware, consider clones rather than the original name brand computer. Only the Macintosh has no clone at this time. If local dealers sell only the big names, this may be problematic.

Fourth, look for possible savings with bundled systems, that is, a discount for buying certain combinations of computer and peripherals or inclusion of desired software with a computer. One example was inclusion of Microsoft *Works* with the IBM PS/2 Model 25.

Stretching the Software Budget

Since software costs may exceed hardware, careful shopping is again called for. There are a number of possibilities:

1. Not all software is priced similarly, despite comparable capabilities. Unless there is an absolute need for product X, it may well be that product Y will fill the bill at lower cost. Just as hardware has clones, so do many popular software products, especially MS–DOS spreadsheets and data bases. Also consider the cost benefits of a modestly priced integrated package like *Works* or *AppleWorks* compared to separate programs.
2. There is a small category of inexpensive software aimed particularly at education. *Joe Spreadsheet* may be a quite suitable substitute for *Lotus 1-2-3* at a fraction of the cost. *Norton Textra Writer* costs less than $25 per copy including spell checker and manual. Many of the leading products are available in limited student editions for a fraction of the full package price, including *Lotus 1-2-3* and *dBase*. The performance limitations are seldom

problematic for a school user. For high school level, you may find useful software through Kinko's Academic Courseware Exchange at your nearest Kinko's copy center. Most products are for the Mac and originated in colleges and universities. Prices are nominal.

3. A few companies market major software (mostly MS–DOS) to education at prices up to 80 percent below retail. Request information from:

> Campus Technology Products Co., P.O. Box 2909, Leesburg, VA 22075.
> Chambers Intenational Corp., 5499 North Federal Highway, Suite A, Boca Raton, FL 33487.
> Diskovery Educational Systems, Corp., 1860 Old Okeechobee Road, Suite 105, West Palm Beach, FL 33409.

4. *Shareware*, primarily for MS–DOS, is software which its creator distributes on a "try it and pay me if you like it" basis. It is widely available from user groups, by mail from companies specializing in it, and via many bulletin boards and information services (*see* Chapter 6). Companies charge a nominal fee for handling shareware, normally less than $10 per disk. The software is usually fully functional and comes with documentation on disk which you can print yourself. The creator specifies a price to "register" your copy, often $50 or less. In return, you receive complete, bound documentation and upgrades to the software as they are made. There is a lot of very good shareware. Harris (1988) discussed his experiences with shareware and recommends it for appropriate situations.

5. *Public domain software*, for all popular computers, can be used, copied, and shared as you wish. You pay little or nothing for it initially, there are no restrictions, and you are not asked to pay the developer.

    Why use public domain? First, the price is within all school budgets. Second, there are no copyright issues, so libraries can circulate it without concern, and schools can copy it as much as needed. Third, many templates for programs like *AppleWorks* are available, often only this way.

    Why doesn't everyone use public domain software? First, quality varies. Some programs are great, more are average to very poor. Data files and templates are more likely to be good than are programs. Second, documentation is often limited to what you read on the screen. Third, educators often do not know of it.

    How do you find public domain software? *The Computing Teacher* runs a column called "The Price is Right." There are also many guide books. We list a few in the references, such as Glossbrenner (1989).

6. CUE Softswap distributes low-priced, freely copiable educational software. Originally Apple II-oriented, many data diskettes are now available in Mac and MS–DOS format as well. Softswap programs can be freely given away or shared with students and colleagues, but may not be sold.

7. Although neither free nor public domain, *Softdisk* offers a lot of Apple programs at very low cost. *Softdisk* is available by subscription for around

$40 for six issues of two disks each. Programs are generally interesting, even entertaining. It's not a bad way to keep new software coming without breaking the budget. Contact: *Softdisk*, P.O. Box 30008, Shreveport, LA 71130–0008; 800-831-2694, 318-221-8718. Softdisk got rave reviews in the January 1989 *Electronic Learning*.

8. Finally, there are countless mail-order firms selling software below retail. They advertise in computer publications.

Outside Funding

Don't overlook the potential of grants, usually of equipment rather than cash, which are available for innovative, creative applications. Often there is a particular funding theme for each grant cycle. For information, contact:

Tandy Education Grants Program, One Tandy Center, Fort Worth, TX 76102.

Apple Education Grants, Apple Computer Inc., 20525 Mariani Avenue, Cupertino, CA 95014.

ARTICULATION—WHAT'S THAT?

Regardless of how computers are implemented, some coordination across grade levels is essential. Except for kindergarten, a teacher needs to know what skills may have been taught previously to plan what to do at another grade level. Just as curriculum is articulated, computers within the curriculum also require such attention. This is further reason for having a designated coordinator at the district and building level. Moursund (April 1987) cited inadequate attention to articulation issues as a common, serious flaw in long-range planning.

WHERE CAN I GET HELP?

Numerous resourses are available to help educators plan for and implement computers in their schools. *Computer Applications Planning* (1984), Lengel (1983), and Klein and Strother (1983–1984) are still potentially useful despite their age. For an extremely detailed resource handbook, consult Batey (1988). McCarthy (1988), Moursund and Ricketts (1987), Biggs (1988), Bennett (1987), and Solomon (1988) all provoke thought and offer valuable advice. Preskill (1988) describes a four-phase training model for in-service.

Among implementation resources, Collis (1988) is particularly strong. Her fundamental premise is integration throughout the curriculum. The book includes over 100 lesson plans for "curriculum-classroom-computer integration."

The International Society for Technology in Education publishes a series *Computer-Integrated Instruction: Effective Inservice for _____ Teachers*, covering elementary and several secondary fields. Each volume includes a *MacWrite* disk of the text materials to encourage modification. Mitchell Publishing is the source for a large group of subject-matter-specific books with the title *The Computer in the* _____ *Curriculum.* Virtually all areas are covered. For science, Vernier (undated) gives instructions on 14 lab interfaces for Apple. The approach is very flexible, with open-ended suggestions to get you going.

Once you know what you want to do, Pelfrey (1988) can show you how to approach the school board. In the case reported, the board approved three times the original budget request despite lack of support from the superintendent!

Finally, a unique resource for curriculum integration is EPIE's Integrated Instructional Information Resource (IIIR). IIIR is a data base containing detailed information on textbooks, software, instructional TV programs, and tests. There are also specific strategies for integrating these resources into one's teaching. In EPIE's terms, the goal is curriculum alignment, bringing all possible resources to bear on an educational problem. Users can determine the degree of correlation between their curriculum objectives, current materials, and any testing program in place. They can also get advice on the most closely correlated materials available (Komoski, 1987, *ERIC/IR*). EPIE's address is in Appendix F.

SUMMARY

In this chapter we outlined one view of the course of computer implementation through the 1980s. We suggested that the initial goal was probably incorrect, and provided possible explanations for less progress than we had anticipated. We proposed a new direction for the 90s.

We revisited the goal of invisible integration articulated in Chapter 15. To implement that goal, we recognize that only some teachers are now prepared to implement computers, and that others may slowly join them. Within that context we presented issues and ideas concerning staff development, hardware and physical facilities, budget and making the most of available funds, and the need for articulation. We also mentioned many sources of further assistance.

In 1988 the Department of Education established a national educational technology research center at Bank Street College of Education. This center is working to identify the conditions which lead to successful curriculum integration of technology. Other thrusts to be developed include studying the ways in which technology integration differs by subject area, how technology can best be used in school reform, how to better measure the impact of technology on student learning, and the impact of cognitive science on technology integration. For information, contact: Center for Technology in Education, Bank Street College of Education, 610 West 112th St., New York, NY 10025.

CHAPTER 16 ACTIVITIES

1. Interview teachers or administrators who were involved early in their school's implementation of computers. How do their experiences compare to our "history?"

2. Contact several school districts to inquire about their plan for computers. Try to obtain copies of written plans and other documents (such as a district mission statement) which refer to computers. Analyze what you obtain.
3. State and defend a position on which teachers to involve in computer implementation.
4. Based on your own knowledge and views, articulate the most compelling reasons why teachers do not use computers. Try to interview several non-users to get their views.
5. Propose a staff development plan congruent with activities 3 and 4 above.
6. Thoroughly research the comparative merits of Apple II, MS–DOS, and Macintosh computers. Write a position paper on their applicability to K–12 education.
7. Interview persons experienced with computer labs and mobile or room-based computers. Synthesize our commentary and their experiences.
8. Outline a plan for computer usage in a one-computer classroom.
9. Examine available shareware and public domain software. Would you consider using such software? Why?

REFERENCES

Allen, C. A. "Social Interactions Between a Teacher and Small Group of Students Working with a Microcomputer." *Computers in the Schools*, 1988, 5(1/2), pp. 271–284.

Balajthy, E. "Evaluation of a Pre-Service Training Module in Microcomputer Applications for the Teaching of Reading." *Computers in the Schools*, 1988, 5(1/2), pp. 113–128.

Barile, J. "One Computer Can Work with a Group." *Electronic Learning*, May/June 1985, p. 20.

Bates, B. G. and Trumbull, V. H. "There *Is* Software to Motivate and Teach the Learning Handicapped." *The Computing Teacher*, May 1987, pp. 27–29, 54.

Batey, A., ed. *Planning for Computers in Education*. Portland, OR: Northwest Regional Educational Laboratory, 1988.

Beaver, J. F. *A National Search for Quality: An Examination of High-Quality Elementary School Instructional Computing Programs*. Unpublished doctoral dissertation, Michigan State University, 1988.

Becker, H. *Microcomputers in the Classroom. Dreams and Realities*. Eugene, OR: International Council for Computers in Education, undated.

Bennett, R. E., ed. *Planning and Evaluating Computer Education Programs*. Columbus, OH: Merrill, 1987.

Biggs, P. "Create Ownership in Your Long Range Plan with a Technology Audit." *The Computing Teacher*, October 1988, pp. 31–33.

Bitter, G. "Computer Labs—Fads?" *Electronic Education*, May/June 1985, pp. 17, 35.

Black, T., and Mishler, T. "How One District Handles Technology In-Service Education." *Electronic Learning*, September 1988, pp. 32–34.

Blankenbaker, R. "A Connection to Learning: Video Networking Systems." *The Computing Teacher*, December-January 1986–87, pp. 19–20.

Bracey, G. W. "Two Studies Show Students Gain When Teaming Up." *Electronic Learning*, January 1988, p. 19.

Bring, C. R., and Nickman, P. J. "Characteristics and Managerial Philosophies of Computer Leaders." *Educational Technology*, August 1988, pp. 32–36.

Bunson, S. N. "Design and Management of an IMC Micro Center." *Educational Technology*, August 1988, pp. 29–32.

Caissy, G. A. *Microcomputers and the Classroom Teacher.* Bloomington, IN: Phi Delta Kappa, 1987. Also ERIC document ED 290 447.

Coburn, P., Kelman, P., Roberts, N., Snyder, T., Watt, D., and Weiner, C. *Practical Guide to Computers in Education.* Reading, MA: Addison-Wesley, 1982.

Collis, B. *Computers, Curriculum, and Whole-Class Instruction.* Belmont, CA: Wadsworth, 1988.

Collis, B. "Research Windows." *The Computing Teacher*, March 1988, p. 24.

Collis, B. "Research Windows." *The Computing Teacher*, August/September 1988, pp. 6–7.

Collis, B. "Research Windows." *The Computing Teacher*, December/January 1988–89, p. 7.

Computer Applications Planning. Chelmsford, MA: Merrimack Education Center, 1984.

D'Ignazio, F. "Setting Up a Multi-Media Classroom: A Quickstart Card." *Computers in the Schools*, Summer 1987, pp. 5–30.

Dockterman, D., and Snyder, T. *Bringing the Computer into Your Classroom.* Cambridge, MA: Tom Snyder Productions, 1988.

Eisenberg, M. B. and Berkowitz, R. E. *Curriculum Initiative.* Norwood, NJ: Ablex, 1988.

Farrell, M. L., and Kaczka, A. "Integrating the Computer into Resource Room Instruction." *Computers in the Schools*, 1988, 5(1/2), pp. 213–223.

Fisher, G. "Developing a District-Wide Computer-Use Plan." *The Computing Teacher*, January 1983, pp. 52–59.

Friedman, D. "I Like Computers but They Don't Like Me." *Electronic Education*, September 1985, pp. 14–15.

Fullan, M. G., Miles, M. G., and Anderson, S. E. *Strategies for Implementing Microcomputers in Schools: The Ontario Case.* Toronto: Ontario Ministry of Education, 1987.

Gader, B., and Hodar, M. V. *Apple Software for Pennies* (1985), *Free Software for the IBM PC* (1984), and *MAC Software for Pennies* (1986), New York: Warner.

Glasser, W. "Quality: The Key to the Disciplines." *National Forum*, Winter 1989, pp. 36–38.

Glossbrenner, A. *Master Guide to Free Software.* New York: St. Martin's Press, 1989.

Harris, J. "Loading for Free Without Freeloading." *The Computing Teacher*, August/September 1988, pp. 51–53.

Hatcher, P. L. and Palmer, W. J. III. *Free Software Handbook.* Plano, TX: PeopleTalk Associates.

Heller, D., and Heller, D. *Free Software for Your Apple.* San Jose, CA: Enrich/Ohaus. (Also versions for other machines.)

Hill, M., Manzo, F., Liberman, D., York, J., Nichols, C., and Morgan, P. "A Plea for Computer Integration: Let's Bring Computers into the Classroom." *Educational Technology*, May 1988, pp. 46–48.

Johnson, D. L., Maddux, C. D., and O'Hair, M. M. "Are We Making Progress? An Interview with Judah Schwartz of ETC." *Computers in the Schools*, 1988, 5(1/2), pp. 5–22.

Kinzer, C., Sherwood, R., and Bransford, J. *Computer Strategies for Education: Foundations and Content-Area Applications.* Columbus, OH: Merrill, 1986.

Klein, K., and Strother, D., eds. *Planning for Microcomputers in the Curriculum.* Bloomington, IN: Phi Delta Kappa. Center on Evaluation Development and Research (CEDR). Hot Topics Series, 1983–1984.

Komoski, P. K. *Educational Technology: The Closing-In or the Opening-Out of Curriculum and Instruction.* Syracuse, NY: ERIC/IR, Syracuse University, 1987. Document IR–77.

Komoski, P. K. "Beyond Innovation: The Systemic Integration of Technology into the Curriculum." *Educational Technology,* September 1987, pp. 21–25.

Knupfer, N. N. "Teachers' Beliefs About Instructional Computing: Implications for Instructional Designers." *Journal of Instructional Development,* 1988, *11*(4), pp. 29–38.

Laney, J. D. "The Successful Introduction of New Educational Technologies: Breaking the Cycle of Circus Oversell." ERIC document ED 290 437, 1984.

Langhorne, M. J., Donham, J. O., Gross, J. F., and Rahmke, D. *Teaching with Computers.* Phoenix, AZ: Oryx Press, 1989.

Lee, H. *Where to Find Free Programs for Your Microcomputer.* Pasadena, CA: Pasadena Technology Press.

Lengel, J. G. *Computer Considerations for Vermont Schools.* Burlington: Vermont Department of Education, 1983.

Levin, H. M. *Cost-Effectiveness of Computer-Assisted Instruction: Some Insights.* Reported in Collis, B. "Research Windows." *The Computing Teacher,* March 1987, p. 56.

Lindsey, J. D., ed. *Computers and Exceptional Individuals.* Columbus, OH: Merrill, 1987.

Mathinos, D. A., and Woodward, A. "The Status of Instructional Computing in an Elementary School: Removing Those Rose-Colored Glasses." Reported in Collis, B. "Research Windows." *The Computing Teacher,* December/January 1988–89, p. 8.

McCarthy, R. "Making the Future Work." *Electronic Learning,* September 1988, pp. 42–46.

Moursund, D. "CAI or Teachers? Not Either/Or—But Both." *The Computing Teacher,* October 1988, p. 5.

Moursund, D. "Education Would Be Better If. . ." *The Computing Teacher,* August/September 1988, p. 5.

Moursund, D. "Long-range Planning," *The Computing Teacher,* April 1987, pp. 4–5.

Moursund, D. "More on Long-range Planning." *The Computing Teacher,* June 1987, pp. 4–5.

Moursund, D., and Ricketts, D. *Long-range Planning for Computers in Schools.* Eugene, OR: Information Age Education, 1250 E. 29th Place, Eugene, OR 97403–1621, 1987.

Norton, P. "In Search of a Computer Curriculum." *Educational Technology,* March 1988, pp. 7–14.

Norwood, D. "Hold the Hardware: Here's a Logical Way to Plan for Microcomputers." *Illinois School Board Journal,* March/April 1983, pp. 22–24.

Olson, J. *Schoolwords/Microworlds. Computers and the Culture of the Classroom.* Elmsford, NY: Pergamon Press, 1988.

Pelfrey, R. "How to Sell a School Board by Really Trying." *Electronic Learning,* February 1988, p. 16.

Plomp, T., Steerneman, A., and Pelgrum, W. J. "Curriculum Changes as a Consequence of Computer Use." Reported in Collis, B. "Research Windows." *The Computing Teacher,* December/January 1988–89, p. 8.

Pogrow, S. "The Computer Movement Cover-Up." *Electronic Learning,* April 1988, pp. 6–7.

Pogrow, S. "How To Use Computers To Truly Enhance Learning." *Electronic Learning,* May/June 1988, pp. 6–8.

Poirot, J., and Heidt, M. "Planning for Educational Computing." In *Planning for Educational*

Computing. Guidelines for Administrators. Lyndhurst, NJ: Scholastic, Inc., 1983, pp. 4–7.

Pollard, J., ed. *Ideas for Integrating the Microcomputer into Science Instruction.* Portland, OR: Northwest Regional Educational Laboratory, 1987.

Preskill, H. "Teachers and Computers: A Staff Development Challenge." *Educational Technology,* March 1988, pp. 24–26.

Roblyer, M. D., Castine, W. H., and King, F. J. "Assessing the Impact of Computer-Based Instruction." *Computers in the Schools,* 1988, 5(3/4).

Ruthen, C. "One District's Victory: Overcoming Computer Resistance." *Electronic Education,* September 1985, pp. 15, 38.

Salisbury, D. F. "How to Decide When and Where to Use Microcomputers for Instruction." *Educational Technology,* March 1984, pp. 22–24.

Solomon, C. *Computer Environments for Children.* Cambridge, MA: MIT Press, 1988. (Potentially valuable background work.)

Staff. "Two at a Terminal? Cooperative Learning and Computers." *The ASSIST Journal,* 1988, Issue 1, p. 7.

Stieglitz, E. L. and Costa, C. H. "A Statewide Teacher Training Program's Impact on Computer Usage in the Schools." *Computers in the Schools,* 1988, 5(1/2), pp. 91–98.

U.S. Congress, Office of Technology Assessment. *Power On! New Tools for Teaching and Learning,* OTA–SET–379. Washington, DC: U.S. Government Printing Office, September 1988.

Venier, D. *How to Build a Better Mousetrap.* Portland, OR: Venier Software, 2920 SW 89th St., Portland, OR 97225.

SELECTED SHAREWARE OR PUBLIC DOMAIN SOURCES

APPLE II

Big Red Computer Club, 423 Norfolk Avenue, Norfolk, NE 68701.

Computer Budget Shopper, 2203 Park Avenue O.V., Cheyenne, WY 82007.

Educational Resource Center, P-700, National Air and Space Museum, Smithsonian Institute, Washington, DC 50560.

Facts on File, 460 Park Ave South, New York, NY 10016.

Pandora Software, Box 590, Clearfield, UT 84015.

MACINTOSH

EDUCOMP, 742 Genevieve, Suite D, Solana Beach, CA 92075.

Quantum Access, Inc., 1700 West Loop South, Suite 1460, Houston, TX 77027. This is the source of *ClubMac,* a CD-ROM collection of Mac software, user-submitted articles, reviews, classifieds, and notices, sold by subscription.

MS–DOS

Multipath, Inc., Box 487, Montville, NJ 07045.

PC-SIG, 1030-D East Duane Ave., Sunnyvale, CA 94086. (A CD-ROM of the total collection is available.)

Public Brand Software, P.O. Box 51315, Indianapolis, IN 46251.

Shareware Express, 27601 Forbes Rd, Suite 37, Box 6849, Laguna Niguel, CA 92677-6849.

Software Shopper, Gallaudet University, Pre-College Outreach, Washington, D.C. 20002.

Computer Shopper, widely available on magazine stands, prints directories of bulletin boards and lists of user groups.

SPECIAL EDUCATION RESOURCES

Access Unlimited—Speech Enterprises, P.O. Box 7986, Houston, TX 77024; 713-461-1666.

ARTS Computer Products, Inc., 145 Tremont St., Suite 407, Boston, MA 02111; 617-482-8248.

COMPUPLAY Resource Centers, INNOTEK Director, National Lekotek Center, 2100 Ridge Ave., Evanston, IL 60204; 312-328-0001.

Computer Aids Corporation, 124 W. Washington, Suite 220, Fort Wayne, IN 46802; 800-647-8255.

Computer Options for the Exceptional, 85 Market St., Poughkeepsie, NY 12601; 914-471-2765.

Heath Resource Center (Higher Education and Adult Training for People with Handicaps), One DuPont Circle NW Suite 800, Washington, DC 20036-1193; 800-544-3284 or 202-939-9320 (voice/TDD).

LINC Resources Inc., Publications Division, 91 Vine St., Pawtucket, RI 02861; 401-725-3973.

Laureate Learning Systems, Inc., 110 E. Spring St., Winooski, VT 05404; 802-655-4755.

Personal Touch Corp., 4320 Stevens Creek Blvd., San Jose, CA 95129; 408-246-8822.

Trace Center, Waisman Center, University of Wisconsin-Madison, 1500 Highland Ave., Madison, WI 53705; 608-263-5408.

CHAPTER 17

□ Issues and Implications □

OBJECTIVES

After completing this chapter, you will be able to:

□ *List and discuss several ways in which computers are affecting the world of work.* □

□ *Discuss several issues related to computers and personal privacy.* □

□ *List and describe four areas of concern related to ethics.* □

□ *Discuss the issues of gender and socioeconomic equity in computer access.* □

□ *Defend a position on potential overreliance on computers.* □

□ *Analyze changes occurring in the traditional roles of teachers, students, and parents in education.* □

Too often considerations of computers in education are so totally positive as to appear naive. Many educators seem quite content to accept blindly whatever fate technology brings to them, never questioning, never wondering. The bandwagon continues to move and pick up riders.

The computer does not deserve such blind devotion. Rather, the entire course of computerization of our society should be closely scrutinized. It is difficult to argue against the claim that society is already so computerized that there is no turning back. By now it should be obvious that we have no wish to turn back. However, greater attention to the impact of computers on our lives may serve to better guide the course of future progress.

This chapter, then, is devoted to considering some of the major issues and implications raised by computers in society and, within it, education. It is critically important that computer education programs not neglect these issues. We do not claim to provide answers, but rather seek to alert you to the issues and the need to consider them personally and with students.

SOCIAL ISSUES

Within the broad category of social issues, we will look at the impact of computers on the world of work and on personal privacy. The underlying concern is what computers are doing to individuals and thus to society.

IMPACT ON WORK

Major works such as *Megatrends* have popularized the concept that society has moved past the industrial age. The most common terms applied to the present are the Information Age or the Information Society. Some believe the transformation has occurred; others see it as under way, but far from complete. These are mostly semantic differences. The major "product" of our society today is indeed information.

Bozeman (1985, p. 173) pointed out some of the changes that have occurred. Farmers have dwindled from some 35 percent of the work force in 1900 to less than 3 percent. From over 50 percent in the 1930s to 1950s, the percentage of persons involved in production of goods has fallen to 10 percent. Of some 20 million new jobs created in the 1970s, nearly 90 percent were information- or service-related. What are some of the ramifications of these changes that should be considered?

Labor Unions
The labor movement developed from concerns over working conditions in industry. Traditional union strongholds, such as the automobile industry and mining, employ far fewer persons than at the peak of union strength. Membership is down accordingly; robots in factories are not potential union members.

What is the future of labor unions? What will be the rallying cries among information workers, if they become unionized? What are the new labor issues in the Information Age? What will become of persons displaced by technology? Technology may create more jobs than it destroys, but not for the same people.

Perhaps retraining of workers is the answer. Some question whether the present work force can be retrained for new responsibilities. Is there any incentive for industry to retrain older workers if younger people are available with the needed skills? Is it possible that we are approaching an era when blue-collar workers in their 40s and 50s will become permanently unemployable?

Job Qualifications

It might surprise you to look up the latest statistics on the percentage of young people who even today do not complete high school. Many think lack of a high school diploma is a thing of the past. Even if this were true, is a diploma regarded as significant in today's world?

What kind of education is required to get a job in the information sector? Jobs of a more physical or menial nature are rapidly disappearing. School dropouts are unlikely to find decent employment except, perhaps, in the lowest-paying areas of the service sector at minimum wage. How long will a diploma alone lead to anything? What does it mean for the educational system if more than a high school education is the minimum for getting a meaningful job?

Where One Works

Particularly in urban areas, it has become quite common for people to spend a great amount of time just getting to and from work. Expressway systems become parking lots at 7 a.m. and 5 p.m.; mass transit, where it exists, is crowded. For some years now, this waste of potentially productive human time has been of concern. It was clear in the age of factories that the worker had to go to the factory. Is this still true in information industries?

Technologically, we have long had the potential for employees in certain kinds of jobs to work from their homes via telecommunications. A terminal and a modem can link a home office to the "physical" job site. What would it mean if large numbers of workers were no longer required to be physically "on the job"? What would this mean for family life at home? What would it mean for the real estate industry if huge office complexes were no longer needed? How would you like to work alone at home rather than with other people? Past experiments with working from home have tended to founder on the lack of socialization with others. Is this likely to change?

PERSONAL PRIVACY

Computers have permitted corporations, government, and other groups to create data banks on a scale previously undreamed of. How wonderful it may be to be able to make a purchase anywhere in the world by credit card, which the merchant can instantly verify. How nice to be able to write a personal check in a distant city because the store can quickly determine if the check will clear.

For all the convenience, these things are possible only because somewhere a computer has a lot of information on file concerning you and your finances. How willingly would you share such information with strangers, if they simply asked you for it?

Law enforcement officials in many areas can learn a great deal about you almost instantly by entering your automobile license number or driver's license number into a computer terminal, even a portable one in a squad car. The benefits of such a system are enormous in crime prevention, but what are the less-benign possibilities?

Westin (cited in Bozeman, 1985, p. 169) defined the essence of personal privacy as "the claim of an individual to determine what information about himself or herself should be known to others. This also involves when such information will be communicated or obtained, and what uses will be made of it by others." Have we already passed the point where personal privacy can be maintained?

Do you consider the ramifications of filling out a credit card application? Of responding to information requested for a city directory? Of applying for a job? Of subscribing to a magazine or completing a "marketing survey" that comes in the mail? All of these things provide data about you to others.

Data banks have been around for a long time, first on paper, then as computer files. The remote access potential of the latter is a major source of concern. Even if one is not concerned about improper use of personal data by those who gathered it, what about use by persons who obtain access to data banks without authority? The newspapers regularly report on the latest cases of "computer invasion." Is there such a thing as a secure computer system, where only those duly authorized and strictly supervised can gain access to your information? The evidence suggests there is not.

Other electronic wonders are creating trails of information on individuals as never before. Consider the use of automatic teller machines and other systems for electronically transferring funds. All transactions must be fully documented, which means a paper trail possibly open to misuse, though its intent is the opposite. As electronic mail becomes more common, there may be a concern for the privacy of one's written communication. Or is this really any more of a problem than the possibility of someone opening and reading your letters now?

It is not our desire to cause massive outbreaks of paranoia over the privacy issue. We have yet to see evidence of problems so severe as to bring the entire system into question. However, the issue is one that requires continual scrutiny. Students must become aware of the situation and become part of a monitoring system to insist that necessary laws, standards, or policies are implemented to protect personal rights. (*See* Mandell and Mandell, 1989, pp. 251–254; Kinzer, Sherwood, and Bransford, 1986, pp. 141–143.)

ETHICS

According to Hamilton (cited in Bitter, 1984, p. 293), "Today's computer is intellectually a moron, and morally permissive. Provided it is instructed in a language it understands and is programmed to receive the instructions, it will do as it is told whether this be right or wrong."

Thus, we turn our attention to concerns over what people are doing to or with computers. With the widespread availability of computers have come significant areas of difficulty in ethical and even legal behavior. We will consider these matters in four categories: copyright, hacking, viruses, and white-collar crime.

It is interesting to speculate on what permits individuals who might otherwise never cross the legal line beyond overtime parking to alter their behavior when it comes to computers. Is this somehow another effect of computers on individuals? What makes the situation sufficiently different from others to affect moral behavior?

COPYRIGHT

The cost of software development is truly enormous for quality products. As in all other areas of business, it is not unreasonable for software producers to expect a profit from their venture. Copyright law is the mechanism for protecting the right to profit from sale of one's products.

Most people seem to adhere to copyright restrictions on items we are long familiar with, such as books and films. Few would attempt to make copies of such products in violation of the law. Computer software is no different in principle. Still, individuals both in and outside of education think nothing of making illegal copies of software for their own use or that of friends. Resale for profit is rarely at issue. (*See* Mandell and Mandell, 1989, pp. 254–256.)

The practice of software piracy can be found among very young computerists as well as adults. To some extent, it must fall to teachers to attempt to deal with this issue (Bear, 1986). We believe piracy is better dealt with as a matter of ethics and practical ramifications than as a major legal concern. The fact remains that few casual software pirates are apt to be prosecuted; apprehension is simply too difficult. Rather, computer users need to consider the significance of their actions.

First, potential pirates must understand that their actions are in fact larceny. It seems likely that many attach no such stigma to their actions at all. They would hardly stoop to burglary or in any other way set out to rob an individual. Yet through illegal copying of software they are denying compensation to the creator of that package. As soon as children are old enough to learn to duplicate disks and to understand that software is a purchased item, they should be gently introduced to the ethical issues involved in software copying.

Second, computer users must become aware of the magnitude of the problem. Producers of computer games generally expect to make their major profits in the first few months on the market. Within six months, more pirated copies may be in use than purchased ones, and the market will drop off accordingly. The case with applications software such as word processors and data bases is similar, although the time frames tend to be considerably longer. Shelly and

Cashman (1984, p. 18.9) estimated that four illegal copies will ultimately exist for every copy sold! Mandell and Mandell (1989) reported speculation that as much as 50 percent of the software *in the schools* may have been illegally copied. Collis (1988) put the figure at 40 to 90 percent! Translate these figures into lost sales, and the sums become enormous.

Third, educators should be mindful of the by-products of the piracy problem. Publishers are wary of teachers in many cases, because teachers have always been "borrowers" of other materials. For instance, educators are notorious for not adhering to the letter of the law on photocopying. But even then, the concerns are not all that great, since photocopying any lengthy work is often more costly than buying it. Still, teachers already have a bad image among publishers and producers of educational materials. Software copying is not improving this negative image.

Ways must be found to meet the legitimate concerns of educators over the cost of the multiple software copies required to remain within the law. However, mere concern over the limits of the school budget does not justify piracy. Furthermore, schools *must be role models for their students.* We cannot preach what is right, then practice the opposite. There is no place for pirated software in a school.

In addition, the ultimate result of piracy is counterproductive for all. If producers cannot reasonably expect to recoup developmental expenses and make some profit, the entire motivation for the industry disappears. We do not question the longevity of producers of popular business software products. Business can and will pay for what it uses. It is education that will suffer most if producers are driven from the market.

The International Society for Technology in Education has published a statement on copyright ("1987 Statement on Software Copyright," 1987) and a code of ethics ("Code of Ethical Conduct," 1987). Educators who use computers should be thoroughly familiar with both documents. They are reproducible for distribution or for use with students. Another guide to ethical and legal software use is available from ERIC ("Using Software," 1987). Concerns pertaining to the library are treated by Talab (1986–87).

HACKING

A somewhat peculiar offspring of the computer age is the *hacker*. A hacker may be characterized as a young person (usually) who is totally caught up in working with a computer, often to the virtual exclusion of other activities. Such people are typically very skilled programmers. With telecommunications access to computers around the world, hackers delight in finding ways around the security checks of systems so that they can just "browse" through the computer's files. Many also use illegal means to avoid long distance telephone charges.

Some hacking can almost be understood as youthful exuberance, a sense of power over mechanical objects. At least at the start, hackers are rarely malicious. However, hacking has led to unauthorized access to government and corporate computers and the changing or destruction of data in them. Cases have been publicly reported of records being altered in hospital files, which could mean life or death to patients. Thus, what may have begun as "play" can become deadly serious. Initially, hackers were treated as curiosities and generally escaped punishment, often because of their youth. However, prison sentences are possible ("Computer Hacker," 1989).

Just as schools must bear some responsibility for educating youngsters about software piracy, so, too, must they attack the issue of unauthorized entry to a computer system.

VIRUSES

Physicians often diagnose an illness as a virus—a submicroscopic agent that causes disease. Today a different virus is receiving attention: the computer virus. A *computer virus* is typically a small program planned and written specifically to cause mischief or damage to computer systems. A virus enters a computer's software where it remains undetected and inactive until a specific date or particular set of conditions occur. At that point it becomes activated and begins its malicious task—perhaps denying access to users, deleting or altering files, or possibly reformatting disks. Some viruses reproduce themselves, taking up more and more memory and/or disk space until they cause the system to crash.

For example, at George Washington University, students noticed that data was disappearing from their disks. When the suspicious disks were examined, a virus program was discovered. At Lehigh University in Bethlehem, Pennsylvania, students are permitted to borrow computer software. Students who were in charge of the check-out program noticed that several diskettes were faulty when returned from use. It was discovered that a virus destroyed all the files on the original disk after it had made four copies of itself. Each of these four copies would make four copies of itself and the master files would then be destroyed (Winter, 1988). While not all viruses have thus far proven to be this harmful, the potential for such destruction obviously is great.

Viruses are often acquired from software downloaded from bulletin boards. They are then unwittingly passed on from individual to individual as the software is shared. Hence, caution should be taken when using such software packages. While there are commercial anti-viral programs available, they remain imperfect and will not guarantee protection from all viruses. Chaffin (1989) suggested ways of preventing viral infections: frequently back up your hard disk, download onto a single computer rather than a networked system, and carefully check software before adding it to your system. As further protection against computer viruses she also suggested that one avoid storing data on program disks and regularly write-protect program disks.

WHITE COLLAR CRIME

Although piracy and hacking are crimes, they are often viewed as less serious than other computer crimes. There is no realm of our existence that is totally free from the potential for crime within it. The computer has merely presented new avenues for criminal conduct, what Scrogan (1988) referred to as the "on-line underground."

This area of concern entails both fraud and direct theft. Bitter (1984, pp. 290–295) provided many examples of computer fraud and misuse, ranging from sale of nonexistent securities to improper transfer of funds from one account to another to insurance policies for fictitious purchasers. Bozeman (1985, pp. 174–177) presented in some detail such crimes as theft of computer services (e.g., using the company computer for personal activity), theft of data to sell or hold for ransom, and falsification of data ranging from financial records to vote counts.

It is unfortunate that the computer age has spawned its own contributions to criminality, but hardly surprising. As more individuals come into regular contact with computer systems, the potential for such abuses seems to grow naturally. In addition, the frailties of computer security are major contributors to the problem, as well as intriguing challenges to the dishonest. Students must confront the potential for computer crime and, as with piracy, be helped to see that there are no modern-day Robin Hoods in the computer world. Theft is theft, regardless of the method.

For further information, the August/September 1984 issue of *The Computing Teacher* had as its theme ethics in computer use. Activities related to ethical behavior are provided by Gilliland and Pollard (1984) and Shelly and Cashman (1984, p. 18.11). The latter describes eight representative situations and asks the user to classify the behavior as ethical, unethical, or computer crime. One issue, for example, is use of a company computer for personal work when it is not being used otherwise.

EQUITY

Although we have just presented a dark side of computing, we remain convinced that by and large computers are beneficial. However, equity of access to the benefits of computers is a source of concern. Equity issues divide along two lines, gender and socioeconomic level. As Pantiel and Petersen (1984, p. 170) wrote, "Probably the most critical question of the decade is whether computers are going to be available to everyone."

GENDER

The gender side of the issue stems from a perception that females are not involved to an appropriate extent in computing today. In countless schools, elective computer classes are filled with boys; girls seem less interested. Yet if the future depends so much on computers and computer skills, this situation cannot be tolerated.

Reasons for this gender gap are many. According to Demetrulias and Rosenthal (1985), computer producers deliberately play to men, with male models in most advertising, unless the person depicted is clearly the secretary. Beyond this, girls are less attracted to typical shoot-'em-up video games, which are the source of much enthusiasm among boys (Linn, 1985; Hess and Miura, 1985).

Collis (1988) suggested that reasons for females being less confident with computers than males include male dominance of computer labs, perceived lack of relevance of school computer offerings to girls' goals, female preference for cooperative as opposed to competitive work, and teachers who accept the assumptions that girls are less interested in computers and less capable with them than boys.

Flake, McClintock, and Turner (1985, p. 339) suggested that the age at which computers are introduced also affects the gender issue. If computers appear in schools in the lower elementary grades, interest appears similar among boys and girls. If the start comes at the middle school level, girls appear to be more passive about their involvement.

Another reason for male dominance at this time may be the identification of the computer with math and science, rather than throughout the curriculum. These two fields have tended to be male dominated, so that a carry-over of attitude toward computers seems only natural (Rosenthal and Demetrulias, 1988; Swadener and Hannafin, 1987).

Educators must guard carefully against problems of gender equity in computer access and use. We do not foresee this as a long-term problem if computers are truly integrated into the curriculum at all grade levels.

ECONOMICS

The economic side of equity is probably far more difficult. In fact, the issue has very little to do with computers per se and a great deal to do with all of American education and society. It is obvious that wealthy suburban schools typically have much more comprehensive computer programs than do some inner city and poorer schools. After all, computers cost money.

Similar problems abound for everything from basic school supplies like paper and pencils to library resources and even the quality of teachers. It is a simple fact that schools in the U.S. are anything but equal. The computer era may add more weight to the injustice of the situation, but it is certainly not the source of the problem.

Not only is a student's access to computers in school linked to the economics of the community or neighborhood, there is also the issue of home access. It is far more likely that the suburban child will have a computer at home and that the child in an impoverished district will not (Stone, 1987). Since the computer is such a powerful and useful tool, how will it be feasible or practical to finance large-scale purchase of hardware and software both for individuals and for schools?

Will computers only be available in homes of the economically privileged? Will only those schools that are well financed be able to do an adequate job using microcomputers within their educational program? As microcomputer knowledge becomes more important in the employment marketplace, will previous microcomputer availability only increase the separation of those who are adequately prepared to compete from those who are not? Although a complete solution to the equity problem is far beyond the local teacher and school, Stone (1986, 1986–87) offers many practical suggestions. Equity is an issue we must be aware of, though our individual contributions toward a solution may not be great. The obvious fear is that inequity further exacerbates the problem of haves and have nots, extending into control of one's destiny. If the future will rely more and more on computers, and the poorest among us have no opportunity to gain the needed skills, the gulf will widen further. Equity becomes a major *social* issue, not just an education issue.

For further reading on equity issues, the reference list contains numerous relevant citations. Sanders and Stone (1986) are especially worthwhile for class activities and specific strategies for encouraging broad computer use and interest.

EXCESSIVE RELIANCE ON COMPUTERS

Another issue that seems to be discussed very little is the ultimate effect of our growing personal dependence on computers in daily living. We raise this issue because we have heard it expressed by teachers who are not yet committed to extensive integration of computers into the curriculum. Few can still doubt that computers are here to stay, yet many blindly accept them with little thought for long-range implications. Perhaps the skeptics among us have concerns that need to be addressed, as Vockell and Schwartz (1988, pp. 126–132) seek to do.

There is clearly potential danger in the thoughtless rise of so potent a force in our lives. Several such issues have already been presented. The kinds of concerns we now refer to fall into two major curriculum areas, mathematics and written communication. A third is the seeming infallibility of computers.

MATHEMATICS

When calculators first appeared on the scene, there were cries of anguish from many teachers that students would no longer really learn arithmetic. Instead, pupils would simply punch keys to enter figures and then accept the displayed result without question. While this no longer seems to be a burning concern, the computer as the ultimate calculator raises the issue anew.

Ultimately, the question of computers as mathematical tools is: What is really important in the curriculum? With calculators, math teachers have not given up the expectation that students should still learn basic arithmetic facts and processes. Rather, calculators are being employed to achieve goals previously unattainable or that had to be delayed until later in a pupil's life. They have not given up the principles of the field, only the drudgery of routine operations. Can the same approach also work for microcomputers?

We believe it can and that changes in curriculum can and must result. For instance, we have already learned that calculators necessitate increased attention to estimation of answers, so that errors in keying in values will be apparent to the user. When a computer is used for even more sophisticated calculations, the same concept applies. We must never lose sight of the need to examine results critically, so that errors in data or programming do not lead to false conclusions. Is there anything wrong with reducing the time devoted to low-level activity and replacing it with more sophisticated work? We think not and hope that underlying concepts may, in fact, be more clearly understood as a result.

Perhaps an example from graduate school will further illustrate the potential. We remember well the days of graduate courses in statistics, when students spent hours memorizing formulas and learning to analyze data using calculators. It was not uncommon for doctoral students to be told what procedures to use to analyze their research data, only to find that they could not independently explain why a given test was used or what the results really meant. Just getting an "answer" was enough, it seemed. Today, there is little reason to learn to hand calculate even relatively simple statistics, and anyone can readily apply far more sophisticated techniques to their data. Statistics classes can now focus on conceptual understanding of procedures and their proper application, since time need not be devoted to learning the raw mechanics. This is a positive influence of the computer on curriculum.

WRITTEN COMMUNICATION

Teachers have also expressed grave concerns over the impact of word processors and related programs such as spelling checkers on students and writing. We have heard comments to the effect that, whatever the benefits of computerized writing, one cannot always expect to have such devices at hand with which to write. If students know no other way to write, how will they cope with impromptu writing needs? If the computer will correct their spelling errors, why should students bother learning to spell?

There is a temptation to dismiss the concern over access to word processing equipment with the notation that portable, even lap-top computers have become quite popular today. It may well be that one can have access to word processing at all times. Still, it seems obvious that this change in how we write is more significant than the switch, say, from chalk and slate to paper and pencil. The latter offered some new independence to write when needed. The computer adds many advantages, but certain burdens, whatever the equipment. We do not foresee an end to handwriting and believe that it remains a viable element of the curriculum, most importantly because it teaches hand coordination skills.

There is no reason why the two approaches to writing cannot coexist or even complement each other. The decision must be when to rely on each.

Concerns over electronic dictionaries may also be misplaced. They are properly viewed as aids to poor typists, not a crutch for those who cannot spell. Spelling and grammar checkers can contribute greatly to better final products, largely free of mechanical errors. They may, over time, help students improve their initial writing by pointing out errors that would otherwise have been part of the submitted work. Immediate feedback promotes learning better than red marks on a paper. The creative teacher may wish to establish some incentive for the fewest errors found by a writing aid to reinforce the importance of careful initial work.

COMPUTER INFALLIBILITY

The reverence with which some still view computers can be a frightening thing. We have already referred to the problem of unquestioning acceptance of a computer's results in the discussion of mathematics and computers. But the issue goes well beyond this.

Riedesel and Clements (1985, pp. 268–269) offered two interesting examples of the potential problem. One involved a student not being allowed to enroll in a course because the computer said the classroom had space for only 25 students, when in fact 30 could be accommodated. The real problem was not the error in the computer's information, but the unwillingness of the registration staff to find a solution. In essence, there was a denial that a problem existed.

The second example was drawn from the famous computer analyst Eliza created by Joseph Weizenbaum, an artificial intelligence researcher at MIT. This program essentially attempts to simulate a Rogerian counseling session, with the computer responding in a nondirective manner and probing for more information based on what the "client" has said. For Weizenbaum, the program was merely an early experiment in artificial intelligence. He was totally unprepared for the acceptance given his creation by users, even professional psychiatrists, who saw in it something far beyond Weizenbaum's intent. He has since become a vocal critic of attempts to further anthropomorphize the computer.

These examples deal with two separate aspects of the issue: outright computer errors and misapplication of programs. Computer users must never lose sight of the fact that errors do occur, both in programs and in the data provided to them. Many credit card holders have already encountered problems with an account and were horrified at the difficulty in correcting them. Of the arguments mustered for requiring students (and teachers) to have some modest experience in programming, the claim that this alone can engender appreciation for the true source of computer errors has definite merit. Within the computer education program, it is critical that students develop understandings of the real nature of computers, their capabilities and limitations, and their proper application.

CHANGING ROLES

The influx of computers into education has the potential to profoundly alter the roles of all concerned: teachers, students, and parents. Let's briefly consider each group. For a much more detailed and philosophical approach to these issues, refer to Ragsdale (1988).

TEACHERS

In our discussion of implementation concerns in the previous chapter, we suggested some of the issues related to staff development. We agree with many observers who see teacher knowledge as the single greatest obstacle to integration of computers into education. There is much new content knowledge that teachers suddenly need to acquire. There are skills to be developed in computing. But what of the teacher's classroom role?

As computers enable the individualization of instruction so long dreamed of by educators, the role of the teacher will truly change from dispenser of knowledge to facilitator and guide through the learning process. Teachers will need to help students learn to use their electronic assistants effectively. They will need to be guides to the vast resources available to the student.

For the foreseeable future, many teachers will also have to accept the fact that some of their students know far more about computers than they do themselves. This is a most difficult realization for many, and yet the problem is almost solely the teacher's. Few students are bothered by the fact that they must help the teacher with something on the computer. Rather, it can be an interesting contribution to the student's emerging self-image to be able to do things that an adult cannot.

All teachers will one day be computer-competent, but not all will be computer teachers. The goal must be for the computer to be no more noticeable in the educational process than is the pencil today. This obviously cannot occur until teachers have assimilated computers into their own professional lives.

There are practical issues that are vitally important. How does one educate teachers in the potential and practical use of the microcomputer as an important education tool? One could answer this by responding that computer education will eventually become part of all teacher-training curricula. But then, what about the teachers who are currently in our schools? Again, one could answer that continuing education will remedy this dilemma. But both of these solutions must be put into practice. This will take time and is already meeting resistance from those who are not familiar with the educational potential of microcomputers.

Finally, we must be cognizant of the time demands placed on teachers using computers. The time requirements in selecting appropriate courseware compared to other learning materials were discussed in Chapter 9. In addition, support materials may need to be developed. Student progress must be monitored and finally assessed. While these are familiar activities, they often require that time be spent at a computer to even begin, rather than being mulled over during lunch or while driving. Teaching with computers is more work and more difficult than traditional teaching.

Ragsdale (1988, pp. 187–208) provided extensive discussion of the role of the teacher in the computer era. He analyzed five aspects of teachers and teaching: theoretical, dispensing, guiding, collaborating, and professional. Readers will find this work thought-provoking.

STUDENTS

The role of the student is also changing in the Information Age. The exponential growth of knowledge and information makes it impossible for students to "learn" everything they will need in their lives. Rather, they must learn how to obtain and manipulate the information they need from the multitude of resources at their disposal.

Today's younger students are growing up with computers as a natural part of their lives. They do not view them as something unusual, but simply as a normal tool for daily living. The promise of computers for students is that they are being "acted upon" less by the educational process and becoming more active shapers of their own growth and development. This is well illustrated by the experiences of students with Logo and data bases, to single out just two examples. Students are confronting their world differently than their parents did. They are becoming more sophisticated problem solvers and have new opportunities to develop thinking skills. These are essential life skills of the Information Age.

At the same time, educators dare not lose sight of the fact that living is more than just information management. However sophisticated students become in using computers for the "mechanical" side of life, they must still develop interpersonal and social skills to cope with "human" concerns. The educational system may be able to devote far less time to traditional concerns, but it dare not abdicate responsibility for assisting in the development of the complete human being. It is in this area that the personal touch will never be lost (Ragsdale, 1988, pp. 159–186).

PARENTS

The traditional role of parents in educating children is also changing. This has been nearly the total responsibility of the schools in the past, with parents providing encouragement and perhaps some help with homework. Computers are altering this role (Ragsdale, 1988, pp. 209–224).

To really allow the microcomputer to become an effective partner in the educational process, not only must the teacher become familiar with its effective use, but parents of children should similarly become familiar with microcomputer educational usage. This need for parent education may be a considerably more difficult problem than present or future teacher preparation, but is nonetheless almost as important if the microcomputer is to reach its full potential in our educational system.

Many families have already brought a computer into the home, opening up new possibilities for learning. More will follow in coming years. In those homes where parents are themselves computer-competent, they will be able to assist their children in new ways. They may, however, be unprepared for the task of selecting computer learning materials for home use, as material selection has long been a school responsibility. Educators should consider establishing ways of assisting parents in this task.

Even greater problems loom for parents who perceive a need for a computer at home but are strangers to the technology themselves. Just as the new math caused many difficulties for parents seeking to help their children, so too may computers, probably to an even greater extent. Again we see a role for the schools to play in developing computer competence in parents through adult education programs.

Computers in the home raise new fears of educational equity, an issue touched upon previously. Just as differences in school budgets are contributing to a potential widening of the gap between the haves and have nots, so too may technology in the home (Stone, 1987). Some districts have addressed this issue by providing parents with the opportunity to borrow computers for home use. This is a concept worthy of serious consideration.

SUMMARY

In this chapter we have sought to identify and provide perspective on issues arising from the spread of computers throughout society. Consideration of such issues is a critical component of any computer education program, however difficult to address.

The social impact of computers requires careful attention, lest we awaken too late to changes that profoundly affect our lives. Educators must guide their students in thinking about all aspects of the computer's impact on where and how we work, and our personal privacy. Computers have come to pervade society today with little thought given to their effects on individuals. It is not too late to develop a critical stance.

Schools must take a leading role in developing understanding of ethics related to computers. The earliest and most obvious area of concern is software piracy. By example and by teaching, computer users must learn that software is property, which is protected both legally and ethically. Attention to this matter can come in the early grades. Somewhat later, students should be exposed to concerns over abuse of computer systems, ranging from seemingly innocent "hacking" to full-scale computer crime and the release of computer viruses.

Major concerns for education and society arise from the issue of equity. While the computer as an educational tool offers genuine potential to benefit all students, economic reality suggests that not all will have access to it. How should this problem be approached? In addition, where computers are readily available, concerns exist over use of them by both sexes. To the extent that computers are now more of a "male" experience, what should and can be done to correct the imbalance?

Computer education must also guard against the danger that students will come to see the computer as the answer to all concerns. We must learn *when* and *when not* to use the computer, and *how* to use it wisely. Thoughtless acceptance of computer output could be enormously harmful.

Finally, the computer is having a significant effect on the educational roles of teachers, students, and parents. To produce the most positive outcome, these changes need to be confronted directly. Both teachers and parents require special help in adapting to their new roles, so that students gain maximum benefit from the technology at hand.

CHAPTER 17 ACTIVITIES

1. What do you see as the major areas of computer impact on work? Are there concerns with any of these that should be addressed?
2. Ask acquaintances in different kinds of jobs how computers have changed their work in the past few years.
3. If possible, talk with someone who works from home through telecommunications.
4. Identify several aspects of the effects of computers on personal privacy. How might privacy be better protected? Interview local police, credit bureaus, or banks about the kinds of information available in their data bases, the importance of computers to them, and their perceptions of privacy issues.
5. What is your position on software duplication that goes beyond the copyright law? Is there such a thing as "fair use" of software? How should schools present this issue to students?
6. What, if anything, should be done if a student were to bring an illegal copy of a software product to school for personal use?
7. Should such ethical issues as hacking and white collar crime be considered in the curriculum? If so, where? How?
8. What do you see as the major equity issues of computing? How can schools contribute to solution of these issues? Interview a school superintendent, board member, and community activist for their views.
9. Is it possible to become overly dependent on computers? If so, how would you as a computer educator deal with the issue? Research the controversy over calculators in arithmetic instruction.
10. Describe your perceptions of the changing roles of teachers, students, and parents. How can this change be managed? Talk with teachers who use computers to obtain their experiences.

REFERENCES

"1987 Statement on Software Copyright." *The Computing Teacher*, March 1987, pp. 52–53.

Bear, G. C. "Teaching Computer Ethics: Why, What, Who, When, and How." *Computers in the Schools*, Summer 1986, pp. 113–118.

Becker, H. *Microcomputers in the Classroom. Dreams and Realities*. Eugene, OR: International Council for Computers in Education, undated.

Bitter, G. *Computers in Today's World*. New York: John Wiley and Sons, 1984.

Bozeman, W. *Computers and Computing in Education*. Scottsdale, AZ: Gorsuch Scarisbrick Publishers, 1985.

Campbell, P., and Fein, G. *Young Children and Microcomputers*. Englewood Cliffs, NJ: Prentice-Hall, 1986.

Chaffin, E. "Computer Viruses: An Epidemic Real or Imagined?" *Electronic Learning*, April 1989, pp. 36–37.

"Code of Ethical Conduct for Computer-Using Educators." *The Computing Teacher*, February 1987, pp. 51–53.

Collis, B. *Computers, Curriculum, and Whole-Class Instruction*. Belmont, CA: Wadsworth, 1988.

Collis, B. "Sex Differences in Secondary School Students' Attitudes Toward Computers." *The Computing Teacher*, April 1985, pp. 33–36.

Collis, B., and Ollila, L. "An Examination of Sex Difference in Secondary School Students' Attitudes Toward Writing and Toward Computers." *The Alberta Journal of Educational Research*, 32(4), 1986, pp. 297–306.

"Computer Hacker, 18, Gets Prison for Fraud." *Chicago Tribune*, 15 February 1989, Section 2, p. 3.

Demetrulias, D. M., and Rosenthal, N. R. "Discrimination Against Females and Minorities in Microcomputer Advertising." *Computers and the Social Sciences*, April–June 1985, pp. 91–95.

Fetler, M. "Sex Differences on the California Statewide Assessment of Computer Literacy." *Sex Roles*, August 1985, pp. 181–191.

Fisher, G. "Access to Computers." *The Computing Teacher*, April 1985, pp. 24–27.

Flaherty, D. "Computers and the New Culture: Where Are the Role Models?" *Educational Technology*, June 1985, p. 34.

Flake, J., McClintock, C., and Turner, S. *Fundamentals of Computer Education*. Belmont, CA: Wadsworth, 1985.

Gantz, J. "Of Unix, Worms, and Viruses: Science Fiction Becomes Real." *InfoWorld*, 21 November 1988, p. 40.

Gilliland, K., and Pollard, M. "Ethics and Computer Use." *The Computing Teacher*, August/September 1984, p. 19.

Hess, R. D., and Miura, I. T. "Gender Differences in Enrollment in Computer Camps and Classes." *Sex Roles*, August 1985, pp. 193–203.

Hoffman, C. "Access and Equity: Computers for Everyone." *T.H.E. Journal*, May 1985, pp. 72–74.

Hollis, R. "Government Computers Under Siege." *MacWEEK*, 26 April 1988, pp. 1, 8.

Jorde, P. "Microcomputers and the Pro-Innovation Bias." *The Educational Digest*, February 1987, pp. 36–39.

Kinzer, C. K., Sherwood, R. D., and Bransford, J. D. *Computer Strategies for Education*. Columbus: Merrill Publishing, 1986. (Chapter 7)

Linn, M. C. "Gender Equity Computer Learning Environments." *Computers and the Social Sciences*, April-June 1985, pp. 19–27.

Lockheed, M. E., and Frakt, S. B. "Sex Equity: Increasing Girls' Use of Computers." *The Computing Teacher*, May 1984, pp. 16–18.

Lockheed, M. E., Nielsen, A., and Stone, M. K. "Determinants of Microcomputer Literacy in High School Students." *Journal of Educational Computing Research*, 1985, *1*(1), pp. 81–96.

Maddux, C. D., and Woods, R. "Equity for the Mildly Handicapped." *The Computing Teacher*, February 1987, pp. 16–17, 49.

Mandell, C. J., and Mandell, S. L. *Computers in Education Today*. St. Paul, MN: West Publishing, 1989. (Chapter 11)

McCarthy, R. "Making the Future Work." *Electronic Learning*, September 1988, pp. 42–46.

McMeen, G. R. "The Impact of Technological Change on Education." *Educational Technology*, February 1986, pp. 42–45.

Miura, I. T. "The Relationship of Computer Self-Efficacy Expectations to Computer Interest and Course Enrollment in College." *Sex Roles*, March 1987, pp. 303–311.

Naron, N. K., and Estes, N. "Technology in the Schools: Trends and Policies." *AEDS Journal*, Summer 1986, pp. 31–43.

Olson, J. *Schoolworlds/Microworlds*. Oxford (UK): Pergamon Press, 1988.

Pantiel, M., and Petersen, B. *Kids, Teachers, and Computers*. Englewood Cliffs, NJ: Prentice-Hall, 1984.

Peterson, D. "9 Issues. Will Education Be Different (Better) in the Year 2000?" *Popular Computing*, Mid-October 1984, Special Issue—*Guide to Computers in Education*, pp. 10–18.

Ragsdale, R. G. *Permissible Computing in Education. Values, Assumptions, and Needs*. New York: Praeger, 1988.

Riedesel, C., and Clements, D. *Coping with Computers in the Elementary and Middle Schools*. Englewood Cliffs, NJ: Prentice-Hall, 1985.

Rosenthal, N. R., and Demetrulias, D. M. "Assessing Gender Bias in Computer Software." *Computers in the Schools*, 1988, *5*(1/2), pp. 153–163.

Sanders, J. S., and Stone, A. *The Neuter Computer: Computers for Girls and Boys*. New York: Neal-Schuman Publishers, 1986.

Scrogan, L. "The Online Underworld." *Classroom Computer Learning*, February 1988, p. 58.

Shelly, G., and Cashman, T. *Computer Fundamentals for an Information Age*. Brea, CA: Anaheim Publishing, 1984.

Siann, G., Durndell, A., Macleod, H., and Glissov, P. "Stereotyping in Relation to the Gender Gap in Participation in Computing." *Educational Research*, 1988, *30*(2), pp. 98–103.

Stone, A. "Action for Equity." *The Computing Teacher*, November 1986, pp. 54–55.

Stone, A. "Action for Equity—II." *The Computing Teacher*, December-January 1986–87, pp. 54–56.

Stone, A. "Computers in the Home—A Learning Advantage for the Affluent?" *The Computing Teacher*, June 1987, pp. 54–55.

Swadener, M., and Hannafin, M. "Gender Similarities and Differences in Sixth Graders' Attitudes Toward Computers: An Exploratory Study." *Educational Technology*, January 1987, pp. 37–42.

Talab, R. "Copyright, Software and the School Librarian." *The Computing Teacher,* December-January 1986–87, pp. 43–45.

"Technology and the At-Risk Student." *Electronic Learning,* November/December 1988, pp. 35–49.

Turkle, S. *The Second Self: Computers and the Human Spirit.* New York: Simon and Schuster, 1984.

Using Software. A Guide to the Ethical and Legal Use of Software for Members of the Academic Community, ERIC Document Reproduction Service, ED 288 494, 1987.

Vockell, E., and Schwartz, E. *The Computer in the Classroom.* Santa Cruz, CA: Mitchell Publishing, 1988.

Winter, C. "Viruses Threatening Era of Computer Freedom." *Chicago Tribune,* 21 February 1988, Section 7, pp. 1, 8.

□ PART 6 □

Looking Ahead

C H A P T E R 18

□ *Today and Tomorrow* □

O B J E C T I V E S

After completing this chapter, you will be able to:

□ *List and briefly describe at least three trends in computer hardware that should continue into the future.* □

□ *Explain what future directions in software are apt to be.* □

□ *Synthesize your knowledge and experiences into your own scenario for the future of computers in education.* □

□ *Define and critically evaluate the role you foresee for yourself in the realization of your scenario.* □

Before we address the final topic in our survey of microcomputers in education, let's recap what you have accomplished thus far.

LOOKING BACK

GETTING STARTED

This book began with a look into the past. In Chapter 1 you gained an overview of the gradual development of data-processing devices and early computing equipment. Covered in more detail were the past hundred or so years that saw the creation of first our modern mainframe computers, then microcomputers geared particularly for individual use. This set the stage for our focus on microcomputers for educators and how they can be used in the learning processes of both children and adults.

To explore the potential uses of microcomputers, you first must gain an understanding of what this new type of computer really is. Chapter 2 focused on the hardware of the microcomputer system and presented a brief look at how this hardware is controlled. There are two basic ways that you can direct a microcomputer to perform useful and desired tasks: use a program that has been written by someone else, or personally write a program.

THE COMPUTER AS TOOL

The typical user controls a microcomputer with a program written by other individuals and simply purchased. You considered fundamental "tool" applications, software capable of helping teachers and students in common tasks. Such programs can be grouped by function.

The first major function examined was word processing. Chapter 3 presented the concepts of writing via microcomputer and some of the supporting software available in this area. Chapter 4 introduced the second function, file management or data bases, and Chapter 5 examined the third function, electronic spreadsheets. Again, both concepts and software were presented, with special attention to their application in an educational setting.

In Chapter 6, you explored telecommunications and many applications areas related to teacher support. Programs of this type are of special interest to classroom teachers and can be helpful in many aspects of materials preparation. Integrated software, presented in Chapter 7, combines multiple functions into a single package. You considered advantages and disadvantages of this approach.

THE COMPUTER AS TUTOR

Next, you turned to direct intervention of the computer in the learning process. Chapter 8 focused on applications for learning in the classroom. You examined computer-assisted instruction (CAI) in detail. Drills, tutorials, and simulations can become an integral part of the instructional process.

Chapter 9 suggested frameworks useful in evaluating educational software. There is a considerable quantity of software available today. Some of it is very good, while much is not. You, the professional educator, must choose wisely. You developed guidelines for prudent and informed program selection.

The section concluded with consideration of the principles and potential of computer assistance in organizing and administering educational programs. We referred to this as computer-managed instruction (CMI) in Chapter 10.

THE COMPUTER AS LEARNER

Next, attention turned from using prewritten programs to the computer learning to perform tasks required by the user. Chapter 11 presented an overview of computer programming and the various levels of languages.

In Chapter 12 you met Logo, a graphics-oriented language that is often used with young children. It is also a language that approaches programming from a specific philosophical and psychological perspective. Most other microcomputer languages are a downward extension of mainframe programming languages, for which applications development is the guiding criterion.

The most widely used language for microcomputer programming is BASIC. Chapter 13 presented this language and attempted to provide you with a conceptual foundation for understanding programming in BASIC.

Chapter 14 surveyed other programming languages in use today. Consideration was given to both general-purpose languages taught in schools and specialized authoring tools, including *HyperCard* and expert system shells, that can simplify teacher and student development of original software.

MICROCOMPUTERS IN EDUCATION

In the last section of this book, you looked at the historic buzzword topic of *computer literacy* (Chapter 15), considering what it has meant and how it has given way to *curriculum integration*. Practical concerns of implementation were the theme of Chapter 16. The knowledge base developed in previous chapters is of minimal value until a coherent program of computer education is created. Finally, Chapter 17 raised issues and implications of computers in society and education. *You* will contribute to developing answers to the issues presented.

LOOKING AHEAD

You have now reached this final chapter. Having covered the past and the present, you will now examine future directions. The discussion is divided into the areas of hardware, software, and computers in education. We offer our observations with no claim to possessing a crystal ball. Predicting the future is both difficult and risky. As Naisbitt (1982) wrote in *Megatrends*, ''The gee-whiz futurists are always wrong because they believe technological innovation travels in a straight line. It doesn't. It weaves and bobs and lurches and sputters" (p. 41). We may do no better. We also agree with Naisbitt (p. 2) that "The most reliable way to anticipate the future is by understanding the present." Some trends seem clear.

TRENDS IN MICROCOMPUTER HARDWARE

MICROPROCESSORS

The internal processing speeds of microprocessors will continue to increase. We have already witnessed the change from an Apple II operating at 1 MHz (megahertz) to 80386 and 80486 PCs operating at 30 MHz and more. As faster and more complex chips are developed and integrated into microcomputer systems, programs that execute faster and more complex tasks become feasible for micros. The lines between micros and "larger" computers continue to blur.

MEMORY

Memory sizes (and needs) will increase further. Whereas initially the upper memory limit for microcomputers was 48K of RAM, most of today's machines are being delivered with 128K to 2 MB of memory. As the capacity of memory chips increases and their cost decreases, even greater memory sizes will become commonplace. Some machines can already be expanded to 16 megabytes of memory. Microcomputers with memories equal to mainframes of the early 1980s are already here.

With such increases in memory, the sheer power available to the educator in each microcomputer becomes enormous, and the variety and sophistication of potential uses increases, as appropriate software is developed.

MASS STORAGE

To accompany increased memory sizes, storage devices such as diskettes also have to increase in capacity. The roughly 100K floppy diskette has given way to the 200K floppy that, in turn, has been replaced by the 400K floppy. Already on the market are 800K and 1.5 megabyte (1500K) diskettes. Early hard disks held 5 megabytes, then 10 megabytes. Today, 20 megabyte and larger hard disks are readily available at reasonable cost, with capacities to 300 MB available. These trends will also continue. For the educator, this may one day bring an end to fumbling with quantities of floppy diskettes for each class.

Storage devices that use different approaches to data retention will become common. Probably the most interesting of these are optical discs similar to audio compact disks (CDs), with capacities in the hundreds of millions of bytes. This CD–ROM technology will advance beyond its original read-only form, suitable for on-line encyclopedias and stable data bases, to read-write forms

CDs and laser discs offer many benefits.

paralleling the capabilities of magnetic devices. CDs will provide an inexpensive way to distribute data by subscription, thereby updating the information regularly. Educators will have never-before-dreamed-of data at their fingertips as optical drives become standard equipment.

Aside from data storage, optical discs offer the solution to the comparative crudeness and large memory requirements of computer graphics. There will be less need to "simulate" reality when the real thing can be shown and even overlayed with computer text or drawings. Animation will give way in many situations to actual motion segments on a videodisc. CD format may replace the 12″ laser disc, possibly in the digital video interactive format (DV–I).

INPUT/OUTPUT (I/O)

Spurred by artificial intelligence research, computers will become easier to use by requiring less accommodation on the part of users. Keyboard use will be minimized by advances in touch screens, alternative devices derived from the mouse concept and from scanner technology, followed eventually by voice recognition.

Voice synthesized output also will become more common. Flat screen monitors will increase in resolution until common systems deliver an image comparable to 35mm photography. Prices of laser printers will fall sufficiently to displace other types of printers for hardcopy. Color laser printing will become affordable for schools.

PHYSICAL SIZE

Advances in microelectronics produced the portable computer, then the battery-powered laptop, then the miniature laptop that fits in a briefcase. The *Wizard,* introduced by Sharp in 1988, may foretell the dawn of the pocket computer with real power. Telecommunications capabilities make such small packages far more useful than would otherwise be true. The day of the computer as paper and pencil is rapidly approaching. However, small computers will never replace desktop models.

TELECOMMUNICATIONS AND NETWORKING

Telecommunication will become increasingly common. The linking of computer to computer via phone lines for the fast and efficient exchange of information will develop to the point of being easy and cost-effective. Already, large-scale data bases are available in many fields, including law and medicine, and have begun to appear for the educator.

Networking is another area that is becoming increasingly important. An individual will not only be able to communicate with other microcomputers, but also tie into larger mainframe computers and make use of their unique capabilities as needed. In addition, microcomputer users will gain access to sophisticated peripherals such as large laser printers and massive storage systems that are not cost-effective for single users. Electronic mail systems are also common on networks.

Among educators, telecommunications and networking will gain, particularly in rural areas where they may represent the most cost-effective solution to distance education problems before they attain comparable status in more urban settings.

COSTS

The general trend in hardware cost has been downward from the beginning. Partly this is a result of economies of scale resulting from increased demand, partly from intense competition in the marketplace. However, prices of memory chips have fluctuated, sometimes drastically. Clearly, there is instability in pricing, just as there is in other industries.

It appears that at least a temporary system price plateau has been reached, now that a *complete* entry-level microcomputer system, including color monitor, can be purchased for $1000 or less. Prices for PC–XT clones and basic Apple II systems have held at that level for some time. There is clearly no cost justification for schools to delay purchasing hardware. Each term or year waited carries with it significant "opportunity cost," that is, lost opportunity to improve education.

In some cases, costs have not fallen, but a given price purchases more: a faster CPU, more standard memory, built-in features that were previously optional. This trend will continue to the benefit of all.

THE FUTURE OF SOFTWARE

Almost from the beginning, advances in hardware have outpaced progress in software development. High-performance hardware readily available in 1990 had little or no software which actually capitalized on the potential. Software will evolve, but remain far behind the hardware for the foreseeable future.

SELECTION

Rapid growth in the number of microcomputer users will create demand for software to which the market will respond. Software writers will not only produce high-quality software in the areas that are now important, they will also search for additional areas of microcomputer applications where there is presently little if any software available. Who knows what the next *VisiCalc* will be, but you can be sure there will be one.

COMPLEXITY

Software will grow in capability; i.e., packages will do more than ever before. As memory size and storage capacities increase and computers become faster, the programs themselves will become more comprehensive in their scope. No longer constrained by small and inefficient hardware, the program writer can develop software that meets the needs of today's complex situations.

Related to this is the trend toward easier-to-use software. At the same time that more powerful and more efficient hardware allows for more complex programs, it also allows for the programming to make such programs easier to use, the so-called human-machine interface. Some of the gain will come from nearly universal adoption of GUI (Graphical *U*ser *I*nterface) and WIMP interfaces (*W*indows, *I*cons, *M*ouse, *P*ointer) which Apple popularized with the Macintosh. Still more may come from artificial intelligence research. For instance, *neural networks* are an aspect of artificial intelligence (AI) which seeks to directly model the human mind. Neural networks can recognize patterns, reach decisions, and learn from their experience. In fact, in a sense one does not program a neural network; one "teaches" it by example. Software such as *The Cognitron, NeuralWorks,* and *NeuroShell* are already on the market as we write. Applications programs which include such concepts behind the scenes will represent a whole new generation of "intelligent" software.

COST

Software may more clearly split into low- and high-cost sectors. Significant reductions in cost for educational software seem unlikely. Typical products are already relatively inexpensive, and the availability of heavily discounted multi-disk lab packs and network versions leaves little room for further reductions. As software complexity grows, development costs also increase. Thus, truly sophisticated software is and will remain costly, at least until a significant market for each product type develops. Eventually, some advances pioneered in high-cost products filter down into the less-expensive ones as well.

SOFTWARE FOR LEARNING

Higher-quality educational software will be developed for in-school use. As both the theory and application of microcomputer teaching and learning are better understood, a new generation of educational software will be developed. This software will take better advantage of the capabilities of the microcomputer as part of the educational process and will better assist the teacher. It will interact with students in far more sophisticated ways, thanks again to developments in artificial intelligence.

With the heavy involvement of traditional publishing houses in the software industry, expect to see more and more software as part of a complete set of teaching materials accompanying text series and individual books. One can envision a day when every textbook sold to schools will come with correlated software, possibly even "free" to stimulate book sales. Books, however, are not likely to disappear.

Home use of educational software will increase to supplement the educational programs of schools. Education will no longer be confined to the school with the home as the place where "homework" is done. The home should become a more integral part of the total educational process.

MULTI-MEDIA

Computer courseware will expand in scope and realism with further developments in interactive video technologies. The experimentation now under way outside of education will soon benefit teachers and students as well. Using still and motion sequences, simulations will take on new levels of sophistication. Dual stereo sound tracks will serve many purposes, including bilingual and foreign language education. In effect, multi-media courseware built around optical discs unites the potential of all other media into truly interactive instruction. The impact will be greatest when courseware on CD becomes available and CD drives become common in microcomputer systems, as already included in Steven Jobs' NeXT computer.

COMPUTERS IN EDUCATION

Whatever exciting developments there may be in hardware and software, their ultimate significance to teachers is their future in our schools.

GLIMPSES OF THE FUTURE

Countless views of the future have been offered, and we list many in the chapter references for your perusal. In most cases, the projections of the early 1980s have not yet been achieved. Will they ever? In many cases, we believe the answer is no. Predictions have been made that the computer will save education! This reflects "the danger of the technofix mentality" (Naisbitt, 1982, p. 52). Realists do not see computer technology as the answer to all the ills of education. In fact, Dede (1987) maintained that we really have no idea yet how best to use computers in education. His arguments merit consideration.

Others like Collis (1988) present visions of the future which are easy to embrace, but which, upon reflection, lack enabling practicality. Who would not wish for a networked lab in every elementary school, multiple labs in every high school, several computers for each classroom with modems where useful, computers for home loan, and so on. While not exceeding reason in terms of expected outcomes, such visions do not seem to take into account the cold reality of school finance, for instance.

Still others share the approach to the future that we took in the first edition of this book (e.g., Lillie, Hannum, and Stuck, 1989). That was to posit three potential scenarios. One is a very gloomy view that computers are just a fad and will soon go the way of film loop projectors. The evidence we offered to support such a view was unclear academic benefits, funding problems, technological backlash, and lack of trained teachers. Slightly less pessimistic was the view that the computer status quo would prevail; schools would drift along on the current plateau. We suggested that limited equipment and teacher training and an absence of clear goals supported such a view.

However, our dream and hope was that advances in computer use would occur. We justified this view from the standpoints of software improvement, the undeniable need for new life tools in the information age, declining costs, and pressures external to the schools.

ASSESSMENT OF THOSE FUTURES

As we enter the 1990s, where do we stand? How do our three scenarios stand up?

We see no evidence that computers have declined. It is probably also inaccurate to claim that the status quo has prevailed. Academic benefits are clearer today and the feared backlash has not developed. There is more hardware in the schools than ever before, but funding, teacher training, and clear goals for computers in education remain problematic.

This leaves only the third view of advancement and, in fact, there has been progress. The factors we cited to support an advance remain true, but progress has been slower than we had hoped. In fact, as you learned in chapters 15 and 16, the whole thrust has changed somewhat. We now see the goal differently than we did, and with it, our view for its realization. No longer do we project a scenario in which most teachers quickly make peace with the computer, nor is this necessary.

TOWARD THE 21ST CENTURY

The future of computers in education should not be described as a revolution. That implies fast, pervasive change. Has there ever been an educational revolution? Is one truly thinkable?

The proper goal for computers in education is *invisible integration*. The computer becomes such an essential part of education that we cease to notice or think about it. It is no more remarkable than a book or chalkboard. It is unique in its power and capabilities, but still fundamentally a tool in the service of learning. Children are expected to learn to read, write, cipher, spell, and behave in school. They will also experience the computer as a resource, a tool, not something as uncommon as a field trip.

As a tool, the computer has the potential for application to all parts of the curriculum. Ideally, it should be used throughout, and it will be one day. For now, we must acknowledge the realities of education and human nature. The best we can honestly project is evolution toward the goal. Those teachers already convinced of the benefits of computers who are filled with ideas for their application deserve full support. The number of such teachers in any school will increase in two ways. Schools will demand computer competence of those seeking positions. They will also provide frequent *opportunity* for non-users to be exposed to potential uses. This will not be the typical large institute day, but targeted experiences that are as informal as possible, demonstrations conducted by credible peers. The goal is to present so conclusively the benefits of using computers that teachers will *want* to use them. Effective usage will spread as more teachers understand the benefits and schools provide the support systems they need. The days of putting a computer, its manuals, and some diskettes in the back of the room and hoping for change will end.

Where will this lead us? Initially, there may be only isolated pockets of computer use in a given school. To use an analogy, such pockets can be like small sparks in a pile of leaves. There is likely to be only a little smoke at first, but if you fan that smoke enough, flames will burst forth. As the flames spread, add sticks, then branches, finally logs to the pile until you have a blaze. It's not as fast as pouring something flammable on the pile to begin, but it will work. In retrospect, we thought we were using a flammable material to spread computers throughout our schools, but it may have had the effect of water instead.

A core of willing and able teachers exists in most schools. They can get the ball rolling. But is that enough to justify the computers already in our schools? Don't we need to move more decisively? Won't the board of education object to a modest goal?

The real question is, What do we have now? We know of schools where there is a computer in every room. Most are unused. Is that better than putting all of them in the room of the one teacher who *would* use them? We think not. Is that better than sending unused ones home with teachers? We think not. Have we achieved anything of consequence when a student can say, "Yes, we have a computer in my classroom, but we never use it." We think not.

What all of this comes down to is a realization that we must accept less in the short run than we had hoped for. We do so in realistic expectation of greater results in the long run. In some respects, computers are like technologies that have gone before them. They arrived with great fanfare and with high expectations. Reality sank in fairly soon. Many educators were disappointed with what was achieved.

But that does not mean failure. Rather, it is like a partially filled glass of water. The pessimist views such a glass as half empty, the optimist sees it as half full. Again, to extend this analogy, the "computers in education" glass is half-full, and a slow trickle is flowing into it. We'd still like to turn the trickle into a real flow, but experience suggests a need for patience. Whatever we accomplish along the path toward our goal, we will be ahead compared to having done nothing at all. It has been a lesson in setting more realistic goals.

REFLECTIONS

The ultimate vision of the future is one in which the computer attracts no more attention than a calculator does today. Students will interact with computers through varied input devices with no more thought than is given to pressing a button in an elevator to signal one's destination. The computer will merely be one of our daily servants, enabling us to do more than previous generations could dream of. The potential for impact is throughout the curriculum. So must be the implementation.

As a teacher, you are critical to the future. With a vision of what the computer can mean in the curriculum, you can develop skills to implement your vision. You alone with one computer in your classroom can accomplish more than many schools have with 20 unused computers. Your example and enthusiasm can encourage others to explore the possibilities. Your willingness to share your knowledge and skills can ease the transformation of a skeptical or technophobic colleague into a hesitant, then comfortable computer educator. *You* are the key to the future of computers in education.

CONCLUSION

This book has attempted to present an overview of the expanding field of educational microcomputing. This is a field that has quickly become important to all of us as educators and one that cannot be ignored. It will become increasingly important in most aspects of the educational process. You have already made a commitment to become both a more knowledgeable user of microcomputers and a better teacher using microcomputers. In this way, it is our hope that you will make microcomputers count.

CHAPTER 18 ACTIVITIES

1. Which of the trends in hardware developments do you believe will be most significant for education? Why?
2. What developments in software would you most like to see? What, if any, evidence gives you hope that these will occur?
3. Develop and justify your own vision of the future. What contributions do you foresee making personally to that vision?

REFERENCES

Abrams, A. "Twelve Modest Proposals for Tomorrow's Technology." *TechTrends*, January/February 1987, pp. 18–20.

Ambron, S., and Hooper, K., eds. *CD–ROM 3. Interactive Multimedia*. Redmond, WA: Microsoft Press, 1988.

"Archives in Miniature." *PC Magazine*, 31 January 1989, pp. 185–200.

Blankenhorn, D. "The Latest in Accessories for the Laptop on the Go." *Chicago Tribune*, 19 March 1989, Section 20, pp. 19, 26.

Bove, T., and Rhodes, C. " 'Interactive Multimedia' Bringing It All Together." *Chicago Tribune*, 19 March 1989, Section 20, pp. 17, 20, 26.

Brownstein, M. "Bellcore Works on Chip Using 'Neural Network' Technology." *InfoWorld*, 26 September 1988, p. 24.

Brownstein, M. "Sharp's Wizard Device Can Upload and Download Data from Any PC." *InfoWorld*, 17 October 1988, p. 27.

Brownstein, M. "To Boldly Go Where No PC Has Gone Before. . ." *InfoWorld*, 8 February 1988, pp. 20–21.

Bulkeley, W. M. "GTE Test Offers View of Video Future." *Wall Street Journal*, 29 December 1988, p. B1.

Collis, B. *Computers, Curriculum, and Whole-Class Instruction*. Belmont, CA: Wadsworth, 1988.

Colvin, L. B. "An Overview of U.S. Trends in Educational Software Design." *The Computing Teacher*, February 1989, pp. 24–28.

Dede, C. J. "Empowering Environments, Hypermedia, and Microworlds." *The Computing Teacher*, November 1987, pp. 20–24, 61.

Dertouzos, M. L. "Introduction: Trends in Computing." *Scientific American Trends in Computing*, Special Issue, Vol. 1, 1988, pp. 8–13. (The entire issue merits reading.)

Elmer-DeWitt, P. "Computers of the Future. Fast and Smart." *Time*, 28 March 1988, pp. 54–58.

Evans, N. *The Future of the Microcomputer in Schools.* Houndmills, Basingstoke, Hampshire (UK): Macmillan Education Ltd., 1987.

Friedman, D. "A Fantasy: Educational Computing in 2010." *Electronic Education,* May-June 1985, pp. 10–11, 33.

Galloway, P. "Say Hello to a 'True' Talking Computer." *Chicago Tribune,* 18 December 1988, Section 5, p. 1.

Ginn, P. L., and Price, C. L. "The Facile WORM." *Instruction Delivery Systems,* September/October 1988, pp. 8–15.

Green, J. O. "Artificial Intelligence and the Future Classroom." *Classroom Computer Learning,* January 1984, pp. 26–31.

Hannaford, S. "Optical Illusions and Realities: The Medium Conveys the Memory." *MacWEEK,* 6 December 1988, pp. 40–42.

Lillie, D. L., Hannum, W. H., and Stuck, G. B. *Computers and Effective Instruction.* White Plains, NY: Longman Inc., 1989.

Lipson, J. I., and Fisher, K. M. "Technologies of the Future." *Education & Computing,* *1*(1), January 1985, pp. 11–23.

Little, A. "Technology Helps Rural Schools." *Chicago Tribune,* 5 March 1989, Section 20, pp. 7–8.

Magel, M. "Write-Once and Erasable Alternatives." *AV Video,* November 1988, pp. 45–47.

Mandell, C. J., and Mandell, S. L. *Computers in Education Today.* St. Paul, MN: West Publishing, 1989.

McClintock, R. O. "Marking the Second Frontier." *Teachers College Record,* Spring 1988, pp. 345–351.

Naisbitt, J. *Megatrends.* New York: Warner, 1982.

Nix, D. "Should Computers Know What You Can Do with Them?" *Teachers College Record,* Spring 1988, pp. 418–430.

Preparing Schools for the Year 2000. Chicago: Society for Visual Education, Inc., June 1988.

Priesmeyer, H. R. "Integrating Educational Software and Textbook Development." *Academic Computing,* September 1988, pp. 32–33, 50–51.

Ragsdale, R. G. *Permissible Computing in Education. Values, Assumptions, and Needs.* New York: Praeger, 1988.

Reed, S. "Voice-activated Computers Often Just the Answer" and "For the Handicapped, New Ways to Communicate." *Chicago Tribune,* 15 November 1987, Section 18, pp. 15, 17, 18.

"The Saturn School of Tomorrow." *Pioneer DiscTopics,* February 1989, p. 8.

Scully, J. "The Knowledge Navigator." *PC AI,* January/February 1989, p. 31.

Turner, J. A. " 'Consulting Scholars,' Backed by IBM, Help Colleges Explore the Role of Computers in Academic Life." *Chronicle of Higher Education,* 2 March 1988, pp. A11–A12.

Tyre, T., and Jones, P. "The Heart of an Apple II Hides in MS–DOS Micro." *T.H.E. Journal,* August 1988, pp. 12–13.

Visions 2000. A Vision of Educational Technology in Alberta by the Year 2000. Edmonton: Alberta Education, May 1987.

Westborough Technology Education Project, c/o Rick Hebert, Westborough Middle School, Westborough, MA 01581.

Whitmer, C. "HyperTV En Route to Desktop Reality." *MacWEEK,* 31 January 1989, pp. 1, 8, 20.

APPENDICES

APPENDIX A

SOFTWARE MENTIONED IN THE TEXT WITH SOURCES

1st Class (1st Class Expert Systems)
Activitymakers (Teacher's Aide, Inc.)
Adventures with Charts and Graphs: Project Zoo (National Geographic)
All of the Above (C & C Software)
All Star Drill (Tom Snyder)
Amanda Stories (Voyager)
Analogies Tutorial (Hartley)
Appleworks (Claris)
APPSTATS (STATSOFT)
Authorware Plus (Authorware)
Balance of Power (Mindscape)
Bank Street Filer (Sunburst)
Bank Street Writer (Scholastic)
Bibliography (PRO/TEM)
Black Magic (Ntergaid)
BOOKBRAIN (Knowledge Access)
BookWhiz (Educational Testing Service)
Cloze Plus (Milliken)
The Cognitron (Cognitive Software)
Compton's Encyclopedia (CD–ROM—Encyclopedia Brittanica)
CrossCountry California (Didatech)
Crossword Magic (Mindscape)
Data Warehouse (McGraw-Hill)
Dataquest series (MECC)
DB Master (StoneEdge Technologies)
dBASE (Ashton-Tate)
Decisions, Decisions (Tom Snyder)
Double Helix (Odesta)
The Election of 1912 (Eastgate Systems)
Electronic Mailbag (Exsym)
Electronic Village (Exsym)
ESL Picture Grammar (Gessler Software)
Excel (Microsoft)
Facemaker (Spinnaker)
The Factory (Sunburst)
File Express (Expressware)
Framework (Ashton-Tate)
FrEdBase (CUE Softswap)

FrEdWriter (CUE Softswap)
Friendly Filer (Houghton-Mifflin)
GeoWorld (Tom Snyder)
Ghost Writer (MECC)
The Golden Spike: Building America's First Transcontinental Railroad (National Geographic)
Gradebook Deluxe (Edusoft)
Gradebook Plus (Mindscape)
Grammatik III (Reference Software)
Guide (Owl International)
GW–BASIC (Microsoft)
Hometown: Local Area Studies (Active Learning Systems)
Homeword (Sierra On-Line)
HyperCard (See Apple dealers)
HyperStudio (Roger Wagner)
IEPWorks (K–12 MicroMedia Publishing)
Imaginator 3–D (Hearlihy)
Immigrant (CUE Softswap)
The Incredible Laboratory (Sunburst)
Joe Spreadsheet (Holt, Rinehart, and Winston)
KidMail (CUE Softswap)
KidWriter (Spinnaker)
Learning DOS (Microsoft)
Lego® TC logo (Logo Computer Systems, Inc.)
LinkWay (IBM)
Logo Plus (Terrapin)
LogoWriter (Logo Computer Systems, Inc.)
Lotus 1-2-3 (Lotus)
MacProof (Claris)
MacWrite (Claris)
Magic Slate (Sunburst)
MagnaCharta (Third Wave Technologies)
Management Master (MECC)
Math Man (Scholastic)
Mavis Beacon Teaches Typing (Software Toolworks)
Microsoft Chart (Microsoft)
Microsoft Word (Microsoft)
Microsoft Works (Microsoft)
Modemless CMS (CUE Softswap)
Multiscribe (Scholastic)
NeuralWorks (NeuralWare)
NeuroShell (Ward Systems)
New Electronic Encyclopedia (CD–ROM—Grolier)
NewsMaster (Unison World)
Newsroom (Springboard)
Norton Textra Writer (Norton)
Notebook (Window, Inc.)
Notebook II (PRO/TEM)
One World (Active Learning Systems)
Operation Frog (Scholastic)

Opus I (Roykore Software)
Oracle (Oracle Corp.)
The Oregon Trail (MECC)
The Other Side (Tom Snyder)
PageMaker (Aldus)
Paradox (Borland)
PC-Quintet (TimeWorks)
PFS: File (Software Publishing)
PFS: First Publisher (Software Publishing)
PFS: Report (Software Publishing)
PFS: Write (Software Publishing)
The Power of Nation States (ISTE)
Power Point (Microsoft)
Presidents (*HyperCard* stack—ISTE)
Print Magic (Epyx)
PrintMaster (Unison World)
The Print Shop (Broderbund)
Publisher's Paintbrush (Z-Soft)
Publish-It! (Timeworks)
Quattro (Borland)
Quick BASIC (Microsoft)
Raise the Flags (Apple Computer, Inc.)
Readability (Scandinavian PC Systems)
Readability Machine (Prentice-Hall)
Reader Rabbit (The Learning Company)
Reading Strategy series (Prentice-Hall)
Reference File (Reference Software)
RightWriter (RightSoft)
SAS (SAS Institute)
SchoolArt (*HyperCard* stack—P-Productions)
The School Publisher (Mindscape)
SchoolWorks (K–12 MicroMedia)
Science Literacy—the Lio Project (Encyclopedia Brittanica)
Search Series (McGraw-Hill)
Sensible Grammar (Sensible Software)
Sensible Speller (Sensible Software)
Sideways (Funk)
SimmuComm (CUE Softswap)
SlideShop (Scholastic)
Springboard Publisher (Springboard)
SPSS (SPSS Inc.)
StateFacts (*HyperCard* stack—P-Productions)
STATISTIX (N H Analytical Software)
Stickybear series (Weekly Reader)
StoryBoard Plus (IBM)
Story Maker (Scholastic)
SuperCalc (Sorcim)
SuperPrint (Scholastic)
Symphony (Lotus)

TenCORE Computer Managed Instruction (Computer Teaching Corporation)
TestMaker (Sage Productions)
TestWorks (Micro-Computers for Education, Inc.)
ThunderView (Thunderware)
TimeOut series (Beagle Brothers)
True BASIC (True BASIC, Inc.)
Turbo BASIC (Borland)
Turbo PROLOG (Borland)
Tutor-Tech (Techware, Inc.)
Understanding Multiplication (Hartley)
Ventura Publisher (Xerox)
Verb Usage (Hartley)
VisiCalc (Visicorp)
The Voyage of the Mimi (Sunburst)
VP-Expert (Paperback Software)
Weather and Climate Lab (Scholastic)
Weather Machine (National Geographic)
What Will Happen? (Macmillan)
Where in Time Is Carmen SanDiego (Broderbund)
Where in the USA Is Carmen SanDiego? (Broderbund)
Windows on Telecommunications (Exsym)
WordPerfect (WordPerfect Corp.)
WordStar (MicroPro)
World Data (HyperCard stack—ISTE)
World Development Indicators (World Bank Publications)
World Geograph (MECC)
Writer Rabbit (The Learning Company)
Writer's Helper Stage II (Conduit)
Writing to Read (IBM)

APPENDIX B

SELECTED SOFTWARE AND INTEGRATED LEARNING SYSTEMS

Selected Software Producers/Sources

Active Learning Systems, 5365 Avenida Encinas, Suite J, Carlsbad, CA 92008; 619-931-7784, 800-423-0818.
Addison-Wesley, One Jacob Way, Reading, MA 01867; 617-944-3700.
Advanced Ideas, 2902 San Pablo Ave., Berkeley, CA 94702; 415-526-9100.
Aldus Corp., 411 First Ave. South, Seattle, WA 98104; 206-622-5500.
Apple Computer, Inc., 20525 Mariani Ave., Cupertino, CA 95014; 408-996-1010.
Ashton-Tate, 20101 Hamilton Ave., Torrance, CA 90502; 213-329-8000.
Authorware, Inc., 8621 Pine Hill Rd., Bloomington, MN 55438; 612-941-5752.
Beagle Bros., Inc., 6215 Ferris Square, Suite 100, San Diego, CA 92121; 619-452-5500.
Borland International, 1800 Green Hills Rd., Scotts Valley, CA 95066; 408-438-8400.
Broderbund, 17 Paul Dr., San Rafael, CA 94903; 415-492-3200, 800-527-6263.
C & C Software, 5713 Kentford Circle, Wichita, KS 67220; 316-683-6056.
CBS Interactive Learning, One Fawcett Place, Greenwich, CT 06836.

CBT/McGraw-Hill, 2500 Garden Rd., Monterey, CA 93940; 800-538-9547.

Claris, 440 Clyde Ave., Mountain View, CA 94043; 415-960-1500, 800-334-3535.

Cognitive Software, Inc., 703 East 30th St., Fall Creek Building—Suite 7, Indianapolis, IN 46205; 317-924-9988.

COMPress, A Division of Wadsworth, Inc., P.O. Box 102, Wentworth, NH 03282.

Computer Teaching Corporation, Illini Plaza, 1713 S. Neil, Champaign, IL 61820; 217-352-6363.

Conduit, The University of Iowa, Oakdale Campus, Iowa City, IA 52242; 319-335-4100.

Cross Educational Software, P.O. Box 1536, Reston, LA 71270.

CUE SoftSwap, P.O. Box 271704, Concord, CA 94527-1704; 415-328-2248.

D.C. Heath Software (Collamore), 2700 North Richardt Ave., Indianapolis, IN 46219; 800-428-8071.

Davidson & Associates, 3135 Kashiwa St., Torrance, CA 90505; 800-556-6141.

DesignWare, 185 Berry St., San Francisco, CA 94107; 415-546-1866.

Developmental Learning Materials (DLM), P.O. Box 4000, Allen, TX 75002; 214-248-6300.

Didatech Software, Ltd., 3812 William St., Burnaby, BC Canada V5C 3H9.

Eastgate Systems, Inc., P.O. Box 1307, Cambridge, MA 02238-9924; 617-924-9044.

Educational Testing Service, Princeton, NJ 08541; 609-734-1909.

Edusoft, P.O. Box 2560-PR, Berkeley, CA 94702; 800-EDU-SOFT.

Encyclopedia Brittanica Educational Corporation, 425 North Michigan Ave., Chicago, IL 60611.

Epyx, 600 Galveston Dr., Redwood City, CA 94063; 415-366-0606.

Expressware Corp., P.O. Box 230, Redmond, WA 98073; 206-481-3040.

Exsym, 7016 Dellwood Ave. NE, Albuquerque, NM 87110; 505-881-3670.

1st Class Expert Systems, Inc., 526 Boston Post Rd., Wayland, MA 01778; 508-358-7722, 800-872-8812.

Funk Software, Inc., 222 Third St., Cambridge, MA 02142; 800-822-3865.

Geo-Soft, 253 Lake Thomas Dr., Winter Haven, FL 33883; 813-299-8421.

Gessler Software, 900 Broadway, New York, NY 10003; 212-673-3113.

Grolier Electronic Publishing, Inc., Sherman Turnpike, Danbury, CT 06816; 203-797-3500.

Hartley Courseware, 133 Bridge Street, P.O. Box 419, Dimondale, MI 48821; 517-646-6458, 800-247-1380.

Hearlihy & Co., 714 W. Columbia St., P.O. Box 869, Springfield, OH 45501; 800-622-1000.

Heizer Software, 1941 Oak Park Blvd., Suite 30, Pleasant Hill, CA 94523; 800-225-6755.

Holt, Rinehart, and Winston, Inc., The Dryden Press, 111 Fifth Ave., New York, NY 10003.

Houghton Mifflin Company, Educational Software Division, Mt. Support Road, Lebanon, NH 03766; 603-448-3838.

HRM Software, 175 Tompkins Ave., Pleasantville, NY 10570; 914-769-6900, 800-431-2050.

IBM Educational Software, 1 Culver Rd., Dayton, NJ 08810; 800-426-2468.

ISTE (International Society for Technology in Education), University of Oregon, 1787 Agate St., Eugene, OR 97403-9905.

K-12 MicroMedia Publishing, 6 Arrow Rd., Ramsey, NJ 07446; 201-825-8888.

Knowledge Access International, 2685 Marine Way, Suite 1305, Mountain View, CA 94043.

The Learning Company, 6493 Kaiser Dr., Fremont, CA 94555-3612; 415-792-2101, 800-852-2555.

Lego Systems, Inc., 555 Taylor Rd., Enfield, CT 06082; 800-243-4870.

Logo Computer Systems, Inc., 121 Mount Vernon St., Boston, MA 02108; 617-742-4042.

Lotus Development Corporation, 55 Cambridge Parkway, Cambridge, MA 02142; 617-577-8500.

Macmillan Publishing Company, 866 Third Avenue, New York, New York 10022.

McGraw-Hill, Webster Division, 1221 Avenue of the Americas, New York, NY 10020; 212-512-2000.

MECC (Minnesota Educational Computing Corporation), 3490 Lexington Avenue North, St. Paul, MN 55126; 612-481-3500, 800-228-3504.

Micro-Computers for Education, Inc., 4246 Schneider Dr., Oregon, WI 53575; 608-835-5922.

Micro Power and Light Company, 12820 Hillcrest Rd., #120, Dallas, TX 75230; 214-239-6620.

MicroPro International Corp., 33 San Pablo Ave., San Rafael, CA 94903; 415-499-1200.

Microsoft Corporation, P.O. Box 97017, Redmond, WA 98073-9717; 206-828-8080.

Millenium Software, 1970 South Coast Highway, Laguna Beach, CA 92651; 714-497-7439.

Milliken Publishing Company, P.O. Box 21579, St. Louis, MO 63132-0579; 314-991-4220, 800-643-0008.

Mindscape, Inc., 3444 Dundee Rd., Northbrook, IL 60062; 708-480-7667, 800-221-9884.

N H Analytical Software, 1958 Eldridge Ave., Roseville, MN 55113; 612-631-2852.

National Geographic Society, 17th and M Streets NW, Washington, DC 20036; 301-921-1330, 800-368-2728.

NeuralWare, Inc., Penn Center West, Building IV, Suite 227, Pittsburgh, PA 15276; 412-787-8222.

W.W. Norton & Co., Inc., 500 Fifth Avenue, New York, NY 10110; 800-223-2584.

Ntergaid, 2490 Black Rock Turnpike, Suite 337, Fairfield, CT 06430; 203-368-0632.

Odesta Corp., 4084 Commercial Ave., Northbrook, IL 60062; 708-323-5423.

Oracle Corp., 20 Davis Dr., Belmont, CA 94002; 415-598-8000, 800-672-2531.

Owl International, Inc., 14218 NE 21st St., Bellevue, WA 98007; 206-747-3203.

P-Productions, 1508 Illinois St., Racine, WI 53405.

Paperback Software, 2830 Ninth St., Berkeley, CA 94710; 800-255-3242.

Pergamon Software, Maxwell House, Fairview Park, Elmsford, NY 10523; 914-592-7700.

Polarware (Penguin) Software, 2600 Keslinger Road, Box 311, Geneva, IL 60134; 800-323-0884.

Prentice-Hall, Education Publishing Group, Englewood Cliffs, NJ 07632; 201-757-9277.

PRO/TEM Software, Inc., 814 Tolman Dr., Stanford, CA 94305-9965; 415-947-1024.

Queue, 562 Boston Ave., Bridgeport, CT 06610; 203-335-0906, 800-232-2224.

Reference Software, 330 Townsend St., Suite 123, San Francisco, CA 94107; 415-541-0222.

RightSoft, Inc., 2033 Wood St., Suite 218, Sarasota, FL 34237; 800-992-0244.

Roger Wagner Publishing, Inc., 1050 Pioneer Way, Suite P, El Cajun, CA 92020; 619-442-0522.

Roykore Software, Inc., 749 Brunswick St., San Francisco, CA 94112; 800-227-0847.

Sage Productions, 5677 Oberlin Dr., Suite 102, San Diego, CA 92121; 619-455-7513.

SAS Institute, Inc., SAS Circle, Box 8000, Cary, NC 27512–8000.

Scandinavian PC Systems, Inc., 51 Monroe Street, Suite 1101, Rockville, MD 20850.

Scholastic Software, 2931 East McCarty Street, Box 7502, Jefferson City, MO 65102; 800-325-6149.

Science Research Associates (SRA), 155 N. Wacker Drive, Chicago, IL 60607; 312-984-7000.

Sensible Software, 335 E. Big Beaver, Suite 207, Troy, MI 48083; 313-528-1950.

Seven Hills Software, 2310 Oxford Rd., Tallahassee, FL 32304-3930; 800-627-3836.

Simpac Educational Systems, Route 2, Box 676, Newberry, FL 32669; 904-472-3299.

Society for Visual Education, Inc., 1345 Diversey Parkway, Chicago, IL 60614.

Softsync, Inc., 162 Madison Ave., New York, NY 10016.

Software Publishing Corporation, P.O. Box 7210, 1901 Landings Drive, Mountain View, CA 94039; 415-962-8910.

The Software Toolworks, 13557 Ventura Blvd., Sherman Oaks, CA 91423; 818-907-6789, 800-245-4525.

Sorcim Corporation, 2195 Fortune Dr., San Jose, CA 95131; 408-942-1727.

Spinnaker Software Corp., One Kendall Square, Cambridge, MA 02139; 617-494-1200, 800-323-8088.

Springboard Software, 7808 Creekridge Circle, Minneapolis, MN 55435; 612-944-3915, 800-445-4780.

SPSS Inc., 444 N. Michigan Ave., Chicago, IL 60611.

STATSOFT, 2325 E. 13th St., Tulsa, OK 74104; 918-583-4149.

Stone Edge Technologies, P.O. Box 1200, Maple Glen, PA 19002; 215-641-1825.

Sunburst Communications, 39 Washington Ave., Pleasantville, NY 10570; 914-769-5030, 800-431-1934.

Teacher's Aide, Inc., P.O. Box 1666, Highland Park, IL 60035; 708-432-8860.

Techware, Inc., P.O. Box 151085, Altamonte Springs, FL 32715; 407-695-9000.

Terrapin, Inc., 400 Riverside St., Portland, ME 04103; 207-878-8200 or Fax 207-797-9235.

Third Wave Technology, Inc., 11934 Lorain Ave., Cleveland, OH 44111; 216-671-8991, 800-233-WAVE.

Thunderware, Inc., 21 Orinda Way, Orinda, CA 84563; 415-254-6581.

Timeworks, 444 Lake Cook Rd., Deerfield, IL 60015; 708-948-9200.

Tom Snyder Productions, 90 Sherman St., Cambridge, MA 02140; 617-876-4433, 800-342-0236.

True BASIC Inc., 39 South Main St., Hanover, NH 03755; 800-TRBASIC.

Unison World, Kyocera Unison, Inc., Box 3056, Berkeley, CA 94703; 800-443-0100.

Vernier Software, 2920 S.W. 89th St., Portland, OR 97225.

Visicorp, 2895 Zanker Road, San Jose, CA 95134; 408-946-9000.

The Voyager Company, 2139 Manning Ave., Los Angeles, CA 90025; 800-446-2001.

Ward Systems, 8013 Meadowview Drive, Frederick, MD 21701; 301-662-7950.

Weekly Reader Software, Optimum Resource, 10 Station Place, Norfolk, CT 06058; 203-542-5553, 800-327-1473.

Window, Inc., 469 Pleasant St., Watertown, MA 02171; 617-923-9147.

World Bank Publications, Dept. 0552, Washington, DC 20073-0552.

Xerox Corporation, 360 North Sepulveda Blvd., El Segundo, CA 90245; 800-445-5554.

Z-Soft, 450 Franklin Rd., Suite 100, Marietta, GA 30067; 404-428-0008.

Selected Integrated Learning Systems Sources

Computer Curriculum Corp, 700 Hansen Way, P.O. Box 10080, Palo Alto, CA 94303-1016; 800-227-8324, 800-982-5851 in CA.

Control Data Corp., PLATO Educational Services, 8800 Queen Avenue South, Bloomington, MN 55431; 800-328-1109.

Educational Systems Corp., 6170 Cornerstone Court East, Suite 300, San Diego, CA 92121-3710; 619-587-0087.

Ideal Learning Inc., 5005 Royal Lane, Irving, TX 75063; 214-929-4201 (Ideal Learning System).

Unisys Corp., Box 500, Blue Bell, PA 19424-0001; 215/542-2243 (the Icon Series).

WICAT Systems, Box 539, Orem, UT 84057; 801-224-6400.

APPENDIX C

SOURCES OF CD–ROM AND RELATED PRODUCTS

Bowker Electronic Publishing, 245 West 17th St., New York, NY 10114-0418; 800-323-3288.

Dialog Information Services, Inc., 3460 Hillview Ave., Palo Alto, CA 94304; 415-858-2700, 800-3DIALOG.

Disclosure Information Group, 5161 River Rd., Bethesda, MD 20816.

Encyclopedia Brittanica Educational Corporation, 425 North Michigan Ave., Chicago, IL 60611.

Geovision, Inc., 270 Scientific Dr., Suite 1, Norcross, GA 30092.

Grolier Electronic Publishing, Sherman Turnpike, Danbury, CT 06816; 203-797-3500, 800-356-5590.

Knowledge Access International, 2685 Marine Way—Suite 1305, Mountain View, CA 94043; 415-969-0606.

Microsoft Corporation, P.O. Box 97017, Redmond, WA 98073-9717; 206-828-8080.

OCLC, 6565 Frantz Road, Dublin, OH 43017-0702.

Optical Media International, 495 Alberto Way, Los Gatos, CA 95032.

SilverPlatter Information, 37 Walnut St., Wellesley Hills, MA 02181; 617-239-0306.

TESCOR, Inc., 461 Carlisle Dr., Herndon, VA 22070.

U.S. Bureau of Census, Data Users Service Division, Washington, D.C. 20233.

H.W. Wilson, 950 University Ave., Bronx, NY 10452.

World Book, Inc., Merchandise Mart Plaza, Chicago, IL 60654.

APPENDIX D

SOURCES OF VIDEODISCS AND RELATED PRODUCTS

ABC News Interactive, 7 West 66th St., New York, NY 10023; 212-887-4060.

Allen Communications, 140 Lakeside Plaza II, 5225 Wiley Post Way, Salt Lake City, UT 84116; 801-537-7800.

CEL Educational Resources, 515 Madison Ave., New York, NY 10022.

The Consortium for Research and Exploration of Advanced Technologies in Education (C.R.E.A.T.E.), Southwest Texas State University, c/o Michael Farris, San Marcos, TX 78666.

Edudisc, 1400 Tyne Blvd, Nashville, TN 37215; 615-373-2506.

FITNE, 28 Station Street, Athens, OH 45701; 614-592-2511.

Future Systems Incorporated, PO Box 26, Falls Church, VA 22046.

ISC Educational Systems, 3700 Electronics Way, Box 3040, Lancaster, PA 17604-3040; 800-537-7950, 717-898-0890.

MECC Etc., 3490 Lexington Avenue North, St. Paul, MN 55126; 800-228-3504, 612-481-3500.

Optical Data Corp, 30 Technology Drive, Warren, NJ 07060; 800-524-2481, 201-668-0022.

Pioneer Communications of America, Inc., 600 East Crescent Avenue, Upper Saddle River, NJ 07458-1827.

SelectraVision, Box 5497, Walnut Creek, CA 94596; 415-283-1670.

SYSCON Corporation, 2686 Dean Drive, Virginia Beach, VA 23452.

Systems Impact, 4400 MacArthur Blvd NW, Suite 203, Washington, DC 20007; 800-822-4636.

Teaching Technologies, 75 Zaca Lane, Suite 110, P.O. Box 3808, San Luis Obispo, CA 93403; 805-541-3100.

Videodisc Publishing, Inc., 381 Park Avenue South, Suite 1601, New York, NY 10016.

VideoDiscovery, P.O. Box 85878, Seattle, WA 98145-1878; 800-548-3472.

Visual Database Systems, 614 Bean Create Road, Scotts Valley, CA 95066; 408-438-8396.

The Voyager Company, 2139 Manning Ave., Los Angeles, CA 90025; 800-446-2001; 213-474-0032.

Whitney Educational Services, Box 25371, San Mateo, CA 94402; 415-341-5818.

Wisconsin Foundation for VTAE, Inc., Instructional Video Division, 2564 Branch Street, Middleton, WI 53562; 608-831-6313.

VIDEODISC REFERENCE GUIDE

The Videodisc Compendium lists and describes hundreds of videodiscs for education and training from many sources. From Emerging Technology Consultants, Box 12444, St. Paul, MN 55112; 612-639-3973.

APPENDIX E

TELECOMMUNICATIONS RESOURCES

AppleLink. See your Apple dealer.

BRS Information Technologies, 1200 Route 7, Lathan, NY 12110; 800-227-5277.

CompuServe Information Services, P.O. Box 20212, 5000 Arlington Centre Boulevard, Columbus, OH 43220; 614-457-8600.

Delphi, 3 Blackstone St., Cambridge, MA 02139; 800-544-4005.

Dialog Information Services, 3460 Hillview Ave., Palo Alto, CA 94304; 800-3-DIALOG.

Dow Jones News/Retrieval, Box 300, Princeton, NJ 08540; 609-452-1511, 800-257-5114.

Einstein, Addison-Wesley Publishing Co., Information Services Division, 2725 Sand Hill Rd., Menlo Park, CA 94025; 800-227-1936.

GEnie Online Services, 401 N. Washington Street, Rockville, MD 20850; 800-638-9636.

Prodigy, P.O. Box 8159, Gray, TN 37615–9961, 800-759-8000.

SpecialNet, National Association of State Directors of Special Education, 2021 K Street NW, Suite 315, Washington, DC 20006; 202-296-1800.

APPENDIX F

PROFESSIONAL ASSOCIATIONS AND ORGANIZATIONS OF INTEREST TO COMPUTER EDUCATORS

American Educational Research Association (AREA)
This organization of educational researchers has an interest group for members interested in computer-based learning. The annual meeting includes many computer-related research reports. Publisher of *Educational Research, American Educational Research Journal,* and *Review of Educational Research,* among others.
Address: 1230 Seventeenth Street NW, Washington, DC 20036.

Association for Computers in Mathematics and Science Teaching
An organization of secondary and post-secondary math and science teachers with computer interests. Publisher of the *Journal of Artificial Intelligence in Education, Journal of Computers in Mathematics and Science Education,* and *Journal of Computing in Childhood Education.*
Address: P.O. Box 4455, Austin, TX 78765.

Association for Computing Machinery (ACM)
This professional association has local chapters and supports various special interest groups (SIGs), including SIGCUE for computer users in education. Publisher of *Communications of the ACM* and *SIGCUE Bulletin.*
Address: 11 W. 42nd St., New York, NY 10036.

Association for the Development of Computer-Based Instructional Systems (ADCIS)
This group seeks to promote computer-based learning by stimulating and fostering communication among educational institutions at all levels, government agencies, and the private sector. Publisher of *The Journal of Computer-Based Instruction.*
Address: Computer Center, Western Washington University, Bellingham, WA 98225.

Association for Educational Communications and Technology (AECT)
Devoted to applications of all technologies to the learning process, AECT members come from all levels of education and from business and industry. The Division of Information Systems and Computers (DISC) is a special interest group for computer educators and other users. Publisher of *Tech Trends,* and *Educational Technology Research and Development.*
Address: 1126 Sixteenth Street NW, Washington, DC 20036.

Computer Using Educators (CUE), Inc.
CUE is a nonprofit corporation founded by teachers in 1978 to promote development and growth in the use of computer and other technologies in

education and to contribute to development of information, materials, and software for all interested educators. As an organization, it serves California educators with statewide conferences. Others benefit from Softswap, its distribution system for low-priced, freely copiable educational software. (*See* Appendix B for the CUE Softswap address.)

Address: P.O. Box 2087, Menlo Park, CA 94026.

Educational Products Information Exchange (EPIE) Institute

The "Consumers Union" of educational computing, responsible for very stringent testing of courseware. See Chapter 9 on courseware evaluation for further information.

Address: P.O. Box 839, Water Mill, NY 11976.

International Society for Technology in Education (ISTE)

This group is the result of the 1989 merger of the International Council for Computers in Education (ICCE) and the International Association for Computing in Education (IACE), formerly the Association for Educational Data Systems. The organization focuses on K-12 educational technology. Publisher of *The Computing Teacher, Journal of Research on Computing in Education, Update* newsletter, and a wide range of computer publications and materials.

Address: ISTE, University of Oregon, 1787 Agate Street, Eugene, OR 97403-1923.

Microcomputer Software and Information for Teachers (MicroSIFT)

MicroSIFT has been a leader in developing software evaluation practices and itself collects and assesses educational software. Refer to Chapter 9 on courseware evaluation for further information.

Address: Northwest Regional Educational Laboratory, 100 S.W. Main, Suite 500, Portland, OR 97204.

National Council of Teachers of Mathematics (NCTM)

Professional organization for mathematics teachers at all levels, with a strong commitment to applications of computer technology in math education. Publisher of *Mathematics Teachers*, a source of many reviews of mathematics software.

Address: 1906 Association Drive, Reston, VA 22091.

National Science Teachers Association (NSTA)

Similar to NCTM, but aimed at science teachers. Publisher of *The Science Teacher*.

Address: 1742 Connecticut Avenue NW, Washington, DC 20009.

Society for Applied Learning Technology (SALT)

An organization concerned with technological innovation. Geared largely to higher education, business, and the military. Sponsors seminars and workshops on interactive video and other emerging technologies. Publisher of *Journal of Interactive Instruction Development.*

Address: 50 Culpepper Street, Warrenton, VA 22186.

Technical Education Research Center (TERC)

TERC is an educational computing research and development center, with special interest in science applications, including interface of laboratory instruments to microcomputers. Publisher of *Hands On!*

Address: 1696 Massachusetts Avenue, Cambridge, MA 02138.

APPENDIX G

PUBLICATIONS OF INTEREST TO COMPUTER EDUCATORS

Journals and Magazines

AI Expert, Miller Freeman Publications, 500 Howard Street, San Francisco, CA 94105.

BASIC Teacher, P.O. Box 7627, Menlo Park, CA 94026.

BYTE, McGraw-Hill, Inc., 70 Main St., Peterborough, NH 03458.

Call—A.P.P.L.E., TechAlliance, 290 S.W. 43rd St., Renton, WA 98055-4936.

Classroom Computer Learning, 2451 East River Rd., Dayton, OH 45439-9907.

Computer Science Education, Ablex Publishing Corp., 355 Chestnut St., Norwood, NJ 07648.

Computers and Composition, Michigan Technological University, Department of Humanities, Houghton, MI 49931.

Computers in the Schools, Haworth Press, Inc., 12 West 32nd St., New York, NY 10001.

Computers, Reading and Language Arts, Modern Learning Publishers, Inc., 1308 E. 38th St., Oakland, CA 94602.

The Computing Teacher, International Society for Technology in Education, University of Oregon, 1787 Agate St., Eugene, OR 97403-9905.

Educational Technology, 720 Palisade Ave., Englewood Cliffs, NJ 07632.

Educational Technology Research and Development, Association for Educational Communications and Technology, 1126 Sixteenth St. NW, Washington, DC 20036.

Electronic Education, Electronic Communications, Inc., 1311 Executive Center Drive, Suite 220, Tallahassee, FL 32301.

Electronic Learning, Scholastic, Inc., Box 2040, Mahopac, NY 10541-9963.

Future Generations Computer Systems, Journal Information Center, Elsevier Science Publishers, 52 Vanderbilt Ave., New York, New York 10017.

Hands-On! Technical Education Research Center, 1696 Massachusetts Ave., Cambridge, MA 02138.

Instruction Delivery Systems, Communicative Technology Corporation, 50 Culpepper Street, Warrenton, VA 22186 (Free to qualified professionals).

Interact, International Interactive Communications Society, 2120 Steiner St., San Francisco, CA 94115.

Interface: The Computer Education Quarterly, Mitchell Publishing, Inc., 915 River St., Santa Cruz, CA 95060.

Journal of Artificial Intelligence in Education, P.O. Box 60730, Phoenix, AZ 85082.

Journal of Computer-Based Instruction, ADCIS, Western Washington University, Miller Hall 409, Bellingham, WA 98225.

Journal of Computers in Mathematics and Science Teaching, P.O. Box 4455, Austin, TX 78765.

Journal of Computing in Childhood Education, P.O. Box 60730, Phoenix, AZ 85082.

Journal of Educational Computing Research, Baywood Publishing Company, Inc., Box D, Farmingdale, NY 11735.

Journal of Educational Technology Systems, Baywood Publishing Company, Inc., Box D, Farmingdale, NY 11735.

Journal of Interactive Instruction Development, Society for Applied Learning Technology, 50 Culpepper St., Warrenton, VA 22186.

The Journal of Logic Programming, Elsevier Science Publishing Co., Inc., P.O. Box 882, Madison Square Station, New York, NY 10159.

Journal of Research on Computing in Education, ISTE, 1787 Agate St., Eugene, OR 97403-9905.

Learning, P.O. Box 2580, Boulder, CO 80322.

Logo Exchange, International Society for Technology in Education, University of Oregon, 1787 Agate St., Eugene, OR 97403-9905.

Machine-Mediated Learning, Taylor & Francis Inc., 242 Cherry St., Philadelphia, PA 19106-1906.

MacUser, P.O. Box 56972, Boulder, CO 80321-6972.

MacWEEK, P.O. Box 5821, Cherry Hill, NJ 08034.

Media and Methods, American Society of Educators, 1429 Walnut St., Philadelphia, PA 19102.

Media in Education and Development, Taylor & Francis Inc., 242 Cherry St., Philadelphia, PA 19106-1906.

Microcomputers in Education, Two Sequan Road, Watch Hill, RI 02891.

MIPS—the Magazine of Intelligent Personal Systems, 400 Amherst St., Nashua, NH 03063.

PC AI, Knowledge Technology, Inc., 3310 West Bell Rd., Suite 119, Phoenix, AZ 85023.

PC Computing, Ziff-Davis Publishing Company, Computer Publications Division, One Park Avenue, New York, NY 10017.

PC Magazine, Ziff-Davis Publishing Company, Computer Publications Division, One Park Avenue, New York, NY 10017.

PC World, P.O. Box 78270, San Francisco, CA 94107-9991.

Personal Computing, Hayden Publishing Co., Inc., 10 Mulholland Dr., Hasbrouck Heights, NJ 07604.

Personal Publishing, Hitchcock Publishing Company, 191 South Gary Ave., Carol Stream, IL 60188.

T.H.E. Journal—Technological Horizons in Education, Information Synergy, Inc., 150 El Camino Real, Tustin, CA 92680.

Teaching and Computers, Scholastic, Inc., P.O. Box 2040, Mahopac, NY 10541-9963.

TechTrends, AECT, 1126 Sixteenth St. NW, Washington, DC 20036.

Newsletters

Apple Education News, Apple Computer Inc., 20525 Mariani Ave., Cupertino, CA 95014.

Education Computer News, BPI, 951 Pershing Dr., Silver Spring, MD 20910-4464.

Online Searcher, 14 Haddon Rd., Scarsdale, NY 10583.

The Sloane Report, P.O. Box 561689, Miami, FL 33256.

Syllabus—An Information Source on Computing in Higher Education, P.O. Box 2716, 1226 Mandarin Dr., Sunnyvale, CA 94087.

GLOSSARY

Abacus An ancient computing device consisting of several rows of rods that represent columns, and small beads that move on these columns to represent digits.

Acoustic coupler A modem that functions through a standard telephone handset rather than connecting directly to the phone line.

Ada Computer language named for Lady Ada Augusta Lovelace, colleague of Babbage and daughter of Lord Byron.

ALGOL *ALGO*rithmic *L*anguage. A high-level language designed for numeric calculations on mainframe computers.

Algorithm Step-by-step procedures for obtaining a specific result.

Alphabetic variable A variable that can store only the letters of the alphabet.

Alphanumeric variable A variable that can store the letters of the alphabet, numbers, and/or special characters.

ALU *A*rithmetic *L*ogic *U*nit. That part of the central processing unit (CPU) of a computer which performs calculations and logical functions.

Analog computer A computer that represents values by a continuously changing physical variable, such as amount of electrical current. Cf. Digital computer.

Applications software Computer programs designed and written to perform specific useful tasks; e.g., a spreadsheet. Normally purchased by users.

Arithmetic logic unit *See* ALU.

Articulation Agreement as to what is taught at each grade level and which therefore can be assumed at succeeding levels.

Artificial intelligence A branch of computer science concerned with the development of machines and programs to simulate human reasoning.

ASCII *A*merican *S*tandard *C*ode for *I*nformation *I*nterchange. A standardized format for coding numbers, letters, and special characters.

Assembler A program that translates assembler language source code into executable machine language object code.

Assembler language A low-level language that relies on mnemonics to represent machine-level instructions. This source code must be translated into executable object code by the appropriate assembler.

Authoring language A specialized high-level language that allows the user to write limited types of computer-assisted instruction without extensive programming knowledge or experience.

Authoring system Software designed to allow non-programmers to create computer-based learning materials by responding to prompts or completing simple forms.

BASIC *B*eginners *A*ll-purpose *S*ymbolic *I*nstruction *C*ode. A high-level language used extensively on microcomputers.

Baud rate In data communications, the number of bits per second transmitted between computers or from one computer to its terminals.

Binary Any system that is composed of only two alternate states, such as 0 and 1, on and off.

Bit *Binary* dig*it*. The smallest unit of information meaningful to a computer, usually represented as 0 or 1. Multiple bits together form a *byte*.

Boot/Boot up The process of starting up a computer so that it is ready for normal operation. Often involves the loading of an operating system from disk into RAM.

Branch The process within a program of skipping to a nonsequential step or selecting among alternate nonsequential steps.

Buffer A storage area or device that can temporarily hold data being transferred from one part of the computer system to another, from one computer to another, or from a computer to a peripheral device.

Bug A mistake within a computer program.

Bulletin board (BBS) Computer system set up for posting and exchange of messages and software.

Byte A series of bits, usually seven or eight, that is used to code numbers, letters, and special characters.

C A highly-structured computer language developed by Bell Laboratories for the Unix operating system. Now available for microcomputers.

CAD *Computer-Aided Design*. The use of computers to create and modify graphic designs, such as in drafting and engineering.

CAI *Computer-Assisted Instruction*. The use of the computer as an instructional tool. Cf. CMI.

CAL *Computer-Aided Learning*. *See* CAI.

Card A single screen in a hypermedia product such as *HyperCard*. Similar to a data base record.

CBI *Computer-Based Instruction*. *See* CAI.

CD–ROM *Compact Disc–Read Only Memory*. An optical-disc technology with massive storage capability. Derivatives include CD–I (*Compact Disc–Interactive*) and DV–I (*Digital Video–Interactive*).

Chip A small piece of semiconducting material such as silicon upon which electrical circuits are etched.

CMI *Computer Managed Instruction*. The use of the computer in the organization and management of instructional and classroom activities. Cf. CAI.

Classroom publishing Use of inexpensive software to approximate desktop publishing.

COBOL *COmmon Business Oriented Language*. A high-level language for business applications that uses English phrases and sentences.

Code Instructions to a computer. Usually modified to indicate the nature of the code; i.e., machine code, source code, COBOL code.

Command An instruction to a computer system to perform a specified input, processing, or output task.

Communication The process of one computer transferring data to and from another computer through communication channels such as telephone lines.

Compiled language Any high-level language whose source code must be translated into machine-executable object code by the appropriate compiler.

Compiler A program that translates an entire program in a high-level language into machine code prior to execution. Cf. Interpreter.

Computer An electronic device consisting of interrelated components that can accept, process, and display data under program control.

Computer literacy Term used to describe the knowledge and skills necessary to function adequately in an environment utilizing computer and information technology.

Conferencing Real time communication between two or more parties via computer. Contrast to electronic mail which does not require participants to be on-line simultaneously.

Connect time In telecommunications, the time spent online from signing on to signing off the host system.

Courseware Computer programs and related materials specifically designed for instruction.

CPM Control Program for Microcomputers. One of the first disk operating system programs used by microcomputers. See DOS.

CPU Central Processing Unit. The "brain" of a computer system, consisting of the control, arithmetic, logic, and primary memory sections where processing is actually performed.

CRT Cathode Ray Tube. The TV-like video display of a computer system. See Monitor, Terminal.

Cursor A movable spot of light that indicates current location on a computer screen.

Daisy wheel printer See *Letter quality printer.*

Data Information that a computer uses in its processing.

Data base Information stored in an organized system of electronically accessible files.

Data processing The procedures used for computer manipulation of information, from input through processing to output.

DBMS Data Base Management System. An application program for creation and manipulation of data bases.

Debugging The process of locating and correcting errors in a computer program.

Desktop publishing Use of sophisticated and costly software to compose text and graphics into near-typeset-quality pages.

Digital computer A computer that represents values discretely using a coding system of binary digits (bytes). Cf. Analog Computer.

Disk A small platter that is capable of retaining data coded as magnetic charges upon its surface.

Disk drive A computer peripheral that can write data to and read data from a removable diskette.

Disk file A collection of related records that are treated as a single unit when stored on a disk.

Diskette A small, flexible disk with limited storage capacity. See Floppy disk.

Documentation The manuals and accompanying materials that explain the functioning, use, and possible applications of computer hardware and software.

DOS Any *D*isk *O*perating *S*ystem. *See* Operating system. Also part of the name of specific systems, such as MS–DOS and PC–DOS (used by IBM–PCs and compatibles), DOS 3.3, and ProDos (used by Apple II computers).

Dot matrix printer An impact printer whose characters are patterns of dots formed by small pins striking against an inked ribbon.

Download The transferring of data from a mainframe computer or minicomputer to a microcomputer. Cf. Upload.

Drill and practice A form of CAI that provides repetitive opportunities for a student to respond to questions and receive feedback.

Electronic mail Transmission and receipt of files, typically messages, among users of a computer network.

Expert system Computer program which performs some task at the level of an expert. Consists minimally of a knowledge base, an inference engine to manipulate it, and a user interface.

Expert system shell An expert system development tool consisting of user interfaces, an inference engine, and a structure for handling the knowledge base, but which is empty. Analogous to spreadsheet software.

Field In data management, the smallest meaningful unit of information; e.g., last name, ZIP code. *See also* File, Record.

File A group of related records, such as an inventory. *See also* Field, Record.

Firmware Programs that are permanently stored on ROM chips.

Floppy disk A flexible disk used by microcomputers for external storage. *See* Diskette.

Floppy disk drive *See* Disk drive.

Flow chart A graphic representation of an algorithm or program.

Font The physical type style of a printer, plotter, or screen display.

FORTH A high-level language used for application and system software development.

FORTRAN *FOR*mula *TRAN*slator. A high-level language particularly suited to mathematical and scientific applications.

Freeware Software distributed at no more than duplication cost, such as *FrEdWriter*.

Graphics Computer output in the form of figures, charts, graphs, etc., as opposed to alphanumeric information.

Graphics pad/tablet An input device for creating graphic images on a computer system.

Hacker An individual who accesses and uses a computer system without authorization.

Hard copy Printed output from a computer system.

Hard disk A rigid magnetic disk that is capable of retaining very large quantities of information.

Hard disk drive A computer peripheral capable of reading from and writing to a hard disk at much greater speeds than a floppy disk system. The magnetic hard disk is generally not removable from the drive.

Hardware The physical components of a computer system.

High-level language A computer programming language whose instructions resemble English statements more than computer codes. These statements must be converted into machine code by an interpreter or compiler before they can be executed. Cf. Low-level language.

High-resolution graphics Highly detailed images resulting from control of very small screen or printer dots. Cf. Low-resolution graphics.

Host The computer which controls a telecommunications network, onto which you log or sign after calling from your computer.

HyperCard Software for the Apple Macintosh which implements hypertext and hypermedia concepts.

Hypermedia Software which links differing data formats in a nonlinear fashion. Text, graphics, sound, animation, laser disk segments can all be interrelated in a lattice or network of information.

Hypertext Text with cross-reference links among words, which allow for non-sequential reading.

Impact printer A printer that forms characters by striking paper through an inked ribbon. *See* Letter quality printer, Dot matrix printer.

Infusion The physical presence of significant numbers of computers in a school or district, apart from their actual use.

Ink jet printer A nonimpact printer that sprays ink onto paper to form characters.

Input Information/data received by a computer system.

Input device A device that transmits information/data from an outside source to a computer system. Examples include a keyboard, mouse, disk drive, and modem.

Instruction A command interpretable by a computer system. An ordered list of such instructions constitutes a program.

I/O Input/output. *See* Input, Output.

Integer variable A variable that can store only whole numbers. Cf. Numeric variable.

Integrated circuit (IC) A complete complex electronic circuit etched on a single piece of semiconductive material, usually silicon.

Integrated learning systems Systems which combine CAI and CMI, and, in many cases, hardware and software.

Integrated software A single program that can perform more than one major application and is capable of transferring information easily among the applications.

Integration Use of computers to support and enhance curriculum goals and objectives in all content areas and in any appropriate manner.

Intelligent CAI (ICAI) Any form of CAI in which branching decisions are made by program components based on artificial intelligence.

Interactive computing A mode of computer utilization characterized by interaction between the user and the computer, either in writing programs or running software.

Interactive Video Instruction (IVI) Multimedia CAI in which a computer controls a videodisc player for graphics and/or motion segments.

Interface The mechanisms that allow connections between separate parts of a single computer system or between different computer systems.

Interpreted language A high-level language whose source code is processed by an interpreter. BASIC is the most widely used language of this type.

Interpreter A program that translates and executes, one instruction at a time, a program written in a high-level language. Cf. Compiler.

Iteration Repetition of one or more statements in a program. *See* Loop.

Joystick An input device that allows the user to control the movement of the cursor on the screen by the hand movement of a stick or lever.

Keyboard An input device that allows alphanumeric input to a computer by striking keys.

Keyboarding Use of a computer keyboard without need to look at one's hand movements. Differs from touch typing in that keyboarding does not involve page layout concerns.

Kilo (K) A prefix used to represent 1000. In computing, technically refers to 1024, or 2^{10}. Used to measure memory or disk capacity in bytes.

Language A set of words, syntax, and rules that allows humans to communicate with a computer.

Laser disc Optical disc containing data that is read by a laser beam. Includes compact discs (CDs) and videodiscs.

Laser printer A nonimpact printer that uses laser technology to produce high-quality text and graphic output.

LCD Liquid Crystal Display. A digital output display device that is constructed of character-forming segments of a liquid crystal material sandwiched between two pieces of polarizing and reflecting material.

LCD Panel Device connected to video output of a computer and placed on an overhead projector to project computer images onto a large screen for group viewing. Typically much lower in cost than data projectors.

LED Light Emitting Diode. A digital output display device that produces alphanumeric characters and graphics from electronic segments that emit light.

Letter quality printer An impact printer that uses a round wheel with fully formed characters on the ends of spokes.

Light pen A pen-like photosensitive input device that is used to control a computer system, to draw, and to modify images by its movement across a monitor screen.

LISP LISt Processing. A high-level programming language designed to process nonnumeric data. Particularly useful for writing programs dealing with artificial intelligence. Cf. PROLOG.

Local area network (LAN) Connection by cables of multiple microcomputers to permit sharing of peripherals such as large hard disks and laser printers and exchange of data among users.

Logo A high-level language that is based on the teachings of the Swiss psychologist Jean Piaget and emphasizes learning by discovery in a computer-based learning environment.

Loop A sequence of operations that may be repeated within a program.

Low-level language A computer programming language one level above machine language. Instructions are in symbolic notation rather than binary code, but remain closely linked to the computer's architecture. *See* Assembler language. Cf. High-level language.

Low-resolution graphics Pictures or images that are not as clear, precise, or detailed as high-resolution graphics because they are formed from larger dots or blocks. Cf. High-resolution graphics.

Machine language Binary coded instructions that a computer can process without any form of translation.

Mainframe computer The largest type of computer system, capable of operating at very fast speeds, handling very large data sets, and servicing many users simultaneously.

Mark sense scanner An input device that reads data into a computer by scanning specially prepared sheets marked with pencil in designated areas, such as test answer sheets.

Mega A prefix used to designate approximately one million. Used to measure disk capacity or memory in bytes.

Memory The capacity of a computer to store information temporarily or permanently in the form of patterns of binary 1s and 0s.

Microcomputer A small computer system built around a microprocessor that performs most of the functions of a mainframe computer, but at slower speeds, handling smaller data sets, and usually servicing only one user at a time.

Microelectronics Miniaturized electronic components, such as the chips used in computers.

Microprocessor A single silicon chip containing the central processing circuits of a computer system.

Mid-level language A language such as C which offers the advantages of both low and high level languages while minimizing their disadvantages.

Minicomputer A computer system whose capabilities are between a microcomputer and a mainframe computer.

Modem An input/output device that *MO*dulates/*DEM*odulates information, enabling a computer to send and receive data over a telephone line.

Monitor A computer output device similar to a high-quality television that displays text and graphics on its screen.

Mouse A hand-held input device that is moved on a flat surface to position the screen cursor.

Multimedia CAI CAI which incorporates media beyond the computer, such as film, filmstrips, laser discs, and CDs.

Music synthesis The process whereby a computer creates or replicates the sounds of music.

Network Two or more computers electronically linked together in a system that allows them to share hardware, software, and data.

Numeric variable A variable that can store any type of number, but no other characters.

On-line Commonly refers to the ability of a user to gain immediate access to information through a computer system.

Operating system Software that controls and manages a computer system and its various peripheral devices.

Optical disk A round platter that is capable of storing a very large quantity of information in digital form.

Optical disk reader A device that is capable of reading the information on an optical disk using a laser beam.

Optical scanner An input device that "reads" pages of text and graphics and converts them into computer files.

Output Information sent from the computer after processing to any peripheral device.

Output device Any device that is capable of receiving output from a computer system. Examples include a printer, disk drive, display screen, and modem.

Packet switching A type of telecommunications service that permits on-line connection to information services at lower than normal long distance charges.

Parallel The mode of data transmission in which data are transferred more than one bit at a time through parallel lines, such as from a computer to a printer. Cf. Serial.

Pascal A high-level language known for features that promote structured programming. Named for the seventeenth-century French mathematician Blaise Pascal.

Peripheral Any device that is connected to a computer and under its control.

PILOT Programmed Inquiry, Learning or Teaching. A CAI authoring language designed primarily for use by educators.

Piracy The illegal copying of copyrighted software.

PLATO A computer-based educational system and related software developed at the University of Illinois for delivering computer-assisted instruction to multiple remote users.

Plotter An output device that uses pens to create high-resolution graphic images, often in multiple colors.

Port A part of the computer where connection can be made to a peripheral device, e.g. serial port, parallel port.

Presentation graphics Software for production and display of graphics screens, combining text and images; used as replacement for traditional overhead transparencies.

Primitive Any word, such as FORWARD, which the Logo language understands under all circumstances, the fundamental Logo vocabulary.

Print graphics Software for production of hard-copy graphics, originated by *The Print Shop.*

Printer A device that produces "hard copy" computer output.

Problem solving A form of CAI in which students seek to understand a problem, develop possible solutions, and test them.

Program A series of instructions that, when executed, result in the performance of a specific processing application.

Programmer A person who writes computer programs.

Programming language The words, structure, and syntax that are used to write instructions to a computer.

PROLOG *PRO*gramming in *LOG*ic. A major language used for work in artificial intelligence. Cf. LISP.

Prompt A symbol on the screen of a microcomputer which informs the user that the computer is ready for further input.

Public domain Not copyrighted. Software legally copiable by anyone.

RAM *R*andom *A*ccess *M*emory. Memory chips that can be both written to and read from by the computer. RAM is volatile, that is, data stored in it are lost when the power is turned off. Cf. ROM.

Real time Processing of data with results immediately available; without delay, as in telecommunications.

Record A group of related fields that contain information treated as a logical unit; e.g., all data on John Doe. A group of related records make up a file. *See also* Field, File.

Relational Data-base software which can link multiple files together based on a common "key."

ROM *R*ead *O*nly *M*emory. Nonvolatile memory chips that can only be read from but cannot be written to by the computer. The contents of ROM cannot be altered. Cf. RAM.

Scanning The process of transferring information from a printed page directly to a computer system.

Secondary storage Storage external to RAM and ROM in a computer system, such as disk and tape drives, which serves both input and output functions.

Serial The mode of data transmission in which data are transferred one bit at a time in sequence.

Shareware Software distributed on a try-it, then pay-if-you-like-it basis.

Silicon The chemical element that is used in the manufacture of electronic chips such as RAM, ROM, and microprocessors.

Simulation A form of CAI in which the learner assumes a role within a structured environment.

Software Programs that are used to direct a computer to perform specified tasks.

Special characters Characters on a keyboard that are neither letters nor numbers, e.g., punctuation marks.

Spreadsheet An electronic tabular workspace that can be used to enter and manipulate data.

SQL *S*tructured *Q*uery *L*anguage. An interface in advanced data base software which permits access to data on differing computers through common commands.

Stack Collection of related hypermedia cards among which the user can move about in a non-linear manner. Similar to a data base file.

Storage A place where information is stored. Within the computer, this is RAM and ROM. External to the computer, storage may be on tape, floppy disks, or hard disks.

Streamer A high-speed tape drive with large capacity used for hard-disk backup.

String variable A variable that can store letters, numbers, and/or special characters. Also called alphanumeric variable.

Structured programming An approach to programming that employs a limited set of logical constructs, minimizes the use of branching instructions, and emphasizes modularity and documentation.

Subroutine A segment of a computer program that performs a specified task when called and executed from within the main program.

Systems analysis A step-by-step approach to determining the best solution to a problem.

Tape drive An external storage device that can write upon or read from magnetic tape. Used when speed of access to data is not critical.

Telecommunications The use of communication lines (telephone, microwave, satellite) to transfer information from one computer to another or to a remote terminal.

Terminal An input/output device usually consisting of a keyboard for entering information and a screen for displaying output.

Text editor Computer program for manipulating text, but with much more limited functions than a word processor. Included within some publishing software and within MS-DOS.

Time-sharing The simultaneous use of a computer system by more than one user.

Tutorial A form of CAI in which the computer carries on a dialogue with the learner, presenting information, posing questions, and providing feedback.

Unit record Data specific to one instance, such as the census data for an individual. Also the cards developed by Hollerith to record such information in the early days of automated data processing.

Unix Operating system originally for minicomputers, now on microcomputers, noted for capacity to execute multiple tasks simultaneously.

Upload The transferring of data from a microcomputer to a mainframe or minicomputer. Cf. Download.

Utility programs Computer programs that perform a wide variety of commonly needed housekeeping and control functions.

Variable A symbol used in programming to identify memory locations containing different values and types of information.

VDT Video Display Terminal. *See* Terminal.

Videodisc A round plastic platter that can retain data and audio and video material in digital form.

Videodisc player A device capable of reading a videodisc using a laser beam. Transmits data into memory, audio material to a speaker, and/or video material to the monitor of a computer system.

Virus A program planned and written to cause mischief or damage to a computer system. Can spread through computer networks or from infected diskettes.

Voice recognition The ability of a computer system to understand human speech, i.e. translate speech into computer code.

Voice synthesis The ability of a computer system to produce intelligible speech from computer-coded representations.

Window A portion of the computer screen, used for a different purpose than the rest of the screen, such as a help window.

Word processing The application of computers to the creation, modification, printing, and storage of written material.

Worksheet A specific application of a spreadsheet, such as the student records for one class or one specific budget. Often used as synonym for spreadsheet.

Writing aids Software such as spelling checkers and grammar or style analysts which extend the composition assistance provided by a word processor.

Index

Abacus, 4
Activitymakers, 133
ADA, 5
Adding machines, 4
Adventures with Charts and Graphs, 185
Algorithm, 250–255
All of the Above, 134
All Star Drill, 169
Amanda Stories, 78
Analogies Tutorial, 172
Analytical Engine, 5
Applelink, 120–121
Appleworks, 39–40, 44, 69, 77, 80–83, 134,
    146, 152, 156–159, 372
Application software, 90–92, 144
APPSTATS, 138
Arithmetic/logic unit, 18
Artificial intelligence (AI), 188–189,
    324–325, 336–338, 407, 409
Assembler language, 260
Atanasoff, John, 9
Authoring software, 326–338
    authoring languages, 328–331
    authoring systems, 331–334
    expert system shells, 336–338
    HyperCard, 334–336
Automated loom, 5

Babbage, Charles, 5, 9
Balance of Power, 176
Bank Street Filer, 67, 77, 80–81
Bank Street Writer, 39, 45
BASIC, 80, 166, 289–314, 316–318
    advantages and disadvantages, 309–313
    development, 290–291
    interactivity, 291
    key features, 291
    structured, 292–309
    use of line numbers, 291
BBS. *See* Bulletin boards.
Bernoulli Box, 26
Bibliographic aids, 139
Bibliography, 140
Black Magic, 336

Bloom, Benjamin, 278
BOOKBRAIN, 77
BookWhiz, 77
Budget, 371–374
Bulletin boards, electronic, 121–123
Bush, Vannevar, 73

C (language), 318–320
CAD, 20
Cards. *See* Hypermedia, *HyperCard*.
Cassette drives, 25
CD-ROM, 26, 74–75, 78–79, 188, 406–407,
    424
Cells. *See* Spreadsheets, cells.
Central processing unit (CPU), 18–20,
    24–27
Chain writing, 123
Classroom applications
    of data bases, 75–83
    of integrated software, 155–159
    of spreadsheets, 105–109
    of word processing, 52–57
Classroom Computer Learning, 207
Classroom publishing, 118–120
Cloze Plus, 137
Cloze tests, 55, 137
COBOL, 321–324
Coding, 257–259
The Cognitron, 409
Community of Living Things, 188
Compact discs, 74–75. *See also* CD-ROM;
    Laser discs.
Compilers, 261–262
Compton's Encyclopedia, 78
CompuServe, 79, 83
Computer-assisted instruction (CAI),
    163–200
    and achievement, 190–191
    and attitudes, 192
    characteristics, 164–165
    effectiveness by level, 191
    evolution, 165–167
    intelligent, 188–189
    interactive video, 186–188

Computer-assisted instruction (*continued*)
  multimedia, 185–186
  and problem solving, 192–193
  and rate of learning, 191–192
  research findings concerning, 190–193
  and retention, 191–192
  types, 167–185
Computer education. *See* Implementation.
Computer infallibility, 392
Computer literacy, 347–352
  literacy curriculum model, 349–351
  problem model, 351
  programming model, 348–349
  tools/applications model, 351–352
Computer-managed instruction, 231–242
  concepts, 232–233
  concerns regarding, 238–240
  evaluating a system, 240
  integrated learning systems, 237–238
  as performance monitoring and
    analysis, 234–236
  student users, 237
  as test-scoring and testing device, 236–
    237
Computers
  appropriate usage, 65
  dependence upon, 390–393
  future in education, 411–413
  generations, 11–15
  history, 4–13
  impact on roles, 393–395
  implementation in schools, 359–380
  issues and implications, 381–399
  as learner. *See* Programming.
  social impact, 382–384
  and student needs, 165
  and system security, 383–384
  as tools, 33–160, 404
  as tutor, 161–242, 404–405
Computing Teacher, The, 207
Conferencing, 121
Control unit, 18
Cooperative learning, 368
Co-processors, 18
Copyright and software, 385–386
Core Concepts, 188
Courseware, 201–229
  evaluation, 205–229
  quality issues, 202–205, 240
  reviews, 207–209
Cross-Country California, 175
Crossword Magic, 134–135
Crossword puzzles, 133–135
Curriculum applicability

  of drill and practice, 171
  of problem solving, 184–185
  of simulations, 177–178
  of tutorials, 174
Curriculum integration, 352–359, 362–365,
    412–413
  advantages, 354–355
  national view, 355
  scope, 353–354
  what comes beyond, 355–356
Curriculum planning, 360–361, 374–375

Data, defined, 4
Data base management system (DBMS),
    68
Data bases, 61, 66–68, 87
  classroom applications and resources,
    75–82
  concepts, 66–71, 73–74
  national, 78–79
  programmable, 70–71
  relational, 70
  research on learning, 83–84
  visual, 74–75
Data files. *See* Files.
Data management, 61–87, 138–139
  benefits of electronic, 63–64
  in education, 64–65, 138–139
Data processing, 4, 63
  applications areas, 147
Data redundancy, 69
Dataquest, 77
Datasaurs—An Experience with Dinosaurs,
    80
dBase, 68, 77, 372
DB Master Version 5 Professional, 68
Debugging, 259
Decisions, Decisions, 176
Dedicated word processor, 36
Desktop publishing, 153–155
Dialog/Classmate, 79
Discovery learning, 279
Disk drives, 25–26, 74–75
Diskettes, floppy, 25
DOS. *See* Operating systems.
Double Helix, 68
Dow Jones, 79
Download, 122
Drill and practice, 167–171
  applicability in the curriculum, 171
  appropriate learning tasks, 168
  characteristics of good, 170
  debate concerning, 170
  types, 168

Educational Software Selector, The, 208, 326
Educational Testing Service (ETS), 47,
  167, 312
EDVAC, 9, 11
Election of 1912, The, 176
Electronic Learning, 207
Electronic mail (E-mail), 121–123
Electronic Mailbag, 124
Electronic Software Delivery System, 210
Electronic Village, 124
ENIAC, 9, 11
EPIE Institute, 76, 208, 326
Equity in computer access, 388–390
  gender, 388–389
  economic, 389–390
ESL Picture Grammar, 169
Ethics and computers, 122, 384–388
  copyright, 385–386
  hacking, 386–387
  viruses, 387
  white-collar crime, 388
Evaluation of courseware. *See*
  Courseware.
Evaluation forms, courseware; 222–226
Events of instruction, 213–217
Excel, 148, 158
Expert systems, 336–338

Factory, The, 183–184
Feedback, 215
Field, 67–68, 139
File Express, 69
Files, 6, 67–73
  exporting and importing, 145
  setting up, 671–731
  sharing, 145
  transforming, 145–146
Filing systems, 69–72
  classroom applications and resources,
    75–82
  selection, 70–71
  special purpose software, 138–139
  storage capacity, 70–71
Flowcharting, 252–255, 293–295, 300–302,
  306
Fonts, 117
Formulas. *See* Spreadsheets, concepts.
FORTRAN, 320–321
Framework, 147
FrEdBase, 71, 82
FrEdWriter, 54, 133
Functions. *See* Spreadsheets, concepts.
Future. *See* Trends.

Gagné and Briggs, 213–217
GeoWorld, 80
Ghost Writer, 45
Glossary, 431–441
Golden Spike, The, 185
Grade Book Deluxe, 138
Grade Book Plus, 138
Grade book programs, 138
Grammar assistance, 44–45
Grammatik, 45, 137
Graphics software, 114–120
Graphics pad, 20
Graphing programs, 125–131
  and data interpretation, 125
  student applications, 125, 131
Graves, Donald, 49–51
Grolier's *New Electronic Encyclopedia,* 78
GUI interface, 409
Guide, 336

Hacking, 386–387
Hangman, 178–180
Hardware, 18–26, 365–371
  adaptive, 370
  to take home, 371
  trends, 406–409
High-level languages, 261–262
Hollerith, Hermann, 6
Hometown: Local Area Studies, 80
Homeword, 39
Hopper, Grace, 322
HyperCard, 72–74, 77–78, 81, 176, 188,
  334–336
Hypermedia, 72–74, 334–336
HyperStudio, 336
Hypertext, 73, 336

ICAI. *See* Intelligent CAI.
IEPWorks, 157
Imaginator 3-D, 125
Immigrant, 157
Implementation, of computers in
    education, 359–380
  budget, 371–374
  cooperative versus individual learning,
    368
  curriculum planning, 360–361, 374–375
  facilities, 366–370
  goals, 362–365
  hardware, 365–371
  history, 360–362
  outside funding, 374
  planning and coordination, 363, 374–
    375

Implementation (*continued*)
  software and hardware acquisition, 365–374
  staff development, 364–365
  teacher involvement, 363–364
Improving Teacher Effectiveness, 188
Incredible Laboratory, The, 183–184
Individualized instruction, 165, 233
Information services, 79–80, 121–124
Information society, 348, 382–383
Input devices, 20–22
Instant Pascal, 318
Instructional games, 178–181
  characteristics, 178
  debate concerning, 180–181
  types, 178
Integrated circuits, 12
Integrated Instructional Information Resource (EPIE), 76, 325, 375
Integrated learning systems, 237–238, 423–424
Integrated software, 143–160
  advantages and disadvantages, 151–153
  classroom applications, 155–159
  concepts, 147–151
  windows, 148
Intel Corporation, 166
Intelligent CAI (ICAI), 188–189
Intelligent tutoring systems, 189
Interactive video, 186–188, 424–425
Interactivity, 164, 211, 273–274
International Business Machines (IBM), 7, 11–12, 168
Interpreters, 261
Introduction to Economics, 188
Issues in educational computing
  changing roles, 393–395
  equity, 388–390
  ethics, 384–388
  overreliance on computers, 390–393
  social, 382–384
Item analysis, 237
Iteration construct, 257–258, 305–309

Jacquard, Joseph Marie, 4–5, 9, 11
Joe Spreadsheet, 372
Joystick, 20

Keyboard, 19
Keyboarding, 49–50
KidMail, 124
Kid Writer, 54–56
Kids' Network, 81

Labels, 93. *See also* Spreadsheets, concepts.
Languages, programming, 260–262, 316–325, 328–331. *See also* specific languages.
Laser discs, 26, 74–75, 186–188, 406–407, 410, 424–425
Learner-controlled instruction (LCI), 167
Learning DOS, 172
Learning retention, 191–192
Learning time, 191–192
Leibnitz, Gottfried, 4
Lemonade Stand, 218
Lego® TC logo, 276
Light pen, 20
Linkway, 336
LISP, 324–325, 338
Living Textbook, The, 188
Local Area Network (LAN), 370
Logic programming, 324–325
Logical operators, 11
Logo (language), 265–287, 291, 312
  characteristics, 268–275
  conceptual foundations, 266–267, 277
  derivatives, 275–277
  ease of use, 274
  establishing the environment, 279–280
  and human development, 281–282
  implementation, 267–268
  primitives, 268–269, 291
  procedures, 269–273
  rationale for teaching, 277–278
  recursion, 272–273
  relationship to Bloom's hierarchy, 278
  research findings concerning, 281–284
  role of the teacher, 279–280
  teaching strategies, 280–281
Logo Plus, 276
LogoWriter, 275–276
Loops, 257, 305–309
Lotus 1-2-3, 77, 146, 151, 174, 372
Lovelace, Lady Ada, 5
Low-level languages, 260
Luehrmann, Arthur, 348–349, 351

Machine language, 260
MacPascal, 318
MacProof, 45
MacWrite, 40, 374
Magic Slate, 39
MagnaCharta, 125
Mailing list software, 139
Mainframe computer, 14, 165–167
Mark I, 9

Mark sense scanner, 21
Mastery learning, 232–233
Math co-processors, 18
Math Man, 169
Mavis Beacon Teaches Typing, 50, 189
Memory, 19–20, 25–26, 62, 406
Microcomputers, 14–15, 17–31, 406–408
   in education, 345–399
Microelectronics, 12, 406
MICROgrams, 208
MicroSIFT, 207–208, 226
MicroSoft *Chart*, 125
MicroSoft *Word*, 118
MicroSoft *Works*, 147, 158, 372
Modem, 26, 120
Modemless CMS, 124
Modern computer era, 11–12
Modularity, in programs, 256
Monitors, 22–23
Motivation, 213
Mouse, 20
Multimedia CAI, 185–188, 216, 410. *See also* Hypermedia.
MultiScribe, 40, 118
MYCIN, 337–338

NASA *SpaceLink*, 122
Networks, 24, 26, 210, 218, 369–370, 408
Neural networks, 409
NeuralWorks, 409
NeuroShell, 409
Newsmaster, 118
NewsRoom, 118, 124
Norton Textra Writer, 372
Notebook, 71
Notebook II, 139

One World, 77
One computer classroom, 368–369
On-line, 79–80, 236–237
Operating systems, 27–29
Operation Frog, 369
Optical discs. *See* laser discs.
Optical scanner, 21
Opus 1, 336
Oracle, 67
Oregon Trail, 83, 177, 218
Organizations, for computer educators, 426–427
Output devices, 22–24

Pagemaker, 153
Papert, Seymour, 266–268, 275
Paradox, 70–71
Parallel interface, 24

Parents' role, 394–395
Pascal (language), 311–313, 316–318
Pascal, Blaise, 4, 317
PC-Quintet, 147
PFS: File, 72, 76–77
PFS: First Publisher, 118
PFS: Report, 77
Piaget, Jean, 266–267
PILOT, 328–331
PLATO system, 166–167, 238
Plotters, 24
Power of Nation States, The, 157
PowerPoint, 117
Powers, James, 6–7
Presentation graphics, 117–118
Presidents, 78
Prewriting, 41–42
Print graphics, 114–117
Print Magic, 114
PrintMaster, 114
Print Shop, 106, 114, 366
Printers, 23–24, 153, 155
   Interface methods, 24
Privacy, impact of computers on, 383–384
Problem solving, 76–82, 181–185, 277–278, 282–283
   applicability in the curriculum, 184–185
   characteristics of software, 184
   debate concerning, 183–184
   and Logo, 277–278, 282–283
   as principles, 182
   as procedure, 181–182
   role of motivation, 182–183
Procedures. *See* Logo, procedures.
Prodigy, 79
Programming, 27, 90, 245–263, 348–349
   concepts, 248–259
   and languages, 259–262, 315–325, 328–331
   rationale for teaching, 246–248
   and students, 247–248
   and teachers, 246–247, 326–328
Programs, 27. *See also* Courseware; Software.
Project PLAN, 233–234
Projection, of images, 117–118, 366, 368–369
PROLOG, 324–325, 338
Prompt area, 93. *See* Spreadsheets, concepts.
Publications, for computer educators, 428–429
Publish-It!, 118
Publisher's Paintbrush, 153

Publishing software. *See* Classroom publishing; Desktop publishing.
Puzzle generators, 131–134

Quattro, 146
Quick BASIC, 313

Raiders of the Lost Ark, 188
Raise the Flags, 179, 181
RAM (Random Access Memory), 19–20, 27
Readability, 44–45, 137
Readability analysis, 137
Readability Machine, 137
Reading Strategy Series, 136
Reader Rabbit, 209
Recalculation, 100. *See also* Spreadsheets, concepts.
Records, 65, 139
Recursion, 272–273
Reference File, 71
Reinforcement, 216
Remington Rand Compnay, 7, 11–12
Repurposing, 190
Research findings
    on CAI, 167, 190–193
    on learning with data bases, 83–84
    on Logo, 281–284
    on word processing, 45–52
Resolution, of monitors, 22–23
RightWriter, 45, 137, 189
ROM (Read Only Memory), 20, 27

SAS, 138
Scanners, 21
School Art, 78
School Publisher, 118
SchoolWorks, 157
Science Literacy: The Lio Project, 176
Search Series, 177
Secondary storage, 24–26, 406–407
Selection construct, 257–258, 298–305
Sensible Grammar, 45
Sequence construct, 257–258, 292–298
Serial interface, 24
Sesame Street software, 209
Shareware, 373, 379–380
Sideways, 151
SimuComm, 124
Simulations, 174–178
    applicability in the curriculum, 177–178
    debate concerning, 176–177
    types, 174–175
Slide Shop, 117

Slide shows, 117–118
Social issues and computers, 382–384
Softdisk, 373–374
Softswap, 124
Software, 26–29, 202. *See also* Courseware.
    authoring, 326–338
    piracy, 385–386
    products mentioned, 417–420
    public domain, 373, 379–380
    rationale for development, 326–328
    shareware, 373, 379–380
    sources, 420–425
    trends, 409–410
Software Reviews on File, 208
Special Education resources, 370, 380
Spelling checkers, 43
Spreadsheets, 89–112
    add-in programs, 102–103
    categories of applications, 103–105
    cells, 92–94
    classroom applications, 105–109
    concepts, 92–97
    creating, 98–100
    how to use, 94–102
    templates, 102
    windows, 94
Springboard Publisher, 118
SPSS, 77, 138
Stacks. *See* Hypermedia; *HyperCard.*
Stanford Drill and Practice System, 168
Starkweather, John, 328
Statistical packages, 137–138
STATISTIX, 138
Stickybear series, 209
Stored program control, 9
StoryBoard Plus, 117
Story Maker, 42–43
Structured programming, 255–257
    in BASIC, 292–309
Structured Query Language (SQL), 70
Style assistance, writing, 44–45
SuperCalc, 146
Super Context, 136
SuperPrint, 114
Super Skills, 136
Suppes, Patrick, 166
Support tools, 124–140
Symphony, 147

Teacher support tools, 124–140
Teacher's role, 393–394
Telecommunications, 79–80, 120–124, 151, 383, 408
    applications, 123

Telecommunications (*continued*)
    bulletin boards, 122–123
    conferencing, 121
    electronic messaging, 121–123
    e-mail, 121–122
    implementation, 124
    resources, 425
Templates. *See* Spreadsheets, templates.
Terminology. *See* Glossary.
TESS, 208, 326
Test Center Database, 76
Test generating programs, 134–136
Test item bank, 76
Test Maker, 134
Text editor, 118
The saurus, electronic, 45
Thinking skills, 82
Thread writing, 123
Thunder Scan, 117
Thunder View, 117
TICCIT, 166–167
TimeOut series, 40, 45, 151
Tool programs, 90
Top-down design, 255–256
Touch screen, 20–21
Transistors, 12
Trends
    in educational computing, 411–413
    in hardware, 406–408
    in software, 409–410
Trigland, 188
True BASIC, 313
TurboBASIC, 313
Turing, Alan, 11
Turtlegraphics, 268
Tutor Tech, 336
Tutorials, 50, 171–174
    applicability in the curriculum, 174
    characteristics, 172–173
    debate concerning, 172
    types, 171–172

Understanding Mathematics, 172
Unit record data processing, 6–7
UNIVAC, 11–12
UNIX, 318–319

Vacuum tubes, 11
Values. *See* Spreadsheets, concepts.

Variables, 296
Ventura Publisher, 153–154
Video Encyclopedia of the 20th Century, 188
Videodisc. *See* Laser discs; Interactive video.
Viruses, 387
VisiCalc, 90–91, 409
Voice synthesizers, 24, 407–408
Von Neumann, John, 9–11
Voyage of the Mimi, 185, 216

Weather and Climate Lab, 156
Weather Machine, 79
Westinghouse Learning Corporation, 233
"What If" applications, 104–106
Where in the U.S.A. Is Carmen SanDiego?, 179, 366
Where in Time Is Carmen SanDiego?, 179
White collar crime, 388
WIMP interface, 409
Windows, 94, 148
Windows on Telecommunications, 124
Wirth, Niklaus, 316–317
Word. See MicroSoft *Word*.
Word Perfect, 40, 45, 118, 172
Word processing, 35–60
    basic concepts, 36–37
    benefits, 45–49
    classroom applications, 52–57
    compared to typing, 36
    group projects, 55–56
    issues, 49–52, 391–392
    and keyboarding, 49–50
    page layout control, 37
    and revision, 51–52
Word processor, 36, 53, 118
    functions, 39–40
Word search programs, 132–133
WordStar, 172
Work sheet generators, 136
Works. See MicroSoft *Works*.
World Data, 78
World Development Indicators, 77
World Geograph, 77
Writer's Helper Stage II, 417
Writing across the curriculum, 56–57
Writing aids, 40–45
Writing as process, 40–41, 50–51, 118, 123
Writing to Read, 47, 170